ALSO BY JOHN U. BACON

Bo's Lasting Lessons (with Bo Schembechler)

THREE AND OUT

THREE AND OUT

RICH RODRIGUEZ

AND THE

MICHIGAN WOLVERINES

IN THE CRUCIBLE OF

COLLEGE FOOTBALL

JOHN U. BACON

FARRAR, STRAUS AND GIROUX | NEW YORK

Farrar, Straus and Giroux
18 West 18th Street, New York 10011

Copyright © 2011 by John U. Bacon
All rights reserved
Distributed in Canada by D&M Publishers, Inc.
Printed in the United States of America
First edition, 2011

Library of Congress Cataloging-in-Publication Data
Bacon, John U., 1964–
     Three and out : Rich Rodriguez and the Michigan Wolverines in the crucible of
  college football / John U. Bacon.
        p.   cm.
     ISBN 978-0-8090-9466-0 (hardback)
     1. Rodriguez, Rich, 1963–   2. Football coaches—United States.   3. University
  of Michigan—Football.   4. Michigan Wolverines (Football team).   I. Title.

  GV939.R622B34 2011
  769.332—dc23

                                                                    2011022040

Designed by Abby Kagan

www.fsgbooks.com

10   9   8   7   6   5   4   3   2

To my mom, who always told me, "Your character is what you do when you think no one's watching." And to my dad, who said, "When you're on the floor, you can't fall out of bed." This book proved them right many times over.

||||| CONTENTS

THREE AND OUT

"When I was still in grade school," coach Rich Rodriguez told me, "I knew I wanted two things: to spend my life in sports, and to do it on the biggest stage possible."

It was late July 2010, just a few days before the Michigan Wolverines' summer camp started. Rodriguez sat at the big desk in his office in Schembechler Hall, a warm, comfortable space, with his stocking foot resting near pictures of his wife, Rita, and his children, Raquel, fourteen, and Rhett, twelve. He had set up more photos of them on the dark wooden shelves behind him, including one of Rhett jumping up to touch the famed GO BLUE banner before Rodriguez's first game at the University of Michigan two years earlier.

It is a picture of pure exuberance. Ten years old at the time, before he hit his growth spurt, Rhett had to give it his all just to reach the bottom of the banner—and he touched it, barely. Now, two years later, he had grown five inches and matured from a deadly serious fourth grader who forced himself to quit wearing Nike (because Michigan had become an Adidas school and he was playing it by the book) to a preternaturally calm young man with a dry wit who seemed to be going on thirty, not thirteen. Living in the epicenter of Michigan football had a way of making you grow weary, or grow up—fast.

Rodriguez had filled the shelf above that photo with Michigan's iconic winged helmets from different eras, starting with a barless version all the way up to the current five-bar model. The two in the middle sported the numbers 47 and 87, representing the retired numbers of Bennie Oosterbaan and Ron Kramer, two of the greatest athletes in Michigan history. On the next shelf over, Rodriguez had stacked the canon of Michigan football literature, including tomes covering the history of Michigan Stadium and the first book on Bo Schembechler, *Man in Motion*, written in 1973.

Throughout Rodriguez's second-floor office, in the locker room, the weight room, and the museum below, he was surrounded by the trappings of Michigan football lore—gigantic photos and displays of the banner, the winged helmet, the 109,901-seat stadium, and the players and coaches who had made the program the biggest stage in college football.

Rodriguez had not merely pursued his childhood dreams. He had actually achieved them.

Michigan football had been a model of stability and success since the Wolverines played their first game in 1879. The six coaches who preceded Rodriguez, dating back to 1938, averaged twelve years on the job—one good reason the Wolverines had won more games, and owned a higher winning percentage, than any other team in the country. They had built the biggest stadium, the largest alumni base, the most heated rivalries, and the richest tradition in the nation. More people have seen the Wolverines play football—in person and on TV—than any other team in the history of the game.

It made sense, then, when Lloyd Carr stepped down in 2007, that the Wolverines would want the hottest coach in the country. And after a stumbling search, they found him.

In late November 2007, Rich Rodriguez, the inventor of the spread option offense that most college teams now use, had led West Virginia University to the cusp of the national title game, until lowly Pittsburgh upset his alma mater 13–9. A week later, when Rodriguez asked the school president for higher salaries for his assistants, he was surprised not only to be turned down but also to be told, "We have done all we can. Take it or leave it."

Although Rodriguez had turned down the University of Alabama the year before, when Michigan offered him the top post, he accepted, becoming only the fourth outsider in over a century to lead the Wolverines. Both parties thought their problems were over. After all, plug a big-name coach into a big-name program, and what could go wrong?

As it turned out, just about everything.

Before Rodriguez had even left Morgantown, West Virginia sued him for full payment of his $4 million buyout. He and the University of Michigan ultimately paid it, but only after six months of one-sided silence, which West Virginia exploited to tarnish Rodriguez's name.

He still assumed, however, that his troubles were behind him—which helps explain why he didn't see the troubles ahead.

During the three years this book covers, Michigan changed athletic directors once, head coaches three times, defensive coordinators four times, and quarterbacks at least five times, depending on who's counting. All play central roles in this story, of course; their actions affect the plot in ways both expected and surprising. But one character affected events perhaps more than any other—and not by his actions, but by his absence.

When Bo Schembechler passed away on November 17, 2006, the Wolverines were 11–0 and ranked second in the nation. They proceeded to lose their next four games, including the infamous upset at the hands of Appalachian State, which one popular website refers to simply as "the Horror." There is no need to explain to any Michigan fan what that means, or to underscore that the team's aura of invincibility had vanished with that loss.

A few months after Schembechler's passing, his former quarterback, Jim Harbaugh, who had become Stanford's head coach, publicly lambasted his alma mater and the football program's academic advisers for allegedly talking him out of majoring in history. Michigan's time-honored practice of keeping conflicts in-house no longer seemed to apply, either.

Lloyd Carr's retirement had been rumored for years; it finally occurred the Monday after his fourth straight loss to Ohio State in 2007, at age sixty-three. Yet it seemed to catch athletic director Bill Martin by surprise. Instead of having several strong candidates lined up, or one already sewed up for a seamless transition, Martin was at a loss; no one seemed to know who or what he was looking for.

Martin's bumbling month-long search for a leader only deepened the fault lines that first appeared after Schembechler's death. The Michigan football family quickly cleaved into camps that wanted to see Louisiana State's Les Miles, Michigan defensive coordinator Ron English, or another candidate succeed Carr. By the time Martin finally hired Rodriguez, unbeknownst to the incoming coach, the "Michigan Men" had become bitterly divided, agreeing on just one thing: "None of this would have happened if Bo were still here."

When Schembechler died, Michigan lost more than a coach, and the university lost more than a leader. The Michigan family lost its father. For the first time in almost four decades, it was not clear who the head of the household would be. Almost five years later, it's still not.

Probably all of the off-field ordeals—from the mudslinging coming out of Morgantown to the factionalism growing in Ann Arbor—would have simmered down if Rodriguez's first Michigan team had posted a winning season. But a funny thing happened on the way to the Wolverines' twelfth national title. With the whole football world watching, Rodriguez's team struggled, stumbled, and finally fumbled its way to an anemic 3–9 record, breaking the program's forty-one-year streak without a losing season and its thirty-three-year run of bowl games. The lowlight was a 13–10 home loss to a weak University of Toledo team, which snapped Michigan's perfect 24–0 mark against Mid-American Conference teams, a record that reached back to the nineteenth century.

Rodriguez's debut sharpened the divisions some, but hope was still alive on the eve of his second season—until the *Detroit Free Press* published a front-page story six days before the 2009 opener, claiming, among other things, that Rodriguez forced his players to spend fifteen or twenty-one hours a week on football in the off-season, more than twice the NCAA limit. It prompted investigations by the university and the NCAA itself, the first that Michigan's football program had ever suffered, which entailed interviewing dozens of players and coaches in the middle of the season.

Despite the distractions and the seemingly nonstop negative nation-wide publicity, the 2009 Wolverines, led by freshman quarterback Tate Forcier, started the season with four straight victories—including a thrilling last-minute win over Notre Dame—but then fell apart, going 1–7 the rest of the way, once again falling out of the bowl picture.

Wolverine Nation winced. How much of its pain derived from Rodriguez's 8–16 record at Michigan and how much from the taint of the NCAA's ongoing investigation was impossible to say. But when you added it all up, by the time we had that conversation in Rodriguez's office in July 2010, just about every sports outlet in the country had Rodriguez sitting squarely on the hottest seat in college football.

The opportunity to write this book popped up largely through dumb luck, and it's been luck—of all kinds—that has reshaped it every year since.

After graduating from Michigan, I taught history and coached hockey at Culver Academies in northern Indiana. One of my star students, Greg Farrall, went on to become an All–Big Ten defensive end at Indiana, before pursuing a career in finance. His boss in 2008, Mike Wilcox, just happened to be one of Rodriguez's financial advisers. When Farrall sent Wilcox my most recent book, *Bo's Lasting Lessons*, Wilcox asked if I'd be interested in following Rodriguez's first Michigan team at close range.

The idea was to publish a series of stories to a magazine, in the hope of turning them into a book coauthored with Rodriguez, similar to the one I wrote with Bo Schembechler in 2007. After that first season ended at 3–9, however, I came to two obvious conclusions: this story wasn't over, and I had to write it myself. A bit to my surprise, Rodriguez didn't think twice.

The deal we arrived at was simple: I would be granted unfettered access to the team's meals and meetings, practices and games—from the sidelines to the locker room—an almost unheard-of opportunity for any journalist. In exchange, Rodriguez would get to read the manuscript for factual accuracy, period, though I was under no obligation to agree to his suggested changes. I was free to report whatever I observed and experienced. It is fair to say that no one involved in this project had any idea what we were getting ourselves into, but to everyone's credit, no one ever tried to renege on the agreement.

Rodriguez never flinched, I believe, because he firmly believed he had nothing to hide and was willing to bet that a fair portrayal of him and his program, warts and all, would be a considerable improvement over the rumors and recriminations coming out of West Virginia after he left. Rodriguez thought it was a chance worth taking.

Of course, at that time it might not have seemed like that big a gamble. When I first met Rodriguez in August 2008, he said, "I've told my wife, Rita, that Charles Manson is also from West Virginia, and right now he's more popular than I am."

As someone who has spent nearly two decades researching and writing about Michigan football, I found the offer especially enticing. I was born at University of Michigan Hospital, grew up in Ann Arbor, and earned two degrees from the school. After a couple of years away, I returned to Ann Arbor and started my writing career at the local paper, covering high school football games for fifty bucks a pop. I moved on to the *Detroit News*, where my position as a sports feature writer allowed me to produce longer pieces on, among other things, Michigan's 1996 NCAA-champion hockey team, its storied football stadium, and its resident living legend, Bo Schembechler.

Most reporters will tell you Michigan has done as good a job running a big-time college athletic department as has any school in the nation, but it surely has not been perfect. I was the first reporter to expose Fielding Yost's racist past and initiated the investigation into the Michigan basketball program, which culminated in serious NCAA sanctions. I wrote a feature piece for *The New York Times* in 1999 explaining how the very department that once stood for unequaled stability, achievement, and integrity was about to hire its fifth director in a decade, under the cloud of a $3.9 million deficit and investigations into its basketball program by the NCAA, the IRS, and even the FBI. "Michigan's problems run deep," I wrote, "and the consequences will spread nationwide."

I left the *Detroit News* in 1999 to freelance for magazines and write books, but I never thought I'd be writing one like this.

The book you have in your hands is not the book I expected to write.

I started out thinking I was writing *Rocky*—the small-town outsider who gets his shot on the big stage. By the middle of 2009, though, the story had morphed into something more akin to *The Shawshank Redemption*, and there was reason to wonder whether Rodriguez would ever be able to escape his detractors. But when Rich Rodriguez's tenure as Michigan's head football coach came to an end on Wednesday, January 5, 2011, I realized I was witness to the final moments of college football's *Titanic*. The unsinkable ship had just gone down.

Now the most pressing question is this: How did the game's hottest coach combine forces with the game's strongest program to produce three of the worst seasons in school history?

Many other questions, however, arose unexpectedly.

I thought I knew college football, and particularly Michigan football, as well as anyone. But after three years of seeing everything up close, I can tell you this unequivocally: I had no idea.

Looking at Michigan's past three seasons, it's not hard to divine dozens of management lessons—starting with the perils of arrogance on just about all fronts—but none of them would resolve college football's central conflict: It's a billion-dollar business whose revenues can fund entire athletic departments and whose leaders personify our biggest universities, but it's all built on the backs of stressed-out coaches and amateur athletes.

The contemporary college athletic department now resembles a modern racehorse: bigger, faster, and more powerful than ever but still supported by the same spindly legs that break with increasing frequency. Michigan's $226 million renovation of its stadium—already the largest in the country, and almost twice as big as many NFL stadiums—the spiraling salaries (Rodriguez made $2.5 million a year at Michigan, the market rate), and the seemingly insatiable desire for new facilities for the university's twenty-eight other varsity programs all depend on selling football tickets, seat licenses, luxury suites, and TV rights.

And all that still depends on the arm of a nineteen-year-old quarterback and the foot of a twenty-year-old kicker.

From the inside, I soon discovered how complicated the game had become, requiring coaches to work 120-hour weeks recruiting, practicing, and watching endless hours of film—only to see that twenty-year-old kid miss the kick. When that happened, Rodriguez would get hundreds of nasty e-mails and very little sleep, and have to hear stories of one of his daughter's teachers making jokes about her father being fired in front of her classmates.

Big-time college coaches ask their players to work almost as hard—not just on the field but in the weight room and in the classroom, too. I followed quarterback Denard Robinson for one day, which started at seven a.m. with treatment for his swollen knee, followed by weight lifting, classes, an interview with ESPN Radio, more treatment, meetings, practice, a third round of treatment, dinner, and film. When he walked out of Schembechler Hall after ten p.m., two middle-aged men who had been waiting all night for him in the parking lot asked him to sign a dozen glossy photos.

I went home exhausted, and all I'd done was follow him around and take notes. But working out with the strength coaches proved to be far tougher. In just six weeks, they doubled my bench press and tripled my squat. They also showed me you could puke from running *or* lifting weights (I hadn't known that). After each workout I collapsed on my couch—not to nap, mind you, but to whimper in the fetal position for a couple hours.

How those players got any work done after their morning workouts was a mystery to me—and thanks to Michigan's self-imposed penalties, the Wolverines actually worked fewer hours than the NCAA allowed.

If Robinson—or any of the 124 other players—did any of these things poorly, or not at all, that was Rodriguez's problem. And whenever such missteps hit the papers, the talk shows, or the blogs, they quickly became much bigger mistakes before breakfast the next day.

This beast Michigan has created is just about the biggest, strongest, and fastest animal of its kind, but the coach's job security and the athletic department itself still rest on kids who weigh three hundred pounds and can squat twice that but can't grow respectable mustaches.

Everyone knew Rodriguez was on trial in 2010—not least Rodriguez, who hadn't had a single good night's sleep since he had moved to Michigan.

What seemed to get lost in the endless discussions about him and his future, however, was that Michigan was on trial, too.

Michigan has long been considered one of the game's "destination jobs." It is not the means to some greater position but an end in itself. When you accept this job, you've arrived once and for all.

Only one head coach in Michigan's long history went on to become a head coach anywhere else. That coach, Gary Moeller, left only because he was fired for one bad night at a restaurant. When the NFL's Detroit Lions later hired him, it was considered a demotion. They fired him after only seven games, perhaps because he had become the only Lions coach to post a winning record since 1972, a no-no in the Motor City.

Michigan has a lot to offer a head coach—as much as any college program in the country—but, like most elite programs, open-mindedness, flexibility, and patience are not among its selling points. Because the Michigan family had not needed those attributes in decades, they had atrophied by the time Rodriguez arrived.

Rodriguez shared many of Michigan's blind spots, including his soaring ambition and admitted impatience, which occasionally created secondary problems. He made his share of mistakes, no question, but Michigan was hiring him, not the other way around. Its very constancy meant it had no recent experience accepting an outsider and preparing him to succeed.

The last time Michigan did so, in December 1968, Bo Schembechler asked his new athletic director, Don Canham, how many years he had. Canham, characteristically, pulled no punches. "You've got the same tenure I have. I think we have about five years. If you guys don't succeed [by then], we're all going to be out of here."

Schembechler knew where he stood, and Canham's word was good.

But by December 2007, Schembechler was gone, Canham was gone, and so was their way of doing business. Thanks to a century-old tug-of-war between Michigan's presidents and athletic directors, which had turned decisively in the presidents' favor after Schembechler retired as athletic director in 1990, Michigan's presidents had hired four straight athletic directors who did not have a single day of experience coaching or administering college athletics. Before Rodriguez's third season, Michigan hired a fifth.

They all brought serious strengths to the post, but none of them seemed to know what coaches went through and how best to help them.

The questions about Rodriguez started the day he arrived in Ann Arbor and multiplied each year he coached the Wolverines.

Could Rodriguez adapt to the unique culture that is Michigan football? Would he embrace the tradition, or fight it? Could his high-flying offense succeed in the stodgy Big Ten, and could he build a defense to match?

But questions about Michigan arose, too. Would the Wolverines, who cherish their past like no one else, seize the future in the form of the spread offense? Could they accept an outsider for the first time in four decades—and the first West Virginia accent in a century—and give him the support he needed to get the Wolverines back to BCS games, where everyone felt they belonged? How would the Michigan family respond if Rodriguez failed to win enough, fast enough?

Many Michigan Men would come to Rodriguez's aid and help him any way they could—sometimes at considerable personal cost. Others immediately rejected him as a "bad cultural fit." Still others came to that conclusion only after the losses piled up.

Rodriguez had not made it all the way from tiny Grant Town, West Virginia, to the biggest stage in the nation by playing it safe. As we sat in his office that July day in 2010, he told me that, for the third straight season, he would be starting a new quarterback in the opener—sophomore Denard Robinson, this time—with former freshman phenom Forcier demoted to third string.

Rodriguez knew he had to win, and he had to do it the right way—just one more reason the outcome of the NCAA investigation seemed so important. He also had to become, in the well-worn phrase of the day, a "Michigan Man"—a leader so exemplary that alums and fans were proud to see him serving as the voice of the program and, truly, the face of the university itself.

Sports fans invest great hopes and dreams in their teams. College football fans invest even more, I think, because of the stronger connection they feel with the school and the players. But I've never seen any fans ask more of their team than Michigan football fans ask of theirs.

There are only two groups who are more devoted to the Wolverines—

the coaches and the players themselves. They have the most to gain and the most to lose. They know the stakes. And they accept them—even embrace them. It's why all of them, from Rich Rodriguez to Tate Forcier to Denard Robinson, came to Ann Arbor. Not to be average, or even good, but "the leaders and best."

Anything less would not do.

This book attempts to explain how the coach and his team fell short—and what happened when they did.

|ı|ı|ı| 1 LEADERS AND BEST

This is a story that could happen only in America.

When you travel abroad you quickly realize it is impossible to explain why a university would own the largest stadium in the country. It is, literally, a foreign concept, one as original as the U.S. Constitution.

Indeed, it was Thomas Jefferson who drafted the Northwest Ordinance, providing for the funding of public schools and universities in the states that now constitute most of the Big Ten. "Religion, morality, and knowledge being necessary to good government and the happiness of mankind, schools and the means of education shall forever be encouraged." The idea is so central to Michigan's mission—even its very existence—it is engraved on the façade of its central building, Angell Hall.

If Ken Burns is right that the national parks are "America's best idea," our state universities—another uniquely American concept—might be a close second. The United States has spawned more colleges and graduates per capita than any other country in the world and created college towns rising out of cornfields, another American phenomenon.

Ann Arbor's founders, in an effort to attract settlers and make money on their real estate venture, first bid for the state capital—and lost to Lansing. Then they bid for the state penitentiary—and lost to Jackson. Finally, they bid for the state university—and won, the best bronze medal ever awarded a brand-new town.

But as the university grew, Ann Arbor experienced problems common to all college towns. Put thousands of healthy young men in one place with little adult supervision, and all that testosterone has to go somewhere—which explains why the game of football was born and raised not in the city or the country but on college campuses.

Football was already so popular at Harvard by 1860 that the school's president felt compelled to ban it for being too violent. That, of course, only piqued the young men's desire to play it. When Rutgers played the College of New Jersey—now called Princeton—on November 6, 1869, the game was a little different from the one Michigan and Connecticut would play in 2010. In the 1869 version, each team had twenty-five men who played the entire game and, because they hadn't yet conceived the forward pass, engaged in a glorified melee.

Rutgers actually won 6–4, marking the first time Rutgers was the nation's top-ranked team—and the last. When Princeton beat Rutgers in the rematch a week later, Rutgers's brief moment at the summit was over.

The college boys that day could not have imagined that their wide-ranging scrum would become one of their nation's most popular spectator sports—a billion-dollar American obsession worthy of stadiums holding over one hundred thousand people, with luxury boxes that would start at $55,000 per season. But that's exactly what they set in motion that day. They also started something the students, the alumni, and the reporters would love—and the university presidents would hate just as much.

Just two years after that first game, Andrew Dickson White—who had left his post as a history and English professor at the University of Michigan to become Cornell's first president—received a request from a group of students to take the train to Cleveland to play football against Western Reserve (now Case Western). He famously replied that he would not permit thirty men to travel two hundred miles just to "agitate . . . a pig's bladder full of wind!"

But he was fighting a losing battle. Ten years later, in 1879, a group of Michigan students traveled to Racine, Wisconsin, to play the first football game on the far side of the Alleghenies—or "the West," as they called it then. The Wolverines won 1–0, starting a tradition that, 131 years later, would be described by athletic director and former regent Dave Brandon as the most prominent feature of Michigan's "brand."

The college presidents responded to this relationship like fathers of debutantes who find their pristine daughters falling for hooligans. It was not simply a Hatfield marrying a McCoy. It was a *Vanderbilt* marrying a McCoy.

If they could have annulled the marriage, they would have. But, conceding the impossibility of preventing this ungodly union of academics and athletics, Purdue president James H. Smart wrote to the presidents of Minnesota, Wisconsin, Illinois, Northwestern, Chicago, and Michigan, inviting them to meet on January 11, 1895, in a wood-paneled room at the Palmer House in Chicago. If they were going to have to put up with this shotgun marriage, they at least wanted to put down some ground rules.

They started with the premise that they, the presidents, should have complete authority over all sports played in their universities' names, and then created rules ensuring that everyone on the field was a bona fide student and an amateur athlete—issues schools still struggle with today.

This was a "radical departure from the prevailing norm," former Big Ten commissioner Tug Wilson wrote, and he was right. The Big Ten was the first major organization of its kind, predating high school associations, other college conferences, and even the NCAA itself. Soon the rest of the country's colleges and high schools followed suit, forming their own leagues based on the Big Ten model.

The American marriage of academics and athletics—something no other country in the world would even consider—had been officially consummated.

It's been a rocky relationship, to say the least, and presidents to this day chafe at having to work with the unruly beast down the street. But it's lasted over a century, and even a trial separation seems out of the question.

Of the seven schools that day that created what would become the Big Ten, one would emerge as the conference's crown jewel. But if the Big Ten penned its Magna Carta at the Palmer House in 1895, the Wolverines would wait three more years to craft their constitution. They needed inspiration, and they found it in the Big Ten's first rivalry.

When John D. Rockefeller decided to bankroll a university to open in 1892, he called it the University of Chicago and hired Yale's William Rainey Harper to become the school's first president. Neither Rockefeller nor Harper was stupid. They knew the fastest way to put their new school on the map was to make a splash in the sensation sweeping the nation: college football, thereby becoming one of the first schools to leverage the game to enhance its academic reputation.

One of President Harper's first hires was his former Yale Hebrew student Amos Alonzo Stagg, a man trained by Walter Camp, the father of football and the author of its first rule book. The investment in Stagg quickly paid off when he turned the Chicago Maroons into a regional power, strong enough after just four seasons to join the nascent Big Ten.

Three years later, on November 24, 1898, in front of twelve thousand fans at Chicago's Marshall Field, the undefeated Wolverines took on the 9–1–1 Maroons to see who could claim their first Big Ten title. Late in the game, Michigan's little-used Charles "Chuck" Widman broke loose for a 65-yard touchdown, followed by Neil Snow's crucial two-point conversion—just enough for a 12–11 victory and the first of Michigan's forty-two conference crowns.

"My spirits were so uplifted that I was clear off the earth," said Michigan music student Louis Elbel. The surprising finish started a song in his head. Some accounts have him finishing the melody by the time he got to his brother's house, others on the train back to Ann Arbor. Either way, Elbel worked with amazing efficiency—perhaps because he seems to have lifted the renowned melody of "The Victors'" from "The Spirit of Liberty," which his friend George Rosenberg had copyrighted seven months earlier.

But no one questions that the powerful lyrics are all Elbel's. A year later John Philip Sousa performed the song in Ann Arbor and reportedly declared it "the greatest college fight song ever written."

One overlooked aspect of "The Victors" separates it from all others. Most school songs urge their teams to make a great effort in the hopes of winning. "On, Wisconsin!" ask the Badgers to "fight on for her fame . . . We'll win this game." "The Buckeye Battle Cry" exhorts the "men of the Scarlet and Gray . . . We've got to win this game today."

"The Victors," in contrast, celebrates a contest already won.

Hail! to the victors valiant
Hail! to the conqu'ring heroes
Hail! Hail! to Michigan
The leaders and best!

Hail! to the victors valiant
Hail! to the conqu'ring heroes
Hail! Hail! to Michigan,
The champions of the West!

There is no wiggle room in those words. No hoping, no wishing—just a clear-as-day declaration that the Michigan Wolverines are "the leaders and best," and everyone else will simply have to deal with it.

Of all the trappings of Michigan's vaunted tradition, the first is something you cannot see or touch. It's just a song. But more than the marching band, big house, or banner, "The Victors" established the most important element of Michigan's identity—confidence—which served as the North Star for all that followed.

He wasn't raised in Michigan, he didn't play there or even take a single class in Ann Arbor, but no one did more to shape Michigan's reputation for excellence—and arrogance—than Fielding H. Yost.

The son of a Confederate veteran, Yost was born in Fairview, West Virginia, in 1871, about five minutes from Rodriguez's future home. He earned two degrees from the state's flagship university in Morgantown before embarking on his coaching career. After one-year stints at Ohio Wesleyan, Nebraska, Kansas, and Stanford, by December 1900 Fielding Yost was out of a job yet again, because no one had the wealth or the will to hire a full-time football coach.

Michigan's first athletic director, Charles Baird, wrote to Yost: "Our people are greatly roused up over the defeats of the past two years," which was an interesting comment for a school that had just gone 7–2–1 and 8–2, establishing another Michigan tradition: high expectations and the impatience that comes with them.

Baird assured Yost that "a great effort will be made" and backed up his promise with a $2,300 salary for just three months' work, far more than a full professor made. Yost snatched up the offer.

Yost had never been to Ann Arbor until the day he showed up to start his new job. He pronounced his adopted team "Meeshegan," which legendary broadcaster Bob Ufer mimicked so often ESPN has picked up the habit.

The day Yost arrived, he grabbed his bags and literally ran from the station up State Street to the campus. When he got there, a reporter asked him how the Wolverines would do that season. Yost hadn't yet seen a single player, but that didn't stop him from predicting, "Michigan isn't going to lose a game."

Then he delivered for fifty-six consecutive contests, going undefeated in 1901, 1902, 1903, and 1904, winning national titles every year—the first team other than Harvard, Yale, Princeton, and Penn to win even one— while beating opponents by scores like 119–0, 128–0, and 130–0, that last one against West Virginia, his beloved alma mater.

According to Yost's biographer John Behee, "No other coach and no other football team ever so dominated their era as Fielding H. Yost and the Michigan teams for 1901–05." And no other coach ever will.

But all was not well with this new game. Incredibly, in 1905 alone, eighteen college students died on football fields.

President Theodore Roosevelt called the coaches and presidents of Harvard, Yale, and Princeton to the White House that year to urge reforms to save the sport. This meeting gave birth to the Intercollegiate Athletic Association, which we now call the NCAA.

Yost's best counter to the many critics of football, however, might be his greatest gift to the game: In an era when football was considered a social ill run by renegade coaches, Yost argued that, when properly coached, football developed valuable qualities in students that the classroom could not. The belief that football builds character has been repeated so often it is now a hoary cliché, but when Yost espoused it, it was a fresh, even radical idea.

But that wasn't enough for James B. Angell, Michigan's longest-serving and most important president. He took office in 1871—eight years before Michigan's first football game—and served until 1909, charting a course for Michigan that the university still follows and other schools adopted. A Brown University alum, Angell's vision for Michigan was to create a university that could provide "an uncommon education for the common man."

He was thrilled to see the sons and daughters of farmers and factory workers becoming philosophers, but he couldn't stand the game of football they loved so much. Having seen firsthand the hysteria the sport created on campus, Angell wrote his fellow Big Ten presidents during that momentous 1905 season with great concern: "The absorbing interest and excitement of the students—not to speak of the public—in the preparation for the intercollegiate games make a damaging invasion into the proper work of the university for the first ten or twelve weeks of the academic year. This is not true of the players alone, but of the main body of students, who think and talk of little else but the game."

Sound familiar?

If the University of Chicago's new president saw football's unparalleled ability to market a private school to the public, Michigan's failed to see its value in pitching his public school to the taxpayers, who picked up over 90 percent of the budget until the 1960s, missing the point that for many Michiganders, there were few other reasons to support the state school.

Football, then and now, serves as the front porch for most schools, the one place on campus where everyone feels welcome.

As Notre Dame coach Frank Leahy said, "A school without football is in danger of deteriorating into a medieval study hall." To which Bear Bryant added, "It's kind of hard to rally around a math class." Football matters.

Angell didn't get this, but what really rankled him were the reporters and students who valued these "men of brawn rather than the men of brains," and he warned his peers that, with so much money "handled for such purpose, the temptations for misuse are not wanting."

Current college presidents know exactly what Angell was talking about.

Yost didn't care. The minute he became Michigan's third athletic director, in 1921, he was on a mission to construct the very best athletic complex in the nation—and because Baird had set up the athletic department to keep its profits, Yost had the means to do so. "We've got the first field house ever built on a campus," former athletic director Don Canham told me. "We've got the first intramural building. We've got the largest stadium in the country. That was no accident. That was Fielding Yost."

That demand had been boosted by Yost himself by winning titles and popularizing the forward pass in 1925 and 1926 with his famed "Benny-to-Bennie" passing combination: Benny Friedman tossing to Bennie Oosterbaan. The forward pass had been legalized in the wake of the NCAA reforms of 1905 to spread the players out and reduce collisions, but two decades later it was still used primarily as a desperation measure. Yost and his stars demonstrated it could be used as an effective, controlled tactic on any down from almost anywhere on the field.

Friedman took the weapon to the embryonic NFL, where he set a record of eleven touchdown passes in 1927. New York Giants owner Tim Mara took note and bought Friedman's entire Detroit franchise just to get the quarterback. Friedman made Mara look smart when he shattered his own record with twenty touchdown passes in 1929. The NFL inducted Friedman posthumously to the Hall of Fame in 2005, along with Dan Marino and Steve Young, for expanding the forward pass that made those later careers possible.

Yost contributed more to Michigan's tradition than victories, buildings, and innovations. When he officially retired in 1941, his admirers put on a tribute in his eponymous Field House, broadcast on NBC radio and titled "A Toast to Yost from Coast to Coast" (which was also the title of a popular song).

After the speeches, Yost said, "My heart is so full at this moment and I am so overcome by the rush of memories that I fear I could say little more. But do let me reiterate . . . the Spirit of Michigan. It is based upon a deathless loyalty to Michigan and all her ways; an enthusiasm that makes it second nature for Michigan Men to spread the gospel of their university to the world's distant outposts; a conviction that nowhere is there a better university, in any way, than this Michigan of ours."

Whether you call it confidence or arrogance, Yost had it and spread it.

Michigan hit pay dirt again when it hired another innovative outsider, Fritz Crisler. In 1938, after Crisler's sixth season at Princeton, Michigan invited him to name his price—and he did, asking for complete autonomy over the team (he knew Yost had all but sabotaged his first two successors), the position of athletic director (effective when Yost stepped down), and more money than any football coach had ever made: $15,000 a year. "I thought my terms were so far out of line," Crisler confessed, "that they would be unacceptable." But Michigan called his bluff, met his terms, and got a legend in the bargain.

During Fritz Crisler's tenure as Michigan's athletic director, from 1942 to 1968, the Wolverines won eighteen national titles, in everything from baseball to ice hockey to men's tennis—plus two in football.

But it was as a football coach that Crisler made his greatest impact.

In 1945, thanks to the war, Crisler had to fill his roster with a bunch of seventeen-year-olds—no match for Michigan's fifth opponent, the loaded Army squad, which was undefeated, ranked number one, and featured "Mr. Inside," Doc Blanchard, and "Mr. Outside," Glenn Davis, who would both win the Heisman Trophy.

Desperate, Crisler combed the rules looking for a loophole, and he found one in the substitution section. Before the war, players could enter or leave a game only once each quarter, but in anticipation of the player shortages World War II would create, in 1941 the NCAA started allowing players to come and go "at any time." Eureka.

"Those three little words changed the game," Crisler said. He divided his team into "offensive" and "defensive" units, creating the sport's first specialists.

"It was no ingenuity on my part," Crisler claimed. "When the other fellow has a thousand dollars and you have a dime, it's time to gamble."

The seventy thousand fans packed into Yankee Stadium were stunned to see Crisler substitute freely—and even more shocked to see Michigan hold Army scoreless in the first quarter and trail only 14–7 in the third before the far more powerful Cadets settled matters, 28–7.

Afterward, it was not Army's victory—which was expected—but Crisler's strategy—which wasn't—that had people talking. Two years later, 1947, the press dubbed Michigan's offense the "Mad Magicians" for their Globetrotter-like ball handling in the backfield. On a single play, as many as seven players might touch the ball. "For Michigan's specialists," a *Time* magazine cover said, "poise, fury, finesse, utter abandon."

Crisler's invention helped Michigan win national titles in 1947 and 1948. The platoon system—the most revolutionary innovation since Benny-to-Bennie unleashed the passing game—caught on fast and also necessitated aggressive, year-round recruiting, something Crisler himself loathed.

But no one ever questioned Crisler's loyalty to Michigan.

"Tradition is something you can't borrow," he said. "You cannot go down and buy it at the corner store, but it's there to sustain you when you need it the most. I have watched countless Michigan football coaches, countless Michigan players call upon it time and time again. There is nothing like it, I hope it never dies."

Converts, of course, make the most fervent believers.

Crisler's successor as Michigan's athletic director, Don Canham, confessed, "I was not a popular choice to succeed Crisler. I think the average Michigan alumnus was saying something to the effect of, 'Who the hell is this track coach to take Fritz Crisler's place?'" The reason was simple: Canham's hiring marked the first split between the positions of football coach and athletic director since 1921.

But it worked exceedingly well. Canham modernized Michigan's marketing methods so dramatically that *Sports Illustrated*'s Frank Deford felt compelled to write a major feature on him in 1975—the same year Canham started Michigan Stadium's string of 100,000-plus crowds—which resulted in summer workshops to teach athletic directors nationwide how to emulate Michigan's success. Soon, every school was marketing their teams the Michigan way.

If Canham's marketing methods received too much attention, his hiring skills received too little. He had the uncanny ability to pluck talented young coaches from the collegiate minor leagues. This savvy approach increased the candidates' devotion to Michigan and decreased the amount of money Canham had to pay to get them there.

Nonetheless, when Canham hired Schembechler, Michigan fans asked, Bo who?

Canham realized that Schembechler's current employer, Miami University, could have thrown more money at Schembechler. But, he said, "they couldn't compete with Yost's hole in the ground or with the prestige of Michigan."

Canham knew he was offering something special, and so did Schembechler. Although Schembechler made an ill-advised crack during an early speech about changing the team's funny-looking helmets (he maintained it was a joke, though others aren't so certain), he quickly received the help of Canham, Bob Ufer, and his predecessor, Bump Elliott. He learned Michigan's gospel and how to preach it.

When Schembechler and his assistants arrived in Ann Arbor, they had to dress in the second-floor locker room of Yost Field House, sit in rusty folding chairs, and hang their clothes on nails in the wall. "My coaches were complaining, 'We had better stuff at Miami,'" Schembechler said. "I said, 'No, we didn't. See this chair? *Fielding Yost* sat in this chair. See this spike? *Fielding Yost* hung his hat on this spike. And you're telling me we had better stuff at Miami?! No, men, we didn't. We have *tradition* here, *Michigan* tradition, and *that's* something no one else has!'"

Schembechler never introduced any eye-popping innovations like the forward pass or the platoon system. But he did plenty to advance Michigan's reputation for excellence, winning thirteen Big Ten titles in twenty-one years while running a famously clean program.

When Canham stepped down as athletic director in 1988, it marked the end of an era of unequaled steadiness and strength—sixty-seven years led by only three athletic directors, each one a leader in the field.

But after Schembechler succeeded his boss as athletic director—partly to ensure he could name the next football coach—it took him less than two years to realize that the new president, James Duderstadt, was intent on diminishing the AD position, and he quit.

"It didn't change until Bo left," Canham told me, "and then it changed almost overnight."

Those changes soon threatened the very foundation of Michigan athletics—and reverberated straight through the Rodriguez era.

In 1901, the same year Fielding Yost ran up Ann Arbor's State Street to jump-start Michigan's modern era, a new village was incorporated just a couple miles down Paw Paw Creek Road from Yost's native Fairview, West Virginia. The Federal Coal and Coke Company had just opened a mine called Federal No. 1 and decided to call the new place Grant Town.

Rodriguez's grandfather Marion emigrated from Spain to work in that mine, and after Rich's father, Vince, spent a few years in Chicago with his wife and three young boys, they moved back to continue the family tradition.

"It's a different world down there," said the soft-spoken Vince, sitting in the family's backyard on a beautiful spring day. "The hole is no wider than a trash can. You look up and see that circle of light getting smaller. It's scary at first, but after a while, you get used to it, until it's like going down to your basement."

Maybe so, but your basement is not likely to collapse on you, as that mine did on Marion—three times. He always escaped, but he couldn't elude black lung disease.

"You could see it coming," Rich said. "And if you've ever seen anybody die of black lung, you know it's pretty hard to watch. It's slow, and it's painful. It definitely made an impression."

Unlike most of his classmates, who went down that shaft after graduation for $100 a day, Rich Rodriguez had other plans.

Ask Arleen Rodriguez when she knew her second son was going to be a coach and she'll tell you, "When he was born!"

When Arleen and Vince tried to get Rich to take a bath, he would hold his breath until he actually passed out—at thirteen months. Stubbornness was in his genes, and so were sports. From the time he could hold his rubber ball, all he wanted to do was bounce it off the wall, the stairs, and the roof. "That was his life," Arleen says.

He also developed a unilateral rivalry with his brother Steve, who was just thirteen months older but much bigger, topping out in high school at 6'3", 250, and a natural athlete himself.

"When we taught Steve how to ride a bike," Arleen says, "Rich learned the same day. Anything Steve did, Rich wanted to do it better."

"And he *did* do it better," Vince added.

Almost all of Grant Town's six hundred people lived off the mines, shopped in the company store, and sent their kids to Miner Camp for two weeks every summer—where Rich won Best Camper three years in a row.

"Looking back on it, we lived pretty modestly—not that I knew it," Rodriguez told me. "We never went on vacations. Our house had no heat upstairs. I wore three sweat suits at night. And you'd wake up to see ice on the windows—on the *inside*. But we always had everything we needed, and everyone loved playing sports. That saved me."

Most of the townspeople had emigrated from Poland, Italy, Spain, and Mexico, and were just as ambitious as Rich was.

"They did not come here for the hell of it," said Joe Weir, Rodriguez's assistant high school football coach. "They were willing to work, but it made the town very competitive. If you're just playing marbles, *that* was really competitive. You wanted to win! *Everyone* was competitive."

Locals like to point out that this cluster of tiny towns in north-central West Virginia has produced far more than its fair share of big-name athletes and coaches. The list includes Hall of Fame linebacker Sam Huff; Frank Gatski, an All-Pro center for the Cleveland Browns; Nick Saban, who grew up fifteen miles away in Monongha, and Florida State coach Jimbo Fisher, from Clarksburg. Mary Lou Retton's father grew up in nearby Fairmont and played basketball with Jerry West at West Virginia. Retton was a friend of Rich's dad, and Rich played ball against all her brothers.

Rodriguez's teachers often told his mother he was the smartest boy in the class, but Rich admitted that there were only three boys in his class. "It was small potatoes, man."

The potatoes got a little bigger before Rodriguez's junior year, when four-hundred-student Fairview High School, Yost's alma mater, and three other small schools consolidated with North Marion to make it one of the bigger schools in the state.

Some of his classmates hated it, but Rodriguez thrived on the tougher competition. He was named All-State in football and basketball—leading the state in scoring part of his senior year, which helped his basketball team get to the finals—and became the school's first athlete to letter in four sports.

But football was the sport he loved, and his upbringing was uniquely suited to provide the young Rodriguez with the incentive, the competition, and the coaching necessary to reach the top in his field.

He was lucky to play tight end and safety for head coach Roy "Punk" Michaels, for example, who won three state championships without ever suffering a losing season.

Using methods similar to Schembechler's, Coach Michaels whittled down the roster from 140 to 50. In one loss, Rodriguez got turned around trying to make tackles so often, he was on his knees all night. Before the next practice, he looked in his locker to discover that someone had cut the knee pads off his practice pants. When he asked Michaels about it, the coach replied, "Maybe this way you'll get off your knees."

There was no point arguing with a coach in coal country. Rodriguez had scabs on his knees for weeks. But when he had finally learned to stay off his knees a month later, he found a new pair of practice pants hanging in his locker, complete with new knee pads.

"But by then, I'd grown proud of the pants I had," Rodriguez said. "I told him, 'Thanks, but I'll keep the old ones.'"

Rodriguez also showed signs of being a budding tactician. "When everyone else was just doing what they were told," Weir recalled, "Rich was having conversations with the coaches about strategy. In those days, quarterbacks timed their passes—one, two, three seconds, and throw—but Rich was already thinking about a different approach."

That came to light during their annual alumni game. Rodriguez started talking to Weir on the sidelines about tempo and timing, a conversation so unusual that Weir still remembers it.

"He thought you could speed things up with a no-huddle offense— which was almost never used in those days—and catch them off guard. And instead of just making the quarterback throw the ball to a certain spot after three seconds, he thought the quarterback could read the defense *before* the snap and run away from a defender if they're in man-to-man, or find his receivers sitting down in soft areas if the defense was in a zone.

"You got to understand: This guy was talking about the beginnings of the spread offense, in *high school*. Are you kidding me?

"I tell you, that kid was way, way ahead of his time."

Davidson, Marshall, and West Point offered Rodriguez basketball scholarships, but Rodriguez wanted to play football for West Virginia, even if the Mountaineers weren't that interested in him.

The Rodriguez boys could probably have qualified as minorities, but they never considered it. Rodriguez had been elected junior class president and narrowly missed out on being the valedictorian, so he was able to cobble together enough academic scholarship money to last one year. When that ran out, he had to either earn a full scholarship or drop out and go to one of the cheaper state schools like Fairmont State, which cost only $325 a semester at the time.

Rodriguez decided to bet on himself.

On his first trip to Morgantown, his father dropped him off on the wrong side of the stadium. Rodriguez still remembers how long that walk felt, circling the stadium, trying to figure out where he was supposed to go.

When he finally found the rest of the wide-eyed walk-ons gathered in the locker room, an assistant coach started yelling names off his clipboard, telling each player where he'd been assigned. After he'd finished, the assistant barked at Rodriguez.

"What're you doing here? Move!"

Rodriguez screwed up his courage and said, "You never called my name. Where do you want me to go?"

"Aren't you Gonzales?" he asked.

"No, sir, I'm Rodriguez. Rich Rodriguez."

"Ah, you're all the same anyway. I can't tell you apart."

Once Rodriguez concluded they had no idea who he was, his plan was simple: "I was going to get in as many fights as I could the first week, just so they would know my name. I played desperate—because I was."

"Rich was a very solid player," head coach Don Nehlen said. "He certainly was not very flashy. He was like his coach—slow! He was a 4.8 or 4.9 guy. But he was smart, and he could read a play."

At the end of his freshman year, Nehlen gave Rodriguez a full ride for his sophomore season. He'd made it.

His first big bet on himself had paid off—and with it, a mind-set began to take hold. Whenever Rodriguez faced a crossroads, he would bypass the safe route, take a chance on doing it his way, and usually make it pay, often quite handsomely.

Once again, Rodriguez's timing was impeccable. He joined the Mountaineers right as Nehlen started turning a program of perennial losers into a perennial bowl team, finishing all four of Rodriguez's seasons in the top twenty. Rodriguez got to learn from another master, one who had learned from Bo Schembechler when he assisted him in Ann Arbor.

"When I got to West Virginia," Nehlen said, "about all I did was turn the 'M' upside down. Whatever Bo did, we tried to do here."

After Rodriguez graduated in 1985, he spent a year on Nehlen's staff as a graduate assistant, then took a job as an assistant coach at a small school called Salem College. There he served under the unforgettable head coach Corky Griffith. Whenever Griffith's assistants presented him with a problem, he'd invariably say, "I'll solve your problem, Jack!" And he'd come back the next day with a solution you could never have imagined.

When they were having trouble recruiting, Corky put an ad in *USA Today*. "WANTED: Football players at Salem College. No experience necessary. See the country."

When Rodriguez told Corky they needed thigh pads, he returned the next day with boxes of *Reader's Digests*. "They're the Christmas issues!" he boasted. "Twice as thick as the normal ones!"

When Rodriguez told him they had no grass on their field, and no money for seed or turf, Corky said, "I'll be back tomorrow, Jack! Solve your problem!" And he returned the next day with a few guys in hazmat suits, who started spraying something on the field. The backs of their suits read HUMAN WASTE FACILITY. Corky had brought them down to shoot shit all over the field—for free. It smelled like shit, but the grass grew.

After Rodriguez's second season at Salem, 1988, Corky Griffith called him into his office and said, "It's all yours, Jack!"

"What is?"

"The team, Jack! I went out and bought a bar and a pontoon boat, and that's what I'm going to do."

So, at the ripe age of twenty-four, Rich Rodriguez became the youngest head coach in the country. He also got a raise, from $16,000 to $20,000 a year.

On Rodriguez's first team, he started fourteen true freshmen, including one player who "couldn't play dead in a Western." (That player, however, would go on to play a role in *Porky's II: The Next Day*.)

The team finished 2–8, but Rodriguez felt optimistic about the season ahead, until his phone rang one morning. The man claimed to be a reporter from the Associated Press. "How do you feel about your program being canceled?"

Rodriguez knew a prank when he heard one. But a few minutes later, the school's athletic director walked in to tell Rodriguez, "We're going to have a press conference to make an announcement that will be detrimental to your program."

There is detrimental, and there is detrimental. In this case, "detrimental" meant they were killing the football program, effective immediately. A Japanese university had just bought the school and had no interest in funding a football team—though, in fairness, no one outside the United States would ever understand why any college would fund a football team, or any other team.

Rodriguez had already proposed to Rita Setliff, a former West Virginia University cheerleader from Jane Lew, a town of about four hundred people just down Route 79 from Grant Town, where her family could get only channels 5 and 12. Since her dad would not let her watch *Three's Company* because it was too risqué, that left one channel, so she focused instead on basketball and tennis, and played both well enough to win the Lewis County High School Female Athlete of the Year award—to go with her homecoming queen crown.

"I liked her immediately," Rich said of their first meeting in the school cafeteria. "She was good-looking, had a great personality, sharp as can be—and she liked sports, too."

When Salem killed football, however, he realized he had a new car to pay for, a new house, and a fiancée who was betting on him.

"'Honey, I've got some good news, and I've got some bad news,'" he recalled telling her. "'The bad news is, the school just cut football, I don't have a job, and I've got no idea how I'm gonna pay for the car or the house.

"'But the good news is, I'm still gonna marry you!'

"And, God bless her, she still said yes."

For their honeymoon, all they could afford was Cedar Point for one night, but they remember it fondly.

Faced with the kinds of problems that make most new husbands head for the hills, the mines, or the cubicles, Rodriguez didn't hesitate. He returned to Morgantown, where Coach Nehlen welcomed him back as a volunteer assistant coach. Rodriguez paid his bills teaching driver's education on the side. But he was still in football. To Rodriguez, that's what mattered.

The next year, 1990, the Glenville State Pioneers came calling for a head coach. The pay was meager, the Pioneers hadn't won a single game the previous year, and it wasn't even an NCAA school. But it was a paid position, and a head coaching one at that. Rodriguez didn't sit around waiting for a better offer. He grabbed it.

To say Glenville, West Virginia, is in the middle of nowhere is not fair. It's actually fifteen miles off the interstate, which goes through the middle of nowhere. When Rodriguez moved there, it took forty-five minutes to get to the nearest McDonald's.

The Pioneers had 105 players, and only nine scholarships to divvy up among them. Rodriguez would take his broken-down tackling sleds to his dad to weld them back together, and Nehlen let Rodriguez ransack West Virginia's bins of used stuff. "Practice pants, jerseys, shoes, you name it," Nehlen recalled. "Rich grabbed everything he could."

One day one of the assistant coaches told Rodriguez, "We've got 105 guys out for the team and only 95 helmets."

"I figured the competition for those last ten helmets would be intense," Rodriguez said. "And it was!"

The program off the field matched the team on the field. "We were so bad that first year," Rodriguez admitted, "the crowd would literally give us a standing ovation if we got a first down. I'm not kidding. And they didn't have to do it very often."

The Pioneers finished that first season 1–7–1.

But the locals still loved him. "He lived in Glenville, right in the faculty apartments," his star receiver Chris George said. "He played in the local softball league, he played on the local nine-hole golf course. Rita played there. They *lived* there. He knew everyone, and everyone knew him."

"That's what made him so loved around this state," longtime sidekick Dusty Rutledge noted. "He was one of them."

But all that love was no substitute for winning. In need of leftover players, Rodriguez went back to the same place he got his leftover equipment: Morgantown. Nehlen told him he had about fifty walk-ons, and if Rodriguez could offer them at least room and board, he could probably get a few of them. Rodriguez scooped up a bunch, including quarterback Jed Drenning and receiver Chris George.

"Remember the Land of the Misfits?" Rodriguez asked. "Well, that was Glenville: the Land of the Misfits. A bunch of Rudolphs and Herbie the Dentists, and none bigger than me!

"But I've got to say, the kids we got were *hungry*. We might have all been misfits. We might have all been a little lost, trying to find something better. But we all wanted it, and wanted it *badly*. And we were willing to sacrifice to get it."

It will come as a surprise to Michigan fans who felt Rodriguez did not embrace Michigan tradition that right before Rodriguez's second season in Glenville "he puts that sign up in our weight room," George recalled, "THOSE WHO STAY WILL BE CHAMPIONS. And he didn't just put it up, he explained what it meant. He said, 'This is going to be hard. We're going to have people leave. We're going to have guys who can't handle it. But if you stick with me, you'll be rewarded. Trust me.' And we did."

The Pioneers still had a long way to go. "My first year," George said, "teams were laughing at us when we got on the field."

They had reason to. The Pioneers headed into their fifth game of Rodriguez's second year at 1–2–1, and they weren't likely to win against West Virginia State. "They were good," George said. "They beat [Drenning] to a pulp. He needed help just getting to the training room the next day."

In fact, he'd been sacked thirty-two times over his last two games, a season's worth even for a bad team. Worse, the Pioneers were about to face Wingate, which had whipped them 63–0 the year before. To say things looked grim is to understate the case considerably.

They say necessity is the mother of invention, and sometimes it's actually true. In 1945, Fritz Crisler had a bunch of seventeen-year-olds who were no match for the undefeated, top-ranked Army squad, with a bunch of twenty-five-year-old guys who had already swept Italy, Germany, and Japan. They were not scared of a bunch of teenagers. Crisler knew it was time to gamble.

Pioneer Stadium would never be confused with Yankee Stadium—your average suburban high school soccer field is nicer—but Rodriguez's desperation was every bit as great as Crisler's. And what he decided to do on that field that day would change the game more than anything since Crisler created his platoon system forty-six years earlier.

Quarterback Jed Drenning was so bruised from all those sacks that he begged his coach to use the shotgun formation. Drenning didn't know it,

of course, but he was talking to the right guy. Rodriguez had been thinking about using the shotgun on every play since his conversation with
Coach Weir on the high school sidelines. The Monday before the game
against Wingate, Rodriguez surprised his quarterback by asking, "How
often do you want to run out of the gun?"

"Coach, I'll run the clock out in the gun if you want."

Rodriguez nodded. Ideas that had been knocking around in his head
for years started coming together. He thought back to his days as a defensive back and asked himself: What was the toughest thing to defend? The
answer came to him in a snap: the two-minute drill.

Rodriguez surprised Drenning when he took it to its logical extreme:
"Let's see if we can do that the whole game." They would skip the huddle, go
to a shotgun snap on every play, put four or five receivers on the field,
spread them out as far as they could, and throw the ball all over the
place—and keep it up for sixty minutes.

Like Army in 1945, Wingate still won—but barely, escaping 17–15.

Using their never-ending two-minute drill, the Pioneers won three of
their last four games. Rodriguez was onto something.

"Whatever incarnation of Rich's offense exists today," Drenning told
Tim Layden, "it was born that day when we played Wingate. And he turned
the place around pretty quickly after that."

During a routine practice the next season, in 1992, Drenning inadvertently provided another piece of the puzzle for his coach, who was smart
enough to recognize it when he saw it.

As Tim Layden recounts in his excellent book *Blood, Sweat and Chalk*,
Drenning bobbled the snap and failed to hand the ball to the running
back in time. Normally when this happens, the quarterback simply follows
the running back to salvage what he can, but Drenning noticed that the
backside defensive end had already started bolting down the line to tackle
the running back, whom he thought had the ball. Drenning decided to
go in the opposite direction, to the spot where the backside defensive end
had started—which was now completely vacant.

Rodriguez blew the whistle. But he wasn't mad. He was curious. "Why
did you do that?"

"Do what?" asked Drenning.

"Why did you run *that* way?"

"The end pinched," Drenning said, though he could have just as easily
quoted Wee Willie Keeler: "I hit 'em where they ain't."

Every football coach in the country has seen his quarterback bobble a snap and run the wrong way on a broken play. And thousands of those quarterbacks probably did so for the same reason Drenning did. But not every coach had the curiosity to ask why and the insight to recognize what he'd just seen and heard for what it could be.

In fact, only one coach did: Rich Rodriguez.

Yost didn't invent the forward pass, of course. But when he saw Benny Friedman toss pass after pass to the sure-handed Bennie Oosterbaan, he knew they were going to change the game.

Likewise, Layden points out that Rodriguez was not the first coach to use the run and shoot with the shotgun, but he was almost certainly the first to come up with the zone read, in which the quarterback is a potential ball carrier, forcing the defensive end to cover him or chase the tailback. Spread them out, and the defender simply can't cover both.

Another secret was changing the way his quarterback gave out the ball. Instead of simply sticking it into the runner's gut, or faking it by holding the ball while putting his empty hand against the runner's stomach, in Rodriguez's zone read, the quarterback holds the ball with two outstretched hands and places it against the runner's belly—and lets it ride for a few feet, like a swinging gate, while he watches to see if the end is following the runner or staying put.

If the defensive end stays put, the quarterback releases the ball, and the runner senses that it's time to clamp down on it—with one fewer defender to worry about. But if the end starts heading after the runner, the quarterback pulls the ball and runs where the end had started.

It is an elegant, simple solution to an age-old problem that any chess player can appreciate. When you have eleven players and your opponent does, too, how do you gain an advantage? Knocking one of them over is one way, but it takes a lot of effort, you can always miss, and unless your guys are a lot bigger and stronger than the other guys, it probably won't work very often. But with the zone read, you force the defender to tip his hand first, and if you read his movement correctly—which any decent high school quarterback can do—you have successfully removed him from the play.

A pianist has eighty-eight keys at his disposal, and a chess master has sixteen pieces—and both of them must use their limited arsenal in ways no one has thought of before. A football coach has only eleven players, but on that fall day, on a scruffy practice field in Glenville, West Virginia, fifteen miles from the interstate to nowhere, Rich Rodriguez figured out a way to eliminate a defensive player without even touching him.

No one knew it yet, but the game had changed forever.

With this new key, the Pioneers started unlocking defenses that had been impenetrable just two years before.

"The defense didn't know what we were going to do next," Rodriguez said, "and they were chasing their tails, gasping for air. They had to respond to *us*. Given our record the previous year, that really impressed me."

While Rodriguez and his staff were still learning how their new weapon worked, they soon realized that it forced the opponent's defense to spread out, too. And once they did that, they couldn't help but show you how they planned to defend your play before you even snapped the ball—and not just the ends, either, but the linebackers, the corners, and the safeties, too.

This gave the Pioneers a great advantage, but only if they were smart enough to recognize it. The coaches started teaching their quarterbacks to look where the defenders were setting up and, based mainly on that information, call the play seconds before the snap. Once they got the hang of it, they could not only make the defensive ends chase the wrong guy but also send three or four defenders so far off the scent, they were no more dangerous than rusty tackling sleds sitting in the middle of the field.

That's when Drenning "started picking them apart," Rodriguez recalled. "*That* was fun!"

Even if the quarterback didn't make a complete read on the defense, or if the defense caught on to at least part of the joke being played on it, Rodriguez still held an advantage. If he could simply force all the defenders to cover all his players—including, crucially, the quarterback—he could make the defense play man-to-man against his receivers. That might not sound like much of an edge on paper, but when you consider that the receiver knows where he is going *and* where and when the ball is coming, it's a considerable advantage over the defender, who can only guess at all three questions.

It *is* like chess, with a catch: You get only three seconds to make your move, the opponent's pieces can weigh up to three hundred pounds, and if you make the wrong move, they'll smash you into the ground. If just one player blew his assignment, not only was the advantage instantly lost, but the ball carrier—usually the fleet-footed quarterback or a speedy little slot receiver—was badly exposed to getting blown up by a big, angry defender who was not going to pass up his chance to hurt the little guy who'd been making him look dumb all day. So, for Rodriguez and his system, being "all in" wasn't merely a motto; it was a necessity. By all accounts, he was not notably tolerant of missed assignments.

Off the field, Rodriguez was tougher. Commitment on the field started with commitment to the program, which entailed a commitment to being at Glenville—not the easiest sell. Dissension in the ranks at any level threatened the efficacy of the spread. "You got to remember these guys who came in who were outstanding athletes but didn't like Glenville," said Ike Morris, a local millionaire who bought the team a new field, "Rich got 'em out. Didn't care how good they were. This is very important about this guy, and one of those many qualities that endeared [him to me]."

"Being a good player, for Rich, was not a hall pass," said George, and he knew of what he spoke. More than once, the record-breaking receiver found himself running the hill behind the stadium for missing just one class. "After I graduated, I helped out at Fairmont [State University], and being good there was a hall pass. Good players got preferential treatment, which is usually how it is. Not Coach Rod. I think the world of him.

"You almost want to say he *demands* you're going to win. He instills it. All he needs is guys buying in—and it's over."

When Rodriguez started coaching, he spent his summers working at a camp run by Florida State University's head coach, Bobby Bowden, who told him, "When you're trying to build a program, you go through four stages: You lose big, you lose close, you win close, and finally you start winning big."

And that, he said, is how you build a program.

Rodriguez's first year at Glenville State, they mastered the lose big stage. His second year, after they started using the shotgun snap on every play, they learned how to lose close—witness the near-upset over Wingate—and win a few close ones, too, finishing with a 4–5–1 record. Rodriguez's third year, the Pioneers got the hang of winning close, going 6–4.

And by his fourth year, 1993, just as Bowden had promised, they started winning big—*very* big—beating up teams by scores like 45–0, 50–0, and 57–0, the last a whitewashing of former nemesis West Virginia State, the team that had crushed Drenning two years earlier. Fielding Yost himself would have been impressed.

"That year, it all came together," George recalled. "You didn't have guys who weren't bought in, quitting and falling off. We were all *his* guys."

The Pioneers had a tenacious defense and strong special teams, too, but the foundation was finding and developing the right players for this new offensive system.

"Jed Drenning was perfect for it," Rodriguez said. "He threw for more than ten thousand yards! You still see his name in all the record books. And the guy he was throwing to, Chris George, broke some of Jerry Rice's records. Four hundred and thirty catches in his career, and 144 in *one season*."

To put that in perspective, Anthony Carter, the three-time All-American receiver who shattered just about every Michigan receiving record a decade earlier, caught 161 passes in his entire collegiate career.

"Those guys were posting just ridiculous numbers," Rodriguez said, "Ridiculous. We had a hell of a team."

The Pioneers won their league title that year, 1993, with a 6–1 conference mark and took a 9–2 overall record into the NAIA national semifinal game.

The bad news: They would have to face Central State Ohio, a power-house. Most teams at that level might have fifteen to twenty-five scholar-ships to give out. Glenville State had nine, while Central State Ohio had ninety-nine, fourteen more than Michigan, Notre Dame, or any other Division I school, which are limited to eighty-five. Central State used theirs to get Division I players who might have gotten in trouble here or there, or didn't want to sit out a year after transferring.

To say they were loaded is to put it lightly. Their quarterback, Charles Thompson, had started at Oklahoma—the Sooners, that is—but got in trouble with the law and had to resort to the NAIA. They also put two de-fensive linemen in the NFL, one of whom, Hugh Douglas, would become a first-round draft pick, the Rookie of the Year, a three-time Pro Bowler, and a ten-year veteran. It would be men against boys.

The Pioneers had home field, but their stadium was too small to hold the fans, so they moved the game just down the road to Summersville High School. On game day in late November, "it was a monsoon!" Arleen Rodri-guez remembered. "No umbrella could save you that day!"

On the first play, Hugh Douglas all but obliterated the Pioneer ball carrier. "I remember going back to the huddle," George said, "and thinking, 'That didn't end well.'"

But Rodriguez's spread offense was still so new that no one else was using it, so it was hard to prepare for the Pioneers. Glenville State didn't score much, but they controlled the ball as well as Central State—well enough to pull off the upset, 13–12.

Rodriguez's players were ecstatic and dumped the water jug on him.

"Rich *dove* in that mud after they won!" Arleen said.

"That was about as happy as I've ever felt coaching," he said. "Yeah, we were living in a small town, working at a small school, and playing in a small league. But it didn't *feel* any smaller. So that win's as good as it gets for me. It was the culmination of everything we'd been working for."

After Canham stepped down in 1988, Schembechler accepted the post. But because he was still coaching, President James Duderstadt assigned former campus administrator Jack Weidenbach to assistant AD.

When Weidenbach asked Canham, an old friend, about Duderstadt's offer, Canham said, "Jack, there is no way you're qualified for the job as athletic director at this school or any other school at this level. This is not some backwater high school situation. Someone must be kidding."

They weren't, but it didn't seem to matter at the time.

When the Big Ten presidents voted Penn State into the conference in 1990 without even informing their athletic directors they were going to do so, "I knew right then and there that the old days were over, when an athletic director was expected to run his department," Schembechler told me. "That did it for me. I knew I was out that day."

As Canham had feared, Weidenbach became the full-time athletic director. He was rapidly followed by Joe Roberson, Tom Goss, and finally Bill Martin before the 1990s closed. Yes, the same department that had needed only three directors for sixty-seven years had to hire five in the next twelve.

All of them had done something impressive before accepting the post—usually in business or on the Hill, which is what athletic directors call the central administration—but three of them didn't seek the job, two were hired as interim directors, and, after Schembechler, not one of them had any experience working in athletics.

As odd as hiring five straight athletic directors with no direct experience seems, especially for one of the foremost athletic departments in the country, it wasn't an accident. It was the *point*.

At Duderstadt's retirement banquet in 1996, he said that being Michigan's president for eight years was not always easy, but there were some nice perks. He even got the chance to meet the man thousands of people consider God.

"No," he said, "not Bo Schembechler, but the Dalai Lama."

It got a laugh, but it also revealed one of the truths of Duderstadt's reign. He was acutely aware of the coach's power, and he resented it.

Michigan presidents since James B. Angell have believed athletic directors and football coaches have had too much autonomy, and they have often dreaded dealing with them.

The solution? Hire a handpicked outsider more familiar with their world than the coaches were. And, after a century-long struggle stretching all the way back to the battles between Yost and Angell, they finally had the power to fulfill their wish.

"It's become more of a business situation than it used to be, but the biggest thing is still to help your coach succeed," said Bump Elliott, who had been an All-American on Crisler's Mad Magicians before becoming Michigan's head coach and finally Iowa's AD. "If your [football] coach doesn't win, it doesn't matter how good a businessman you are."

"They say it's more important nowadays to have a business background than an athletic one," Canham said. "I disagree. You have to have an athletic background first, or you don't know what's going on. You cannot run a hospital without medical people. You cannot run an athletic department without sports people. You just don't know what to look for."

Duderstadt obviously disagreed, but the former administrators' very weakness and inexperience resulted in more scandals in the 1990s alone—with twenty-eight separate headline grabbers on the Detroit papers' front pages—than Michigan had suffered in the previous eight decades combined. The biggest problem proved to be the basketball program, when it was discovered Chris Webber and other Michigan basketball players had received hundreds of thousands of dollars from a corrupt booster.

The NCAA gave the Wolverines four years' probation and took away 113 wins, plus every NCAA, NIT, and Big Ten banner Michigan had won during that ugly era.

"That's my point," Canham said. "The administrators under [the outsider ADs] have never been in the trenches and don't know what to look for."

It was also the presidents who approved conference basketball tournaments, conference football title games, the BCS bowl system, and the twelfth regular-season football game—while limiting the number of walk-ons each team could have.

"It's all being driven by money," Weidenbach told me. "I can think of no other reason. It's hard enough to be a student athlete already. Bo was against it, I was against it—but nobody asked us."

James B. Angell would have been proud of President Duderstadt's intentions—but likely appalled by the results.

When Michigan athletics entered its second century in the Big Ten, the fate of its vaunted tradition and autonomy were both in jeopardy.

In 2000, then president Lee Bollinger fired Tom Goss, who served as the fall guy for Bollinger's ill-considered "maize halo." Bollinger talked his good friend, local real estate tycoon Bill Martin, into taking the job for just six months or so until they could find a permanent replacement.

Bollinger had good reason to tap Martin for the temporary post. When Martin was still a Michigan MBA student in the 1960s, he had parlayed an emergency student loan into the largest private real estate empire in the county—so big that the university today has to spend over $5 million every year just to lease his property. (Michigan's biggest landlord, however, is Domino's Farms.)

When Martin was in business school, he realized that "I was not driven by wealth or fame. I was driven to be independent and not have to answer to anyone."

Even on the weekends, he went his own way. He was famous for saying, "Why would I want to sit inside a packed stadium on a perfectly good day for sailing?" In Ann Arbor, the statement was virtually blasphemous.

But Martin sailed to win—and often did. He was appointed president of the U.S. Sailing Association, then USOC sailing director and USOC board member, serving on its budget committee.

When Martin accepted Bollinger's offer, the athletic facilities hadn't been updated in a decade, the department was $3 million in debt, and the basketball program was about to get hammered by the NCAA investigation.

Bollinger gave him no job description, simply telling him, "Go down there and see what you can do."

When it came time to find a permanent replacement, Martin declined to throw his hat into the ring. His company was very successful, but very private, with just a handful of employees—not exactly the environment the Michigan athletic director finds himself working in. But when the coaches presented Bollinger with a petition to keep Martin, he accepted Bollinger's request on one condition: that his salary be one dollar a year. Bollinger wisely did not make a counteroffer.

At the end of Martin's first year, *The Ann Arbor News* named him "Citizen of the Year." During his term as chairman of the Big Ten athletic directors, he was part of the negotiating team for the league's contract with ESPN—in which ESPN paid about a third more dollars for a third less programming, and gave the Big Ten its library of old games—and aided the effort to launch the league's own network. After a rocky start, the Big Ten Network has succeeded wildly, providing a measure of financial stability to every member, which helped lure Nebraska.

But Martin's bailiwicks were bricks and budgets. Under Martin's tenure, Michigan would create or renovate no fewer than twelve major buildings. Football received $226 million for the stadium renovation (plus a new $26 million practice building and a $3 million locker room), basketball would get a new $23 million practice facility, and the hockey arena added a $2 million club level.

But the sports formerly called "nonrevenue" also made out quite well under Martin. For baseball, wrestling, women's gymnastics, and softball, Martin built brand-new state-of-the-art facilities, for a total of $32 million, not to mention facilities that benefit all sports, such as the Junge Champions Center, the ticket office, the administration building, and the academic center, totaling $21 million.

The facilities are not only first-rate functionally, they are architecturally consistent, classic, and appealing—in contrast to the pell-mell buildings on the Hill.

The decadelong building boom cost a total of $333 million. Yet, when Martin stepped down, the Michigan athletic department enjoyed a $20 million annual surplus, he had doubled its "piggy bank" of unrestricted operating reserves to $35 million, and its endowment had almost tripled to $56 million.

As a result, the department has no trouble footing the bill for the five hundred athletes' scholarships it pays for each year. In 2010–11, that came to roughly $15 million each year, for which the department wrote an actual check to the folks up on the Hill. Despite the considerable cost, Michigan never nudges the coaches to recruit more in-state kids to save money. "We pay retail," Martin told me. "So I suppose that makes the athletic director the biggest dad at U-M."

When it came to bricks and budgets, no one—not even Fielding H. Yost or Don Canham—outperformed Bill Martin.

In 2006, Martin attended the regents' meeting in Dearborn that approved his plan to add luxury boxes to the Big House, the pièce de résistance of his building program. On the way back, Martin and five employees stopped for a celebratory beer at an Ann Arbor pub. They felt relieved, happy, even satisfied. In just six years, Martin had fulfilled his ambitious agenda—out of the red, off probation, with great facilities covering Ferry Field and beyond. The rest was just filling in the blanks.

After they toasted Martin's success, PR man Bruce Madej said, "You know what you should do?"

"What's that?"

"Walk straight into [President] Mary Sue [Coleman's] office and retire tomorrow."

Martin laughed.

"He thought I was kidding," Madej says today.

"If he had decided to ride off into the sunset after the luxury boxes were approved," says Percy Bates, the longtime faculty representative on Michigan's athletic board, "he would have gone down as one of the greats."

When Gary Moeller was let go in 1995, athletic director Joe Roberson tapped Lloyd Carr to be the interim coach. After struggling through two 8–4 seasons, Carr's 1997 squad captured Michigan's first national title in fifty years. It was probably the best thing to happen to him, and maybe the worst. After the Michigan faithful had gotten a taste of life at the very top, it seemed like nothing else was good enough.

From 1997 through 2004, Carr's teams played one hundred games, winning a remarkable seventy-eight of them, averaging almost ten wins a season while grabbing five Big Ten titles. But, incredibly, criticism of Carr actually seemed to grow. The complaint went like this: His teams were boring, his offense was outdated, and his defense couldn't stop mobile quarterbacks in general and the spread offense in particular—the last point punctuated by a loss to Northwestern in 2000 when the once lowly

Wildcats beat the Wolverines for the third time in six years, that time by the unheard-of score of 54–51.

Michigan fans are uncommonly loyal and knowledgeable, and gracious toward opponents—even in defeat. They do not believe in a win-at-all-costs approach, and take great pride in the sterling reputation of the program.

But they can also be very fickle. If Episcopalians are "God's frozen people," then a segment of Michigan backers could be called the Episcopalians of college football—less fans than opera critics, sitting quietly in their seats, waiting for someone to screw up so they can show their friends how much smarter they are than the coaching staff. More than a few Michigan fans are simply not happy unless they're not happy. That's probably true of the fans of most elite programs, but it doesn't make it any more appealing.

To test this theory, in 2003 my Sunday morning radio cohost and I posed a challenge to our listeners. The day before, the Wolverines had smoked fifteenth-ranked Notre Dame 38–0—the series's first shutout since 1902—in a nearly flawless performance. So, we asked our listeners, what can you find to criticize? We thought we were making a joke. But to our amusement, and our amazement, the callers had no problem filling two hours with a stream of original complaints.

While such talk wouldn't have mattered much to Schembechler, who possessed an almost superhuman immunity to criticism, it affected Carr. This is a man who would walk out to his secretary's desk between lunch and practice each day, ask for the mail, then shut his door and go through each and every letter, including the angry ones. (He was generous enough to compose handwritten replies to the nice ones.)

Each week he went through the game program and circled everything he didn't like—right down to an ad for Velveeta cheese featuring former Ohio State quarterback turned ESPN analyst Kirk Herbstreit—and told the sports information people to make sure it was pulled by the next week. Inside the department, such stories earned him the nickname "Paranoid Lloyd."

While Carr's psychology was not ideally designed for the overhyped era in which he coached, it was also part of his charm. If he voraciously consumed all the gossip coming in, he was utterly disciplined about not letting it out. In press conferences, he could be closed off, curt, and even condescending—often appropriately, given the inanity of the questions—but I cannot recall a single gaffe in his thirteen years at the helm.

When Carr spoke to a large class I was teaching, he told the students if he was not a college football coach, he would have been a high school teacher, and a very happy one. The shelves in his office groaned under the weight of books by Doris Kearns Goodwin, Stephen Ambrose, and Jon Krakauer. He also kept, just outside his office door, an unabridged dictionary on an oak table.

I once teased him about it. "I haven't seen too many coaches look up words in a dictionary."

"Don't be impressed," he said. "It's only because I don't know them."

When I first reported this several years ago, I was surprised how quickly it became part of Carr lore—exactly the kind of image, of course, Michigan wanted for its football program: a wordsmith who won games.

At Schembechler's public memorial service at Michigan Stadium, they assembled an all-star team of eulogists, most of them national figures. But Carr gave the most polished and touching talk of the day. He was simply an outstanding spokesman for the team and the school.

To the day Schembechler died, he was the godfather of the Michigan football family. If a former player or coach got out of line, he could be confident Schembechler would be calling within twenty-four hours. The conversation would be brief, one-sided, and highly effective.

"That was the good thing about Bo," said Jamie Morris, who broke Michigan's career rushing record in the 1980s. "He would get you in his office, and say, 'You need to shut up,' and that was it. Wasn't much to talk about after that!"

But if you were a Michigan Man in good standing—whether an All-American or a walk-on—and you needed something, even $150,000 for a bone marrow transplant, Schembechler would mobilize the Michigan family immediately, and you could be assured help was coming, and fast.

When Canham said, "It didn't change until Bo left, and then it changed almost overnight," he was talking about the athletic department, but he could have been talking about the Michigan family.

Within months of Bo's passing, Harbaugh accused Michigan football of slipshod academics, Mike Hart replied that Harbaugh was not a Michigan man, and suddenly none of the old rules seemed to apply, with everyone airing his laundry in public, and the media taking shots it wouldn't have dared to do just a year earlier.

The institutional discipline that had ruled the program since its inception was eroding—and fast—with serious consequences in the years to come.

Near the end of Schembechler's life, he had lunch with Morris and his beloved quarterback, John Wangler. "When I leave this earth," Schembechler told them, "we are going to see the true Michigan Men come out."

"I didn't know what he was saying then," Morris said.

"I do now."

Most fans assume once a football coach has had some success, the bigger programs will start beating a path to his door.

Not always.

At Glenville State, Rodriguez posted a 43–28–2 record over seven seasons, with four consecutive conference title teams that never lost more than one league game each season—all while introducing the game's most important innovation of the decade.

Didn't matter.

Year after year, Rodriguez not only didn't get any calls from Division I schools looking for a coordinator or an assistant coach, even the bigger schools in his own conference—teams he was beating regularly—never called when they had an opening. Rodriguez was initially puzzled, then frustrated, and finally curious. But, he said, the minute he quit worrying about his next job and focused on the one he had, things started stirring.

In his fourth year at Glenville, Rodriguez added the position of athletic director, which boosted his salary from $35,000 to $50,000. If he stayed one more year he stood to receive a $50,000 annuity: "Big money to me," he said. But in 1997, Tulane head coach Tommy Bowden called out of the blue. Rodriguez didn't know Tommy as well as he knew his dad, Bobby, and he knew even less about Tulane. But he was willing to listen.

After a brief bit of small talk, Bowden asked point-blank, "So, would you like to come down?"

"What's the job?"

"Offensive coordinator."

"Wow, that's something," Rodriguez said. "But you know I run this spread offense, right?"

"Run whatever you want."

It was the break he'd been waiting for, but Rodriguez still had his doubts. Rita had just given birth to Raquel, they had never lived out of the state, and the money at Glenville was getting better. Rodriguez also wasn't sure if the spread option offense would work in Division I.

Rita wasn't having it. "If you don't take this, you might not get another chance."

"As usual," Rodriguez noted, "Rita was right."

But in his first spring game at Tulane, his offense couldn't even get a first down. "It was like our first year at Glenville all over again." Rodriguez's fancy new offense was so pathetic that Tulane's defensive coach let one of his student trainers call the defense—and her plays were producing sacks, too.

"Don't worry about it," Bowden told Rodriguez. "It'll come together. This is what I hired you to do."

When Bowden's crew took over, the mayor of New Orleans, a Tulane grad, told them Tulane football succeeds only when the city's with them. When Tulane opened the 1997 season in the Superdome against Cincinnati, only fifteen thousand fans bothered to show up to see the debut of the spread offense. The city was clearly not with them.

The Bearcats had little trouble jumping ahead 10–0, while Tulane couldn't seem to move the ball at all.

"We are in some serious trouble here," Rodriguez thought. "But all of a sudden—and I remember it like it was yesterday—[quarterback] Shaun King calls a play-action pass, and he hits the fullback on a wheel route, and it goes for a 40-yard touchdown."

Tulane won 31–17, and the Green Wave started to roll. Rodriguez kept tinkering with his new machine, adding wrinkles, including a slot check for every running play. If the slot receiver—who sets up between the tight end and the wide receivers—was not covered, the quarterback was instructed to forget the run and just throw it to him. That's why slots don't have to be tall, just fast, which allowed Rodriguez to recruit players most teams overlooked.

Rodriguez also wanted King to utilize the zone read more often. Originally, whenever the defensive end started chasing the ball carrier, Rodriguez wanted his quarterback to pull the ball and run into the space just vacated, like Drenning did that memorable day in Glenville. But King knew he could get crushed, and he wanted no part of it. He made a deal with Rodriguez: If no receivers were open, *then* he'd run it.

Rodriguez wisely adapted, the Green Wave kept winning, and the crowds started coming. Tulane finished the 1997 season at 7–4, the kind of mark that would create complaints at Michigan but generated something closer to euphoria at Tulane. It was the program's best season since 1980, producing twenty-five school and conference records.

After starting the 1998 season with three straight victories, Shaun King broke his left wrist. They devised a special cast for his nonthrowing hand, taught the center to hike the shotgun snap to his right, and kept tearing up the record book. King threw thirty-eight touchdowns against only six interceptions, breaking Danny Wuerffel's record 178 quarterback rating with a 183.

"I can't remember Shaun missing a single open touchdown pass all year," Rodriguez said.

In a 49–35 win over Navy, King became the first quarterback in NCAA history to pass for 300 yards and run for 100 in the same game.

With Shaun King showing just what the spread offense could do, the Green Wave rolled into its last regular season game against Louisiana Tech with a 10–0 record and a seventh-place national ranking—but there were already rumors that Tommy Bowden might be headed to Clemson.

The Superdome was packed—a far cry from the paltry fifteen thousand who showed up to see their first game the year before. The fans got what they wanted. Tulane scored on its first possession. And the next. And the next. And kept it up for ten straight possessions. Well, except two: at the end of the first half, and at the end of the game, when Shaun King took a knee.

"That place was rockin'!" Rodriguez recalled. "Everybody was happy."

When the team ran off the Superdome field, the crowd started chanting, "Stay, Tommy, Stay!"

But a few days later Bowden announced he had accepted the job at Clemson. The papers and radio shows all figured Rodriguez was the heir apparent.

Tulane interviewed Gary Crowton, the head coach at Louisiana Tech; Chris Scelfo, a Louisiana native and assistant at Georgia; and Rodriguez. After Rodriguez's interview with athletic director Sandy Barbour went smoothly, "she tells me the next step is to meet with the president at his house that Saturday night.

"I go through my little speech with him, too. We chat, and after two hours or so, we shake hands and I walk back to my office. Sandy comes over and says, 'The president was really impressed. Everything looks good. We'd like to have a press conference Monday at eleven. I'll call you tomorrow at three to go over the details.'"

But by three o'clock that Sunday, Rodriguez still hadn't heard from anyone. Rita said, "Rich, something's up."

Monday morning, still in the dark, Rodriguez got to the office by six, as usual—but this time he was wearing his green Tulane jacket and tie. He had started on his paperwork when the line coach, Ron West, poked his head in to say, "Looks like we got a new coach."

"What do you mean?" Rodriguez replied, not sure if he was referring to him or someone else.

West held up the *New Orleans Times-Picayune*, which announced Tulane's new coach: Louisiana native Chris Scelfo. As Rodriguez read this, Sandy Barbour stopped by, still wearing her sweat suit from the night before.

"We decided to go in a different direction," she said.

"Yeah, I can see that," Rodriguez said, pointing to the paper. "Tell me, did I blow something in the interview?"

"No, no," she said. "Your interview went great. But we just decided to go in a different direction."

When she left, Rodriguez slumped back in his seat and loosened his tie. He decided he should meet with the team. "Guys, I don't want to have to tell you this, but I'm not gonna be the head coach."

Rodriguez didn't want to go to the press conference, either, but figured if he didn't, everyone would assume he was off pouting somewhere. So he found a spot on the third floor of the athletic department atrium, looking down at the press conference below. "Man, that was embarrassing. I felt like a junior high school kid all over again, like you wore the wrong shirt and everyone's looking at you. 'What kind of loser is that guy in the balcony?'

"I just wanted to go—anywhere."

Bowden couldn't believe it and offered Rodriguez the coordinator job at Clemson. Bowden sent Clemson's private plane, with the Tigers' trademark orange paw painted on the tail, and a bouquet of orange roses waiting for Rita on her seat. They had them.

But Tulane's new head coach, Chris Scelfo, asked all the assistants to stay on to coach Tulane in the Liberty Bowl against Brigham Young. Reluctantly, Rodriguez agreed. The Green Wave drowned the Cougars 41–

27 to finish a perfect 12–0 season, then carried Rodriguez off the field, chanting his name. "For all the ups and downs of this crazy profession," he said, "a day like that goes a long way."

No matter how outlandish the results—maybe *because* of the outlandish results—critics always said the same thing: "Sure, the spread option worked down there, but it will never work up here."

When Bowden and Rodriguez took the spread to Clemson, the critics looked pretty smart—at first.

Clemson opened the 1999 season at home against Marshall, led by future New York Jets quarterback Chad Pennington. But the Thundering Herd had become a Division I, Mid-American Conference team just two years earlier, so no one thought they had much of a chance. The Tigers' fancy new offense, however, could muster only 10 points, and they lost a shocker 13–10.

The natives were not happy, and Rodriguez was about to hear why. Only after the game did he remember that all the coaches had gotten dressed at the field house across the street. No big deal, right? He put his coaching clothes back on, grabbed his bag, and started walking across the parking lot toward the field house, through three hundred yards of tail-gaters, and that's when the thought popped into his head: "Rodriguez, this might not have been the best idea you've ever had."

But then he thought, "Well, I'm new here, and I'm only an assistant coach anyway. Maybe they won't know who I am." But when he looked down and saw he was wearing his bright orange CLEMSON FOOTBALL polo shirt and a bright orange CLEMSON FOOTBALL hat and carrying a bag that said CLEMSON FOOTBALL—well, that's when he realized the odds of his getting across the parking lot unnoticed were pretty slim.

At about the exact moment all these thoughts occurred to him, ten yards into his walk, he started hearing it.

"Hey, nice offense, Mr. Genius!"

"What kind of high school plays you gonna run next week, brainiac?"

"Go back to Tulane!"

"You hear the first one, you tune it out," Rodriguez recalled with a grin. "But once they started in on me, word spread pretty fast, and all of a sudden every damn tailgater in the state turned around to let me have it.

"That was my first experience in Death Valley—and that's when I learned they were serious about that Death part."

The Tigers and Rodriguez redeemed themselves the following week by beating league rival Virginia 33–14. They finished the season at 6–6—up from 3–8 the year before—but they still took those losses hard.

Rodriguez and Bowden ran together every day. They had two paths: If they won that Saturday, they'd run all week decked out in their Clemson gear on the sidewalks through town, waving at all the fans honking their horns. But if they lost, they'd take their "alternate route," wearing gray sweats and baseball caps, through the woods and lakes, risking only angry squirrels.

Fortunately for Bowden and Rodriguez, they needed to resort to the alternate route less and less during Rodriguez's time at Clemson.

In 2000, Bowden's second year there, the Tigers won their first eight games, they were ranked fourth in the nation, and they had an outside shot at a national title game. Things were getting serious when they traveled to play the 5–2 Ramblin' Wreck of Georgia Tech in Atlanta.

The Tigers fell behind 31–28 in the fourth quarter. On third down, with 1 yard to go around Tech's 40-yard line, Rodriguez figured Georgia Tech had to be expecting a run up the middle, maybe even a quarterback sneak.

"So, smart me, I called a reverse—and we lose 6 yards! We're out of field goal range, we had to punt, and there goes the game, the undefeated season, and the shot at a national title. Kerplooie!"

When a dejected Rodriguez got home that night, Rita knew not to say anything to him about the game for a while. But after Clemson beat South Carolina a few weeks later, she finally asked him, "Honey, when you were playing Georgia Tech, why'd you call that reverse?"

"Oh, that? I thought I might surprise 'em. Honestly, why do you always have to second-guess my decisions?"

"Honey, I just want to *understand.*"

"That's her fallback line," Rich said. "Hard to argue with that. But man, I already endured three press conferences the day we lost that game, and here's my fourth, three weeks later. And my wife is always the toughest."

But there was a bigger point: Like all good gamblers, Rodriguez was smart enough to learn his lesson, but strong enough not to be paralyzed by the setback.

Back in Morgantown, on November 4, 2000, Don Nehlen announced he would be retiring at the end of the year. He had delivered twenty-one very good years for West Virginia, breaking just about every coaching record they had, and bringing them to the brink of the school's first national title twice.

About that time, Arleen Rodriguez was sitting in the Clemson stands next to Ann Bowden—Bobby's wife and Tommy's mom—and mentioned that Rich had always wanted to be the coach at West Virginia, where Ann's husband had coached and two of her sons had played in the 1970s.

"I'll never forget it," Arleen recalled. "She turned right to me, and she said, 'Honey, you go right home and talk him out of it. They're gonna break his heart and hurt him. I'm telling you that right now.'

"'Oh, we have lots of friends there.'

"'Honey, listen to me. Our boys went to high school there and played for Bobby and it didn't matter. They hung him in effigy. You don't know what you're getting into.'"

Arleen would have reason to remember that.

Chris Scelfo would go 37–57 at Tulane, never finishing higher than fifth in Conference USA, proving once again that college football is an objective meritocracy for the players, but a club for the coaches, at least when it comes to getting hired. Rodriguez was learning all this the hard way, so he knew—as much as they loved Clemson—if he got a call from West Virginia, where he had lots of support, he'd better take it.

The athletic director, Eddie Pastilong, had promised Nehlen that he would be able to name his successor. But while he was making that promise to Nehlen, he was calling Glenville and West Virginia booster Ike Morris to get his views on Rich Rodriguez. (Pastilong did not respond to requests for an interview.)

"You got to look at him," Morris said. "He's won everywhere he went. If you can win here at Glenville, you can win *anywhere!*"

The Sunday after Thanksgiving, Pastilong announced that West Virginia was hiring Rich Rodriguez to lead the Mountaineers.

This came as news to Nehlen, who had promised his assistant coaches they would all have jobs after he left—the same promise Schembechler had made to his staff when he retired.

"Naturally I was a little disappointed that the administration didn't look at one or two of my guys a little closer," he told me. "But I knew Rich was a very strong candidate, and he was very well connected here, and it's a very political state. They love their own. The governor was from right down the road from Rich's hometown. [Rich] was connected with the AD, and he got the job. But he had good credentials, no question about that."

In the Music City Bowl, Nehlen's last game, the Mountaineers whipped up on Mississippi 49–38 and put their old coach on their shoulders on the way out—a fitting send-off.

After fifteen years of sacrificing to achieve his childhood dream, Rodriguez had finally become a Division I head coach—at his alma mater, no less. He had arrived.

It looked like his path was paved with gold. The home fans were basking in the return of a native son, one who had played and coached for the Mountaineers, then had gone off to figure out his fancy new offense before his triumphant return to an adoring public.

Rodriguez quickly discovered that the job came with some unexpected perks. People in West Virginia will tell you the Mountaineers' head football coach is more powerful than their governor. "Only one person was ever bigger than the head coach," Arleen said, "and that was [U.S. senator] Robert C. Byrd." But some say that's not true: Even Byrd wasn't bigger.

A few months after Rodriguez took over, without any notice whatsoever, the dirt road in Grant Town he had walked on all those pitch-black nights after basketball games suddenly got paved.

Arleen called her son to say, "Thank you!"

"Don't thank me," he said. "I didn't even know they were doing that."

That spring, and again without notice, a sign went up in Rodriguez's hometown.

WELCOME TO GRANT TOWN
HOME OF RICH RODRIGUEZ, HEAD COACH
WEST VIRGINIA UNIVERSITY MOUNTAINEERS

It looked like it was built to last.

He would need that support. In his first year, Rodriguez turned a 7–5 bowl champion team with seventeen returning starters into a 3–8 bottom feeder. Rodriguez was accustomed to bumpy starts—in fact, those were the only kind he knew—but that didn't mean everyone else was. Nehlen, for one, wasn't thrilled. "When I retired, my friends said, 'You're crazy,' because we were going to be 8–3 or 9–2 the next year. We had great talent.

But I knew it was easy to sit in the press box and criticize. It was water over the dam."

It was more than just the losses, though, that separated the two regimes.

"Rich's coaching on the field was so much different than mine, especially after I'd been a head coach for twenty-one years," Nehlen said. "When you know you're about to step down, you're a little mellower, I guess would be the term. Going from me in my last year to Rich—well, he was such a shock to our guys, they didn't know how to take it. A lot of them rebelled. I could tell just from watching the field that they weren't playing for him."

But Nehlen knew what Bump Elliott had done for Bo Schembechler, refusing to talk to his former players who were eager to complain about the new coach, and supporting Schembechler every chance he had, publicly and privately. Nehlen also knew just how much Schembechler appreciated Elliott's class and loyalty to the day he died. So, when Nehlen's former players tried to complain to him about the new guy, he told them if they had a problem, they had to talk to their coach—not him.

Rodriguez's second year didn't start off much better. In their fifth game, the 3–1 Mountaineers got humiliated 48–17 by rival Maryland. They had reason to fear that their upcoming seven-game Big East schedule—the same one that had given them a 1–6 record the year before—could crush them again.

But that's when Bobby Bowden's prophecy—you lose big, you lose close, you win close, and then you win big—proved true once more. The Mountaineers took six of their next seven games, the only loss coming to first-ranked Miami. Along the way, West Virginia knocked off number thirteen Virginia Tech and number seventeen Pittsburgh, earning West Virginia a top-fifteen ranking itself. The 1–6 to 6–1 conference records marked the greatest turnaround in the history of the Big East, which named Rodriguez Coach of the Year.

Rodriguez had dodged disaster—and an early departure. But winning came with a price, too.

Perhaps only Louisiana State University, during the reign of Governor Huey Long, could claim such a close relationship between the state's flagship university and its state capital. During Long's one term in the Governor's Mansion, from 1928 to 1932, he picked LSU's president, he doubled

LSU's enrollment, he quadrupled the size of its marching band, he wrote some of the songs the band plays to this day, and he even designed a play he wanted the football team to run.

Rodriguez's relationship with Governor Joe Manchin was at least as strange.

"It must have been 2005," recalled businessman, booster, and Rodriguez friend Matt Jones. He and Rodriguez were playing golf at the Pete Dye Golf Club in Bridgeport, about forty-five minutes from Morgantown; the club also served as the boosters' base of operations. "We're on the third or fourth tee, and he gets a call on his cell phone. We don't know who it is.

"At first he's walking far behind the tee, trying to be quiet, but then he starts screaming. 'This is bullshit! Why don't *you* run the government and *I* run the football team!'"

"What the hell was that?"

"Damn it," Rodriguez said. "He's going to make us play Marshall."

The "he" in question turned out to be Governor Joe Manchin, who had grown up in Farmington, just a few miles from Grant Town, and first met Rodriguez when he was a teenager working in Manchin's carpet store down the street. Manchin had made a campaign promise in 2004 that, if elected, he would get Marshall on West Virginia's schedule. "And that got him the southern vote," where Marshall is located, Jones said.

The Marshall backers had been begging for the game for years. After Marshall's team plane crashed in 1970 (inspiring the movie *We Are Marshall,* starring Matthew McConaughey), Marshall posted the fewest wins of any major college team the rest of that decade. But they notched the most victories in the 1990s, when Chad Pennington was throwing to Randy Moss. The fans down there were clamoring for a game against their big brothers in Morgantown, who had little to gain and a lot to lose.

Over Rodriguez's private protests, Manchin set up an unconventional three-game series, with the 2006 and 2008 contests to be played in Morgantown, and 2007 in Huntington. Whoever won two out of three would host the game in 2009—with a few hundred thousand in the balance, putting even more pressure on the nineteen-year-old kickers. In 2006, the Mountaineers won big, 42–10, but in 2007, on a blazing-hot day at Marshall's smaller stadium, West Virginia was losing 13–6 at halftime.

Manchin, standing on the sideline near Matt Jones, said, "Boy, isn't this a beautiful day in West Virginia!"

"Governor," Jones said, "you better hope West Virginia wins."

"Why's that?"

"Because if they don't, you'll never win another election."

What would be a joke in almost any other state was probably a fair prediction in West Virginia. The Mountaineers pulled ahead 48–23 and remained undefeated.

Joe Manchin was reelected in 2008 with 70 percent of the vote. Huey Long would have tipped his hat.

After Rodriguez's rough start, the Mountaineers ran off three good marks of 9–4, 8–4, and 8–4, capturing two Big East titles. In 2005, Rodriguez's fifth season, the Mountaineers started winning big, just as Bobby Bowden would have predicted.

The Mountaineers' 2005 conference title and 10–1 overall record earned them a berth in the 2006 Sugar Bowl. But that meant they had to face the eighth-ranked, SEC-champion Georgia Bulldogs. And, because of Hurricane Katrina, the Sugar Bowl moved the game for that year only to the Georgia Dome, right in the Bulldogs' backyard.

Adding to the pressure, the Big East had fared poorly in BCS games. It had never qualified a second-place team for an at-large bid, and had won only three of seven BCS games. Worse, Miami had won all three, then left the Big East for the ACC in 2004. There was serious talk about the Big East losing its automatic BCS invitation.

Finally, all that pressure would fall on the shoulders of three freshman: quarterback Pat White, tailback Steve Slaton, and wide receiver Darius Reynaud. When Las Vegas called the Mountaineers double-digit underdogs, that seemed about right.

"That's one of those games," Rodriguez said, "when you're looking around during warm-ups, going, 'Wooo—I'm losing confidence!' But I could tell our guys were dialed in, because in our last three days of practice we didn't have a single MA [missed assignment]. They were ready."

The freshmen listened to their coach, not Las Vegas, fearlessly leading the Mountaineers to a mind-blowing 28–0 lead early in the second quarter. But the Bulldogs' comeback was just as impressive, cutting the lead to 38–35.

With just 1:26 left in the game, and the Mountaineers facing fourth-and-6 near midfield, Rodriguez contemplated the most courageous call of his career: a fake punt. But after he floated the idea to his assistants on the headsets, they went quiet. Rodriguez thought perhaps they had lost the connection. "Hello? Hello!"

"Sorry, Coach," one finally said. "We're not making that call."

Rodriguez, once again trusting his gambler's instincts, put his chips in.

Punter Phil Brady took the snap, hesitated long enough to let his team-mates run down the field and draw the Bulldogs out of the way, then took off through the left side of the line for a 10-yard gain—more than enough for the first down needed to seal the upset.

"That fake punt, that was a gutsy call," Nehlen said. "That won the game and solidified Rich here." Just as Nehlen's shocking 41–27 upset over the ninth-ranked Sooners at Oklahoma in 1982 established Nehlen as the new leader of the Mountaineers, "the Georgia game really made [Rich] what he was in West Virginia."

Reynaud scored two touchdowns, Slaton scored the other three, running for a Sugar Bowl–record 204 yards, and Pat White won the first of four straight bowl games. The freshmen had come through.

The upset also saved the Big East's seat at the BCS's big-boy table, it confirmed Rich Rodriguez's status as the hottest young coach in America, and it bolstered his belief that instead of seeking a bigger stage, he could turn West Virginia into one.

It also, perversely, increased the tension with his bosses.

"Rich was without a doubt an icon here," said Dave Alvarez, another booster, "and he could have been the Bo Schembechler of Morgantown. But you also have to have support. After the 2006 Sugar Bowl, you'd think Eddie [Pastilong] would be right there giving him a big hug and saying, 'You're awesome!' But Eddie didn't say anything. You could feel it. I think that's when the conflict started." Pastilong was conspicuously absent from the postgame party.

The 2006 Mountaineers picked up right where the 2005 Mountaineers left off, zipping through a 10–2 regular season to earn a bid to the Gator Bowl, where they beat Georgia Tech to finish in the top ten once again. And on December 7, 2006, in between the regular season and the bowl, Alabama invited Rodriguez to become its next head coach.

Rodriguez was then making about $1.3 million, while Alabama was offering $12 million over six years. That works out to an additional $700,000 a year, a 50 percent increase, and the honor of leading one of college football's truly legendary programs.

But the next day Rodriguez publicly declined the offer, explaining: "This was my school, my alma mater, my dream."

The people of West Virginia, whose very identity was tied up with the football team, were ecstatic—and relieved. The leaders of the state, who began to fear Rodriguez's growing influence, were worried, too—but *after* he declined.

"Rich got bigger than the university, and more powerful than the governor," Jones said. "He could have been the football coach *and* governor at the same time—and I'm not kidding! And when it came down to it, that had become a problem for the politicians."

While the governor, school president, and athletic director were growing disdainful of Rodriguez's ambition, Rodriguez was growing impatient with their lack of it. On the one hand, you had an athletic director, Eddie Pastilong, who'd been the Mountaineers' second-string quarterback in the '60s, who "comes in at eleven a.m., goes to lunch at one, and never comes back the rest of the day," said Paul Astorg, a Mercedes dealer who provided cars for some of the coaches. Then you had Rodriguez, who worked fourteen hours a day, every day, "more than Eddie worked all week."

Pastilong seemed safe, however, because he had been Governor Manchin's roommate at West Virginia. But Rodriguez and Manchin were tight, too, from Rodriguez's days working in Manchin's carpet store to Rodriguez's help campaigning for Manchin in 2004. So Rodriguez figured he was safe, too, and had the go-ahead to do what was necessary to make West Virginia one of the nation's elite programs, year in and year out.

Already at the high end of the Big East pay scale (only Louisville's Bobby Petrino's total package of $1.7 million topped Rich's), Rodriguez was not asking for more money for himself. What he wanted were the same things the best programs in the nation already had, including a better locker room, an academic center for athletes, and access to a private plane for recruiting. But the underlying conflict was simpler: Did his bosses share his ambitious vision? Those were the tectonic plates. The rest were tremors.

Rodriguez had been assured by the governor that, once Manchin installed his business associate Mike Garrison as school president in 2007, all Rodriguez's wishes would be granted, Astorg recalled. In fact, the elevation of Garrison, an attorney still in his thirties with no experience leading an academic institution and no support among the faculty, actually made life far tougher for Rodriguez.

"To [Garrison], a new idea was a threat," said Dave Alvarez. The football program's success "was intimidating. It'd gotten so big, so fast. Garrison was young, and new, and under scrutiny. Eddie [Pastilong] was near the end of his career and didn't want to rock the boat.

"But Rich wants to go right in the middle of the ocean and see what that ship can do!"

Given this backdrop, you didn't have to be an organizational psychologist to see trouble ahead. The question was, how would management respond to Rodriguez's grand plans?

"One of our alumni said it best," Alvarez recalled. "You don't tell your best salesman what he needs. You ask him what he wants."

Instead, Rodriguez had to beg for permission just to raise the money himself for a private jet. He and the top donors put their heads together and came up with something they called the 1100 Club: Everyone put in $1,100, of which $100 went for food and drink for a big night at the Pete Dye course, and the remaining $1,000 went to the plane fund.

"We grew that thing to over $300,000 in just a couple years," Alvarez said. The campaign also had the beneficial side effect of getting the busy coach out to meet his strongest supporters, who developed a great bond with him.

"Our first 1100 Club meeting," Jones recalled, "we were up at the clubhouse until two in the morning, everyone having a great time. Man, we had it *going*."

They were winning games and having fun. It seemed like the sky was the limit.

Concerned that Pastilong and Garrison seemed to be doing nothing to keep their coach, boosters like Alvarez, Astorg, and Ike Morris decided they had to take action.

"Ike and Alvarez get a notepad out," Matt Jones said, "and they say to Rich, 'You tell us what it would take for you to stay.' So he did. And then they went over the list to see what we could take care of."

Rodriguez had told them he wanted the following:

- Better pay for his assistants.
- A new academic center.
- Locker room upgrades.
- Free game passes for high school coaches.
- An all-access pass for Rita.
- Control of sideline passes ("to cut off Eddie's drinking buddies," one booster said).
- Program allowing the players to sell their books (and keep the money, as they did at other schools), instead of having the school do it for them. It was a small item, but other schools were using it to recruit against West Virginia.
- A professional website, with any profits to go to the assistants.

"I'm looking at this list," Jones said, "and I'm saying, 'Shoot, this list is *easy*! Let's get 'er done!'"

Rodriguez was raring to go, the boosters were lining up to help him—but the administration wasn't budging. The 2007 off-season dragged out like a cold war. No talking, little progress, just growing fear, anger, and suspicion. "If all they said was, 'Rich, we can do everything you want, if *you* raise the money,' he would have done it!" Rutledge said. "Hell, he *did* do it with the 1100 Club!"

But Rodriguez soon learned that the athletic department had taken the money the 1100 Club had raised for the plane and diverted it to expenses like training table meals. Even the small stuff didn't get done. Rodriguez never got the website. The high school coaches still had to pay to get in. And while the assistant coaches did get a little more money, according to Rodriguez's longtime right-hand man, Dusty Rutledge, it was not anywhere near what Rodriguez had wanted for them. In exchange for all that, they insisted on adding a $4 million buyout into the contract, claiming the boosters insisted on it, which was false.

"Do you want to be here?" Garrison asked Rodriguez.

"Yes, of course I do!" Rodriguez recalled responding.

"Trust me, if there ever came a time where you did not want to be here, we would not stand in your way. What we would do is sit down with the attorneys, cut the buyout in half, and you could be on your way."

"He must have said 'Trust me' a hundred times," Rita recalled. (Garrison declined to be interviewed.)

"We're from the same small area—Fairmont is just a few miles from Grant Town—and I believed him. I thought he was all in. How dumb was that?"

Rodriguez would soon find out just how dumb.

But in the meantime, the unusually high buyout allowed Rodriguez's bosses to drag their feet on his wish list, believing he was virtually trapped.

"Rich has his plan," Astorg said, "and he's working his plan, and the administration is right front and center in the way of his plans."

Something had to give.

The Wolverines' 32–18 loss to USC in the January 1, 2007, Rose Bowl took some of the sparkle off a season that started with a historic 11–0 winning streak, but not that much. Michigan still finished 11–2, marking Carr's sixth ten-win season and his fifth top-ten finish. Not too shabby. It would have been a good year to call it a career, and some thought he might take the opportunity to step down.

Several Carr confidants told me he planned to do just that, but Martin talked him into staying one more year. Martin already had a search under way for a new men's basketball coach, and he needed more time to line up Carr's successor. Perhaps thinking that coaching one more season would increase his odds of naming his successor, Carr agreed.

Martin, however, insisted that was not true. "Lloyd never said to me at any time that he was thinking of retiring. No. Not until his last year, and only toward the end of the season. Until then, I wouldn't have been surprised if he'd said, 'Bill, I want to coach another year.' And frankly I was hoping he would."

What could go wrong?

Since the NCAA split Division I into two subdivisions in 1978, Michigan, Notre Dame, and USC were the only BCS schools that had never scheduled an opponent from the lower tier, then called I-AA and now called the Football Championship Series (FCS). But when the NCAA decreed in

2005 that teams could add a twelfth regular-season game—in what can only be described as a shameless money grab on the backs, knees, and skulls of amateur athletes—Michigan had to scramble to find an opponent before the music ended and everyone else was sitting down.

"I always wanted to schedule opponents that Lloyd would approve," Martin said. "If he said absolutely no, I wouldn't schedule them. He knew our football program. He knew our goals. He knew how important it was to win every single game."

Hawaii was initially at the top of Martin's list. But after June Jones—who refined Mouse Davis's run-and shoot offense, an older cousin of Rodriguez's spread option—and Heisman candidate Colt Brennan, who would break Shaun King's record for passing efficiency, led the Rainbow Warriors to an 11–3 overall record the year before, the Warriors were scratched off.

"I never would have picked up the phone and found Appalachian State," Martin said. Scott Draper, the assistant AD for football and one of Carr's most trusted lieutenants, came up with the idea. "It didn't excite me—I didn't want to play the I-AA schools, but everyone was doing it."

When Appalachian State agreed to the game in February 2007 for a flat fee of $400,000, the few discussions it generated focused on why Michigan had scheduled them and where the heck *is* that school? Their fight song didn't make a very strong argument, either: "Hi-hi-yike-us. Nobody like us. We are the Mountaineers! Always a-winning. Always a-grinning. Always a-feeling fine. You bet, hey. Go Apps!"

"The Victors" it was not.

No ranked I-A team had ever lost to an I-AA team. With most of Michigan's key starters returning, including a stellar trio of Chad Henne, Mike Hart, and Jake Long, they entered the 2007 season ranked fifth.

They seemed safe.

The point spread was set at 27, though some Las Vegas sports books would not even take that bet. Not since 1891, when the Wolverines started the season against the teenagers at Ann Arbor High School, dispatching them 61–0, did the home opener seem like such a complete mismatch.

The Big Ten Network had debuted just two days prior to the September 1 contest. Because the better Big Ten games had already been snapped up by ABC, ESPN, and ESPN-2, the BTN had this one all to itself. Of course, not many homes got the BTN in its first week, and the few that did weren't expected to tune in to this massacre.

Nobody gave the Mountaineers much thought at the time—but they should have. Appalachian State had won the previous two FCS national titles and would win a third straight that year. They weren't big, but they were fast, well-conditioned, and well coached. They had mastered the spread offense, which they learned directly from a visit to Rodriguez in Morgantown, and they ran it very, very well.

The Mountaineers had been studying Michigan since the game had been announced. They knew the Wolverines had a national-title-caliber team, but they also knew their defense had a horrible time against the spread offense.

If the Wolverines weren't ready for the Mountaineers, the Mountaineers were ready for Michigan. On their third play of the game, Armanti Edwards hit Dexter Jackson on a slant route, sending him 68 yards to the end zone. It wasn't a fluke. They poured on three more touchdowns that half and headed to the locker room leading 28–17.

In the second half, despite a slew of turnovers, bad penalties, and a pair of failed two-point conversion attempts, Michigan regained the lead 32–31.

But with 1:37 left and no time-outs, the Mountaineers needed just seventy-one seconds to move the ball from their 24-yard line to Michigan's 7, where they kicked the go-ahead field goal: 34–32.

Chad Henne responded with a 46-yard pass play to Mario Manningham to set up a 37-yard field goal attempt, with 6 seconds left. As crazy as the day had been, the Wolverines were surely about to escape, learn their lesson, and come back stronger the next week against Oregon.

But it wasn't meant to be: A Mountaineer speedster ran straight through Michigan's line and smothered the kick in his stomach.

The Giants win the pennant!

Down goes Frazier!

Do you believe in miracles?

The announcer from Appalachian State made all those famous calls sound about as exciting as a Burger King worker repeating your order at the drive-through speaker. ESPN still plays it.

There was no joy in Arborville.

Mighty Michigan had struck out.

It took a while for the whole thing to sink in: The fifth-ranked Michigan Wolverines had actually lost to the Mountaineers of Appalachian State, a team not even eligible to be ranked.

In the Michigan locker room, no one yelled. No one screamed. No one threw his helmet. They slumped down in their stalls, heads on hands, and stared off into space, dazed. They could not comprehend it.

History is usually presented as something that simply rolls along, one year after the next, and what it produces is the inevitable result of broad, sweeping trends that no one individual or single moment can alter.

Not true. Individuals matter. Moments matter.

Michigan football has plenty of proof: Louis Elbel. Fielding Yost. The 1945 Army game. Bo versus Woody, 1969.

But on September 1, 2007, Appalachian State added one of its own, pulling off what many sportswriters consider the greatest upset in the history of college football. Its effects were both immediate and long-lasting.

A few grown men left Michigan Stadium in tears, and the bars became morgues. You couldn't escape the story, which was broadcast on virtually every channel, even MSNBC.

In one of the easiest journalistic decisions of all time, the editors of *Sports Illustrated* didn't bother to send anyone to cover the game, yet in an equally easy decision, they put the game on the next cover. "My job is to help put major college football developments into perspective . . . ," Stewart Mandel wrote. "But in the case of Appalachian State 34, Michigan 32 . . . I feel utterly unqualified . . .

"What every coach tries to tell his players and the media every week only to be met by perennial skepticism has now been confirmed as true. No one is unbeatable in college football anymore. Anything can happen."

Brian Cook, creator of MGoBlog, the most popular college football website in the country, couldn't even address it, instead opting to run a screen that simply said "Kittens!" It took him three days to bring himself to write about "the Horror," running his story under the headline "Unconditional Surrender," and a picture of a mushroom cloud.

"Let the record show that Lloyd Carr never learns, and that you are right. We suck. We promise not to hope or expect anything except misery until someone named Tedford or Rodriguez or Schiano is coaching the team and to regard all good events as mere preludes to a fall. We are a defeated people. Give us your treaty. We will sign it."

That night the e-mail boxes of Carr, Martin, and University of Michigan president Mary Sue Coleman overflowed with vitriolic missives, occasionally disturbing enough to forward to university security.

But the fans' emotions were real enough. And what many wanted was to see Carr go. The various websites devoted to Carr's departure—sackcarr .com, FireLloyd.com—did brisk business that night. The talk shows didn't need to give out their numbers to get irate fans to call in.

The game was a stinker of historic proportions. There was no spinning it. "We were not prepared," Carr said afterward, "and that's my responsibility."

But it was only one game, hardly dwarfing Carr's accomplishments on the field or off. Carr had won more Big Ten titles than Fritz Crisler and more national titles than Bo Schembechler, yet he remained the Harry Truman of college coaches—unappreciated in his own time.

I stopped by his office later that week to drop off the book I had coauthored with Bo Schembechler, which Carr had helped fact-check after Schembechler passed away, adding a few stories in the process. I found him in his office, the lights off, tilting back in his chair before the reflected glow of a big-screen TV dancing on his face. He looked as though he had swallowed a live grenade and his insides had been hollowed out.

He was philosophical. "I've been warning these guys for years that one of these days a MAC team is going to beat us," he said, "and you don't want to be the team that gets beaten."

I didn't have the heart to tell him that Appalachian State was not even a MAC team. Appalachian State was probably better than most of them, but they still played in the FCS, not the BCS.

A week later, Oregon, a bona fide BCS team with another mobile quarterback running the spread offense, humiliated the Wolverines on their home turf 39–7.

Nationwide, just about every sports pundit said Lloyd Carr was "on the hot seat." But the custom since Charles Baird became Michigan's first AD was clear: Only one vote mattered, and Carr had it. He would leave under his own power, at his own pace. But the rest of the season would be dominated by predictions of Carr's retirement and speculation about who would replace him.

The Wolverines rebounded when they got back to the bigger, slower, less imaginative Big Ten. Despite injuries to Michael Hart and Chad Henne, the Wolverines willed themselves to eight straight wins. Nevertheless, the Horror cast a long shadow. The 2007 season was not the victory lap Carr had hoped for, or deserved.

The Appalachian State loss not only lowered the stock of Carr's coordinators, it also diminished his power to boost them. The ability to name his successor was something he badly wanted, but unlike Schembechler,

Carr was not the AD, and the 2007 season confirmed concerns that his assistants were not the next Lloyd Carr.

In Carr's final Ohio State game, with the Big Ten title on the line, the banged-up Wolverines managed a mere 91 yards of total offense en route to a fourth straight loss to the Buckeyes and an 8–4 record.

Two days later, on Monday, November 19, Michigan football coach Lloyd Carr announced he would retire after Michigan's bowl game.

Two of the University of Michigan's worst-kept secrets that fall were Carr's likely retirement and the possibility of Les Miles replacing him. Both seemed like obvious calls. Miles had played for Schembechler, coached for Schembechler, and was about to lead Louisiana State University into the BCS title game in January.

Hiring Miles would have followed the oldest script in college football: promoting a school's former player to lead his beloved alma mater. Gustave Ferbert was the first alum to coach Michigan to a Big Ten title in that famous 1898 win over Chicago, and Harry Kipke, Bennie Oosterbaan, and Bump Elliott—all great players—followed suit. Miles had not been a star player, but he was clearly a heck of a coach. But a third poorly kept secret was that Carr preferred that someone else get the job—*anyone* else.

Exactly why has inspired both honest speculation and ridiculous rumors. The two most likely theories include bad feelings left over from conflicts when both served on Schembechler's staff—something Schembechler often intentionally stirred up between the old guard and the young Turks, just to get the best ideas out on the table—and the friction generated after Miles took over LSU in 2005, when they found themselves recruiting the same players.

But ultimately, it was less important *why* Carr didn't like Miles than the simple fact that he didn't, which no one denies.

Carr wanted his offensive coordinator, Mike DeBord, or his defensive coordinator, Ron English. But Martin wasn't convinced that either was ready. DeBord had been a successful assistant, but in his four-year stint as head coach of Central Michigan, he compiled a 12–34 record. English had been a coordinator for just two years, with mixed results.

Whatever your opinion of what happened thereafter—from the scattered search to Rodriguez's three tumultuous years in Ann Arbor—all of it could have been easily avoided had Carr prepared a worthy successor from his ranks. In Schembechler's twenty-one years, he hired thirty-six assistant coaches, eleven of whom became Division I head coaches. Three won national titles, and Larry Smith and Don Nehlen came very close.

In his thirteen years, Carr had nineteen assistants, four of whom became Division I head coaches: Stan Parrish, Mike DeBord, Ron English, and Brady Hoke, who had just finished the 2007 season at Ball State with a 7–6 record, giving him a career mark of 22–37.

With no candidates from the Carr tree deemed ready, Bill Martin had to look elsewhere—and that's when things got interesting.

Since leaving Iowa to become Michigan's thirteenth president in 2002, Mary Sue Coleman had gained a loyal following among Ann Arborites and the alums nationwide. A former biochemist, she impressed just about everyone as professional and likable, though she could be surprisingly tough when needed.

She earned particularly high marks for recognizing the economic troubles ahead and deflecting them by spearheading a $2.5 billion fund drive that ultimately produced $3.2 billion—a record for a public university. Then she and her team wisely protected a far larger chunk of the university's endowment than did its peer institutions before the crash of 2008. She also struck groundbreaking partnerships between Michigan's seven-million-volume library and Google (whose cofounder is Michigan alum Larry Page). Coleman would be named by *Time* magazine as one of the nation's ten best college presidents in 2010.

She had more important things to do than monkey around with a coaching search—just one reason why she had given Martin complete autonomy over the search, as she had when he had hired sixteen other coaches. She was neither intimidated by nor mistrusting of Bill Martin, forging one of the best working relationships in college athletics. The month after Carr retired, however, would test all of that.

A year earlier, Martin had decided Kirk Ferentz, whom Coleman had hired when she was Iowa's president, would be his top candidate. Schembechler respected Ferentz, and Carr would have supported him. Martin did not check with President Coleman, however, and she did not tell him until after Carr stepped down that Ferentz was not to be considered, perhaps because numerous Hawkeyes had serious off-field problems that fall. Whatever her reasons, the result was the same: Another solution had been eliminated.

Martin put together a six-man search committee representing a cross section of university leaders, successful businessmen, and former Michigan football stars who'd done well after their playing careers had ended—the kind of opinion leaders a wise executive would work hard to keep on his side.

About a week after Carr's announcement, the committee met for the first time in the glass meeting room in Weidenbach Hall. Martin told them what he was looking for and mentioned that Tony Dungy was his favorite candidate. Dungy had played high school football for Jackson Parkside, a half hour from Ann Arbor, but turned down Bo Schembechler to play for Minnesota. His Indianapolis Colts had just won the 2007 Super Bowl the previous winter, and his book, *Quiet Strength*, had been on the bestseller lists much of the year. Exactly why Martin thought Dungy might be interested in Michigan, however, is a mystery.

The committee then briefly discussed Cincinnati's Brian Kelly, who had won two NCAA Division II titles at Grand Valley State in Grand Rapids and a MAC title at Central Michigan before finishing the 2007 regular season in Cincinnati 9–3 while graduating 75 percent of his players. But Kelly had a well-earned reputation for being unpleasant—even basketball coaches had strong opinions about him—and Martin made it clear he was not a serious candidate.

What was most striking about that first meeting, however, was the number of candidates they barely discussed, if at all: Mike DeBord, Ron English, Jeff Tedford, Rich Rodriguez, and even Les Miles, the committee's first choice. "Bill didn't want him," recalls Ted Spencer, the director of admissions and a committee member. "I have no idea why. He never gave us a reason."

When the first meeting adjourned, the committee had been given no serious candidates to consider, nor any real direction. There was no urgency, no plan. The members left mystified—and miffed.

"If I had to put my finger on anything," said longtime faculty representative Percy Bates, "it's this notion that 'this is Michigan. Once the job is open, they're going to be banging my door down, and I'm going to pick and choose among all these great candidates. The only question is, which of these great coaches will I invite to accept the honor of coaching at Michigan?'

"But never having conducted a big-time football coaching search before, Bill may not have realized how it works. They're not going to be knocking down your door.

"Anybody watching the scene at Michigan would know our program was not where it had been, and there were people who would think twice about coming here."

The takeaway was clear. "There hadn't been any preparation for this that I could see," Bates concluded. "Nothing that said, 'We need to get ready for this.' And then it started to unravel."

Many observers seemed eager to believe that the very absence of any real news or activity emanating from the department was all part of some supersecret master plan that would result in Miles being hired after LSU's bowl game. But the truth was that the silence was simply the result of a slow, sloppy search. There was nothing newsworthy to report.

The public also didn't know that Miles's representatives had been re-peatedly trying to connect with Martin after Carr's announcement, with-out success. Miles's people placed more calls on Thursday, November 29, but Martin and his wife were heading out for a three-day trip to Florida. When Jamie Morris, who worked in the development side of the athletic department and served as an unofficial liaison to the former players, pre-sented Martin with a short stack of pink message slips before Martin left that Thursday, Martin told him he planned to call Miles when he re-turned on Sunday and left it at that.

All this came to a head two days later, on Saturday, exactly two weeks after Michigan's loss to Ohio State, when Miles was preparing his team to play the SEC title game that afternoon against Tennessee. That morning, ESPN's Kirk Herbstreit announced that Miles had accepted Michigan's offer to succeed Coach Carr.

Even while Herbstreit was talking, Miles's agent was trying desper-ately to get in touch with Martin in Florida, to no avail.

"My weekend starts," Morris recalled, "and I'm sitting on the couch about to watch some football when Kirk Herbstreit announces Les is going to Michigan. My phone starts going crazy! I'm getting calls from everyone— the committee members, the regents, people at Schembechler Hall— and all I can say is, 'I can't confirm this.' Then they start asking, 'Where's Bill?' Now *I'm* thinking he must have stopped in Atlanta [where LSU was playing Tennessee] to meet with Les and get him signed before going to Florida."

Thanks to Herbstreit's report, the buzz became so deafening so quickly that Miles felt compelled to give an impromptu press conference of his own just hours before the SEC championship game. "There was some misinformation on ESPN and I think it's imperative that I straighten it out," he said, jaw clenched. "I am the head coach at LSU. I will be the head coach at LSU. I have no interest in talking to anybody else. I've got a championship game to play, and I am excited about the opportunity of my damn strong football team to play in it. That's really all I'd like to say."

After Miles gave his public denial, Morris's phone started burning up again with calls from insiders who wanted to know where Martin was and why they could not get through to him on his cell phone. Before Martin had left Ann Arbor, he had changed cell phones, and he said he didn't know how to use the new one yet. Which, in effect, meant the Michigan athletic director, in the midst of a search for a new head coach for the winningest program in collegiate football that generated the bulk of his department's revenues, was somewhere near the tip of Florida, unable to communicate when the popular front-runner for the post had been forced to refute ESPN's inaccurate report that he had taken the job in a nationally televised appearance.

"Bill was totally oblivious to everything," Morris said. "Finally Mary Sue [Coleman] calls Bill after he gets home Sunday night, and she's pissed off. So now he's finally getting it. He finally figures out he's in deep shit."

The next day, Monday, December 3, with pressure mounting, Martin told the media he had a list of twenty candidates—which seemed like the kind of slate he'd have at the beginning of the search, not in December. The same day Martin flew to New York City under the guise of attending the National Football Foundation's Hall of Fame dinner Tuesday night, when his principal motive was finding a football coach.

Martin met with Rutgers's Greg Schiano, who was a hot commodity after leading the Scarlet Knights from the Big East's basement to a 10–2 regular season record, garnering almost every coaching award available. Rutgers fans hoped Schiano might return the Scarlet Knights to the top of the college football world for the first time since their one glorious week at number one in 1869.

Word quickly got out that Michigan was actively pursuing Schiano, which not only surprised Martin—who had naïvely believed the high-

profile search could be kept quiet—but also came as news to the committee members, who had not been told Martin was even considering Schiano.

"It would be hard for anyone on that committee to say they felt respected, or were happy with the process," Bates said of his piped-in peers.
"I am certain that Bill did not understand how people on that committee
felt about being on the committee."

Although Martin was the director of Michigan athletics, he had not
been a member of the Michigan football family before taking the post,
and he had done little to ingratiate himself with the insiders in the years
since. The careless search confirmed for many Michigan Men Martin's
permanent status as an outsider of the very organization he was leading.

A few days later, a minor embarrassment became a major one when
Schiano, after considering Martin's offer, declined. "I very much liked him,"
Martin said, "and it just didn't work out."

In fewer than three weeks, Martin had lowered his sights from Super
Bowl champion Tony Dungy to Rutgers's Greg Schiano—and he still didn't
have a coach. The sporting public was stunned to see Michigan, one of the
most respected athletic departments in the nation, failing to find a leader.

"The phrase I kept hearing," Bates recalled from his colleagues around
the country, was "the process being 'so un-Michigan-like.' And *that* was
beginning to rise to the highest level of the university as well. Mary Sue
was certainly getting the word from outside, and from the regents and
donors, that this was falling apart."

Detroit Free Press columnist Michael Rosenberg wrote that there were
two possibilities: Martin had decided Miles was not his man and intentionally let him slip away, or he was simply asleep at the wheel. Neither interpretation played well with the former Michigan football alums, who flooded
President Coleman's office that week with respectfully written letters and
e-mails, pointedly not arguing for this candidate or that—though they
generally had strong feelings—but simply asking that the process be conducted in a professional manner, and that Michigan Men be treated with
respect.

They certainly got Coleman's attention. She summoned Martin to her
office and showed him the pile, saying she'd never seen anything like it in
her years as president at Iowa or Michigan. The meeting had all the sub-
tlety of a master rubbing her dog's nose in the rug he'd ruined. From that
point on, Martin no longer had complete autonomy over the process, and
Coleman would be working with him until it was complete.

The natives were getting restless, manifested in a rare public criticism of the athletic director—something that had been virtually unheard-of in Ann Arbor since Charles Baird first took office in 1898.

When Schiano's rejection was announced on WTKA, many alums, fans, and former players were listening. One of them was Bill Dufek—the son and brother of two Michigan greats, and a former All–Big Ten lineman himself—who was working away in his office when the news hit. Like most listeners, he couldn't believe what he was hearing.

"I didn't think I'd see the day," he told me, "that a Rutgers coach would turn down the Michigan job."

Within minutes, John Heuser of *The Ann Arbor News* called Dufek for a reaction. Dufek, who had picked his words carefully for a year on the Sunday morning show I cohost on WTKA, always supporting Carr and the football team even after the losses to Appalachian State and Oregon, spoke his mind.

"Bill Martin might know how to build buildings," he said in the paper, "but he has no feel for running an athletic department."

Another first: Dufek and fellow former teammate Mike Leoni publicly called out Coach Carr. Dufek told the *News* he believed "Carr sabotaged the pursuit of Miles because of personal animosity, or 'petty jealousies.'

"This job is one of the top ten jobs in the country, but frankly for several years we haven't even had a top-25 coaching staff. And people have kept their mouth shut out of respect for Bo, but after this, you're seeing they're not going to keep quiet any more."

The manifestation of the "deathless loyalty" to Michigan that Fielding Yost had honored so memorably back in 1941 had shifted. Many alums felt that in order to protect the prestige of the program, they needed to do something they had never done before: air their concerns and complaints in public. "Basically all [Carr] ever was," Dufek went on, "was a steward of Bo's program. And it's Bo's program that lasted that long."

The response to the article was swift—but mixed. Many agreed, many did not, but every Michigan Man felt passionate about the mismanaged search, which was causing the football family to fracture.

After Schiano's rejection, Martin told the committee they would be postponing the search until after the bowl games—but that's when he kicked the search into high gear.

———

Months before Michigan's problems became public, the West Virginia Mountaineers were having problems of their own.

They entered their 2007 season ranked third in the country, two spots ahead of Michigan, and started their campaign in fine style, dispatching Western Michigan 62–24. Despite losing to South Florida in the fifth week, on the strength of their 10–1 record and victories over three ranked teams (Rutgers, Cincinnati, and UConn), they had climbed all the way to the top spot in the coaches' poll for the first time in school history.

All the Mountaineers had to do to get a trip back to the national title game was win their last game against the 4–7 Pittsburgh Panthers. Rodriguez had not lost to a team with a losing record in five years.

They seemed safe.

Star quarterback Pat White's thumb injury would keep him out most of the game, but with the Mountaineers 28½-point favorites, it barely seemed worth mentioning.

If Michigan faced its Armageddon on the first Saturday of the season, the Mountaineers faced theirs on the last, December 1, when they played the Backyard Brawl for the one hundredth time. It wasn't supposed to be much of a brawl—but then, on a cold, rainy day, West Virginia missed two chip shots and lost 13–9, in what ESPNU called the "Game of the Year," temporarily displacing the Horror.

Like the Appalachian State stunner, this upset created unforeseen by-products. It opened the door for Les Miles's LSU team, which beat Tennessee the same day to take West Virginia's spot in the national title game, and it gave Rodriguez more time and incentive to address the growing chasm between him and his bosses.

"They were scared of him," Matt Jones said. "It was nothing to do with the little things, the list, or any of that. He'd just gotten bigger than them."

"They pushed him in a corner," Paul Astorg said, "and they wanted him to know who the boss was."

Right when it seemed like Rodriguez might be trapped, a door cracked open.

But Michigan's awkward dance with Les Miles wasn't quite done. After Schiano turned Martin down, the Michigan insiders realized Martin's slow search was the sign not of some carefully executed master plan but of an almost complete lack of preparation. They had peeked behind the Wizard's curtain and seen him scrambling. Miles's advocates realized it was time to make their move.

Jamie Morris went to work on Andrea Fisher Newman, Michigan's top-ranking Republican regent, while John Wangler, a close friend of Miles's, opened discussions with Larry Deitsch, the top-ranking Democrat.

That Friday, December 7, Bill Martin made an early-morning call to an intermediary, who told him Les Miles would not speak to Martin, only to President Coleman, but if Martin wanted to listen in on the conversation, that was fine. They arranged a conference call from Coleman's office at 11:00 a.m. that day, marking the first conversation either Michigan official had had with the alleged leading candidate for the position.

It was a simple, pleasant conversation. Neither side committed to anything more than keeping their conversation confidential and having another conversation before LSU's national championship game. Miles did let them know, however, that, "I would never say no to Michigan."

But, incredibly, by 1:30 that afternoon word of the conference call had already started popping up on the blogs—and word quickly traveled down to Baton Rouge. Miles was, understandably, upset.

Three days later, on Monday, December 10, 2007, Coleman and Miles talked again. She said she could not hire Miles without meeting him first, and asked Miles to meet her and Martin in Miami, where Miles had already scheduled a recruiting trip. Miles replied that he could not do any face-to-face meeting until after the national title game. Besides, he pointed out, Michigan couldn't keep a conference call confidential for more than a couple hours, and the media was already watching his every move in Baton Rouge. He already had a great job in a great program, poised to play for a national crown, and he was not interested in leaving LSU unless Michigan—and only Michigan—was truly interested. And if they were, he figured, they could wait until January to seal the deal.

But he added, "If you want me, then after the bowl game, I will be your coach—I just can't do anything before that." Again he added, "I would never say no to Michigan."

After they hung up with Miles, Coleman and Martin met to discuss their strategy with Deitsch and Newman on the phone. When they agreed they should approach Miles, someone raised the question everyone dreaded: "Who's going to tell Lloyd?"

After a pause, President Coleman said, "I will."

Dave Brandon and Jim Hackett, former players who went on to great success in business and remained close to their old coach, both recalled Schembechler, contemplating who should succeed Carr. Although Schembechler was very big on Kirk Ferentz, they remembered, he also told them Michigan should consider the young coach at West Virginia, Rich Rodriguez.

But they did not present Rich Rodriguez's name to Bill Martin. And they were not the first Michigan people to reach out to Rodriguez, either.

No, that happened the night of Michigan's Monday conference call with Miles. In what will likely come as a surprise to most Michigan fans, Rodriguez received a call that evening from Michigan head coach Lloyd Carr. Rodriguez recalled they talked for ten or fifteen minutes.

Carr asked Rodriguez, "Would you be interested in coaching here? It's a great school, with great tradition."

"I've never given it any thought," Rodriguez said.

"Even if you hadn't thought about it before," Carr said, "it's something you should think about now."

"Is there interest in me on Michigan's part?"

"Yeah, they're looking at you."

"It was a very positive call," Rodriguez remembered. "He was definitely encouraging me to think about it."

That next day, according to three sources, including a high-level department administrator and a search committee member, the first person to encourage Bill Martin to think about Rich Rodriguez was none other than Lloyd Carr. (Carr did not respond to requests for an interview.)

That same day, Tuesday, December 11, someone leaked the story of the resurrection of Miles's candidacy to Mark Snyder at the *Free Press* and Bernie Smilovitz at Detroit's NBC affiliate. Naturally, it got picked up in Louisiana—marking the second time the "Miles to Michigan" story had broken, the first being Herbstreit's report ten days earlier. That not only upset Miles, it effectively boxed him in.

That night, Bill Martin—tipped off by Lloyd Carr—called Rodriguez at his home to inquire about his interest in the Michigan job. Both sides were noncommittal but intrigued. Almost exactly a year after Rodriguez had turned down Alabama, he found himself flirting with the Michigan job. Rodriguez called Dusty Rutledge at 11:30 that night.

"Dusty, can you keep a secret?"

"I'm about to go to bed."

"I've got something to tell you, and you can't repeat this to anyone. I just got off the phone with someone high up at Michigan. What do you know about the place?"

Rutledge, who grew up just over the Ohio border, about an hour from

Ann Arbor, was a hard-core Michigan fan. He went to the games, attended the summer camps, met Schembechler once in his office, and knew the team's history and traditions better than just about anyone else. He believed fervently in the Michigan Man and all it stood for. He just didn't believe Rodriguez was serious.

"Well, they've got the most wins of anybody, eleven national titles, three Heismans."

"No, no. What do you know about the university and the town?"

"Now, don't be messing with me, Rich. This is my mecca you're talking about! Let me just tell you this: Everything about Michigan is first-class."

With Miles tied up until January, Michigan returned to Rodriguez. As luck would have it, Rodriguez had already scheduled his annual meeting with his financial adviser, Mike Wilcox, in Toledo that Friday, December 14. Wilcox knew Martin, and he helped arrange a meeting with Coleman, Martin, and the Rodriguezes in his office.

Although the two sides knew almost nothing about each other, the meeting went well, and both Rich and Rita developed a good feeling about President Coleman in particular. "She was the key," he told me. After dealing with Mike Garrison—a lawyer turned president, still in his thirties, who would step down after less than a year when it was discovered that Governor Joe Manchin's daughter received an MBA without doing the necessary work—Rodriguez felt the seasoned Coleman came across as calm, in control, and utterly reliable. (Senator Manchin did not respond to requests for an interview.)

Coleman and Martin got right to it and laid out their offer: a $2.5 million annual salary, about $700,000 more than he was making in West Virginia. But more important, they offered better salaries for his staff, the $226 million renovation to the stadium, the $26 million indoor facility, and the $1 million they promised to put toward revamping the weight room. Michigan not only had the tradition, it was clear they were serious about football and eager to please—echoing the same pitch Charles Baird made to fellow West Virginian Fielding H. Yost 106 years earlier.

Michigan seemed to be offering everything Rodriguez was not getting at West Virginia, including attention and respect. It was music to his ears.

Rodriguez wasn't sure how much football they knew, so he wanted to be certain they were aware of what they would be getting.

"You know the style we play, right?" he asked, referring to his invention, the spread option offense. "It's no-huddle, fast-tempo. It's going to be different than what you're used to."

That's fine, they said. They were eager for an innovative offense.

"Well, that's good," Rodriguez said, but added, "Everywhere I've been, it takes a little while for the players to run the system." He remembered repeating this point several times.

Coleman and Martin seemed excited by the prospect, and wanted Rodriguez to accept the post immediately, without seeing the town, the campus, or the facilities, and without getting to know more about Michigan's history and culture. "We need to know today, right now."

The Rodriguez tour had to be canceled, in any case, when word of their meeting leaked to the media before they had even finished.

Another glitch arose when Bill Martin requested that Rodriguez keep Carr's assistants to appease his predecessor. But the more experienced President Coleman nixed the idea. "No, Bill, you can't ask him to do that."

Rodriguez was clearly intrigued, but he made it clear he had to return to Morgantown and let his bosses respond. On that day, Friday, December 14, Rodriguez still did not believe he would be leaving his alma mater for Ann Arbor.

That afternoon, Paul Astorg and Matt Jones were leaving Parkersburg for Morgantown to take a new car up to Rita Rodriguez. They went to practice, then returned to the Rodriguezes' home to discuss the urgent matter at hand. By the end, Jones recalled, "the only one who wasn't sure about going to Michigan was Rich."

Astorg tried one last time: "'If we want to put all this to bed, what'll it take?" It really all came down to just one thing: money for his assistant coaches.

On paper, at least. The problems Rodriguez had at West Virginia ultimately were not about this plane or that assistant. It seemed like the people running the university never believed Rodriguez would leave, and wanted to put him in his place. That naturally rankled the local boy who had made good.

Ike Morris said, "When this thing started festering—and I know the whole thing, and not just from Rich but from the guys on the other side, too—this was all over assistant coaches, about hiring an academic counselor to make sure the players graduate, about [building] a better locker room. Well, hell! That's what he is *supposed* to ask for, isn't it?

"We used to have forty thousand fans, and now we were getting sixty-five thousand—sellouts. His record was unbelievable. We're in the top five every year. He got us there! We were a contender! If he worked for me and he was one of my best salesmen, I think I'd be inclined to listen to him.

"From the governor to the president to the AD—they all took it the wrong way. They thought it was all about Rich, and *Rich* thought it was all about the program he wanted to build."

"Even that week," according to Jones, "[Rich] was still telling us, 'I want to do something that nobody else has ever done, and that's win a national championship here at West Virginia.'"

With Rodriguez's mind not yet made up, the boosters hastily arranged a meeting between Rodriguez and President Garrison the next night, Saturday, December 15. Dusty Rutledge drove Rich to the president's house and ended up, awkwardly, sitting behind a pillar in the same room where the two men met. Rodriguez thought the meeting was Garrison's idea, which would have been a good sign, but he soon realized that the governor or the boosters or both had put the president up to it. Garrison did not seem pleased to have to meet with his football coach.

"Well, I know it's hard for you, but you've got to stay or go," Garrison told Rodriguez. (Garrison declined to be interviewed.)

Rutledge heard Garrison say at least five times, "You've got a tough decision to make." In other words: Take it or leave it—which is exactly what he came out and said later in the meeting.

"They weren't budging," Rutledge told me. "Hell, they didn't want him to stay. That was pretty clear to me, anyway."

Their conversation lasted only twenty minutes or so. Once Rodriguez realized Garrison didn't want to be there, wasn't going to concede anything, and didn't even seem to want Rodriguez at West Virginia anymore, he knew it was time to leave the meeting—and probably Morgantown, too.

The next morning, President Coleman talked with Les Miles for about ninety minutes—the first time she really got to know him. Despite the good rapport, they had already offered Rodriguez the job and were waiting for his answer. President Coleman wished Miles best of luck in the bowl, telling him to "make Michigan proud" of its alum, and told him they would see how the chips fell. In other words, if Rodriguez declined, they could be talking in January about Miles becoming the next Michigan coach.

Meanwhile, back in Morgantown, President Garrison was telling the press that Coach Rodriguez loved West Virginia and he was never going to leave. But with the dissonant dialogue from the night before still ringing in Rodriguez's ears, he asked his old coach, Don Nehlen, "What do you think I should do?"

"Rich, if you win here in West Virginia, they *think* you walk on water," he said. "If you win at Michigan, you *walk* on water."

Such was Rodriguez's faith in his former coach that he decided to take the job before he had ever set foot in Ann Arbor, seen the stadium, or met his predecessor, the players, or the press he would be dealing with—just as Fielding Yost had in 1901. Rodriguez assumed that moving to Michigan would not only rid him of the problems he faced in Morgantown but would not add any of its own.

Later that Sunday, Rich Rodriguez picked up the phone and called Bill Martin to accept his offer.

"People in West Virginia don't want to believe it happened so fast," Rodriguez said. "They want to think there was some great conspiracy in the works, going back before the season started. Sorry. Not even close. The whole thing started *after* our loss to Pitt and it was a done deal in seven days, start to finish."

When Rodriguez accepted, President Garrison looked pretty ridiculous, and the Mountaineer fans weren't happy.

West Virginia—the state and the university, which are close to one and the same—already felt burned by losing basketball coach John Beilein to Michigan eight months earlier, but losing Rodriguez cut much deeper. It's a football state, and losing a native son hurt more than losing a transplant from upstate New York. Losing two coaches in eight months to the same school didn't feel too good, either.

The governor, the university president, and the athletic director had no reason to spare Rodriguez. The moment he committed to Michigan, the calculus for them became very simple: either paint him as the bad guy in every way they could, or gird themselves to receive the full brunt of the wrath of every student, alum, and resident of the state for blowing the chance to keep their beloved son in West Virginia winning title after title for the Mountaineers.

They didn't waste a lot of time deciding.

While Garrison hit the radio waves, Governor Manchin immediately released a statement that said, in part, "I have known Rich for most of his life, from a boy whose only wish was to play football at WVU to a young man whose only wish was to coach at WVU. His dreams came true, and he brought back with him to West Virginia a love and a loyalty for our state that I thought would never change.

"But, unfortunately, over the last two years, I have seen Rich become a victim of a college coaching system driven by high-priced agents that has turned those dreams into just another backroom business deal. Something is wrong with the profession of college coaching today when a leader's word is no longer his bond, and it does not bode well for the student athletes who entrust these coaches with their futures."

Rodriguez could have said a lot in response. He hadn't asked President Garrison for a dollar more for himself, only better salaries for his assistants and better academic support for his players. When he asked Garrison repeatedly, "Where do you want to take this program?" he'd heard the president reply, "Take it or leave it," just as many times. But because Michigan's attorneys were worried—correctly, it turned out—that a lawsuit was forthcoming, they urged their new coach to keep quiet until it was settled.

This is the kind of sound legal advice lawyers give their clients who aren't celebrities. It works very well in cases that will be tried months later in a court of law, and very poorly in cases that will be tried instantly in the court of public opinion. Giving Rodriguez a gag order was tantamount to being put in stocks in the village square while the townspeople lined up with tomatoes. The longer he kept his silence, the more emboldened his critics became, and the worse he looked.

West Virginia might have done a poor job retaining their coach, but they were miles ahead of him when it came to controlling the narrative.

Rich and Rita didn't have much time to dwell on the backlash; they had to get to Ann Arbor.

That Sunday, December 16, 2007, the day before Rodriguez's formal introduction as Michigan's new head coach, they signed a legal agreement, faxed it back to Ann Arbor, and got on a plane. Rodriguez trusted Michigan the way he had trusted West Virginia—and both times it proved to be a major mistake.

The most visible elephant in the room was the $4 million buyout clause in his West Virginia contract, which Pastilong had finalized in August 2007 when Rich had first gone to him with his list of requests. While he'd not been able to nail down the items on his list, West Virginia had nailed down the new buyout clause.

President Coleman, Martin, and Rodriguez all felt confident they could get the total buyout reduced. If West Virginia insisted on the full amount, however, Coleman and Martin asked Rodriguez to try to get it knocked down—but, failing that, they promised that Michigan would pay $2.5 million and Rodriguez $1.5. He agreed.

Nothing was made public, and no one told the regents of the arrangement.

"I know this from watching it too many times in business," said Jim Hackett, who played under Schembechler before rising to CEO of Steelcase Furniture in Grand Rapids. "We want something to happen so badly that, during the early lovefest, we pass over too many of the specifics because the general discussions are going so well, and the details are lost.

You don't want to add tension in that moment. 'We'll get this roughly right and then iron it out later.' That sounds great—but then it becomes incumbent on the people doing the hiring to follow through."

It didn't help that both sides were reaching their decisions at the eleventh hour.

But that Monday, the day Rodriguez would become the school's tenth head coach in a little more than one hundred years since Fielding Yost arrived in 1901, everyone involved seemed color-blind when the numerous red flags kept popping up.

The Junge Champions Center was packed with five rows of seated reporters, a few more standing by the wall of glass doors, and behind them all, some fifteen TV crews, including ESPN, which carried it live. You could no longer just run up State Street to take the job.

Rodriguez came off well. "I'm tickled to death to be standing here," he said. "It was the most difficult decision I've made in my professional career."

When asked about the decision to leave West Virginia, he was politic: "It was just the opportunity. It was time."

When asked how he felt about being Michigan's third choice—reflecting the common perception that Schiano *and* Les Miles had been offered the job—Rodriguez joked, "I was probably Rita's third choice, too!"

A smart reporter asked him how his spread offense would work at Michigan. Rodriguez replied, "If you want to know our system or philosophy, if you've watched us over the years, that's what you'll see. We're going to do what we've done. That's the only thing we know." But he added, "I know we have the ability to adapt our schemes to our personnel," which just about every coach who brings a different system to a program feels compelled to say, and which invariably sets up a false expectation, because you can adapt any system only so much.

When someone asked him about the anger brewing behind him in Morgantown, Rodriguez referred to a scene in *The Lion King*, which he had watched with his kids, in which a monkey hits a lion over the head and the surprised lion says, "'What'd you do that for?' and the monkey says, 'It's in the past!'"

Rodriguez—who naturally had very strong feelings about the damaging statements being made about him back in West Virginia—felt he was taking the high road and being gracious. The line got a laugh, but if you followed the metaphor, he had just portrayed himself as the guilty party. The actual Rodriguez, in contrast, firmly believed his actions had been completely justified. Rodriguez, the media was learning, was more open, direct, and entertaining than his famously button-downed predecessor, but he lacked Carr's discipline and precision, too.

He'd never before needed to learn that lesson, and no one in Ann Arbor was prepared to teach him.

That became more obvious when he was tossed the most important question of his first day on the job: Do you have to be a Michigan Man to be the Michigan football coach? Rodriguez repeated the question—clearly one he had not considered before—then said, "Gosh, I hope not. They hired me!"

He navigated the issue of Michigan's weighty heritage like a man teetering on a high wire. "I think you have to have great respect for the tradition. I know a little bit about the tradition. I'm studying it." He gave a courteous nod to Lloyd Carr—"I'm excited about following a legend"—then offered three predictions: "I think [the] transition will be relatively smooth because of all the things you already have in place"; "I'm just going to be the way I am"; and "I will plan to retire here." Only one of those would come true.

The takeaway for most fans was this: After a train wreck of a coaching search, in which they were disappointed that Michigan hadn't hired Les Miles, the Wolverines were lucky to land one of the best young coaches out there, who seemed to be a sincere and genuinely likable guy.

But if you watched and listened carefully, you could detect trouble ahead. Coleman had not attended the conference. Martin had, and mentioned the Yost connection, but with little sense for public relations had not staged the event with former coaches and players to show support and continuity, nor had he prepared Rodriguez for the predictable questions.

In short, Martin and Rodriguez missed their lines.

To appeal to the Michigan blue bloods, Rodriguez could have started his answer by noting that Michigan's three greatest coaches—Fielding Yost, Fritz Crisler, and Bo Schembechler—had been outsiders, too, and the first of those had grown up just ten minutes from Rodriguez's hometown.

He could have mentioned that he had learned about "The Victors," the Big House, the winged helmet, and the banner at the knee of his coach and mentor, Don Nehlen, who had learned the value of Michigan tradition from Schembechler himself. In fact, that's what inspired Rodriguez to put up Bo's famous THOSE WHO STAY WILL BE CHAMPIONS sign at Glenville State. True, he could have concluded, he wasn't a Michigan Man, but he knew how special that was and sincerely hoped to become one.

And a "Go Blue!" at the end would have been a nice touch.

Rodriguez could have said all those things because they were all true, and he knew most of them off the top of his head. He didn't need a script. But he didn't say any of those things, leaving doubts about his knowledge of Michigan traditions and his dedication to protecting them. That vital vacuum of information—*who is this new guy?*—would be filled by the people in Morgantown and the media, who did not necessarily have the new coach's best interests in mind.

As the saying goes, you have only one chance to make a first impression. Studies have repeatedly shown that, after we form our initial opinions of someone, we are surprisingly reluctant to change them. Rodriguez hadn't blown the press conference. Far from it. But he hadn't blown it out of the water, either, as he readily could have, while Michigan missed a perfect chance to pass the torch with a choreographed bit of pageantry.

This day marked the first of many that would shrink Rodriguez's safety net until it would be reduced solely to the number of wins he could produce.

In 2011, I asked *Detroit Free Press* columnist Michael Rosenberg if he felt he had any bias against Rich Rodriguez. "I never had personal feelings for Rodriguez one way or the other," he said. The column he wrote about Rodriguez's hiring supports his claim.

"Michigan hired a great football coach Sunday. Not a good one, like Greg Schiano. Not a very good one, like Les Miles. A great one . . . For the Michigan football fan who has complained incessantly for the last ten years, Rodriguez might as well show up at this morning's news conference dressed in wrapping paper and a bow."

The column laid out the pros and the potential cons of the hire in an evenhanded manner—very presciently, in many ways—but his private comments that day suggest a different mind-set.

After Rodriguez's first press conference, Jim Brandstatter, a former lineman turned Michigan color man and one of Schembechler's closest friends, walked out to the parking lot with Rosenberg, when the columnist declared, "I don't like that guy. I don't think he belongs here."

Brandstatter wasn't sure why Rosenberg was so convinced and told him he should at least give the guy a chance. But he went away certain that Rosenberg's mind, at least, was already made up.

Before Martin had hired Rodriguez, just about everyone who followed Michigan football was already apoplectic. They care deeply about the program, after all. It's not a stretch to say many fans feel it represents the very best of their cherished midwestern values, and those who have worn the winged helmet know it will be one of the first things mentioned in their obituaries, no matter what else they do before they die.

All the members of the Michigan family had trusted Bo Schembechler and his heirs to protect it. One fan, whose dad had died young, went so far as to write the AD that "Michigan football is my father." To see the succession handled so carelessly created anxiety and even animosity among the fans, the alums, and especially the former players, who'd done the work to make the program what it was.

Just about every faction was upset, including those devoted to Lloyd Carr, Ron English, and Les Miles. Mary Sue Coleman, the regents, and the athletic department staffers weren't happy, either. People were angry that their favorite candidate didn't get the consideration they felt he was due, and they were angry with each other, too. They all had one thing in common, however: Fairly or not, they were all mad at Bill Martin, who would never again have the full support of any of those constituencies. Whatever ill will Martin had already generated among the Michigan Men and the media was sure to affect the head coach he had just hired.

In fact, a few months later, Rosenberg confessed to several U-M employers his feelings about the athletic director. His comment to one was typical when he said, "word for word, that he hated Bill Martin because he'd lied to him, and he was going to get him run out of his job."

The faster Rodriguez failed, many reasoned, the sooner Martin would have to leave, too. To this faction, Rodriguez was just collateral damage—and so were the players.

Some started leaving immediately. But it turns out the departures might not have been as spontaneous as they first appeared.

After Rodriguez's press conference accepting the Michigan job on Monday, December 17, he flew back to Morgantown to close out his business there. Before he returned a few days later, Lloyd Carr suddenly called a team meeting for his players in the team room on either Tuesday or Wednesday morning. According to five players there, Carr told them he knew some had come to Ann Arbor to play for him, and some to play for Michigan. "But," he said, "you're here to play for Michigan."

"Of course," one player said, "every coach has to say that."

But not every departing coach has to say what Carr said next. He told them he wanted them all to be happy, and he recognized not everyone would want to go through the coaching change to come. So, he said, if any of them wanted to transfer, he would sign the form, since it requires a player's current coach's signature.

On its face, it seems like a simple, generous offer to look out for people he cared about—and, in fairness, that was probably part of his motive. (Carr did not respond to repeated requests for an interview.) But it was also interpreted by many of the players as a vote of no confidence in his successor before Rodriguez had conducted a single team meeting, a single workout, a single practice, yelled or sworn at a single player, or coached a single game. It was an invitation from Carr, someone they knew, admired, and looked to for direction—the man who had recruited them and promised their parents he would look out for them like a father—to execute a preemptive bailout, to transfer, to jump to the NFL, or simply to not come back for a fifth year.

Certainly that's how Michigan's former director of compliance, Judy Van Horn, read the gesture. When former director of operations Scott Draper called over to Compliance as soon as the players left the meeting— to give them a heads-up that a line of players might be asking for their transfer papers in a few minutes, and that Carr was prepared to sign all of them—the compliance officer alerted Van Horn. She told Martin of Carr's offer and said, "Bill, we just can't let this happen. It could be a mass exodus."

Van Horn then called Rodriguez. As Van Horn recalled, "Rich said, 'If a player wants to go, I don't want to make him stay. But I don't want Michigan to give any player a release until I've had a chance to talk with him.'"

That seemed fair, even generous, but Van Horn called the Big Ten office to make sure it would not be a violation of league rules. The Big Ten assured her Rodriguez's request was allowable, because he was not keeping anyone from transferring who wanted to. Satisfied, Van Horn passed on Rodriguez's response to Scott Draper, who replied, "But Lloyd won't like that." The day raised more questions than answers, but no one questioned Draper's devotion to Carr. (Draper declined to be interviewed.)

Carr's feelings aside, that was the policy created that day: Any player who wanted to transfer could do so, provided they talked with the new coach first. But even that low bar was too high for some players, including Ryan Mallett, who only spoke with Rodriguez on the phone before leaving Ann Arbor.

There are about three dozen people who worked directly for both Carr and Rodriguez and know them well. Almost every single one of them told me, at one point, "Lloyd never liked Rich."

In many ways, their styles could not be more different. Carr came across as professorial, while Rodriguez was more comfortable as a good ol' boy. Carr was very private, even closed off. Rodriguez was open and outgoing. As early as the Capital One Bowl, one athletic department staffer observed, "If those two were driving across the country together and couldn't talk about family or football, they wouldn't have anything to say to each other for three thousand miles."

Carr was also no fan of the spread offense, which had tormented his team many times. In the last few years of Carr's tenure, he and his staff sponsored a fantasy camp to benefit the children's hospital. In 2007, a camper asked one of Carr's assistants if they would learn about the spread offense. "The spread offense?" the assistant spat. "That's Communist football!"

Whatever friction might have existed between the two, it is simply impossible to square Carr's making an unsolicited call to Rich Rodriguez to sell him on Michigan, and telling Bill Martin that Rodriguez might be a good candidate, followed almost immediately by his offer to help any of his players transfer. It's even harder to square those actions with his new role as Michigan's associate athletic director, whose job it is to protect and promote the Michigan athletic department, football above all.

When Rodriguez returned to West Virginia to pack up his office and persuade his assistant coaches to join him, all of them seemed ready to go, but they were still curious to see who would succeed Rodriguez as the Mountaineers' next head coach. Rodriguez had recommended offensive coordinator Calvin Magee for the post, even though he wanted Magee to lead his offense in Ann Arbor.

"He was ready," Rodriguez said, "and you can't deny him his chance." But when an administrator told Magee the West Virginia fans might not accept an African-American head coach, Magee decided not to press the issue.

"If that was the case," Magee told me, "I figure it's better to know it and move on than wait around for something that's never going to happen."

Though disappointed for his friend, Rodriguez was relieved to have Magee on board. Ditto Jeff Casteel, who had taken a shaky defense and turned it into one of the nation's ten best in 2007, earning the national Defensive Coordinator of the Year award for his efforts.

Casteel used the 3-3-5—the defensive answer to Rodriguez's spread option offense—which emphasizes speed over size, putting fast, versatile players in space and letting them attack. Like the spread option, the 3-3-5 has its critics, who say it won't work in the Big Ten. But Rodriguez, as usual, wasn't listening to the critics. Besides, he and Casteel worked well together, and their approach to the players was in sync.

Casteel was that rarest of college coaches: content. He cares only about family and football, and in West Virginia he had everything he wanted, including a trailer on a lake where he took his family after home games. He seemed to have no particular desire for wealth, fame, or a bigger stage.

But he knew his next boss could jeopardize his private paradise. Head coaches have strong personalities, and if they don't mesh, you're in for a rough ride. Given the choices, Casteel's best chance to preserve most of what he had was to follow Rodriguez to Michigan—and that's what he decided to do.

"Here's the big thing that most people don't know," said Rodriguez's eventual director of football operations, Mike Parrish, in 2011. "Casteel already had a Michigan cell phone. He was getting ready to go."

Rodriguez tried to retain all his assistants, save one: Bill Stewart, whom Rodriguez had inherited as the quarterback coach until Rodriguez brought in Rod Smith in 2007, moving Stewart to tight ends. Perhaps for that reason West Virginia named Stewart the interim coach for the Fiesta Bowl game against third-ranked Oklahoma, the Big 12 champion. After the ninth-ranked Mountaineers pulled off the upset 48–28, West Virginia surprised almost everyone by tapping Stewart to be the permanent head coach. As a result, the West Virginia staff would have to decide: stay with Bill or leave with Rich.

Many fans recall that when Nick Saban left Michigan State for LSU, not one assistant went with him. "That was my greatest fear," Rodriguez said, "and an even greater fear for Rita. She loved those guys and knew how important they were to our team—and to me."

So after Rodriguez came to Ann Arbor, he sent a plane back to Morgantown to get his assistants. Who was going to get on? How many?

A couple of hours later, Magee called Rodriguez and said, "We're ready to go. The plane's full, and we've got two cars trailing us filled with the strength coaches."

Rodriguez let out a sigh of relief—then decided to have a little fun. He called Rita and told her, "Calvin said no one is on the plane but him."

Rodriguez planned to drag it out, but Rita was so distraught he didn't have the heart to keep the gag going. "Naw, honey, I'm just kidding ya! It's full. Everyone's coming with us."

"Don't you *ever* do that to me again!"

"Honey, I don't ever want another chance."

But one coach did not get on that plane: Jeff Casteel.

Stewart made a play for almost all of Rodriguez's assistants, including Rod Smith, who turned him down to accept less money, a smaller role, and no contract to coach the quarterbacks at Michigan—which is exactly what Michigan expects.

However, when Stewart offered Casteel $275,000 and, more important, a two-year contract, it looked pretty good compared to Michigan's offer: $265,000 and no contract at all. Casteel decided to stay put.

"If they don't hire Stewart," Parrish said in 2011, "Jeff Casteel comes to Michigan."

And if Casteel had joined Rodriguez's staff?

Parrish didn't hesitate: "It would have been completely different."

If Rodriguez came close to batting a thousand on hiring, even with one vital miss, he didn't fare as well when it came to firing.

On Thursday, December 20, Rodriguez asked to meet with everyone—from coordinators to clerical workers—in the team room. He explained that, like any new coach, he had autonomy over hiring, and he had people in mind for most of the coaching positions, but he was willing to talk with anyone who wanted to stay. (In the football business, many new coaches simply clean house before they even meet.)

He told them he would be in the commons—which also serves as the team's second-floor dining hall—and would stay for as long as people wanted to talk.

There is no easy way to complete such a chore, but it's fair to say that, despite good intentions, Rodriguez didn't make any new friends that day. Rodriguez kept all the trainers, equipment managers, video staffers, and secretaries, plus running backs coach Fred Jackson and, at Carr's urging, operations men Scott Draper and Brad Labadie.

All told, Rodriguez kept far more of Carr's employees than he let go. The assistant coaches knew they would be leaving and simply wanted to get on with their lives with their dignity intact.

But that was not the day's lasting memory. Instead of setting up individual appointments, they ended up lined up outside the commons, with some of them sitting on the floor waiting for hours, which did not go over well with a group of men who had won Big Ten titles as players and coaches. When they finally did see Rodriguez, at least two were unimpressed with his lack of eye contact and sincerity.

"The conversation was hollow," former assistant coach Steve Szabo said. "I didn't think he was up-front. I don't think he had any intention of keeping any of us. I can understand that—everyone brings in his own guys—but I wish he'd just said that. He was trying to be nice, but I'd rather he'd be flat honest."

Any labor lawyer can tell you it's not firing employees that generates lawsuits but the way you fire them. And this was not handled well—creating another layer of well-connected insiders who would have no love for Rodriguez, no mixed feelings if he failed, and no hesitation about spreading their views on the matter.

Mike Gittleson, who'd been Michigan's strength and conditioning coach for thirty years, was one of those who felt bitter about the transition, but the fault was not all Rodriguez's.

The coaches were terminated immediately, and lost all benefits except health, which they kept for sixty days—though it is not uncommon elsewhere for even fired coaches and staffers to get benefits and severance pay for much longer.

None of this was communicated directly by Martin, who never met with the staff, but a third party. "They give you a box and say, 'Clean your offices out,'" Szabo recalled. "It was in some ways shocking. I was offended by the way we were treated.

"As much as we disliked the way Rodriguez talked to us, he had nothing to do with that whatsoever. Bill Martin was ultimately responsible for the mechanics of the way we were treated, the dismissal. There were a lot of quality, hardworking coaches there. We were knocking on the door of a national title in 2006, and came back from a bad start in 2007 to knock off the defending national champions.

"But that's not how we were treated. That didn't sit well with anyone. We all resented the way it was handled. The whole thing was just really sad."

Strength coach Mike Barwis planned to name the new weight room after Gittleson—until reports started coming in every week of Gittleson bad-mouthing Rodriguez, Barwis, and his staff around town, at clinics around the country, and even to reporters, recruits, and current players. Of all the disaffected former staffers, no one, it seemed, was more eager to castigate the new coaches than Mike Gittleson.

Coach Carr's final season might have started on the worst note in the history of Michigan football, but it ended on one of the best.

In the 2008 Capital One Bowl, played in Orlando on New Year's Day, Las Vegas oddsmakers calculated that the twelfth-ranked returning national champion Florida Gators would beat Carr's unranked 8–4 Wolverines by double digits.

But the Wolverines, healthy for the first time since the opener, upset the Gators 41–35. The most memorable play of the game occurred *after* the game, when the seniors—who hadn't beaten Ohio State or a bowl opponent until that game—lifted their coach onto their shoulders and carried him across the field.

Sure, the Capital One Bowl has all the tradition of . . . well, a credit card company, but it was the best departure by a Michigan coach since Fritz Crisler's players lifted him up after his 49–0 Rose Bowl victory over USC to cap an undefeated national title season exactly sixty years earlier.

Back in Schembechler Hall, Rodriguez was stumbling out of the gate. On Tuesday, January 8, 2008, the day after his entire staff had moved in, Rodriguez walked into the team room to address the Wolverines for the first time. He said all the right things, and the introduction was well received. "They all stood up and cheered," Parrish recalls, "*wildly*. I mean, *loud*."

But a key group was missing: the outgoing seniors. There was a logic to this. Rodriguez would not be coaching them, of course, which is why most coaches excuse the seniors a few minutes into their last team meeting. Rodriguez hadn't coached that senior class, barely knew them, and—while they were not barred from attending the meeting—he made little attempt to connect with them on their way out, thank them for their contributions, or ask for their support.

Not reaching out to them generated unnecessary ill will among a powerful class that included four-year starting quarterback Chad Henne, Michigan all-time leading rusher Mike Hart, and future number one NFL draft pick Jake Long. Tough guys, good guys, great leaders, and soon-to-be graduates—the very embodiment of the Michigan ideal. They were not the kind of people to spend their time and energy bad-mouthing the new coach. But they could have been the kind of true-blue Michigan Men Rodriguez sorely needed to be ambassadors to the former players and the public. Instead, Rodriguez lost them from the start.

In those testy early months, Rodriguez got some things right. When they finished up their first recruiting class, Rodriguez invited the celebrated '69 team, Schembechler's first, back to speak to the team on Tuesday, February 5, about Michigan tradition and transition.

The event was well organized and well executed. About thirty players showed up, with Jim Brandstatter emceeing the event, and Dick Caldarazzo, Jim Mandich, Reggie McKenzie, and Dan Dierdorf all giving funny but fiery speeches to the team. A few pointed out the parallels between their transition from the gentlemanly Bump Elliott and the bombastic Bo Schembechler to what the current players were going through. Their message was a familiar one: It's not going to be easy, but those who stay . . .

Dierdorf went beyond that, pointing out that, in their era, teams that dared enter the Big House were already half-beaten before kickoff. During warm-ups, Schembechler would walk in front of his players, like a general inspecting his troops, then point to the visitors at the other end of the field. "They're scared, men. You know why? Because you're *Michigan!*"

"Well, they're not scared anymore," Dierdorf told them. "Appalachian State wasn't scared. You need to bring that back."

It was a rare admission from within the Michigan family that Rodriguez wasn't just bringing in a new system but also was restoring the one he had inherited.

The event was a smash hit, with everyone—the coaches, the players, and the alums—doing their part to bridge the gap between the old and the new. "I want everyone who played here to know he is welcomed back anytime," Rodriguez told *USA Today* about the reunion. "Hopefully, this will be one of the first steps toward getting that message out."

It went so well that Martin decided to invite all the former players back on February 16, 2008, to welcome the new coaches and teach them about Michigan tradition.

Of course, Michigan football had held many reunions over the years. They were great successes, cementing the bond not only among teammates who had entered middle age but also across eras. With few exceptions, you met good husbands, good fathers, and good community leaders. To a person, they will tell you Michigan football made them better men. But this was the first such event without their father figure, Bo Schembechler, in attendance—and it showed.

Reports on the evening vary widely, but almost everyone agrees the intentions were better than the execution. About 250 football alums returned for the event, held at the Junge Champions Center, and "95 percent of them were just first-class, great," Parrish recalled. "They really made us feel welcome."

But things took a turn when the speeches started. "Some of you guys come in here wearing sweatshirts, looking like shit," said the always urbane Stan Edwards with a grin. "Well, fuck you guys!" He then tore off his own tie, and the room erupted.

A steady stream of profanity spewed from the podium, eventually from Bill Martin himself. A lot of the japing got laughs, but, as Jim Hackett said, "there was a cheapness to it I wasn't used to. Each one of the talks was less about the virtues that made us great, the values that built this program, and more about reminiscing—unconnected to what we were there to do: build the bridge that would ensure Michigan's success in the next phase of our evolution."

By almost all accounts, the night hit a low point when Eric Mayes took the podium. A walk-on who rose to become a cocaptain of the 1997 squad, he was sidelined by a knee injury in the fourth game but continued to lead during his team's national title run. He went on to earn a Ph.D., but his teammates knew he had a mercurial side. No one was quite sure what he was going to say.

They found out soon enough. Mayes delivered a stern lecture to the new coaches. The message was simple: They were interlopers among proven Michigan Men, who still owned the program, not the newcomers. "I better not see *any* of your friends from *West Virginia* on *our* sidelines!" Mayes declared.

"I remember feeling that if Bo Schembechler had been sitting in that room," Hackett told me, "he would have been appalled at the way the former Michigan Men had been so critical [of the new coaches] and missed the point of the event: to pull us together. I had this urge to get up and chastise everybody that this was about *our* responsibility, not Rich's responsibility. But I didn't do it. And I don't have a good answer as to why."

After the former players finished, it fell to Rodriguez to take the podium. He started out by making a joke—"I haven't been chewed out like that since I was in kindergarten!"—and got a nervous laugh. He gently warned them some change was inevitable, then did his best to span the chasm created that night, but he couldn't finish on the note he had hoped for, and the night's mission had been missed.

"Ultimately, this is a Bill Martin problem," Hackett said. "There is a casualness [to] Bill through all this—from the search to the setup—that often means he doesn't seize the opportunity. He doesn't plan the event very well. He doesn't set the standard on how it needs to flow. It became a bit of a free-for-all, and by the time Rich gets up there, he probably doesn't know what to do or say."

The older alums did. Before the week was over, a couple dozen of them—including such legends as Don Lund, Bob Chappuis, and Jim Conley—felt compelled to make their way to Rodriguez's office to apologize in person.

But Martin said nothing. Nor did Eric Mayes or his peers. After that night, few members of Mayes's generation would speak with Rodriguez again.

Rodriguez's mounting problems in Ann Arbor were nothing compared to those still pending in Morgantown, starting with the $4 million buyout clause in his West Virginia contract. Coleman, who had to be shaking her head at the mess she had been dragged into, and Martin, already under severe scrutiny for the sloppy search, still lacked the temerity to tell the regents they had promised Rodriguez that they would pay $2.5 million of it.

This "overlooked" detail proved damaging to all parties, but especially to Rodriguez. First, Coleman and Martin asked Rodriguez to keep their agreement a secret, which made it appear he was fighting West Virginia strictly out of self-interest and not at the request of his new employers.

Of course, if common sense had prevailed among the media and fans, just about everyone would have realized Michigan must have made some kind of arrangement with Rodriguez or he never would have accepted in the first place. Coaching at Michigan may be a great honor, but not quite a $4 million one.

But throughout the transition, common sense was as rare as public relations savvy—the price for trying to sweep a messy search under the rug.

While Michigan was working to keep a lid on potential embarrassments, West Virginia seemed eager to manufacture them. The day after Rodriguez's introductory press conference in Ann Arbor, he had returned to Morgantown to clean out his office. At about the same time, a story leaked that Rodriguez's West Virginia University–owned cell phone showed dozens of calls each day to a mysterious number in Peterstown, West Virginia, which some suggested was something sinister.

The truth was not so exciting. Rodriguez had asked three employees, including Mike Parrish, to shred stacks of old practice schedules and game plans—things no one wanted lying around—but not transcripts or scholarship information, as reported. "The director of operations and Bill Stewart walked by," Parrish recalled. "We weren't hiding anything."

As for the cell phone number, Rodriguez was curious about it himself. So he gave the number to Jamie Morris, who took all of five minutes to determine it was the number for a cell tower that retrieves your messages.

"It was so comical," Rodriguez said, "we just didn't think we had to worry about it."

But that's not how either story played in the national press.

After promising to help any of his players who wanted to transfer or jump to the NFL, Carr proved true to his word. Shortly after Rodriguez arrived, quarterback Ryan Mallett, following a consultation with Carr, transferred to Arkansas, and receivers Adrian Arrington and Mario Manningham—who never planned to stay for their senior seasons—bolted for the NFL. Carr would also help Justin Boren and Toney Clemons, among others, and encouraged some to leave who hadn't asked him and ultimately stayed. These decisions were almost always preceded by long conversations in Carr's new expanded office at Weidenbach Hall.

No matter what was said in those private "exit interviews," the players' departures would have caught the press's attention, with some particularly eager to report them. But if Carr was discouraging his former players in these meetings from talking to the *Free Press*, at least a few must have gone out of their way to ignore his advice, with no apparent consequences—which was, at the least, very unlike Schembechler's approach to message control among the Michigan Men.

Any coaching change evokes the metaphorical cupboard, inspiring heated debate about how full or empty the previous coach left it for the new guy. In Ann Arbor, few seemed to realize that if the cupboard was emptier than it might have been if Carr had remained, in the months leading up to the 2008 season, Carr himself was helping to empty it. It would be Rodriguez, however, who would be blamed for the wave of defections.

In 2011, Mallett's father said Rodriguez made no attempt to keep his son, but Rodriguez maintained he called Ryan three times—and, considering the alternatives, it makes sense that he would. In their third and final conversation, Rodriguez told him, "Listen, we can fit our offense around a thrower," just as he had with Shaun King at Tulane. But given the switch from Carr's pro-style offense to Rodriguez's spread offense, Mallett made a rational choice. When Mallett's father asked Carr what his son should do, Carr replied, "He needs to leave." Mallett's decision seems like less a choice than a fait accompli. (Carr did not respond to Mr. Mallett's claim and did not respond to requests for an interview.)

But in the press, the departed were portrayed like rats scurrying off a sinking ship—or, worse, passengers being shoved off a perfectly seaworthy one.

Recruiting didn't play much better in the media. Rodriguez kept most of Carr's incoming class—including its star, Mike Martin—and added a few of his own. But when defensive line coach Bruce Tall traveled to Trotwood, Ohio, to reinforce Michigan commits Michael Shaw and Brandon Moore, he checked up on a receiver named Roy Roundtree, whom they had coveted at West Virginia.

Roundtree had since committed to Purdue, the only major school near his home that wanted him. But the dour engineering-dominated school was a bad fit for the ebullient receiver. When Tall told him Michigan would love to have him, Roundtree visited Ann Arbor and changed his mind, well within the unwritten code of football recruiting. "I had to plan for my future and where I wanted to spend those years," he said. "I couldn't pass up the Big House, man!"

But that's not how outgoing Purdue head coach Joe Tiller saw it. He claimed that there was a "gentleman's agreement" among Big Ten coaches—which Minnesota's Tim Brewster refuted from the podium at the Big Ten meetings that summer. Then Tiller added, "If we had an early-signing date, you wouldn't have another outfit with a guy in a wizard hat selling snake oil to get a guy at the last minute, but that's what happened." The line quickly boiled down to "snake oil salesman with a wizard hat," and it stuck.

If there's one thing Rodriguez struggled with during his introduction to Michigan football, it was Michigan tradition—a train stretching back to 1879, with 129 years of momentum behind it when he arrived. If you're on board, barreling down the tracks is one of the game's greatest rides. But if you're caught on the tracks, you're going to get run over.

Before Rodriguez hit the recruiting trail for his first full Michigan recruiting class that spring, he wisely asked Scott Draper which numbers Michigan had already retired. Draper told him, accurately, that Michigan had retired five: 11 (the three Wistert brothers—Whitey, Ox, and Moose), 47 (Bennie Oosterbaan), 48 (Gerald Ford), 87 (Ron Kramer), and "Ol' 98," the legendary Tom Harmon's number. Draper did not tell him, however, about Michigan's special relationship with the No. 1 jersey.

It started in 1979, when Bo Schembechler assigned it to a pelican-legged freshman from Florida named Anthony Carter, who went on to break virtually every school receiving record and become Michigan's first three-time All-American since Bennie Oosterbaan.

An icon was born—but not a tradition. Not yet.

After Carter left, No. 1 went untouched for three years, until Greg McMurtry became the second wide receiver so honored. Since then, All-American receivers Derrick Alexander, David Terrell, and Braylon Edwards (plus a few forgettable ones in the middle) have all been awarded No. 1. The jersey was further elevated after Edwards generously endowed it, as one might endow a professor's chair. But no one told Rodriguez about any of this.

When J. T. Floyd, a safety out of South Carolina, asked to have No. 2, Rodriguez told him that number had already been promised to fellow incoming freshman Sam McGuffie. But, Rodriguez said, Floyd could take No. 1 if he wanted it.

It's hard to know what surprised the new Michigan coach more: that this was considered blasphemous to the Michigan faithful, or that it became national news.

Rodriguez arrived in Ann Arbor with several books about Michigan tradition, and he had already read a couple before this recruiting trip. But by the end of his first spring, Michigan tradition had come to represent not a source of support, as it had for Crisler and Schembechler, but a club used to beat the new coach over the head. He learned to blanch instinctively whenever the subject came up.

When Rodriguez wasn't wrestling with tradition, he was dealing with transfers.

Justin Boren is the son of Mike Boren, a great linebacker under Schembechler who became a successful businessman in Columbus. In 2006, Justin started as a freshman, but after each game he'd drive back to Columbus to hang out with his high school friends.

Boren never bonded with his Michigan teammates. When Lloyd Carr sponsored his "Carr Wash" for the children's hospital, the players would show up in their jerseys and raise thousands scrubbing down fans' cars. Notably absent was Boren, until he pulled up in his SUV, hauling a boat behind it. While he waited in the driver's seat, his teammates washed both his car and boat, after which he drove off without leaving a dollar.

Once the new coaches came to town, one former teammate recalls, "Justin never even gave them a chance." After Boren told Carr he wanted to transfer to Ohio State—something no Michigan player had done since at least World War II—Boren told this teammate that Carr had replied, "That's a good fit for you. That's where you belong. I'll help you."

"If Bo was still around," the teammate says, "I don't see how that would even be considered. But [Carr] was doing stuff to try to get people out." Whatever Mallett and Boren's teammates thought about them and their decisions, they said nothing publicly.

Boren was less restrained. "Michigan football was a family, built on mutual respect and support for each other from Coach Carr on down," he told the media, making more national news. "We knew it took the entire family, a team effort, and we all worked together. I have great trouble accepting that those family values have eroded in just a few months . . . That I am unable to perform under these circumstances at the level I expect of myself, and my teammates and Michigan fans deserve, is why I have made the decision to leave."

A few months later, Rosenberg lent support to Boren's claim: "Rodriguez's staff uses some of the foulest, most degrading language imaginable. I know coaches curse, and I'm no prude, but this goes way beyond a few dirty words. He belittles his players. This is a big part of why offensive lineman Justin Boren left the team. He felt his dignity was at stake."

It was a strong statement, especially for a reporter who had not attended any of the fifteen practices that spring, all of which Rodriguez opened to the press and the staff's spouses and children—a Michigan first. It was even odder coming from the man who celebrated Schembechler in his book, *War as They Knew It*. In it, Rosenberg describes a practice the week after Michigan lost to Missouri in 1969. Because Missouri had blocked a punt the previous weekend, Schembechler's men would practice punt-ing—and lo and behold, another punt got blocked.

Convinced that Jim Brandstatter let his man through, Schembechler jumped up and landed his left elbow into the top of Brandstatter's chest, then grabbed his face mask and yelled, "You dumb son of a bitch! You'll never play another fucking down for Michigan! Get out of here! I never want to see you again!"

Such outbursts were common during Schembechler's first spring, which is one reason why a few dozen players left the team before the spring game. The tough love behind Bo's tirades, however, also explained why so many of his players became lifelong friends, Brandstatter chief among them.

"Let me just say this," said Brandstatter, who has covered the Wolverines and Lions for decades, "I've been on a lot of fields with a lot of coaches, and the language is not pretty. Points of emphasis are made with, let's say, ex-treme prejudice. That's to make sure you get the point across. If you go on a practice field on a collegiate football team and expect a coach to say, 'You're going the wrong way, sunshine,' you're barking up the wrong tree. That ain't gonna happen."

A couple years later, it came to light that Boren's real beef with the Wolverines was their failure to offer his little brother, Zach, a scholarship. But that revelation came too late to prevent another dent in Rodriguez's reputation.

Rodriguez was both mystified and furious. "Boren was barely *here*," Rodriguez told me. "He never wanted to be here. We never said *anything* to him. And Rosenberg had never been to a single practice—and our prac-tices are *open*. I'd never even met him, and he writes all that?"

It would not be the last Rodriguez would hear from Rosenberg.

Because Michigan Stadium was under construction, the Wolverines had to play their 2008 spring game at Saline High School. Given the cold, gray weather and the equally ugly play, it might have been just as well.

"I knew then we weren't going to be very good," Rodriguez said six months later. "During the search, I didn't even look at the roster, because I just figured, it's Michigan. They've got to have some players. Just throw 'em out there and you'll get eight or nine wins."

But when he realized he would be going into battle with only one re-turning starter on offense—sophomore lineman Steve Schilling—and a starting quarterback, Nick Sheridan, who had played his high school games on the very same field they used for their spring game, earning All-Conference honorable mention, Rodriguez knew he had to recalculate his timetable. He still believed they would be going to a bowl game, but he already figured it would take more than three years to get where he wanted to be.

Rodriguez's revised projections were on his mind when he received a call in June of 2008 to meet Mary Sue Coleman and Bill Martin at the president's house. When Rich and Rita arrived, it quickly became clear his bosses were not there to talk football.

"There was a sense of urgency," Rodriguez recalled. "As soon as we sat down, Mary Sue said, 'The lawsuit's becoming a problem.'"

Of course, it had been a problem for Rodriguez for six months—including West Virginia's smear campaign and the gag order U-M had given him—but it became Coleman's problem when West Virginia sought to depose both her and Martin.

This had them suddenly concerned, and Rodriguez soon found out why: Neither Coleman nor Martin had ever told the regents about the buyout agreement they had signed with Rodriguez in December. To avoid that getting out, they wanted Rodriguez to settle with West Virginia immediately.

But Rodriguez wanted his day in court to counter all the claims from West Virginia and had been keeping a legal pad of notes for that purpose. Further, he knew if he settled, it would look like Michigan was bailing him out, and he'd be the bad guy all over again.

Both Rich and Rita remembered President Coleman telling them, "If they find out, I'll be toast."

"And so will I," Martin added.

"I don't want anyone to lose their job over this," Rich finally said, "but I want the truth to come out."

Coleman turned to Rita and asked, "What do you think?"

"And then I got emotional," Rita recalled. "I said, 'What I need to know is that you're still happy you hired us, and you still want us to be here.'"

"Oh, yes," Coleman and Martin said. "Absolutely."

Rich, Rita, and their financial adviser, Mike Wilcox, talked it over in a separate room, then returned to say they'd do as Coleman had asked and settle. But while they were there, they wanted to make sure they understood that Rodriguez had more work ahead of him than he had originally anticipated. Coleman and Martin agreed to adjust his contract to provide for a $4 million buyout from Michigan if they let him go during any of the first three years, instead of his original buyout deal, which diminished by $500,000 after each year. After January 1, 2011, however, it would fall to $2.5 million.

After thanking them, Rodriguez repeated his prediction that it would take him more than three years to get where he wanted the team to go. Coleman and Martin nodded, but both added, "You'll have to remind us, in case we forget." It was an odd comment but, in view of the day's events, easily put aside at the time.

When the press ran the story of the settlement the next day, there was no mention of any prior agreement between Rodriguez and Michigan.

"And sure enough," Rodriguez remembered, "the writers rip my ass for the settlement, with the perception being that Michigan helped bail me out."

Two thousand and eight was one off-season Rodriguez did not mind coming to an end. Almost lost in the nonstop drama of the transition was the upcoming season. For Rodriguez, even with a shaky squad, it couldn't come soon enough.

In the spring of 2008, Rodriguez made a fateful calculation: If he could never say enough of the right things to satisfy the new media and the old guard, and if divulging his deal with Michigan and rebutting Morgan-town's rumor mill were prohibited, then his only hope was to win games fast enough to keep his detractors from bringing him down.

There was one problem with this plan: Beneath the enviable tradition the Wolverines had built over a century was a team in need of serious work.

Before he had coached a single game at Michigan, Rich Rodriguez had probably received more coverage in 2008 than any coach in the country. As the season approached, the attention only increased.

Rodriguez's Michigan debut seemed to be the top story of almost every media outlet's college football preview, from *The Kansas City Star* to *Sports Illustrated*, and it wouldn't stop all season. ESPN's College Game Day ran a story or commentary every week, augmented by almost daily pieces on "Around the Horn," "PTI," and "SportsCenter." The lead story changed, but some mention of "Rich Rod" was a constant, right up to Malcolm Gladwell's piece comparing teachers and spread option quarterbacks in the December 15, 2008, issue of *The New Yorker*.

In *Sports Illustrated*'s 2008 college football preview issue, Austin Murphy devoted his main story to Rodriguez, whom he described as "the progenitor, the Kevin Bacon, the fountainhead of the spread . . . which dominates the sport at nearly every level . . . the most influential trend in offensive football."

The article ran through the checklist of truisms about the spread. You don't need a world-class bulldozer to run the ball in the spread, just a handful of speedy, skilled receivers who can run perfectly timed routes and a quarterback who zips through a protocol of decisions in a few seconds. Problem is, it takes time to recruit and develop players to do all that, and Rodriguez hadn't had much of either before his first kickoff.

That's why, Murphy wrote, "If past is prologue, the Wolverines will grind their offensive gears in Rich Rod's first season. After that, stand back."

The night before his first game as Michigan's eighteenth head coach, and eleventh since 1901, Rich Rodriguez stood on the second-floor balcony of the Campus Inn, gazing over the lobby below. "I usually have a pretty good idea what we have going into battle," he said, standing at the rail. "Not this time. I have never had so many unknowns going into a football game in my entire life, not even in high school."

Rodriguez could no longer kid himself that this team would compete for a Big Ten title that season. The question was, could he get them across the finish line with the program's streaks alive?

He certainly wasn't conceding the upcoming Utah game. They knew Utah ran the spread offense, and they probably ran it better than Michigan would. But Rodriguez hoped his more experienced defense could keep the Utes from lighting up the scoreboard and give the Wolverines' embryonic offense a chance to win.

Beat a solid Utah team, and Miami of Ohio was next. Take a 2–0 record into South Bend the following weekend, where Charlie Weis was already fighting for his job, and who knows? Success breeds success.

Mulling it all over, Rodriguez held on to the railing and stared at the dark windows across the lobby. "I honestly have no idea what's going to happen tomorrow. No idea."

His uncertainty was justified. If ever there was a team with more questions than answers, it was the 2008 Wolverines, beginning with quarterback. Steven Threet had been a four-star prospect out of Adrian—a rural town just forty minutes from Ann Arbor—where he had been the class valedictorian and a baseball star. When it didn't work out at Georgia Tech, he transferred to Michigan in 2007.

After sitting out a season, he was eager to make his mark. He always leaned forward in the quarterback meetings, eyes wide open, nodding and agreeing so vigorously—"Uh-huh, uh-huh"—that sometimes the quarterback coach Rod Smith lost his train of thought.

The coaches considered Threet a nice kid, hardworking, and very smart, but his unorthodox form gave them fits. When he threw the ball, he leaned back on his left foot and flicked his right foot up behind him, like a second basemen flipping the ball to first. They worked every day on it, but it always returned, like a stubborn cowlick, especially under pressure.

The second candidate was walk-on Nick Sheridan. His father, Bill, had assisted Lloyd Carr, but after his dad took a job with the New York Giants, Nick was content to stick to intramural football until one of the former coaches, knowing Nick wanted to become a coach himself, told him to come out for the team. His disposition in meetings was the opposite of Threet's. He leaned back, eyelids relaxed, and rarely made a sound.

Perhaps Sheridan's calm demeanor tipped the balance, since neither quarterback had ever played in the Big House and the coaches knew that jitters would be an issue. The coaches decided they had a slightly better chance starting Sheridan.

When I asked Rodriguez, at the team breakfast before his first game as Michigan's head coach, how he felt about getting back to football, he paused briefly and answered, "Thank God."

The Wolverines piled into four university buses at 1:00 p.m. for the 3:00 kickoff. But this year, instead of just pulling up to the tunnel at the Big House, Rodriguez had the buses park a hundred yards away to let the coaches and players walk through a roped lane with the band playing and—they hoped—fans cheering them on.

When Rodriguez and his troops got off the buses, the Michigan Marching Band was right on schedule, blasting "The Victors." The fans were standing twenty-deep at the rope line, packing the old staircase by the tunnel, and covering the hillside leading up to Crisler Arena. Michigan maniacs were everywhere, clapping and cheering and punching their fists in the air.

When Rodriguez entered the locker room he passed Jon Falk, Michigan's equipment manager since Bo Schembechler hired him in 1973. Falk turned to him, waved his arms over the fans, and yelled, "Was that cool or what?" Rodriguez beamed and nodded.

Then it was back to the coaches' room—which, even at the Big House, isn't very big—where Rodriguez tried to kill time by sitting in his folding chair in the corner, going over his play chart, jotting down a couple of notes for his pregame speech, and looking up at the muted TV bolted to the wall by the door.

Right over that door they had installed a digital clock—the same kind of no-nonsense one-foot-by-half-foot model that littered Schembechler Hall. Unlike those, however, this one didn't tell you the time of day but counted down the big red minutes and seconds until kickoff, reminding you of a time bomb.

For the most part, the players appeared much calmer than Rodriguez, with the possible exception of Steven Threet, whose already eager personality seemed amped up for the occasion. Sheridan remained characteristically cool.

Freshmen Sam McGuffie and Michael Shaw tried to force themselves to mimic Sheridan's calm. The seniors were a mixed bag, about half on board with the new program and the other half unsure at best.

A guy like Will Johnson would work his tail off no matter who the coaches were, and he did, setting weight room records under Barwis. Mike Massey might have felt more comfortable with Coach Carr, but he wasn't going to undermine anyone's efforts to lead the team, even if the spread offense eventually cost the big tight end playing time.

Perhaps no one responded better to the change than junior Brandon Graham. When Rodriguez and his staff arrived, Graham weighed 315 pounds, could bench his weight only once, and was just as weak in the classroom, where his attendance was spotty. But in nine months, he had gotten his weight down to 275, and he was well on his way to bench pressing over 500 pounds, increasing his squat from 275 to 625, and his clean from 185 pounds to 450. He had also become a conscientious student, emerging as a viable candidate for both an NFL contract and a bachelor's degree.

"I just listen to the coaches," he told me, "and do what they tell me. They're not trying to mess you up. They're trying to make you better."

But not all the older players were buying into the new coaches' program. Much of the resistance was the normal consequence of any coaching change, when all seniors lose the goodwill they had accrued with the previous coaches and resent having to start over just like the freshmen. The seniors also had to adjust to an entirely new approach to just about everything, including conditioning, where they could no longer come in to lift when they liked but had to join the morning or afternoon group. And some of them were disappointed by Rodriguez's decision not to name permanent captains but rotate them every week.

More fundamentally, the loss of not only the graduating seniors but also half the rest of their offense—from Mallett to Manningham and Arrington to Boren—gave them a shaky outlook for their senior season. Like everyone else, they did not come to Michigan to be mediocre, and they were genuinely concerned that, with all the changes and departures, they might end their careers that way.

Since Schembechler had posted that famous sign in 1969, the promise at Michigan was straightforward: Those who stay will be champions. But these seniors *had* stayed, and their odds of winning their first Big Ten title that year looked pretty slim. If they fell short, they would be only the second senior class since 1969 to leave without a ring, and the first since 1996. This was not the deal they had signed up for.

When it was finally time for warm-ups, Rodriguez got up from his chair, jammed his "M" cap on, and exhaled. "Let's go out there and see if anyone's shown up."

Dusty Rutledge yelled, "Go through the training room and turn left! Stadium's straight out the tunnel. Can't miss it!"

"Thank God," Rodriguez muttered, "I brought the smart-ass with me."

When the coaches and players jogged down to the end of the dark tunnel, they were met with a blinding sun and a packed house, more than an hour before kickoff.

"You hear about it, you see it on TV," Rodriguez said, gazing up at the stands, "but until you're in the middle of it, you don't quite know."

Rutledge joined Rodriguez in the corner of the end zone, two old friends going back to their days at tiny Glenville State. They looked around the Big House, taking it all in.

Dusty finally broke their reverie. "Coach, we're a long way from Pioneer Stadium."

"Yes, we are, Dusty. Yes, we are."

About an hour later, back in Michigan's locker room, it was time for the real thing. Rodriguez gathered his players around him, his back to the double doors, and gave them his first pregame speech in the Big House.

"Take a knee, men.

"Since we got here, we've heard a whole lot of questions about us, about me. That's fine. That's the price you pay when you come to the greatest program in college football. You're going to get questions, you're going to get critics. Don't like it? Go somewhere they don't care who you are. That'll solve that problem.

"I know the last eight months haven't been easy—the press, the coaches, the workouts. There were a lot of ways you could've gone.

"You could've said, 'Hey, I don't like to work this hard!'

"You could've said, 'I don't like getting yelled at! These guys are tough!'

"You could've said, 'I'm gonna go somewhere else, where it's easier!' But you didn't do that to. You're HERE! You're *here*, and that tells me a lot about you."

He worked the room, making eye contact with each player. They might have been unsure about him as a coach, maybe even as a person, but at this moment, he had them.

"People always talk about Michigan tradition. I ain't from here. I *chose* to come here. You did, too. But I can tell you, the banner, and the band, and the Big House—those are all great. But when I brought back the guys from Bo's first team, I asked 'em, 'What is Michigan football?' They talked about their *practices*. Tougher than Woody's! They talked about Bo's intensity and the confidence they felt when they ran out of that tunnel."

His voice started rising with emotion, warming to his subject, reacting to the response he was getting as the players nodded.

"Now *that*, to me, is Michigan tradition! It's a bunch of guys wearing blue getting after the bad guys wearing white—and making 'em pay! *That* is why everyone's scared to play at the Big House. So when a guy from Utah says that playing in the Big House is not as intimidating as you might think, that's a problem. That's something we need to fix."

It seemed like a spontaneous speech, but there was a clear structure to it. Start by acknowledging all the obstacles, praise them for fighting through it all, and give a hearty nod to Michigan tradition. Then narrow their focus on the task at hand.

"I'll tell you what Michigan football tradition is to us right now, just a few minutes before our first kickoff: It's about a bunch of tough sons bitches getting after them as soon as they get off the bus and staying after them until the minute they get back on that bus and get outta here. It's the pride and intensity Michigan Men have brought to every snap for years. EVERY SNAP! *That* is Michigan football!"

Watching the pregame speech, the contrast between Rodriguez's public reputation and the private reality was striking. Mark Twain famously said that once a man gets a reputation for hard work, he can sleep in until noon. But the flip side is also true: Once a coach gets a reputation for disregarding tradition or being ethically challenged, after a certain point it barely matters what he's really like. One of Rodriguez's biggest battles at Michigan was being waged between reputation and reality.

If Michigan had videotaped this speech and broadcast it to the fan base, it probably would have lured more than a few folks to Rodriguez's side. You could certainly see the effect his speech was having on his players, many of whom were still on the fence themselves. By the time Rodriguez reached his crescendo, he had taken control—temporarily, at least—of an uncertain, jittery bunch and given them a shot of confidence.

"After sixty minutes," he barked, "they will *understand* that when you play Michigan, you better put on a little extra tape, you better tie your cleats a little tighter, and you better put a little more air in your helmet—and strap it on!

"*NOW LET'S GO!*"

"YEAH!"

The coaches and players gathered at the opening of the tunnel, the collection of helmets looking like a swarm of bees from above. That was all it took for the biggest crowd in the country to stand and start cheering. Rodriguez turned back to his new troops and yelled, "Let's go!" sending them storming out toward the banner, their ears pounding with thunderous cheers.

Stages don't come any bigger.

After Michigan's defense recovered a fumble at its own 26-yard line, the offense calmly moved the ball downfield. With first-and-goal from the 10-yard line, Sheridan took the shotgun snap, rolled out, found freshman tailback Michael Shaw open in the flats, and tossed him the ball. From there, Shaw had no trouble zipping into the end zone for the first touchdown of the Rich Rod era, just 3:40 into his first season. 7–0, Michigan.

It's fashionable to say Michigan fans are quieter than most, but not after that play. The place erupted.

On Michigan's following possessions, the offense stalled, and stalled again. Sheridan, with too much new information to sort through on every play, struggled to get his passes off fast enough, and when he did, they were frequently off the mark.

Rodriguez wasn't surprised, or alarmed. He'd been through it four times before, and he expected some bugs with his offense. But he didn't expect the Utes to have such an easy time against Michigan's defense, which boasted nine returning starters. When the Wolverines ran up the tunnel for halftime of Rodriguez's debut game, they were already down 22–10.

Falk met them just inside the door, barking at each player who passed: "Let's go, Blue! Second half, team! Second half, team!"

The players were yelling and whooping, getting pumped up as soon as they got back into the room.

"We've worked too hard for this!"

"This is it, seniors!"

"Everything you've got—now!"

But in the coaches' room, it was all business. They had just seen these players perform in a real game for the first time, and they had a lot of raw data to sift through. They started going over their play sheets and stat sheets and working the dry-erase boards.

"We need to stop their offense, and fast," Rodriguez said, "because our defense is about to pass out. It's hot as hell out there." With the temperature in the mid-eighties, it was at least ten degrees hotter on the field, thanks to the black rubber pellets in the FieldTurf.

Rod Smith said, "The Nick we're seeing today isn't the Nick we saw all spring. No rhythm. No confidence. Let's keep him in there for another series and see how he looks. If he hasn't got it, let's put Steve in there."

Rodriguez nodded grimly, probably the way the *Titanic* captain did when informed of the size of the iceberg they'd just scraped. Like that captain, Rodriguez didn't need his assistant to spell out what the news meant. If you were trying to run the spread option without a confident field general, you were in deep trouble.

Rodriguez looked at the digital clock, which read 8:32. "Let's go."

The offensive coaches fanned out to talk to their position groups, while Scott Shafer, the new defensive coordinator Rodriguez hired from Stanford, addressed his defense in front of a big whiteboard.

With a few minutes to go, Rodriguez addressed the team again: "They're not doing anything that we can't fix. Nothing special. No gettin' our heads down.

"We play sixty minutes of football here at Michigan. That's what we do. That's why Barwis worked your asses off all year.

"We're going to kick off, we're going to pin their asses back deep in their own territory, and then we're going to get the ball back and score. That's it.

"Sixty minutes of Michigan football. Let's go!"

Michigan kicked off, shut the Utes down, and got the ball back, just like Rodriguez had said they would. Trusting his instincts, he spontaneously decided to put Steve Threet in. But Threet didn't get much traction, either, and on the Utes' next possession they kicked a field goal to go up 25–10. When Michigan finally got a drive going, it ended when tailback Brandon Minor committed Michigan's third fumble of the day.

Rodriguez was trying to be calm and patient with his players—not his strengths, he would be the first to tell you—but he couldn't contain himself. "DAMN IT! We are KILLING ourselves!" he yelled at Minor and the other tailbacks. "Hang on to the ball, high and tight, *every* time!"

They needed a break. And with just nine minutes left in the game, still down 25–10, they got it. Walk-on sophomore Mark Moundros—a special teams madman—rushed Utah's punter, blocked the ball, and smothered it deep in Utah territory.

Rodriguez decided to press their advantage immediately, calling for a pass to Junior Hemingway. Threet threw a perfect ball, and Hemingway took it straight in. Utah 25, Michigan 17. Rodriguez, the players, and the crowd were reborn. "Now we got a game!"

On the Utes' next possession, the refreshed defense chased quarterback Brian Johnson around the backfield when sophomore lineman Adam Patterson knocked the ball out of Johnson's hand. A few plays later, freshman tailback Sam McGuffie ran it in.

Utah 25, Michigan 23, with 6:26 left in the game.

Once again, Rodriguez didn't hesitate: "Let's go for two, right now."

For those who knew their Michigan football history—a group that included just about everyone in the stadium that day—the moment harkened back to Lloyd Carr's 1995 debut. Just three months after he'd been named interim head coach, the Wolverines fell behind 17–0—a greater margin than Michigan had ever overcome—and it looked like Carr's next job title could be former interim coach. But the Wolverines capped the comeback on the last play of the game with a lob to Mercury Hayes in the corner of the end zone. The Wolverines won their next four games, and by the eleventh week Michigan removed Carr's interim status.

Thirteen years later, Threet rolled out, scanned the end zone, and saw Toney Clemons wide open, gliding underneath the goal posts. "He's there!" Rodriguez shouted. "Throw it! THROW IT!"

But unlike the seasoned Scott Dreisbach in 1995, the untested Threet hesitated. He pulled the trigger a beat late and threw off his back foot, causing the ball to float high and behind Clemons. No chance.

Six minutes later, Rodriguez was 0–1 as Michigan's head coach—but the crowd cheered anyway.

In January 2011, offensive tackle Elliott Mealer said, "If we beat Utah that first game—it's hard to put it all on one game—but I think things would have been different."

It might sound a little crazy, but Mealer knows that in college football, more than perhaps any other sport, momentum breeds momentum, something Utah proved after narrowly escaping the Big House, then running the table that season, capped by beating Alabama in the Sugar Bowl.

Likewise, if Threet had hit the open Clemons in the end zone to tie

THE EVE OF A NEW ERA | 111

the game, it's not hard to imagine the Wolverines scoring on their next drive, then pressing on to beat at least Toledo and Purdue, which would have been good enough to keep Michigan's bowl streak alive and most detractors at bay.

But the losing started on day one, and so did the doubting. The factions that wanted the heads of Rodriguez or Martin—or both—all received a small gift that day.

The players jogged up the tunnel to the locker room, where they met Falk standing behind one of the big laundry carts. No motivational messages after a loss.

"Turn your helmets in and keep moving! Get inside! Turn your helmets in and keep moving. Hustle up!"

The only sound in the locker room was that of helmets crashing on helmets in those bins. Rodriguez stepped on a leg machine in the center of the room and told them to take a knee. They weren't happy—there was no chatting or laughing—but they weren't crushed, either. The dominant emotion was uncertainty—about their team, themselves, and their new coaches. Rodriguez sought to dispel some of that.

"That was a tough loss, but you guys didn't quit," he said. "We just got beat, and that hurts. It's *supposed* to hurt! If it doesn't hurt, you don't belong at Michigan.

"The coaches have got to do a better job of getting you ready, and that starts with me. No one points a finger. No one. We win as a team, we lose as a team. We'll all take the blame today.

"I promise you this: I will not leave your side, or your back.

"You've got to understand something: I've been here before, and I can assure you, we're going to be okay. Got that? No heads down. We'll be okay. See you tomorrow."

Back in the coaches' room, seven coaches sat in their chairs with their heads down, every one of them. No one said a word.

Dave Ablauf, Michigan's sports information director for football, handed Rodriguez some stat sheets. After a quick glance, Rodriguez whipped them against the wall above his desk. "DAMN IT!" he shouted, then knocked over his metal folding chair.

He believed what he had told the players: They would be okay.

But a loss is still a loss, and for the kid from Grant Town, it always hurt.

When the digital clock in the staff room hit eleven o'clock the next morning, the start time for their postgame meeting, Rodriguez still hadn't walked through the door from his adjoining office. It was unheard-of for a man who was early for everything and expected everyone else to be, too. The assistants knew something was up.

"Who's he talking to?"

"Tate," Rod Smith said. He didn't have to say any more.

Rodriguez's disappointing debut had kept him up most of the night watching tape and writing down observations. Nothing new there. He had enough perspective to realize his team wouldn't be setting college football on fire his first season, anyway.

His staff had worked hard to secure commitments from four-star defensive linemen Pearlie Graves out of Tulsa and DeQuinta Jones from Louisiana, and quarterback Shavodrick Beaver out of Dallas, to commit to Michigan in April. But the coaches were convinced that Tate Forcier, who had just turned eighteen three weeks earlier, could be the guy to lead them to the promised land.

"If you have the right guy running the spread, it's damn hard to stop," Rodriguez said. "But if you don't, you're going to struggle."

Forcier would have enough credits to graduate from high school in December, so he could enroll in January. And that meant he could be working out with Barwis, learning the offense, and be ready to compete for the job the next fall.

When Rodriguez finally entered the coaches' room at 11:12, he was in a much better mood than his coaches expected.

"So?" offensive coordinator Cal Magee asked.

Rodriguez tried to keep his poker face, but he couldn't. "He committed." When you're 0–1, coaching a team weakened by graduation, NFL jumpers, and transfers, you could probably not be blamed for fantasizing about the future. Everyone in that room believed the most important piece of that puzzle had just fallen into place.

Rodriguez won his first game at Michigan the next week over Miami of Ohio, 16–6. It wasn't pretty, but it got the monkey off Michigan's back and put a painted game ball on Rodriguez's shelf, right below the famous helmets.

Next up: Notre Dame. Heading into this classic contest between the two teams with the most wins in the history of college football, Michigan still held a commanding 869–824 advantage, but the race for the highest all-time winning percentage was closer. Notre Dame had led Michigan for eighty-four years until the Wolverines took a razor-thin lead in 2004. At times the difference was a ten-thousandth of a point, but as of that week Michigan's all-time winning percentage stood at .738, with Notre Dame at .736, close enough to take back the lead by the end of the season.

Adding to the intrigue, Notre Dame head coach Charlie Weis's job seemed to be in jeopardy. When the Fighting Irish fired Tyrone Willingham after just three seasons in late 2004, they'd suffered through their own sloppy search. Utah's Urban Meyer, named after a pope, turned down what was once his dream job to take over at Florida. The Irish then offered the post to George O'Leary but rescinded it when they discovered he had fudged his résumé. Finally, they hired Weis from the New England Patriots, though he had never been a head college coach. He arrived with great fanfare, declaring that Notre Dame would have a "decided schematic advantage" thanks to his work as the Patriots' offensive coordinator.

With Willingham's players, Weis's first team jumped out to a 9–3 record, earning him 2005 Coach of the Year honors—and, in midseason, a ten-year extension worth a reported $30–40 million.

In 2006, the Irish finished 10–3. But once quarterback Brady Quinn graduated, the Irish suffered through a faith-shaking 3–9 season—marking the first time Notre Dame had ever lost nine games. Even more embarrassing, the Irish offense finished third from last in school history in points per game—not exactly the decided schematic advantage he had been promising. Besides a healthy helping of Schadenfreude, what many Michigan fans took from Notre Dame's demise was a cautionary tale. "We're in danger," they often wrote on the blogs, "of becoming Notre Dame."

For the Wolverines, few things feel better than beating Notre Dame. For Rodriguez, beating the Irish in South Bend, which Michigan had done only four times since the rivalry resumed in 1978, would go a long way to establishing him as the worthy successor to all the greats who'd come before.

The night before the game, Rodriguez addressed his team in a banquet room at the South Bend Marriott. He started by warning them yet again of the heavy rains expected the next day, then showed them a clip of Weis and his players taking shots at Michigan.

When the tape finished, Rodriguez said, "They don't like us. Weis has popped his mouth off and a few of their players have, too. That's fine. They talk about the Golden Dome and Touchdown Jesus and all those national championship banners. That's fine, too. But let me tell you right now: It wouldn't matter if the pope himself came down and blessed every one of them. From what I know, the pope doesn't coach football!" That got a good laugh. "It's us against them, no one else."

They reviewed a PowerPoint presentation highlighting Rodriguez's "Keys to Victory," then he turned his attention back to his players.

"Now, look. If I have to worry about motivating Michigan football players to get ready to play Notre Dame, then I'm coaching at the wrong school, and you're at the wrong place."

Whenever he addressed his players, it was striking how well he grasped Michigan tradition, relied on it, and broadcast it to his troops better than he ever did to the public.

"I hope you guys aren't listening to anyone outside out of our circle," he said. "Some of this stuff you might not understand for years—even I don't understand it all right now—but we'll get a lot of answers in tomorrow's game.

"One thing I *have* figured out is that the guys in this program have a lot of pride. So you have to take it *personally* when they say, 'We can't wait to play Michigan!' That bothers me. And I bet that bothers you, too."

Rodriguez finished with a classic coaching tactic: the assumptive victory. "I visualize walking across the field after we kick their asses and shaking the fat boy's hand and saying, 'We can't wait to see you again in 365 days.'

"Get your rest. We'll see you in the morning."

The Wolverines got off the bus, carrying their bags and wearing their iPod headphones, navy blue nylon Adidas sweats, and stern expressions, and walked through the stadium's tall black iron gates.

If they had kept walking straight, they would have gone right down the tunnel under Notre Dame's huge national championship banners—running from 1924 to 1988, eleven in all, same as Michigan, with both schools claiming 1947—all the way to the grass field.

Instead, they cut just to the left of the ramp and then turned left at the wall, walking past a small brass plaque identifying the room: VISITORS LOCKER, 1101.

When they walked through the wooden door they entered one of the oldest locker rooms in the country, and it looks like it. Framed by yellow brick walls, a low ceiling, and textured windows protected by iron grilles, the place feels like a vintage Catholic high school locker room.

In the right corner, there's another big wooden door, through which the assistants found their locker room, a cramped little space with old gray metal lockers lining the walls and a few rusty folding chairs. The only thing that's changed since Michigan's Fritz Crisler coached here in 1942 is the addition of fluorescent lighting and a dry-erase board. That's it.

But when Rodriguez turned right again and squeezed through a tiny passageway to an even smaller room—maybe eight by eight—he'd found the place where the head coach gets dressed, replete with two metal lockers and two additional rusty chairs.

Now, when he turned his head toward the little room's only uncovered wall, a six-foot-wide slab of gray-painted brick, he noticed some hieroglyphics drawn in blue. When he looked a little closer, he realized it was some kind of play, an "iso," probably drawn by a desperate coach years ago. And, knowing Notre Dame's record in this place, 299–95–5 at the time, it probably failed.

Standing there, squinting at this play, he probably couldn't help but feel he was looking at the final words of a climber caught in a cave on a failed attempt at Mount Everest, who knew he was going to die there.

If you were not careful, this place could get to you.

Three hours later, under ominously dark clouds, the Irish chose to kick, which proved to be a wise move. During that week's practices, when it had been relentlessly sunny, Rodriguez had the student managers hose down the footballs and dunk them in tubs of water to simulate game conditions, but it wasn't enough. Just a few minutes into the game, Michigan fumbled two kickoffs and a pitch-out to fall behind 14–0.

On Notre Dame's next possession, Jimmy Clausen hit Golden Tate for their third touchdown in the first 10 minutes. It marked the most points Michigan had ever given up in a quarter in 129 years of varsity football.

After all seemed lost, the Wolverines settled down, scoring three times to cut Notre Dame's halftime lead to a slightly less ghastly 28–17.

Michigan had reason to be optimistic. The bad news was pretty simple: Unforced turnovers and Notre Dame's 60-yard pass play accounted for three of Notre Dame's four touchdowns, but the Wolverines seemed to be getting the better of them on most plays. Threet had passed for 116 yards, little Sam McGuffie had already compiled 132 yards rushing, and the team had notched 16 first downs—all higher totals than the Wolverines had produced in the first halves of their first two games. The coaches were convinced if they could just hold on to the ball, they might leave South Bend with a surprise. The players felt it, too.

"Plenty of time, men, plenty of time!"

"We got this!"

Michigan's director of football operations, Brad Labadie, popped his head into the cramped coaches' room and said, "Storm will be here soon, Coach. Supposed to last about an hour."

"Well, all right," Rodriguez said. "Can't drop the ball any more than we already have, can we?" He paused and asked again: "*Can we?*"

Jon Falk spread the word. "Sticky gloves, men! Sticky gloves!"

If the Wolverines could stop Notre Dame on its opening possession, then march down for a touchdown, they would be within a field goal. From there, they believed, their conditioning would take over.

Out in the players' room, offensive line coach Greg Frey assured his charges, "Those guys are dead-ass tired. Whatever you're feeling, they're feeling worse! This is why you did all that work—make 'em pay!"

On Notre Dame's first possession, Michigan's defense got the ball back, and the Wolverines soon found themselves with a first and goal from the 5. They called a play for Kevin Grady, a highly coveted recruit from

East Grand Rapids—but the Irish gang-tackled him, the ball popped loose, and the Irish fell on it at the 7.

The third quarter ended with the score stuck at 28–17.

Then the rains came—and kept coming.

With the sky so dark that they turned the floodlights on, Michigan began to drive, pushing the ball to midfield. But when Threet called for the shotgun snap, it slipped right through his hands and bounced off his chest, then off the grass. The Notre Dame linebacker Brian Smith scooped it right up without breaking stride and lugged it all the way to the end zone.

Michigan 17, Notre Dame 35.

On Michigan's next possession, Rodriguez put Nick Sheridan back in; Sheridan drove the offense down to Notre Dame's 3-yard line.

"It was still a long shot," Rodriguez said afterward in the locker room. "But hell, get into the end zone here, get 2, and you're down by 10. Who knows?" That is what the spread offense was designed for, after all: the endless two-minute drill. But Sheridan dropped back and threw one right at their linebacker, and that was it.

"The worst part?" Rodriguez said days later, after he had cooled down. "We gave them 28 of their 35 points—I mean, *gave* them—and the other seven came off a 60-yard pass we never should have allowed. We fumbled the ball *six* times, lost *four* of them, and gave them an interception deep in the red zone. That's five turnovers, three in their red zone and two in ours. There's your 35 points right there. A giveaway!"

That was enough to drive any coach crazy. But not as crazy as seeing some of your players, in the last minute of a tough loss to an archrival, standing behind your bench, giggling. Exactly what they were laughing at, Rodriguez hardly cared.

The players jogged back to the locker room through the darkness, the rain, and the mud about as miserable as could be, but Rodriguez was so upset he cut through them all and got to the locker room first. He stormed straight to the coaches' room, where his anger boiled over. He hit the metal chairs, banged the chalkboard, and knocked over a trash can. At first he was alone, but after the players got in, his rampage spilled over to their locker room, too.

"DAMN IT!"

He slammed their lockers and kicked over the Gatorade jug—which got everyone standing still, wide-eyed, too scared to move—before he finally spoke.

"We're losing the goddamned game, getting our *asses kicked*, and we've got two guys *laughing* over there on the sidelines," he shouted. "LAUGH-ING! We've got seventy guys out there busting their butts, right up to the very end, and a few guys who think it's *funny*."

There are times every head coach has to act angry to get his players' attention. But this was no act. Rodriguez was white-hot mad.

But he was not out of control. The last thing he needed was to lose his team after two losses, and he had enough sense, even in the heat of the moment, to know that most of the players, if not all, were working hard.

"Now everyone else is going to dump on you—the media, the fair-weather fans, whoever—but I'm not going to leave you. I know how hard you've worked. Those folks haven't seen it. They haven't been at your work-outs, your practices. They've got no idea. But I do. And I'll defend you. But I'll be goddamned if we give away another game like that!"

All that was left to do was shower in silence, get on the bus, and endure a three-hour ride that would feel like a day. But before Rodriguez left the coaches' room, he took one more look at that old play scribbled on the wall.

He knew exactly how that poor bastard had felt.

Just as Rodriguez had warned them, the Wolverines took it like a piñata for a solid week. But Michigan had the next Saturday off, which was probably a good thing for all involved.

When the players returned to Schembechler Hall, they had shaken off the defeat and its aftereffects. They were fresh and ready to work, putting in their best week of practice to that point.

Rodriguez was pleased—and relieved to see them bounce back—but he still had the nagging feeling they were missing something, a certain joie de vivre. Maybe it was because they stood at an uncharacteristic 1–2 for the second year in a row and had ninth-ranked Wisconsin coming to the Big House that Saturday. The Badgers were not just the highest-rated team in the league, they were widely considered to be the Big Ten's best chance—maybe its only chance—to win a national title.

Fresh or not, Michigan's players knew ending the weekend at 1–3 was a very real possibility. The seniors who had endured the 7–5 season in 2005, and the ignoble start to the 2007 season, couldn't be blamed for dreading the onslaught of criticism they'd face if they lost to the Badgers.

"I don't get the feeling they really believe we're going to win," Rodriguez told me that week. "They're intense, but they've got no swagger. We're not having any *fun*."

When Gary Barnett addressed his Northwestern team before their opening game against heavily favored Notre Dame in 1995, the Wildcats hadn't won in South Bend in thirty-four years. Barnett believed they could. But did his players?

Right after their bus pulled up to Notre Dame Stadium, he told them not to carry him off the field when they won. Not if—when. It was a great bit of motivation—and it worked. The Wildcats beat Notre Dame 17–15 that day, the first step in a magical journey that ended in Pasadena.

"Well, that's what I want to do," Rodriguez said, pondering the story. "Plant the seed that maybe, just maybe, we could win this one."

On Thursday, Rodriguez decided it was time to lighten things up. "I want some spirit!" he said in the coaches' meeting that morning. "I want some fight!"

Under Rodriguez, Michigan ended each practice with one play for the offense and one for the defense, just as Schembechler had done for years. The offense was supposed to throw a last-second game-winning touchdown pass, and when it was the defense's turn, it was supposed to knock down a would-be game winner.

On this Thursday, however, after each of those last two plays, Rodriguez wanted them to jump up and down, storm the field, and generally act like they'd just won the Rose Bowl. But when they did it, Rodriguez wasn't satisfied.

"No, no, no," he said. "That's not it, men."

They didn't display half the enthusiasm he had wanted, so they did it again. Once more, however, their celebration fell short.

"Hold up! Hold up! Hold up!" he yelled. "You're not celebrating like you just won some big game. The way you're acting, you look like you just won a *scrimmage*! So we're going to do it again!"

The third time was a little better but not quite the charm. So Rodriguez blew the whistle one more time and gathered the players around him.

"Okay, now you just won a nonconference game—maybe," he said. "But it wasn't any Big Ten game. And it sure as hell wasn't anything like the way you'll be dancing when you beat the ninth-ranked, first-place Wisconsin Badgers on Saturday! So we're going to do it again. And damn it, we're going to *keep* doing it until you guys learn to celebrate like a Michigan team should."

He knew that last threat would get them, because if there's one thing college players want more than anything else, it's for practice to end.

"All right, this is it! Last play of the game! We're beating Wisconsin by two points, they've got three seconds left, *and the crowd is going crazy*. But the Badgers got the ball, and you know what they're going to do. Hail Mary! Here it comes! Let's go—hike the ball—and *be ready*!"

The quarterback dropped back and heaved a bomb. But the defensive backs were in perfect position and knocked the pass to the turf. Normally that would be enough, but on this day it was just the first step. The question remained: Would the players celebrate with enough enthusiasm to satisfy their coach—and get to go home?

They started jumping up and down, doing chest bumps, and screaming and yelling like madmen. The guys on the sidelines came charging onto the field like they were being chased by lions. Mike Massey grabbed the first-down marker and started thrusting it up and down over his head like he was a member of some football tribe initiating a war dance with his shield. Mike Shaw got on his knees and banged the turf with his fists like he was crying. Toney Clemons sprayed water on his teammates as if it were an explosive bottle of champagne, while others high-stepped up and down the field like drum majors.

Rodriguez got into it, too, hooting and hollering and chest-bumping everyone in sight.

They kept it up for a solid two minutes, when Rodriguez finally blew the whistle, signaling the players to get in two lines and slap hands the way they do after each practice. Everyone was still belly laughing.

"Now, men, *that* is how a Michigan team celebrates a great win!" Rodriguez said. "Don't forget it!" Not all the players were "all in" for Rodriguez, but on that day it sure looked like it. And a big win could make a convert out of almost anyone.

In the first half of the Wisconsin game, however, the Wolverines didn't give themselves or their fans much to cheer about. How bad were they? They took only twenty snaps on offense the entire half. They gained a grand total of 21 yards on offense—with minus 7 yards passing. They would have been better off telling Threet to take a knee on every play.

That's not a joke. They got exactly one first down—*one*—and that play ended with a fumble, one of four turnovers that half.

The Wolverines all but gave Wisconsin 19 points. The Badgers' defense was on the field so rarely that their players broke into the Gatorade and oranges not out of hunger but boredom. They had the first half off.

The day marked the five hundredth game in Michigan Stadium, and in all those games, the Wolverines had never come back from so far down, not even in Carr's record-breaking debut. They didn't seem likely to on this day, either.

When the Wolverines ran up the tunnel at halftime, the Michigan fans gave it to them, and good. One veteran said it was the loudest booing he'd heard since Oregon tagged Michigan 39–7 the year before—and that, he said, was the loudest he'd ever heard. "Honestly," he muttered, "I don't know if we're going to win a league game all year."

When the Wolverines ran up the tunnel, they heard the Badgers yelling, "Take a shower, Blue! Ball game's over. Take a shower!"

In the locker room, Terrance Taylor, a senior defensive lineman, yelled at his teammates, "You guys aren't playing like you give a damn! This is it for the seniors. We don't have another shot at the Big Ten title. This is our last chance! It's up to you, offense! How ya gonna respond?"

No one yelled back.

But Rodriguez didn't rant and rave, not even in the privacy of the coaches' locker room. He didn't make a lot of changes, either. "Our strategy wasn't the problem," he said later. "Hell, maybe it'd be easier if it was. You could fix it, then."

He had enough experience with rocky transitions to recognize what he could start changing immediately and what could be improved only over time. And he didn't share Taylor's view that they didn't care.

"The strange thing was, no matter how bad we'd played, no matter how bad we looked, and no matter how loud the fans booed us, our *effort* was good," he said the next day, after he'd seen the tape a few times. "It was our *execution* that was lousy. No, we just had to get in a rhythm. Give Threet something he can execute, get his confidence back, and get a little momentum going."

Before they ran back onto the field, Rodriguez said in a calm voice, "Now look, I'm not gonna pull your chain. That first half right there— well, hell, we just couldn't play any worse. But despite all that, we're only down 19–0. Could be a lot worse. *Should* be a lot worse! They had to settle for four field goals in the red zone. That's got to tick 'em off a little. Our defense is playing their *asses* off!

"We're not going to make many adjustments, because that's not our problem right now. The only change we're going to make is this: Whenever we have a run-pass check, we're going to give the tailback the ball and run it. That's it. Everything else stays the same. Got it?

"Now, maybe some of you aren't sure if we can get back in this game. And I know the fans don't think so. No one likes being booed. But you had to notice one thing: None of them left. They ain't leaving! So somewhere in there, they still believe. And we do, too."

The next day in his office, he said, "Every game you learn something about your team. And I knew I was about to learn a lot about mine—one way or the other."

And they were about to learn something about him: The man could coach.

Michigan opened the second half with the ball, but stalled at their own 43. On fourth-and-1, Rodriguez figured they didn't have much to lose, so he decided to go for it—knowing that if they failed, the cement on their 1-and-3 record would start drying. There wouldn't be any need to celebrate that. But tailback Kevin Grady, fresh from a crucial red-zone fumble against Notre Dame, made Rodriguez look smart by busting through Wisconsin's beefy defensive line for 5 yards.

They stalled again at the Badgers' 26. On third-and-10, Threet found freshman tight end Kevin Koger in the end zone for Michigan's first points of the day. Michigan had been horrible to that point, but the scoreboard said 19–7. They weren't dead yet.

The coaches' decision to simplify Threet's play list had a great effect. Instead of looking lost, confused, and hesitant, he seemed calm, cool, and in control, throwing a series of short, quick strikes all the way down the field. Pop, pop, pop! He suddenly looked like a world beater.

With the Michigan fans on their feet for the second time all day—and the first to cheer instead of boo—Threet handed off to Brandon Minor, who busted through the Badgers' line for a 34-yard dash to the end zone. 19–14. The Big House went berserk, and the Badgers started feeling the heat. On their next offensive play, quarterback Allan Evridge dropped back and fired one over the middle—but Michigan's cornerback, Donovan Warren, read the play perfectly and got a hand on the ball just enough to tip it into the air for linebacker John Thompson to jump up and catch it.

An entourage of eight Wolverines seemed to materialize out of nowhere to escort the less-than-speedy Thompson down the field. No Badger could get within five feet of him. Thompson lumbered 25 yards to the end zone, and by the time he got there, the crowd was so loud that the coaches up in the press box could not be heard through their headsets.

After Michigan's defense, feeding off the crowd's energy, stopped Wisconsin again, Threet took off on an awkward 58-yard run, and McGuffie finished the job.

Michigan 27, Wisconsin 19.

The Badgers finally came back to life with a touchdown—their first points of the half—and then lined up for a two-point conversion to tie the game at 27. They made it, but an official saw that they had lined up illegally and had the guts to make the correct call. On Wisconsin's do-over, Michigan stopped them, and then held on for a 27–25 victory to complete the biggest comeback in the five-hundred-game history of the Big House.

The celebration that followed almost equaled their rampage after Thursday's practice.

Almost.

Unbeknownst to the fans, Rodriguez's crazy prediction had paid off, and his stunt worked like a charm.

"In all my years of coaching," Rodriguez told them back in the locker room, getting a little choked up, "I've never been more proud of a team than I am of you guys today."

It felt like he'd won them over. Winning, of course, solved a lot of problems, but perhaps this one more than most. And maybe, just maybe, Rodriguez might skip the first two stages of Bowden's four-step progression and start winning close.

The 2–2 Wolverines would likely be heavy underdogs against high-flying Penn State and Ohio State—both of whom were in the hunt for BCS bowls—but they still had lowly Toledo and Purdue ahead of them, and winnable games against middle-of-the-pack Illinois, Michigan State, Minnesota, and Northwestern. Six wins seemed conservative.

That might not have been a big deal outside Ann Arbor, but it would mean Michigan would avoid a losing record for the forty-second year in a row and they would go to a bowl for the thirty-fourth consecutive year. The Michigan fans and press made sure Rodriguez was acutely aware of both records.

But if anyone knew the high-wire act ahead, it was Rodriguez. If there was one thing he and his coaches agreed on, it was this: "Year three and four, that's when it takes off," they often said. "You watch. That's when you'll see it."

This is not to say Rodriguez was going to take the losses in the meantime with philosophical equanimity. This is a guy who loved sports as much as he hated losing. When he was still a kid back in Grant Town playing Pop Warner football and his team lost, it put him in a typically inconsolable mood, "crying and moping," Arleen recalled.

On the drive home, Arleen turned to him in the backseat of their station wagon and said, "We're tired of seeing your face like that after every loss. We don't want to see it anymore!' "

So instead of coming out of his funk or faking it, Rodriguez grabbed a blanket in the backseat, pulled it over his head, and kept it there the rest of the ride home.

He had gotten a little better since then—but not much. No matter how expected a loss might be—especially in the early stages of implementing his system—he never took it well. He was good with the players in his postgame speeches and Monday afternoon assessments, but he started taking it out on himself in the coaches' room with a stream of profanity and an occasional relocated play chart or chair. Then he would grumble the whole way home, where only Raquel, if she felt bold enough, could talk to him. If Rita had an unavoidable question, she would send Raquel to ask.

The best competitors are motivated less by a desire to win than an abject fear of failure. At the highest levels, even one loss diminishes them in some deeply personal way. For them, a victory is not a victory. It is simply a loss avoided. Rodriguez was squarely in that category.

He would spend the night watching the tape, back and forth, writing things down, getting a few hours of fitful sleep. He'd get up early and go back to the tape, so by the time his staff met at 11:00, he'd seen it probably four or five times—and he wasn't happy. But after they broke down the game as a staff, and he'd had his final say, they were amazingly good at putting it behind them and focusing on the next one. The mantra was absolute: "Don't let the team that just beat you, beat you twice."

And at age forty-five, he had some perspective and some experience. He knew what the stages looked like. He had faith in his system, and he wasn't going to panic.

He did have some concerns unique to this team, however, including a defense that did not seem to be improving, but there are few problems in a coach's life that winning doesn't solve.

The Illini were 2–2 overall and 0–1 in the Big Ten, but with their electrifying quarterback Juice Williams they could be very dangerous.

Michigan jumped ahead 14–3 in the first quarter, before the Illini pulled in front. In the second half, the Illini blew past Michigan, winning 45–20. Rodriguez wasn't happy, but on a rational level he understood that it was Illinois coach Ron Zook's fourth year, and Juice Williams had put on the best performance of any visiting player in Big House history, with 431 total yards. Rodriguez could also take some solace seeing that the spread offense, run by a great quarterback, could work very well in the Big Ten, too.

He also knew that Toledo was coming to town, the next best thing to a bye week, and maybe better, because you get credit for a win. The Rockets, at 2–4, were not even a good MAC team, and everyone—maybe even the Rockets—assumed Michigan would be right back at 3–3, with their streaks still within reach. After all, Michigan had never lost to a team from the MAC, sitting on a perfect 24–0 record.

"Always remember," Auburn's legendary coach Shug Jordan said, "Goliath was a forty-point favorite over David."

On its second possession of the game, Michigan easily cut through the Rockets' defense, pausing only to let the officials move the chains. The Wolverines soon faced first-and-goal from the Toledo 5-yard line. Steve Threet rolled out to the right, saw freshman Kevin Koger wide open in the end zone, and delivered a perfect strike—right to Rockets' safety Tyrrell Herbert, who caught the ball easily, then took off from the goal line down the Michigan sideline with a half dozen Wolverines on his tail. But they couldn't catch him, and just like that, instead of a quick opening touchdown en route to a blowout, Herbert broke another stadium record—longest interception return—and the Rockets were up 7–0.

More surprising, Michigan's offense failed to get it back, while the defense looked helpless against receiver Nick Moore, who caught twenty passes to set a third record for opponents in the Big House in two weeks.

Down 13–10 in the final minutes, with the Appalachian State debacle in the air, Threet drove Michigan's offense to Toledo's 10-yard line. With just seconds remaining, Rodriguez decided not to risk running out of time and brought out kicker K. C. Lopata. He had been inconsistent so far that season, hitting four out of six field goals of varying lengths, but since this attempt was barely longer than an extra point, Rodriguez felt confident he could send the game into overtime.

Sean Griffin's snap was good, as was Zoltan Mesko's hold. The ball was down, and the laces were out. Lopata stepped into the ball, got good contact, and launched it high—and right. The fans' fears were confirmed when the refs signaled, "No good."

The Rockets celebrated like it was the biggest win of their lives—which it was.

Rodriguez's expression at that moment, captured perfectly by an *Ann Arbor News* photographer, is beyond pain or anguish or even disbelief. It is a face I've seen only on college football coaches, the one where they look like they've swallowed a hand grenade, and it had just detonated.

Rodriguez congratulated Toledo head coach Tom Amstutz, then watched him get swept up onto his players' shoulders. Rodriguez jogged back to the locker room and gathered his team.

This one spoke for itself, so Rodriguez kept it short. He urged the players to keep working hard, to ignore the critics, and to stick together. "We'll be all right," he assured them.

Given the circumstances, Rodriguez was remarkably calm—nothing like the postgame Notre Dame tirade—but once he got back into the coaches' room, his anger burst through. Game plans, chairs, trash baskets—he threw them all against the walls. His language matched his actions. None of the other coaches dared to say a peep. But Rodriguez's anger wasn't directed at anyone, just the results—and himself. There would be no rationalizing his way out of this one. He had failed to get his team mentally ready to execute against a mediocre team from a mediocre league.

While his wife and kids waited for him in the little room down the hall, Raquel asked her mom, with wide-eyed desperation, if she could stay with her friend, the daughter of assistant coach Tony Gibson, that night.

"Yes, honey," she said.

Rhett asked if he could stay with Tony's son, Cody.

"Yes."

If Rita could have stayed with Coach Gibson's wife that night, she might have joined them.

Adding insult to injury, while trying to avoid the traffic on State Street back to their home in Saline, Rodriguez managed to get lost and turn a twenty-minute trip into a forty-minute funeral procession.

Where was a backseat blanket when you needed one?

Rodriguez could not even speak about that game until a few days later, and even then, not much. "God, that was just awful," he said softly. "One of the worst losses of my career."

Toledo, which was supposed to be the only freebie of the season, turned out to be the most painful game of the year. Instead of entering the rest of the Big Ten season at 3–3, the Wolverines now stood at 2–4. That meant if they lost to Penn State and Ohio State, as expected, they would have to beat the rest of their opponents: Michigan State, Purdue, Minnesota, and Northwestern. Of that group, only Purdue, led by new adversary Joe Tiller, was struggling.

All of it made preparing for Michigan's next game, in Happy Valley against undefeated, tenth-ranked Penn State, that much harder.

When David's already knocked you down, how do you get up for Goliath?

Rodriguez didn't seem to give a lot of thought to the Nittany Lions himself, nor did he talk much about them to his team. The coaches had plenty to worry about just getting their guys to play the game hard and smart and not give up. That would be enough.

It could have been the start of an endless, heartless second half of the season, but the Wolverines played with abandon. They also had some history on their side, having won the previous nine straight games against the Lions, including a few last-minute thrillers. Threet looked comfortable, while tailback Brandon Minor looked positively unstoppable. Michigan blasted out to a 17–7 lead, more than enough to get the Lions thinking about the losing streak that started when they were about ten years old. But on the following kickoff, with Penn State probably content to get to the locker room, a Michigan player got into a shoving match, which resulted in a costly penalty, sparking the Lions to a quick touchdown drive.

It was just Michigan 17, Penn State 14—but the momentum had swung 180 degrees.

In Michigan's locker room, Threet sat in his stall by the front door, teary-eyed. Once Michigan's coaches ascertained he wasn't hurt, they made a tight circle around him while the other players passed by.

Rod Smith didn't have anything to say to Threet, instead just turning to Sheridan and saying, "Nick, you're in."

Just like that, Michigan's chance for another upset evaporated. Penn State unleashed all the frustration built up over a decade of losses and whitewashed the Wolverines 32–0 in the second half. Final score: 46–17.

That was Michigan's 2008 trademark: one good half.

With the Wolverines now stuck at 2–5 overall and 1–2 in the conference, a win over Michigan State would go a long way toward saving the season. But, to the Spartans, it would always be worth more.

The history between the schools is long and bitter. The University of Michigan Wolverines have always been the University of Michigan Wolverines. When young General George Custer took command of the Michigan Brigade at Gettysburg, he frequently yelled, "Come on, you Wolverines!" And that became their rallying cry.

Michigan State, in contrast, started life as Michigan Agricultural College, then Michigan State College, and finally, Michigan State University. Their mascot evolved from the Farmers to the Aggies to the Spartans—a direct response to Ann Arbor, the "Athens of the Midwest."

Fritz Crisler did everything he could to keep Michigan State from taking his alma mater Chicago's place in the Big Ten, but the Spartans got in anyway. When they started playing in the Big Ten in 1953, Governor G. Mennen "Soapy" Williams announced the winner would get the Paul Bunyan Trophy—truly one of the game's ugliest awards, for one of the game's ugliest rivalries.

The Michigan players condescendingly said that if they won it, they'd leave it on the field. No matter: Sparty took the game 14–6, and the trophy. The Wolverines did win the next year, however, and, as promised, left the trophy on the field, and refused to get it engraved.

Michigan State got the last laugh in 1973, after Michigan and Ohio State tied 10–10, giving them identical 10–0–1 records. The Big Ten athletic directors broke the deadlock by voting 6–4 to send Ohio State to the Rose Bowl. MSU's athletic director, Bert Smith, a Michigan alum, voted for the Buckeyes. To the day Schembechler died, he never forgave Smith.

The cultural divide has never been breached. The Wolverines' tailgates at their famed golf course are run by the alums, and resemble wedding receptions. The Spartans' at Munn Field are run by the students, and resemble Woodstock.

If the Wolverines' most conspicuous feature is an upturned nose, the Spartans' is a carefully nurtured chip on their shoulder. The rivalry occasionally takes the high road—former MSU coach George Perles and Schembechler enjoyed a great mutual respect—but usually, it's as ugly as the trophy. When Rodriguez became Michigan's head coach, his duel with Mark Dantonio, which had started with West Virginia's two victories over Dantonio's Cincinnati squads in the Big East, grew a lot hotter.

Before the game, Jon Falk rolled the unwieldy wooden colossus that is the Paul Bunyan trophy into Michigan's locker room, so no one forgot what they were fighting for. The Wolverines entered the game rare 4-point underdogs, at home, to the resurgent 6–2 Spartans, though Michigan State hadn't taken Paul Bunyan home in six years.

As usual for the season, the Wolverines put up a good fight in the first half, which ended deadlocked at 14–14. That didn't stop Dantonio from telling Falk he expected Paul Bunyan to be waiting for the Spartans in their locker room before they returned after the game.

Falk wisely said nothing.

At the end of the third quarter, the teams were tied at 21–21, and that's when the Wolverines' wheels came off again, in the form of two unanswered touchdowns, the first sparked by an interception. They lost 35–21.

When the Wolverines got back to their locker room, Paul Bunyan was long gone—not because Falk was eager to fulfill Dantonio's wishes but because he didn't want the players to see the trophy rolled across the tunnel. The Spartans took it from their locker room back down to the field, where they celebrated under the temporary lights long after the Michigan fans had left.

Dantonio had gotten everything he wanted: a win at the Big House, a 7–2 record, and one of the largest trophies in college football—plus the chance to rub Michigan's upturned nose in it. The Wolverines, on the other hand, were left standing at 2–6, with absolutely no margin of error left to keep their bowl streak alive—an almost impossible task.

Michigan multiplied its problems at the postgame interviews. When a reporter asked Calvin Magee to describe Threet's performance, which included three interceptions, he snapped, "Inconsistent, like it always is," before adding, "We just gotta get better. That's it."

Needless to say, the first part of Magee's quote, which was very out of character for the warm, friendly, and optimistic man, made the rounds—and then it made a few more, once Rodriguez's critics and defenders started knocking it back and forth.

Even though Rodriguez hadn't said it, it inevitably came back to him, fueling a criticism gaining traction that he frequently blamed his players for his mistakes. If you listened to everything he told his players, you would conclude, without hesitation, that this simply wasn't true. He constantly urged them not to point fingers at anyone else, and after every loss he always told the players at least once, "That's coaching. That's me."

Likewise, if you added up all his press conferences, you'd find he almost always took responsibility and almost never blamed his players there, either.

The problem, however, was the crucial qualifier: "almost." In Morgantown, Rodriguez had earned a reputation as a buck-stops-here kind of guy. But at Michigan, he could say the right thing ninety-nine times, but if the hundredth came off as a knock or an excuse, it shocked the faithful, who were accustomed to Coach Carr taking full blame for the Appalachian State game, with no ifs, ands, or buts. The attention Rodriguez's off-kilter comments received set up the expectation of more, until everything he said was filtered to find the gaffe.

Example: When one MGoBlog reader came across the quote "I was prepared for some attrition when I became Michigan's coach. I can honestly say we did not lose a guy who really could have helped us. I didn't lose any sleep over anyone who quit that spring," his first response was, "Gee, I really wish RichRod had said this in a nicer way, because it seems awfully rude to the people who left." Then he took a closer look and realized the quote was not from Rodriguez but from Schembechler's last book, talking about the spring of 1969. How things were interpreted at times seemed to depend less on what was said than who said it—and who was doing the interpreting.

But Rodriguez's occasional pleas to be patient while they "rebuilt the program" didn't help, either.

What he was saying was pretty straightforward, especially from a coach's point of view: Whenever a new regime comes in, everybody has to learn to do everything a new way. In Michigan's case, Rodriguez felt they needed to transform how they recruited and trained, to get the right people doing the right things for his system. It was also true that Michigan hadn't beaten the best in years, losing their last four games to the Buckeyes and their last three BCS games, while West Virginia—stocked with two- and three-star recruits—had won BCS bowls in 2006 and 2008 (a few weeks after Rodriguez left) and gone five-of-five against the SEC.

Looked at that way, Rodriguez had a point—similar to the one Dierdorf had made to the current players in February 2008, when he told them their opponents were no longer afraid of Michigan.

It echoed what former All-American center turned attorney Tom Dixon told me on the sidelines before one of the games in 2009. "When I was here, we always had two or three classes of players who'd won Big Ten titles. It was simple: The coaches told you, 'Just do what the seniors are doing.' That's all. The thing didn't run itself, but they didn't have to reinvent the wheel every year, either.

"Not one guy out here has won a Big Ten title. They don't know what it's like, they don't know what it takes. That's what they need now. Win one title, and everyone *knows*—and you're over the hump. From then on, you tell the freshmen, 'Just do what they do.'"

But it's one thing for former Michigan All-Americans to say those things privately. It's quite another for the transplanted coach to say them publicly. To some alums, it sounded like a century of unequaled tradition—from "The Victors" to the Big House to the banner to those forty-two conference titles, the most of any school in any league—wasn't good enough, and Rodriguez felt he had to start from scratch.

This problem, at least, was easily solved: stop saying that.

And that's exactly what Bill Martin advised him to do. Martin's subordinates said two negative e-mails were enough for him to reconsider almost anything, and he once stopped by Rodriguez's office after a tough loss to tell him a regent had complained about his use of the word "ain't." So when he received some feedback saying Rodriguez's "rebuilding" comment had ruffled their feathers, Martin promptly paid another visit. For a man frequently criticized for not helping Rodriguez win over the Wolverines faithful, this time his advice was spot-on. But for some reason, on this point Rodriguez—who as a baby was stubborn enough to hold his breath until he passed out—refused to drop the phrase permanently from his repertoire, angering the Carr crowd every time he said it.

"Bill says you don't need to *rebuild* a program here at Michigan," Rodriguez told me. "But we do! But I knew from West Virginia never to make any comparisons with the way it was done before—I always tell our players never to say anything we do is *better*, just *different*—I didn't then and I'm not doing that now."

Rodriguez sincerely believed this, and he had often bitten his tongue about the state the program was in when he arrived. But he had let slip enough comments that the average fan would disagree with his assessment of his restraint.

And, as was often the case, the man who suffered for it more than anyone else—albeit all out of proportion to the crime—was Rich Rodriguez.

If Rodriguez's trusting nature was his Achilles' heel in negotiations, his candor was his downfall in public relations. The sealed-lips approach Carr had made famous in the Fort Schembechler era might have been boring, but it rarely generated distracting controversies.

At the coaches' meeting the following morning, Rodriguez let himself and his coaches have it. He knew they were in Phase One, he knew they knew they had a very inexperienced offense, and he knew recruiting would be the key. He'd been through it all before. But enough was enough.

"We just got outworked, outplayed, and outcoached," he said, sitting at the end of the long meeting table. "Everything. And now we have to get their spirits up. This is getting *old!*"

The defense was especially puzzling. The experienced group was supposed to be the strength of the team, but it didn't seem to be getting better. Rodriguez, who had hired Shafer virtually sight unseen, wasn't sure what was happening, or *wasn't* happening, on that side of the ball—Was it the players? Was it the coaching?—but he would be watching all of it more carefully in the days ahead.

Rodriguez had also decided they had a better chance to be aggressive with his favored 3-3-5 defense than with the more conventional 4-3-4 that Shafer used, and insisted it be installed for the upcoming game against Purdue.

But it was more than defensive schemes that were bothering him.

"Something is fundamentally messed up. This is the eighth game of the damn year, and we're still doing basic things *wrong*. Either we're *coaching* them to do the wrong things, or we're *letting* them do the wrong things. Either way, I'm getting my nose in it. You can call it micromanaging if you want, but if I've got to, I'll get into every damn position.

"We're going over every damn play today—offense, defense, and special teams—and I'm going to tell you one more time exactly what I expect from you and your players. There won't be a *lick* of doubt when we leave this room today."

And that's exactly what they did. They watched play after play after play, every single one of them. And they didn't just watch them but went back and forth and back and forth and back and forth, stopping, commenting, and correcting each and every one. It took the coaches three hours to finish this grueling exercise, after which they finally escaped into the well-lit hallway, rubbing their eyes like they'd just finished an FBI interrogation.

A few hours later, Rodriguez gave the team a similar message.

"Because shit runs downhill, it ran on your coaches today," he told them in the team room. "I was all over them. And this is something I don't share with anyone else because it ain't nobody's business but ours, but you've got to know that everyone is held accountable. Always. And when we're not doing our jobs the way we should be on the field, your coaches hear about it—and so do I, every day.

"Everyone's asking me, 'You're 2–6, are you gonna change your approach? Whatya gonna do differently?'

"Whatya gonna do differently? You guys know me pretty well by now. Whatya think? And the answer is: *nothing*."

Here he was obliquely addressing the frequent criticism that he should have waited until he had the right players before installing the spread. When I asked him about this, he replied, "The players always struggle at first. But if we tried something else, then *no one* would know what the heck's going on. Is that better?"

In fact, the adapt-to-your-talent argument is largely a canard, one rarely made by experienced coaches. Football is now so complicated that just learning a new offensive or defensive system usually takes more than a year, and few coaches are allowed much more than that if they plan on keeping their jobs. So trying to teach your players one system, then the other, is a waste of valuable time and risks confusing your players and possibly your assistants, too. Yes, coaches can adapt their play calling—witness Rodriguez's shift from running to passing when he went from Jed Drenning at Glenville State to Shaun King at Tulane—but they cannot easily adapt their *systems*.

"We're not going to start having picnics or hit every day," he continued, "and I ain't trading you in, either. I'd still rather have you guys than their guys. We're just going to do what we *know* how to do like we *know* how to do it! That's it!"

They would have been thrilled to win the next four games, including

Ohio State, and get back to a bowl game, but that's not why Rodriguez was taking this tack. He was a realist about the odds they were facing. What he was insistent on, however, was that they get rid of some bad habits, develop some better ones, and become a better team by 2009. He also wanted to determine which players were all in and which weren't.

Of course, Rodriguez had directed this play before. As usual, the older players didn't like the tougher conditioning regimen or the intensity of the coaching.

One change none of them liked was the new Sunday schedule. At West Virginia, the players didn't complain to Rodriguez about coming down for a meeting or weightlifting, then going home for an hour or two off before returning for an evening practice. The upside was getting Mondays off.

But when Rodriguez brought the same schedule they had followed in Morgantown to Michigan, some of the players grumbled to outsiders about it.

It was bad scheduling. But as the 2008 season wore on, Rodriguez reduced the Sunday schedule until it was a simple walk-through, and changed it altogether before the 2009 season. But some things weren't going to change, including the intensity of their new coaches.

If some of the players found Rodriguez and Barwis shocking, that was true about Bear Bryant at Texas A&M and Alabama, Woody Hayes at Miami and Ohio State, and Bo Schembechler at Michigan. It is the well-worn formula for just about every football movie ever made.

But, as Rodriguez said in the coaches' meeting, "something is fundamentally messed up." He sensed that something was different this time, though he couldn't quite put his finger on it.

Rodriguez knew he didn't have all the seniors. That was typical, too, of this phase and mirrored his first year at West Virginia. But he didn't realize that many of them were still meeting regularly with associate athletic director Lloyd Carr across the parking lot. You could certainly argue this was normal, even healthy. Most of the seniors had a deep and abiding affection for their former coach, which Carr reciprocated. Depending on what was said, the meetings could very well have been helpful to Rodriguez and the team. But a reasonable inference could be drawn from what Carr was saying on behalf of Rodriguez in public: nothing. With just a handful of brief exceptions, he avoided the press, the alums, and the subject altogether.

The only model Michigan had of welcoming an outsider into the fold was too old for anybody in the building to remember: the transfer of power from Bump Elliott to Bo Schembechler almost forty years earlier. Elliott is an erudite, modest Midwesterner—who happened to be a celebrated All-American—who rarely swore or even yelled, and if you said you were hurt, that was enough for him. Schembechler yelled, screamed, and swore like a sailor. He grabbed your face mask, literally kicked you in the ass, and cracked your backside with a yardstick—and his were special models, twice as thick and four feet long. He also drew a distinction between being "hurt" and being "injured." The latter was serious and got you medical attention. The former was just pain, and if you missed a practice because of it, you got left in Ann Arbor when the team flew to Minnesota in 1969.

Needless to say, the players who had come to Michigan to play for Elliott, not this raving madman, were less than enthusiastic. It was the casual attitude of thirty or forty players, mostly walk-ons suddenly walking off, that prompted Schembechler to put up his famous sign, THOSE WHO STAY WILL BE CHAMPIONS.

But before they were champions, some of them went to see their former coach, Bump Elliott, who had stayed on as the assistant athletic director, to complain about the new guy.

"If he wanted to," Schembechler said in *Bo's Lasting Lessons*, "Bump could have made life very difficult for me. Hell, he could have set me up for failure. His players loved him, really loved him—and remember, that first year I was coaching all *his* players. I was an outsider, they didn't owe me anything, and it wasn't like I was making life easy for them, either. Bump was a former Michigan All-American, and a whole lot nicer than I was! They could have complained to him—he was still working in the athletic office—and I bet some of them tried, but he would have none of it. He made it clear to everyone that he was on my side."

"I didn't *want* to talk to them," Elliott told me in 2011. "That was Bo's team now. There was no reason for me to be involved in that." As a result, not many made their way to his door. And once they learned where he stood, they stopped completely. Whatever problems Schembechler had in 1969—and he had plenty—Bump Elliott was not one of them. And that is why, when Michigan beat Ohio State that first year, Schembechler gave the game ball to Elliott—and there was not a dry eye in the room.

Thirty-nine years later the situation was quite different. When Carr's former players came to his new office to complain about the Rodriguez regime, Carr was reportedly happy to listen as long as they wanted to talk. But when Rodriguez walked to Carr's office, which he did at least eight times by his count, to personally invite Carr to speak to the team or just visit practice, Carr declined every time.

There were rational reasons for Carr to avoid Schembechler Hall, such as ensuring that his successor had the space to do his job without worrying about Carr looking over his shoulder. But declining Rodriguez's eight personal requests suggests a deeper stubbornness on the subject.

Likewise, there were plausible explanations why Carr refused to comment publicly on Rodriguez and his staff, including Carr's naturally private personality and his desire to avoid making any comment that would invariably be scrutinized, parsed, and twisted out of context. But as the months rolled on, during a rocky transition, Carr's silence became deafening and stood in stark contrast to Schembechler's repeated public and unequivocal statements in support of Lloyd Carr. Exacerbating matters, most of the players from the Carr era—including a few famous faces—followed his lead.

Of course, if Rodriguez had started out 6–2 instead of 2–6, the critics would have been a lot quieter and ignored by the masses. Likewise, if Carr hadn't generated so much well-earned admiration over a distinguished career among Ann Arborites, Michigan Men, and fans, what he said or didn't say would not have mattered so much, either. But Rodriguez was struggling and Carr was respected, making it easier for many players to follow their former coach than their new one.

And that, in turn, made it easy for the fault lines the search had created in the Michigan football family to split wider with each loss.

On a picturesque fall Saturday in West Lafayette, Indiana, Michigan's team buses rolled past a guy in a Michigan jersey standing on a street corner with a sign that said OUR 2–6 TEAM IS BETTER THAN YOUR 2–6 TEAM! That's what the 2008 season had been reduced to. They were in a dead heat with Purdue for the bottom of the league.

Michigan busted out to a 14–0 lead just five minutes into the game, then watched Purdue mount its own 62-yard touchdown drive and convert a fumbled punt into another touchdown. And that's how the game went, with Michigan going up 28–14, falling behind 35–28, and going back up 42–35. The Boilermakers, eager to give their avuncular head coach Joe Tiller a respectable final season—and avenge the "stealing" of Roy Roundtree— scored another touchdown to make it 42–41 but blew the two-point conversion. The shift from the 4-3-4 to the 3-3-5 defense, at least, could not be deemed a success.

All Michigan needed was a game-sealing first down, but Threet, who had been hot and cold all day, couldn't get it. So, with 34 seconds left and the ball on Michigan's 32-yard line, Purdue's Justin Siller dropped back and found Greg Orton in the flats, wide open but facing the wrong way. The Wolverine defenders soon discovered why when Desmond Tardy ran up to Orton, who tossed the ball to him, pulling off a perfect hook and ladder for the 48–42 victory.

That was it. Any chance the Wolverines had to keep their streaks of forty-one winning seasons and thirty-three bowl games was dust. Back in their locker room, a few of the players banged the metal stalls and knocked over stools.

The press conference, held in an annex of the locker room, wasn't much better than the game itself when a Detroit reporter asked, "What's the problem?"

Rodriguez was typically candid: "Blocking, tackling, and holding on to the ball." Then he added, "And that's coaching. That's me."

He would never make it in politics.

The Wolverines stood at an unheard-of 2–7, heading up to face the 7–2 Minnesota Gophers, and they would enter the game without their starting quarterback, Steven Threet, who was home nursing a concussion suffered during the Purdue game.

But putting in Threet's understudy didn't concern the coaches too much. Threet worked hard and was eager to please, but he had never fixed his odd delivery or gotten much better at running the spread. Nick Sheridan, who looked half-asleep in the quarterback meetings, turned out to be listening the entire time. His goal, after all, was to coach—and if he couldn't learn, he couldn't teach. He was also undeniably tough.

Since the Wolverines had won the Little Brown Jug back in 1909, they had kept it seventy-six of ninety-eight years, merely lending it to Minnesota the other twenty-two. This great imbalance probably explains why, when the Gophers do win the most storied trophy in college football, they give it a seat on the team plane and parade it through every restaurant and bar in the Twin Cities, where patrons actually drink from it. (This is not advised.) But when Michigan keeps the Jug, they just put it back in its box, pack it on the truck, and head on home.

That latter scenario didn't seem very likely when they faced off again in 2008. That morning, ESPN conducted a poll to see which team would run up the most points: Ohio State against Northwestern, or Minnesota against Michigan? The viewers voted for Minnesota in the kind of landslide that would have made President Reagan proud.

What the viewers weren't seeing, admittedly along with almost everyone in Ann Arbor—coaches and players included—was that Rodriguez's team wasn't as bad as its record. Far from good, no question; even genuinely bad; just not *as* bad. If Rodriguez could take any solace from 2008, it was watching his team "lose close." Overthrowing a wide-open receiver against Utah. Missing a tying field goal against Toledo. Falling for a last-minute hook-and-ladder play against Purdue. Just a few plays the other way and Rodriguez's Wolverines could have been 5–4, with plenty to play for in the last three games. It was a tin lining, to be sure, but to the farsighted it suggested there was reason to expect better days weren't far off.

The Friday night before the game, the Wolverines gathered, like always, in the banquet room of their hotel. The meeting was scheduled for 8:00, but by now everyone knew the starting time was a myth. The players arrived no later than 7:42. When Rodriguez walked into the room five minutes later, the players shushed each other, and he began his speech.

"We don't play these guys for a couple years, so the Brown Jug is going to be in someone's possession for three years. I think it should be ours.

"Number one: We must play the game with GREAT PASSION. I don't understand why anyone would *not* do that.

"Number two: WE MUST stick together as a TEAM! The most important people in my eyes are my family and my football team. Outside of that, whatever people say really shouldn't matter. On campus, in the press, doesn't matter. Stick together! Everyone wants me to point the finger, and they want you to point the figure. Never gonna happen. Never will.

"Number three: We MUST enjoy being PART of the TEAM! It's as simple as having something bigger than yourself to fight for.

"Think about the opportunities *you* have to make a statement to the entire country. And you get to make that statement *every* time you play! You play for Michigan—everyone's watching! Trust me, if this season has taught me nothing else, it's that *everyone* is watching!"

They all laughed.

"Starting tomorrow, you seniors can make a statement about your last three games in a Michigan uniform. And you freshmen can make a statement about the future. The future of *Michigan football*.

"So let's play the game with great passion. Let's stick together as a TEAM! And let's *enjoy* being part of the team!"

The next morning, instead of packing it in, the Wolverines packed a punch, shocking the experts and just about everyone else with a dominating 29–6 victory over the Gophers. Nick Sheridan, who hadn't started since the season's first game against Utah, played the best game of his life, completing eighteen of thirty passes for more than 203 yards, one touchdown, and no interceptions.

"Now, there's a guy who's taken a lot of heat all year," Rodriguez said afterward. "But look at that! That, to me, was nothing short of heroic. That was the Nick we saw all spring.

"Good for him."

When the gun sounded, Jon Falk brought the Brown Jug out of its box. But this time, the seniors didn't just stuff it back in and store it for another year. They hauled it to midfield, then ran it over to the Michigan fans celebrating in the corner of the end zone, heaved it high, and sang "The Victors" with their fans like they meant it.

With nothing to play for but pride and a five-dollar, 105-year-old water jug, the Wolverines, led by a beleaguered senior class, reminded the country what they were made of.

It's a good thing they enjoyed it, because that was the last highlight of the year. The Wolverines lost their final home game to Northwestern 21–14 on a cold, dark, rainy day before heading to Ohio State.

All week, reporter after reporter asked Rodriguez how the Michigan fans were reacting to this dismal season. "Really, they've been good," he said, and in almost all respects they had been much better than just about anyone could have expected. At which point Rodriguez grew expansive. The entire quote bears repeating. "They're still coming out and supporting us, we get a lot of positive support from fans when they talk to us or send us e-mails. But sometimes we get these amazingly nasty personal attacks on me or my players or my family. Those people need to get a life! But I can understand it. When you're 3–8, no one's happy, and we're not happy, either!"

In a season where very few things went right, on or off the field, Rodriguez's answer was reduced to this headline on ESPN.com: RICH ROD TO UM FANS: "GET A LIFE!"

A week later, around Thanksgiving, *Sports Illustrated* used the comment to name Rodriguez one of its "Turkeys of the Year."

"Man, some days you can't do anything right," he told me, "and this has been a year of those days."

Michigan had enough to worry about without those distractions. The Buckeyes had lost only two games all year, to USC and Penn State, they were ranked tenth in the country, and they hadn't lost to Michigan in four years—a little statistic that seemed to get repeated every half hour.

But as Michigan's buses rolled to Columbus Friday morning, the story's focus shifted far from the field.

Rick Leach, arguably one of the three greatest athletes ever to attend Michigan, along with three-sport stars Bennie Oosterbaan and Ron Kramer, earned All-American honors in both football and baseball. After finishing in the top ten for the Heisman three years in a row, he went on to a solid ten-year career in the major leagues. But he is still best known for being Schembechler's only four-year starter at quarterback and beating the Buckeyes three straight.

In December 2007, right around the time Rodriguez agreed to coach Michigan, Leach received a call from Don Nehlen, whose three years as Schembechler's quarterback coach had overlapped with Leach's last two. "I always had an awful lot of respect for him," Leach said. "Whatever he asked me to do, I was going to do."

Nehlen knew Leach was still a close supporter of Michigan football. On January 1, 1998, when Michigan won the national title at the Rose Bowl, Leach was on the rooftop patio celebrating with Fred Jackson, Lloyd Carr, and the rest of the coaches while recruiting his former Tigers teammate Lance Parrish's son, David, to play catcher for Michigan (He did.) After Carr's 2007 team lost to Appalachian State and Oregon, Leach led a group of forty or fifty football alums down to the tunnel as the team got off the buses for the Notre Dame game, to show their support for the coaches and the players. If the Michigan coach was a good guy, worked hard, and did things the right way, he could count on Leach's support. Nehlen knew that, but the call was still unexpected.

"He said, 'Rich could really use your help getting acclimated,'" Leach recalled. "I told him, 'If Rich ever needs anything, he can just ask. Make sure he has my number. Happy to help.'" But it seemed very informal, and Leach figured Rodriguez would probably never call.

Leach attended a few spring practices and met Rodriguez briefly, but he spent most of the 2008 season watching from afar. "But then I started seeing all the stuff in the papers—about shredding papers and buyouts and everything out there trying to make [Rodriguez] look as sinister as possible—and I'm saying, 'Where is all this coming from?' They're talking about all these things, and I'm thinking, 'I've never seen this at Michigan. What the hell is going on?'"

At first, Leach's few public comments that fall were limited to supporting Rodriguez. But that changed after Mitch Albom's column appeared in the *Detroit Free Press* the Friday morning before the Ohio State game. The column's focus was Rodriguez's suddenly infamous "Get a life" comment. Albom also rehashed the buyout mess, repeating the conventional view that Rodriguez was making Michigan pay for his betrayal of his alma mater. In fairness to Albom, the column was no hatchet job, and only Coleman, Martin, Rodriguez, and his wife knew that Michigan had promised to pay $2.5 million of the buyout from their first meeting, and that they asked Rodriguez to keep quiet about that fact. But for Leach, seeing Rodriguez's character questioned once more was the final straw.

When Sam Webb at WTKA called Leach that morning for his take on the Ohio State game, for the first time Leach didn't merely support Rodriguez but attacked his critics and asked where Carr had been that season, and why hadn't he been defending Rodriguez the way Schembechler had defended Carr?

These charges are now familiar to most Michigan fans, but at the time they seemed shocking and made big news. People on the buses going to Columbus played the interview on their computers again and again, to rapt listeners. It announced that a new battle had started—off the field and in public.

A week later, Webb asked Leach to return to his morning show. Leach had to talk it over with his family.

Both Leach and Bill Dufek are in sales and depend on name recognition and goodwill to make their livings. Both had a lot to lose and nothing tangible to gain if they joined a public fight; they would surely become fair game themselves. Anyone watching the press's treatment of Rodriguez was wise to be leery.

Leach gathered his wife and three sons in their living room and explained what Don Nehlen had asked and what he felt he had to do for Rodriguez and Michigan football. But he needed to know if they supported him in doing this. If they wanted him to leave well enough alone, he would drop it.

"No," they said, one by one. "You need to do this. We're with you."

So Leach agreed to go back on Webb's show, but this time he tried to be as unemotional as possible and keep Carr and others out of it by leading with statistics to support the commonly held view that Rodriguez simply didn't have the personnel previous Michigan coaches all enjoyed. This appearance was less heated, but Leach let it be known that he and Dufek—and soon others—would not sit idle.

Of the seventy players who had earned a seat on Michigan's team buses to Columbus, forty-one were walk-ons or freshmen—not exactly the kind of team poised to upset Ohio State, and a far cry from the eleven All-Americans Schembechler inherited from Elliott, four of whom would be inducted into the College Football Hall of Fame. Likewise, when Schembechler retired, he left Gary Moeller enough talent to win three straight Big Ten titles, extending Michigan's streak to five. And when Carr won the 1997 national title, almost all those starters had been recruited by Moeller and his staff, which included, of course, Lloyd Carr, who had been, by all accounts, an excellent recruiter.

In contrast, Rodriguez had the task of rebuilding an offense that had lost ten starters, five to the NFL—including Chad Henne, Mike Hart, and Jake Long, who set just about every school record at their positions. Rodriguez opened the season with ten returning starters on defense, but just fifteen seniors, fourteen juniors, and only one returning starter on offense (and no seniors), plus two quarterbacks who had never thrown a pass in college. According to ESPN, Michigan was one of the youngest teams in Division I, and would be again in 2009.

At the team dinner the night before the Ohio State game, after the players had filed out, I asked Rodriguez how he felt. He picked up a short piece of silverware and said, "I feel like I'm heading into a gunfight with a butter knife.

"Our guys have been busting their butts all season, and I'm proud of them. But the Buckeyes, almost to a man, are bigger, stronger, faster. Older. We're putting freshman walk-ons against senior All-Americans. That's asking too much."

But the mostly young, inexperienced Wolverines gave the Buckeyes a battle. Ohio State started with the ball, but on its first possession Michigan's Stevie Brown intercepted a Terrelle Pryor pass at midfield and almost ran it in for a touchdown. Instead of going up 7–0 early and giving the Buckeyes something to think about, Michigan's offense stalled once more, so the coaches called for the field goal team on fourth-and-15 from the Ohio State 18. But, once again, Michigan missed the kick.

After the Wolverine defenders pinned the Buckeyes deep in their own territory, freshman Tay Odoms dropped another punt, which the Buckeyes recovered. But they played hard and managed to get to the locker room down only 14–7. Rodriguez's five successors at Michigan had all lost their first games to Michigan State, but all won their first Ohio state games. A season-saving upset was still a possibility.

But just as Michigan's first half held to form, so did its second. The Buckeyes scored four unanswered touchdowns while giving up none, to post another victory over their rivals, 42–7—the worst loss Michigan suffered in Columbus since the infamous 50–14 drubbing in 1968, the year before Bo Schembechler arrived.

Rodriguez's first season at Michigan was, mercifully, finally over. The Wolverines had finished the year 3–9, their worst record since 1961 and the most losses ever in Michigan's 129-year history.

When a writer asked legendary basketball coach John Wooden who the best coaches in the game were, he replied, "The ones with the best players." Even before the start of the 2008 season, Rodriguez and his staff knew their first job was to get the best players and develop the ones they had. Then, with more conditioning, better knowledge of the spread offense, and quarterbacks like Tate Forcier and Shavodrick Beaver—plus two dozen other players who had already committed to Michigan—they might start to demonstrate what their program could do.

And that's why, when the team's buses rolled back through Ohio's cornfields on two-lane rural routes with the sun setting on a fresh blanket of snow, five assistant coaches were staying behind in Columbus that night to start out on recruiting trips that much faster the next morning.

For some of the very reasons that Michigan struggled so much in 2008—a new coach, a new system, and a lot of new players—they were optimistic about 2009 and beyond.

In 2008, seven new players on offense accounted for roughly half of Michigan's rushing yards, passing yards, and touchdowns, and all seven would return in 2009. Brandon Graham, who had transformed himself into a pro prospect, decided to return for his senior season. And, thanks to early commitments, Michigan was already in the thick of the recruiting race.

Shavodrick Beaver, who had committed to Michigan in April 2008, had his mom call Rod Smith on December 19 to tell him her son would be attending Tulsa instead. The main reasons seemed to be proximity to their Dallas home and his upcoming shoulder surgery, which would put him eight months behind Tate Forcier. But, inevitably, Rodriguez took some heat for it.

Michigan also lost its two four-star defensive linemen, Pearlie Graves and DeQuinta Jones, when they flipped to Texas Tech and Arkansas, respectively. Still, Michigan's recruiting class was shaping up to be a very strong one, starting with Forcier. During halftime of the Army All-Star Game in January, Will Campbell, a five-star defensive lineman said to be the top recruit in the state of Michigan, stood in front of a table with the hats of LSU and Michigan before him. With the NBC cameras rolling, Big Will ended months of conflicting reports by picking up the "M" hat, jamming it on his head, and making a muscle-man pose. Forcier and Campbell would join five other freshmen on Michigan's campus in January 2009, which would allow them to participate in the fifteen practices for spring ball to get ready to play that fall.

Rodriguez felt he also had to make some changes on his coaching staff. "When Toledo beats Michigan at the Big House, and their coach still gets fired—well, that tells you what kind of year we had," he said. "If you don't face the facts, you can never fix the problem."

And the biggest problem, in Rodriguez's view, was the defense. Instead of being the team's savior, with ten returning starters—more than the offense and special teams combined—it gave up an incredible 346 points that season, the most in Michigan history. Something had to give.

"The two fastest ways to get fired from my staff are disloyalty and cheating," Rodriguez told me in December 2008. "My first year at West Virginia, my defensive coordinator was disloyal, and he was gone. That's it. But none of these guys are disloyal, and none of them cheat. They're all good guys, and that only makes it harder. I've seen coaches who just let 'em go, with no warning. I can't do that, but we just had the worst defense in the history of the school. You've got to produce, and we didn't. As bad as our offense was, our chemistry on defense was worse—among both the players and the coaches. So expect some changes there. I've given a few coaches a heads-up."

Two weeks after he said this, defensive coordinator Scott Shafer announced his resignation.

There was still the question of recruiting a second quarterback. While Rodriguez had always wanted Denard Robinson to play quarterback, wires crossed with Shafer, who had worked hard to recruit the speedster as a defensive back. But Denard had been adamant. "I wasn't coming to Michigan to play corner," Robinson told me. He had already turned down Florida for the same reason and had explained as much to Shafer.

But about the same time Shavodrick Beaver informed Michigan he was turning to Tulsa, defensive back coach Tony Gibson happened to be in Deerfield to recruit defensive back Adrian Witty for 2010. While there, he checked in on Robinson and was surprised to learn he was still interested in Michigan—but solely as a quarterback. Michigan wisely got him by signing day.

Looking back on the brutal year behind him and the arc of his career, Rodriguez could be philosophical. "People say it's harder to be at the top than the bottom," he told me. "But I guarantee you, anyone who says that has never been at the bottom.

"This year, we've seen the good, the bad, and the ugly. How do we feel about it? I guarantee you this: We feel worse than all the students and alumni and fans combined. We have to live with this. We're responsible for it. But trust me, we know what we're doing, and we're going to get this going. It's happened this way every time. It's not fun, but it's predictable.

"We're going to get there. It won't be tomorrow, and it won't be easy, but we're going to get there."

But crucially, in December 2008, Rodriguez was answering the wrong question. It was not: Could his team get there? but: Could they get there fast enough?

Rodriguez didn't know it yet, but the storm was not behind him. It was building and headed his way.

The 2009 team lost eleven scholarship seniors from the 2008 team, plus Steven Threet, who transferred again, this time to Arizona State; Sam McGuffie, who transferred to Rice; and Toney Clemons, who transferred to Colorado. But they added seven recruits who enrolled in January, and they would add more that August.

This new group gathered in the team room on Friday, January 9, 2009, for its first meeting as a squad.

Rodriguez kept it short, asking all of them to fill out a card listing their individual goals—in terms of academics, conditioning, and football, in that order—against which he would measure them.

The team's goals hadn't changed much: win revenge games (there were plenty to choose from that year), beat their three rivals, win the Big Ten title. But Rodriguez added a new one: "I've asked the academic people what the team's highest grade point has been," he said, "and they told me it's a 2.60." He wrote it on the board in big numbers. "I think we can beat that. I *know* we can beat that. But it's going to take *all* of you, doing your best."

He then explained the Wolverine Olympics, a competition he had devised whereby the seniors drafted eight teams of players, then tried to get the most points—given out for touchdowns and tackles, attending classes, getting above a 3.0, visiting Mott Children's Hospital, and so on—and to avoid demerits.

"Last year, the teams that didn't win fell behind because of the negatives, like missing class, violating the team dress code, or showing up late for a workout. That's the difference between winning and losing here, and in the Big Ten."

Rodriguez assigned each team to a position coach's room. In Bruce Tall's class, he told them that last year his team had come close to winning, and he intended to win it with this bunch.

He introduced himself, gave a sketch of his family, then called on the newly enrolled Tate Forcier to introduce himself.

"Oh! Um, I'm Tate."

"Hi, Tate!" the others said jokingly.

"Last name?" Tall asked. There was a message in that.

"Oh, um—Forcier. Tate Forcier."

"And what position do you play?"

"Huh?"

"Position."

"Ah. Quarterback."

After a few more biographical facts, Tall said, "Glad to have you on board, Tate. David?"

Senior-to-be David Moosman, who played chess in elementary school in a national championship club, encouraged his teammates to come with him to Mott on Thursday nights.

"Don't make it a chore," Kevin Grady added. "Make sure you have fun with it. They need some fun."

Bruce Tall felt compelled to mention a missing team member: Zoltan Mesko, the punter with a 4.3 grade point average in the Ross Business School, which caused a few veteran players to cheer. "Trust me," Tall added, "I know how to pick 'em!"

The next official team gathering five days later wasn't so warm and fuzzy.

On Wednesday morning, January 14, at 7:56, half the team gathered in the weight room, wearing matching white Michigan T-shirts and blue Michigan Adidas shorts, to meet Mike Barwis and his staff. The other half would meet that afternoon.

"Now, you've got to get your mind right, right now!" he said. "Everything we do here, we do the right way—from getting to class to doing your squats. We're going to keep in mind, *every minute of every day*, what we want to be next season—and that's Big Ten champions. Because it all starts right here.

"And for every meeting, your ass is *early*. For every workout, your ass is *early*, and for every class, your ass is *early*. No excuses! This is what we want, and this is how we're going to get it.

"We've got a lot of motherfuckers we've got to pay back this year.

"It all starts right here, right now. Everything we want—revenge, respect, the Big Ten title—it all starts THIS VERY MINUTE!

"So get in. 'Big Ten champs' on three! One, two, three—"

"BIG TEN CHAMPS!"

They didn't walk but *ran* to every station and got to work immediately, a stark contrast to the confusion and reluctance the players showed exactly twelve months earlier.

As the legendary football coach Lou Holtz said: "Motivation is simple. You eliminate those who are not motivated."

Among the most motivated were projected stars like Brandon Graham, Mike Martin, and David Molk, but also two-star offensive lineman Patrick Omameh, who developed stretch marks on his chest from growing from 255 pounds to 305, all muscle, and walk-on Erik Gunderson, who lost 15 pounds in the first three days—and kept losing more. (Despite the amazing gains, steroid use was one of the few rumors Michigan football did not have to deal with under Rodriguez, and from everything I saw, rightly so.)

I'd heard so much about these modern gladiators and their weight room heroics—and seen enough of it, too—that I wanted to find out for myself just how much harder it really is than what we weekend warriors put ourselves through just to avoid buying "relaxed-fit" jeans.

I signed a waiver to work out with Barwis and his staff. Barwis's grandfather broke horses well into his sixties, but Mike was a troubled teenager on Philadelphia's mean streets until he finally leveraged his 151 IQ to find his calling.

And find it he has. Rich Rodriguez accepted Michigan's offer on one condition: Barwis could bring his entire staff and get an unlimited budget to overhaul the weight room. A million dollars later, the Wolverines' gym is world-class.

After eating an uncharacteristically healthy breakfast, I walked through the doors of the Michigan Wolverine weight room Monday, March 16, at 10:00 a.m. for my first ninety-minute workout. I joined a group of pro players from Michigan and West Virginia, who worked out between the two groups of current players. I was to show up three times a week for six weeks—"if you last that long," said Barwis, whose alums call his gym the Barwis School of Pukitude for a reason.

Barwis conducted a baseline test on me. I weighed some twenty pounds over my "playing weight" and carried 26 percent body fat. Not good. But when you're forty-four, eating like a lineman, but exercising like, well, a sportswriter, something was bound to give.

The formalities behind us, the fun began. "Time to get after it!" Barwis yelled in his ridiculously raspy voice. (At the kids' summer football camp, one brave ten-year-old raised his hand to ask Barwis, "Is that your real voice, or is that your 'tough guy' voice?" I can answer: It's both.)

"Bacon! You're working with Foote!"

That would be Larry Foote, the former Michigan All-American linebacker turned two-time Super Bowl champion Pittsburgh Steeler.

Foote was one of more than a dozen professional players who come back every year to work with Barwis, who refuses payment. "Barwis is crazy, but I love him," Foote told me. "He will get you doing things you never dreamed of."

Foote was right. Barwis constantly yelled at me to "move that bar!" Back and forth, all day, through twenty-some different lifts, pull-downs, curls, and all manner of squats. We did everything at least three sets each, consisting of ten reps each time. That's about six hundred reps per workout, for you folks scoring at home, not one of which I would have done without these maniacs pushing me.

Whatever your limits are, they double them—so being in better shape would have spared me nothing—then they make you do twice as many reps as any sane person would do. They're also fascists about form, so each set feels twice as hard as it would doing it your way—that is, the wrong way—which is why your personal records get cut in half when you're working out with these guys.

And you can forget about getting a breather. Between each set, while Foote was lifting, just for fun they made me do plyometrics, like lunge jumps, abdominal crunches, or inclined push-ups, so I could never decide which was going to kill me first: the lifting or the stuff between the lifting.

Just fifteen minutes into my first workout, I was sweating like a pig and panting like a dog. You could have taken my pulse by touching my hair.

By 10:30, I already had the look of a man in deep trouble—mouth breathing, head back, eyes half-closed—when I realized I had to find a trash can, and fast. Barwis just pointed his thumb over his shoulder to the

Rubbermaid barrel in the corner, then calmly returned to loading more plates on Foote's weight bar. I made it just in time and let loose, repeatedly and loudly.

A great cheer went up. "Yeahhhh!"

"Go, Bacon, Go!"

"Get rid of the poison!"

"We have a winner!"

There is a snobbism in the Michigan weight room, but it's not based on your stats or your weights, just how hard you're working. I was the oldest, weakest, and fattest guy there by a long shot, and I was fully prepared to take a lot of crap the minute I walked through the door. But I never took a single shot for any of that. So long as I was sweating, the players would yell and urge me on and high-five me after each lift.

In their eyes, I now had the same status as every other guy who'd puked in that trash can—which is to say, everyone.

When I left Schembechler Hall that day, I had just started going through something called hypertrophy, which occurs when you push your body so far past its limits that "it's basically a catastrophic event to your body," Barwis said. "Like a car accident." And that explains the incredible pain.

When I tried to wipe some sweat off my brow, I discovered I could no longer raise my right arm, so I grabbed the sleeve with my other hand and whacked my face with the powerless limb. Eureka. Walking to my car, my legs felt like prosthetics, as if I needed some kind of remote control to operate them.

When I got home and collapsed on the couch, I filled over two pages with simple tasks that suddenly seemed almost impossible, from tying my shoes to flossing my teeth. Even taking a shower proved problematic, because I could not raise my hands high enough to shampoo my hair.

I then made a second list of all the things that didn't hurt, which consisted of a single entry: blinking. That was it.

Of course, you think I'm kidding, and doing all this for laughs. But any Barwis graduate reading this is nodding: "Yep, sounds about right."

As I lay curled up in the fetal position on my couch, it occurred to me Michigan's players go through hypertrophy twice a year and have to go to classes after each session.

How they do this is a mystery to me.

By the middle of my second week, the hypertrophy started to fade, and it became just a matter of grinding it out. I started getting the hang of it, the ripped blisters on my hands stopped bleeding, and my form improved. Once I figured out that Barwis's goal for us was not making beach muscles but increasing our core strength, I understood why we did so many squats and dozens of balancing tricks.

I was coming so close to competence, I could almost taste it.

After three weeks I was beginning to think I might just make it, until one day Barwis announced I'd be joining the rest of the guys for an additional half hour of laps, hundred-yard dashes, sprints, and suicides after each workout.

"If you're going to go around claiming you did this," Barwis said, poking me in the chest, "you have to do *all* of it."

We ran in two groups, the fat boys and the speedsters. I was lumped with the fat boys, of course, but I couldn't catch even the long snap center recovering from a broken toe.

Near the end of our next workout, Barwis told us we had to run the width of the field and back, three times. "Y'all got to finish in fifty seconds," he said. "Bacon in sixty. But Bacon, if you don't make it, everyone else has to run again."

The glares from the NFLers were all the motivation I needed.

I took off like I was being chased by Larry Foote. But after five of the six widths, I had only kept pace and was running out of gas. This was not good. With one width left, I knew I had to find something extra. Most of the guys had finished and were looking back at me, huffing and puffing. "Move that white ass, Bacon!" I dug deep and pulled and lurched and thrashed every limb of my body toward that finish line.

"Fifty-eight!" Barwis bellowed. I had made it.

The guys cheered and walked up to high-five me, but I ran right past them straight for the trash can, puked again, wiped my mouth, and got back on the line for our final sprints. My threshold for . . . well, just about everything had doubled.

"That's the first time I saw you run," Barwis said, "when I didn't want to punch you in the jaw."

It doesn't get any better than that.

On my last day, with all the guys cheering me on, I doubled my bench press to 145 pounds—doing it their way, which entails keeping your arms wide, your back flat on the bench, and holding the bar an inch above your chest for three counts before pushing back up. I also squatted 180, with much better form, tripling my starting mark. I had lost only ten pounds, but they had reduced my body fat from 26 percent to 16 percent.

If they could get a forty-four-year-old man to do all that in six weeks, you can imagine what they can do with the real athletes in that weight room. In the winter of 2009, I was not surprised to see them setting record after record—and enjoying it.

Over dinner one night, Mike Martin and friends told me a story about the "40 complex," a diabolical regimen that requires you to do eight upright rows, then go right into eight clean and jerks, eight simple jerks (over your head), eight more clean and jerks, then finish with eight bent-over rows. You have to do all of it without ever letting go of the bar or putting it on the floor. You drop the bar, you have to start the entire set over until you finish it the right way.

I knew that drill too well. Larry Foote, no stranger to hard work, asked me while we were warming up one day, "Hey, Bacon, can you count to forty?"

A week earlier, I would not have paused. But three workouts with the Barwis crowd had me doubting just about everything.

"I think so," I finally muttered.

"Well, you're going to find out."

Having finished the first four sets, I forgot about the last set, the bent-over row, and dropped the bar. I will never forget Jim Plocki screaming in my face, alarmed, "NOOOOOO!"

I have never dreaded anything more than picking up that bar and doing it all over again. There is a reason why these football players could not sleep the night before a big workout. They're *scary*.

When Mike Williams, one of Michigan's defensive backs, was in the throes of his 40 complex that March, he was standing with the bar on his chest, doing his reps, when his legs buckled and he fell back to the floor, on his back. Amazingly, he had the presence of mind not to let the bar touch the ground, which would require him to start the whole thing over.

That's when ten teammates ran to help him, but they did not touch him or the bar. When they saw he was all right, they started yelling at him to get up and finish it.

"It was, like, 'C'mon, Mike, you can do it!'" Martin said. "And he was, like, 'I can't, I can't!' Almost crying."

But Williams didn't let it hit the floor, and bit by bit, he found a way to get up. It took him about five minutes to get back on his feet, but he did, and then he finished it.

"And when he did," Martin recalled, "the whole weight room went *nuts*."

"I'll never forget that," Ryan Van Bergen said. "We just know there's no one with a hidden agenda on this team. It's what we do."

On Friday night, March 13, they held the Night of the Wolverine, the culmination of their winter workouts, with stands set up for family, friends, and select fans. It was an Olympic-style competition—whose points counted for the Wolverine Olympics—consisting of events like the medicine ball toss, the Plyo-Box jump, and the sled drive. It wasn't a punishment but a celebration of what they'd accomplished—capped by an egg-eating contest à la *Cool Hand Luke*.

Whenever you asked any of the players about the coming season, the most common remark that spring was "I can't wait."

Rodriguez's vision for what his Wolverines could be was slowly coming into focus.

On Sunday, August 23, the 2009 Wolverines gathered on the practice field for Michigan's Media Day. When the *Free Press* asked freshman Brandin Hawthorne, who had enrolled in January from Pahokee, Florida, what winter conditioning was like, he said, "It's crazy. We'll work out from, like, 8 to 10:30. We come back later, have one-on-ones, seven-on-sevens, a little passing. Then I'll go watch a little film."

The *Free Press* also asked freshman receiver Je'Ron Stokes, who arrived from Philadelphia in June, about Michigan's off-season program. "Hooooo!" Stokes said. "A typical week is working from 8 a.m. in the morning to 6 or 7 at night, Monday through Saturday."

And that was starting in June?

"Yes, sir," Stokes said. "We do the weight room at least three times a week, and seven-on-sevens and one-on-ones. Speed and agility on the other days. Every day we have something new to get ready for the season. The coaches have done a great job of stressing the importance of getting us ready for the big season that we're about to have."

Their answers fed into the aura of Mike Barwis, who had become something of a cult figure—so much so that Michigan State felt compelled to counter, on its website, with the fourteen hours its players endured every Sunday.

The 2009 squad looked better in every way: experience, leadership, and team spirit.

On Thursday, August 27, the team took a "practice road trip" to a suburban Detroit hotel. They devoured another gargantuan team dinner, consisting of salad, clam chowder, potatoes au gratin, chicken cordon bleu, lasagna, and prime rib, washed down with a two-scoop ice cream sundae.

Then the freshmen put on the team's second annual Gong Show. What followed could charitably be described as "energetic." The show hit a low point when four freshmen played a boy band dance troupe—without any of them able to play, sing, or dance. But it was so bad it was funny, and it gave the upperclassmen the chance they'd been waiting for: to stand on their chairs and yell "GONG!" in unison.

More than a few sketches mocked the coaches, including Barwis and Rodriguez, with impunity. The targets took it in good humor.

The boldest of the batch, though, was the freshman who came out wearing a headset over his baseball hat, mirrored sunglasses, and pillows stuffing his sweatshirt and sweat pants while chewing on a white towel wrapped around his neck. The crowd howled, immediately recognizing the character as quarterback coach Rod Smith. But it took a few extra beats to realize the player doing the imitation was Smith's star pupil: Tate Forcier.

Nine days before his first game, the kid was already exhibiting his trademark trait. Whether people called it arrogance or fearlessness would probably depend on whether he won or lost.

The most therapeutic portion of the show was a skit they titled "Dead and Gone," about the fifteen players who had quit or transferred in the previous twenty months, from Ryan Mallett to Justin Boren to Steven Threet. It wasn't the most gracious gesture of the evening, but it was probably the most cathartic—and it got the most laughs. For the 2009 squad, all that business from the previous team was, as the monkey in *The Lion King* says, "in the past."

When the show ended, Rodriguez stepped to the front of the room. "Okay, men, that was a lot of fun, but I don't want to pass up this chance to teach. So let's take a look at the top twenty plays of camp."

The highlights included a few examples of coaches jumping to get out of the way of deadly collisions—and some not quite making it; Carlos Brown tripping over his own feet in the end zone; and center David Molk wiping out and inadvertently kicking Nick Sheridan in the balls.

Most of the plays, though, showed how much better this team might be: Jonas Mouton blasting his man so hard his helmet popped off like a Rock 'em Sock 'em Robot's head; Jordan Kovacs, who'd just made the team from the walk-on tryout, racing across the width of the field to break up a pass; and the most impressive play, Denard Robinson, who set the Florida state record in the hundred-meter dash that spring, running toward the left sideline, planting both feet, jumping to his right like a snow skier making a cut, then continuing down the field untouched. The "Oooooh's" were involuntary.

The lights went up. "Okay, men," Rodriguez said. "We've all heard enough crap over the last sixteen months, and I've had it up to here with all that.

"I gave a speech at a club today, and they all mean well, but you get the same questions every time: 'Are you gonna be better this year?'

"'No, I don't think we are!'" The players laughed. "Hell, we *better* be better this year!

"Well, we've been here almost three weeks, and you can already feel there's something special going on here. I wanted to tell those folks today, 'You have no idea what these guys go through and you have no idea how much these guys want to win.' But I don't want to tell anyone outside this room, because we know it, and that's enough. Everyone else is going to find out soon enough.

"That's why we train the way we train, that's why we coach the way we coach—and that's why we'll play the way we'll play.

"We're going to have adversity, but no one in this room is gonna panic. We're just gonna keep coming after you. I can't *wait* for September fifth."

The previous season, Rodriguez had said a lot of things that sounded something like this—but weren't quite this. The new message was more direct, more confident, but the biggest difference was something intangible: Rodriguez knew he had this team. He believed in them, and they believed in him. The feeling in the room that night was unlike anything they had felt in 2008.

"You freshmen will soon learn," Rodriguez said, "that we have the greatest fight song in the country. After we win a home game we go over to the student section and sing it, and that's great. We love it, they love it. But after that, we run back to the locker room, where it's just us, and sing it again—and that's what I enjoy most."

He had dramatic pauses in this speech. Not for effect, it seemed, but because he was savoring the sentences.

"You talk to guys who've played in the Super Bowl and got all the bling. And I promise you, they will tell you the joy of singing 'The Victors' with 125 brothers in that locker room is the greatest football memory they have. By far."

He let that sink in, looking out at the fresh faces. Believers at a religious revival are not more rapt.

"So you freshmen need to learn it as soon as possible. Seniors? Time for you to get up and teach your younger brothers the greatest fight song in the world!

"Listen to the words closely, freshmen. You'll be singing this on September fifth!"

They got loud, their fists shot up, and they finished with a cheer.

"We brought you here," Rodriguez said, "because we thought you should be part of the greatest football program in the country.

"Go Blue! See you tomorrow."

The next morning, they headed back to Ann Arbor for a scrimmage in the Big House. They touched the banner, the band blasted "The Victors," Dusty Rutledge announced fake scores from around the Big Ten on the stadium PA system ("Michigan State 9, Montana State 47; and in Columbus, we have a final: Ohio State 3, United States Naval Academy 33"), and they ended the game with a 12-lateral play worthy of the Berkeley-Stanford classic.

"Final score," Rutledge boomed on the PA. "Michigan 56, the Rest of the World 0."

They were ready. They were unified. Football was fun again.

On that day, more than any other in the Rodriguez era, it seemed the Rodriguez Revolution was ready to launch, and the sky was the limit.

It had been a cool, gray, drizzly day, but hot showers after the scrimmage got the chill out of their bones. They walked to the adjoining Junge Champions Center and ate a hot dinner while the sun reappeared.

Life for the Wolverines could not have been much better.

But at one of the coaches' tables, cell phones started buzzing in unison.

It was already past five on a Friday, but within minutes, Michigan's associate athletic director for compliance, Judy Van Horn, and her assistant showed up, whispering to the coaches and staffers while they ate. A few of them got up and walked to the lobby to talk more freely.

While the team had been scrimmaging, Bruce Madej, Michigan's associate athletic director for communications, received a visit from Mark Snyder and Michael Rosenberg of the *Free Press* to get their comments for a piece they planned to publish on Sunday.

Rosenberg told Madej they were accusing the football program of violating the weekly time limits, and read him a few anonymous quotes. Exactly how much they divulged to Madej is unclear, but it's fair to say they gave Madej the gist of the piece, without spelling out all the specific charges.

In a 2011 interview, Rosenberg told me, he distinctly remembered Snyder sitting across from him, asking for information. "'We need anything you have,'" Rosenberg recalled Snyder saying. "'We need Rich. We need Bill. We need schedules. Tell us we're wrong—anything you have.'"

"The problem is," Madej told me, "they work on a project for months, and you've got seven or eight hours to respond. That's difficult."

Rosenberg stressed that no one at Michigan asked them to delay the story, though he admitted if they had, the *Free Press* would have "discussed it" without any guarantee of postponing. Knowing how vital it is for any newspaper to publish the Sunday before the season starts for maximum impact, it seems unlikely such a wish would have been granted.

Madej told Rosenberg, whom he considered a friend, they would get back with them. Before they left, however, Madej added, by way of advice as much as warning, "You better make sure your sources aren't exaggerating and know the rules."

"We're covered," Rosenberg replied confidently.

The coaches, including Rodriguez, were initially less upset than confused.

"Practicing too much?" he asked Van Horn. "They know taping doesn't count, getting dressed doesn't count?"

Rod Smith chimed in: "Study table doesn't count, team meals don't count." They wondered, and worried, how well the reporters had mastered the intricacies of an admittedly absurd list of rules.

Rodriguez pointed out that during the unofficial walk-throughs before spring ball, "we didn't even practice with footballs," instead using taped-up towels, which the players didn't bother handing off. He could have added that, before he started his noon workouts, he called down to the weight room to make sure no current players were still lifting, to ensure his presence did not constitute "coaching." He was making the case, through anecdotes, that they were not running a renegade program.

Football sports information director Dave Ablauf whispered to recruiting coordinator Chris Singletary, "Who're their sources?"

Singletary shrugged, but they were able to throw around a few suspects pretty quickly, all of whom had an ax to grind for some reason or other. One was mad he wasn't a permanent captain. Another's NFL career hadn't turned out the way he'd hoped. Another didn't like the new workouts. A fourth didn't fit the spread offense.

Other candidates included half the senior class of 2008. As 2009 senior walk-on Jon Conover later put it, "They worked harder than ever"—particularly on Sundays—"and they go 3–9. Of *course* they were pissed."

Then the coaches started guessing which administrators might have helped the *Free Press*.

"Numero Uno?" one asked, referring to Lloyd Carr.

About a month earlier, at a Michigan alumni luncheon in the resort town of Petoskey, an alumnus asked Carr if his views had been solicited on a successor—an open invitation to comment on Rodriguez.

"I have not commented on that because it's not my responsibility, first of all," he said. "I will say this, I was asked for my opinion." And that was it.

You could argue that, acting in good faith, Carr's Delphic comments reflected his awareness that any statement from him on Rodriguez would inspire endless rounds of splicing and spinning.

But you could also argue that, as the former head football coach turned associate athletic director, drawing an annual salary of $387,000 for a loosely defined position devoted mainly to public relations, showing public support for the current coach was one of his *primary* responsibilities. It was, after all, exactly what Elliott had done for Schembechler, and Schembechler had done for Moeller and Carr—without title or salary.

Of course, given everything that had transpired since Rodriguez had arrived, Carr declining to make comment at all was also grist for media spin. While Carr's tepid answer hardly constituted interference, no one confused it with support, either.

So, thirty-six hours before the *Free Press* story had even arrived on readers' doorsteps, suspicion, paranoia, and divisions were exploding anew in Schembechler Hall—exactly the viruses the coaching staff had been working for nine months to eradicate.

Rodriguez, Singletary, and Ablauf cut dinner short and headed back to Schembechler Hall in complete silence. They weren't sure what was coming next. They knew it couldn't be good, but they could not have predicted that the hard-earned focus the team had achieved was about to be shattered.

Back in the team room, the players waited for their coach to give his scheduled postdinner speech. They were talking and joking, oblivious of the concerns swirling around them. When the digital clock hit 5:56, the seniors started shushing their teammates. They knew their coach would be walking through the door at any second.

After some housekeeping, Rodriguez asked his players: "The foundation of our program is built on what?"

"TRUST!" they yelled back. They knew their lines.

"We've had a good camp. A *great* camp. You've done what I've asked you to do—I *like* this team—and after tomorrow, you need to give me thirteen more weeks.

"Tonight, go home, and get off your feet, and get your rest.

"Sunday we'll get ready to kick some ass next Saturday.

"Go Blue!"

The players still had no clue about the crisis control being conducted down the hallway, and the staffers stewing in those offices didn't know a heck of a lot more. They were scratching their heads, trying to figure out what, exactly, the *Free Press* was up to.

That night, the coaches and staffers went back and forth between Ablauf's secondary office at Schembechler—a glorified walk-in closet—and Rodriguez's far more spacious room down the hall. They started piecing together what information they had. They quickly eliminated money, grades, or steroids as targets, which left . . . what? The best they could come up with were some problems they'd had with something they called the CARA (Countable Athletically Related Activities) form. John Hardt, an influential NCAA staff member who became the director of compliance at Michigan State, developed the form, which Judy Van Horn brought with her when she left MSU for Michigan.

Van Horn graduated from Central Michigan University and started her career as a receptionist in the CMU athletic department in 1989. CMU, like every other school, needed someone to run compliance, but couldn't afford a full-time employee for the position. So, to her credit, Van Horn took the phonebook-fat NCAA rule book home every night to learn the arcane codes therein, and that's how she became Central's compliance director, the first woman to hold that post in the Mid-American Conference.

After a full-time compliance stint at Michigan State from 1997 to 2001, Bill Martin hired her, partly to help with the basketball booster scandal he had inherited.

In 2002, Van Horn created Michigan's CARA form for all its teams to use. Unlike most schools, which require only a sample of student athletes to record their hours each week—much the way the NCAA regularly conducts random drug tests—Van Horn's system required every athlete to fill out a form every day. It was the equivalent, one athletic board member told me, of asking lawyers to keep track of their billable hours every ten seconds.

Scott Draper and Brad Labadie were assigned the onerous task of handling this for the football team each week and were not to submit the forms to Van Horn's office until every player had filled his out—an almost impossible standard for football, which has eight times more players than basketball.

"If 119 of 120 players sign it and you submit it, it gets sent back," Labadie told me. "The irony of the whole situation is this: The only way to get 120 students to do *anything* is to make their coach or their strength coach make them. And once you've done that, you've compromised the whole process." The forms, after all, are intended to protect the athletes from being exploited by their coaches.

But this does not explain why the job had been done much better by Scott Draper, and better still by MSU's Mike Vollmar, who submitted the forms "like clockwork," Van Horn said. Further, every other Michigan team, even those with large rosters like track and women's rowing, were submitting their CARA forms regularly.

Draper and especially Labadie did not put the task at the top of their list of things to do, and stopped submitting them altogether soon after Rodriguez had been hired. "The fact that every form was not signed with 100 percent completion, that's on me," Labadie said.

At the time, Van Horn was spread thin. It was no secret that Van Horn, a very warm and likable person, had ambitions to become an athletic director.

To those ends, she jumped at the chance to add the title of senior women's administrator (SWA). Because Michigan does not have separate athletic directors for men's and women's sports, like most schools, at U-M the SWA is largely a ceremonial title, but it allowed Van Horn to travel to conferences and increase her profile nationwide. In 2005, the National Association for Athletic Compliance (NAAC) named Van Horn the recipient of the Outstanding Achievement Award, and three years later, in 2008, she was elected to a two-year term as president of the NAAC.

But she was still well aware of the problems with the CARA forms, and sought to fix them. After Labadie failed to turn in the forms for the spring of 2008, Van Horn convened two formal meetings that summer with Scott Draper, Brad Labadie, Mike Parrish, and Ann Vollano from Compliance to determine why the forms were not submitted and to remedy the problem for the upcoming academic year. Labadie said he had an improved system and assured Van Horn that football CARA forms would be submitted each month. Van Horn reported to Bill Martin that Labadie's delay that spring appeared to be an aberration, and the forms should be submitted on time in the future.

But they were not. Van Horn's office engaged Draper and Labadie in a slow game of e-mail tag, repeatedly requesting that the forms be submitted. Van Horn informed Martin of the situation and solicited the help of athletic development director Joe Parker, who kept on Draper and Labadie to get them done.

In the beginning, Labadie's explanations seemed plausible to Van Horn, who had enjoyed a good working relationship with Draper and Labadie since she arrived in 2002.

However, as time went on and attempts to get any CARA forms turned in went unheeded, the Compliance staff grew increasingly frustrated. As one former colleague said, "Labadie told Compliance a number of times that the CARA forms were ready and he would hand-deliver them, and then later claimed they'd been lost. Help was offered as well and he and Draper never threw any red flags."

"Looking back, I feel like I was snowed," Van Horn told me. "Thinking on all the written and verbal communication that occurred, particularly with Brad, the explanation or excuses were nothing more than misdirection, or even out-and-out lying to the Compliance staff."

A year later, in the spring of 2009, Van Horn—fed up with the lack of results—brought in the university auditors to examine the situation and bring more pressure to bear on Labadie. Their review resulted in a finding against the football program in the summer of 2009, a few weeks before the *Detroit Free Press* began its investigation.

Rodriguez had been told the department used CARA forms a few weeks after he had taken over, but had largely forgotten about them— which was not an oversight, but how the system was supposed to work— until early August 2009, when Van Horn, Labadie, and others came to him after the internal auditors presented their report.

Rodriguez asked why the CARA forms had not been submitted and, just as important, why he had not been informed of the problem when it was discovered months earlier.

No one had good answers. Van Horn had believed Draper, who reported to Rodriguez, when he told her repeatedly that Rodriguez was in the loop. He was not.

They all apologized and promised neither mistake would happen again. The good news, at the time, was that the problem was easily fixed: submit the forms you've held on to for a year, and stay current from that point on. And that was the last Rodriguez had thought about it, until that Friday night after the scrimmage.

It was still just a boring administrative glitch, however, until the *Free Press* submitted a very specific Freedom of Information Act request asking for interoffice correspondence related to the CARA forms. "Now," Labadie asked, "how could you possibly know about something like that without a leak?"

It's a fair question. Whoever it was, they knew what to look for, and where to send the information.

In the recruiting lounge, Mike Parrish, Dusty Rutledge, and Chris Singletary sat, mulling over the events, feeling like they were on death row.

"Sometimes," Rutledge said, "you're just not wanted. And it just gives [Rich] that much more to think about—like he needs that."

Down the hall in Rodriguez's office, it was obvious Rutledge was right. Rodriguez paced around his desk, angrily muttering to himself or anyone who walked in. "Every day, it's something else. We've given the media complete access, and this is what you get. They *know* when practice begins and when it ends—because they're *there*! Look at your goddamn watch! We're *clean!*"

It is a spacious office, but Rodriguez, a strong man with an overabundance of kinetic energy, seemed to fill it completely, especially when he was worked up. As he paced back and forth—to pick up something from his desk or meet someone at his open door—he would stop and make another point.

"Never seen nothing like the drama of this place," he said, and he was including West Virginia in the comparison. "Ridiculous. Someone at this university has to stand up and say, 'Enough!' But no one ever does. Everyone just listens and surrenders when we're *right*! Why do we always give in to it?"

His office phone rang. He looked to see who was calling and let it go to voice mail.

"It's always 'Trust me, trust me,'" he continued, searching for something on his desk. "They told me in the interview, 'You get to Michigan, and you're gonna be surrounded by great people who're gonna support you.' Oh, yeah? Really? Where are they?

"I want to talk to the regents, directly, and tell them what's going on."

He walked out to his secretary's desk to sift through a small stack of papers.

"People who want to support our program only hear about all the bullshit these guys are making up. What about Mark Huyge? Jared Van Slyke? Tim North?" They were, respectively, an engineering student and starting lineman; the son of a baseball star who chose to be a football walk-on; and a great student with a bright future in business. "What about the guys from Pahokee, who never got three meals a day or a practice jersey until they got here? So many good stories aren't getting told. It grinds you."

Madej walked into the office. For him, it all boiled down to a simple idea: "We need Bo," something all the veterans echoed at some point that weekend. "Bo would say 'Bam!' and all this bullshit would be over. I was worried as soon as he died about what would happen. It started with Harbaugh taking a shot at the program when Lloyd was the coach—and now this."

Rodriguez sat down at his desk, while Madej looked over his shoulder to work through several drafts of a short press release. But they were at a loss, since they weren't sure exactly what they were responding to. Ablauf joined them and suggested they also send out a copy of a week of their practice schedule to all the reporters who cover the team, as proof that they were in compliance.

This is what they finally came up with: "Rich Rodriguez: We know the practice and off-season rules and we stay within the guidelines. We follow the rules and have always been completely committed to being compliant with all NCAA rules."

They had no idea if it would do any good. The progress they had made over the previous nine months, culminating in the unrestrained joy and hope of the past twenty-four hours, was in danger of being wiped out by Sunday's paper.

When Rodriguez woke up Sunday morning, this is what he found on his doorstep:

MICHIGAN FOOTBALL PROGRAM BROKE RULES, PLAYERS SAY
Rodriguez denies exceeding NCAA time guidelines
By Michael Rosenberg and Mark Snyder
Free Press Sports Writers

The University of Michigan football team consistently has violated NCAA rules governing off-season workouts, in-season demands on players and mandatory summer activities under coach Rich Rodriguez, numerous players told the Free Press.

Players on the 2008 and 2009 teams described training and practice sessions that far exceeded limits set by the NCAA, which governs college athletics. The restrictions are designed to protect players' well-being, ensure adequate study time and prevent schools from gaining an unfair competitive advantage.

The players, who did not want to be identified because they feared repercussions from coaches, said the violations occurred routinely at the direction of Rodriguez's staff.

"It's one of those things where you can't say something," one current Wolverine said. "If you say something, they're going to say you're a lazy person and don't want to work hard."

That player was one of six current or former players who gave lengthy, detailed and nearly identical descriptions of the program to the Free Press.

Rosenberg and Snyder stated that Rodriguez and his staff were making their players put in some fifteen to twenty-one hours a week on football during the off season—more than twice the NCAA limit of eight—in an article depicting a head coach exploiting his players for personal gain. The long piece raised more questions than answers, not only about Rodriguez's program, but also about the *Free Press*'s motives and sources. But in the short run, none of that mattered.

Ablauf and company pointed out that the headline and opening paragraph themselves were misleading, because the players interviewed (two of whom—Brandin Hawthorne and Je'Ron Stokes—were freshmen proud of the work they had done) apparently didn't know the difference between "countable" and "uncountable" hours and were not accusing the coaches of breaking those rules, since they didn't know what they were. The writers, not the players, were making that charge.

But as the saying goes, you can't unring a bell, and the *Free Press* had banged this one loudly enough to be heard from coast to coast, drowning out any questions or counterpoints for a news cycle or two.

The coaches met for their regular meeting at 11:00 a.m. and got the day's business behind them before allowing themselves to ruminate on the story making national news as they spoke. Though somewhat shell-shocked, and not yet able to get their heads around the entire piece, they had read enough to poke at the particulars pretty efficiently.

"These guys are claiming our players go forty-five hours a week," the normally easygoing Cal Magee said. "Do *they* even know the fuckin' rules?"

In the reporters' defense, just to cover a small section of this rule, the NCAA needs two pages and thirty-five bullet points. Boiled down, student athletes can spend only eight hours a week on their sports during the off-season, and twenty hours a week during the season. But when you get into which hours count and which don't, things get blurry fast.

Under "countable hours," the NCAA lists eleven core activities, like practice, games, and team meetings. "Uncountable hours" include just about everything else, sixteen items total, including getting taped, receiving physical therapy, eating team meals, and traveling—and, most ill-defined of all, anything deemed "voluntary."

How can you tell the difference? Good question. If you write for *The Michigan Daily* or play in the Michigan Marching Band, you probably should expect to put in extra work if you want to become the editor in chief or the drum major. Does that make it mandatory? Who knows? The NCAA isn't watching them, of course. But it doesn't get much easier to determine what's truly voluntary when you're talking about a football player who's dying to start or get to the NFL.

Even voluntary weight lifting can be tricky. If several strength coaches are in the weight room conducting the session, it's considered mandatory, and it counts. But if only one strength coach is in the weight room *monitoring* the players for safety, that's considered voluntary and does not count. And that's why Rodriguez always called the strength coaches' office to make sure the coast was clear before he headed down for his workout.

Put it all together, and the twenty hours a week the NCAA counts is probably about half the actual time a student athlete puts in every week, in just about any sport.

Which just underscores the self-evident fact that, for the nineteen-year-old quarterback and the twenty-year-old kicker, on whose arms and legs the $100 million athletic department depends, college football is not merely an adventure. It's a job.

But unlike most full-time workers, these guys also have to squeeze in a college education while they're at it.

That's the story the *Free Press* could have pursued with vigor and balance: the silliness and hypocrisy of the NCAA rules, which give the false impression that the workload for student athletes is half what it really is.

Before Michigan's NCAA champion softball coach, Carol Hutchins, and her team play their first home game in April, they make six separate trips south. But none of those hours "count" unless they're in meetings or in gyms or on the field. Their games—like *all* games in the NCAA rule book, no matter the sport—count only three hours, even though Hutchins said, "We get there three hours *before* the game even starts. That's how arbitrary the whole thing is. It's all bogus."

How bogus? Consider the Michigan hockey team's annual trip to play league opponent Alaska-Fairbanks. They leave at 6:00 a.m. on Wednesday and return about 4:00 p.m. on Sunday—a 106-hour trip. While there, they have two one-hour practices, one mandatory twenty-minute skate, and one voluntary twenty-minute skate (which doesn't count), and two games, which count as three hours each. All told, that 106-hour trip adds up to a mere 8:20 in the NCAA's eyes—only 97:40 shy of the total trip.

And that is the difference between countable and uncountable hours.

Impressively, the hockey team graduated over 90 percent of its players until they started leaving early for the NHL, and the softball team consistently has a team GPA over 3.0. But Hutchins is tired of the NCAA's hypocrisy, too. "Just tell us the truth," she said. "If the limit is twenty or thirty or forty hours a week, say so. But make it real."

Knowing the NCAA, however—which former Central Collegiate Hockey Association commissioner Bill Beagan called "Vatican West"—don't hold your breath. Until the NCAA does "make it real," however, the crux of this rule will always be the distinction between countable and uncountable hours.

And that was a distinction Rosenberg and Snyder—experienced, hardworking sportswriters with a deep knowledge of Michigan athletics—did not mention once in their three thousand-word package accusing Rodriguez of breaking that very rule.

"It was in the story at some point," Rosenberg told me, "but it went through a lot of edits. Hindsight is twenty-twenty. We should have explained that to the readers. [But] for whatever reason, I don't think that ended up being in the story."

To some readers it was a major oversight. To others, it was inside baseball. But to every journalist I've discussed this with—including colleagues of Rosenberg and Snyder—it was a jaw-dropping omission, tantamount to accusing General Motors of tax fraud without mentioning the difference between gross revenue and net profit.

The people sitting around the table had other problems with the piece. "A four-hour workout?" Barwis asked, referring to another claim made in the story. "You'd be dead. Forty-five minutes of running? You'd be dead."

I could vouch for both. Two hours with these guys was the rough equivalent of ten hours at your local gym. Barwis did not need to break the rules to get his people in shape, and to prove it, the pro players he worked with—including Morgan Trent—usually finished well under two hours each day, though they were obviously free to work as long as they liked.

"You guys aren't doing anything different than they did before," added a former player.

In fact, a few veterans said, if the *Free Press* had talked with people from Carr's era, they would have found out about "Torture Tuesdays," when players were punished for missing class (one of the NCAA violations Rodriguez would be accused of) and receiver Antonio Bass was cited for working out with the coaches—not the quality control staff—and, significantly, a football before spring ball started (yet another violation Rodriguez would be charged with).

But the article inspired at least one immediate change: That evening, Michigan State removed the piece on its official football website bragging about the fourteen-hour Sundays their players put in to get ready for the season, as a counter to all the attention Barwis's weight program had been getting that year.

"I don't understand," Rodriguez said, looking more hurt than angry. "When it's just hearsay and you've got no facts, how can you publish this? We just got the highest GPA ever. If they're overworked, how does that happen?

"And the two freshmen they quoted, all they said is 'We work hard.' No kidding?! Aren't they *supposed* to say that? They're *proud*! What if they said, 'This isn't any harder than high school'? They'd want me fired—and they should!

"We bust our ass to try to help these kids. That's what really bothers me. They've got more people trying to help them than any other students on campus. We give them tutoring, counseling, strength coaches, trainers— and when you graduate, we take you back, for free, to help you some more. And this is the thanks you get from some of the alums."

Although the article did not distinguish between the current and former players, the coaches did, separating the benign quotes of the freshmen from the damaging comments of the anonymous players they suspected were mostly from the 2008 team.

That brought the subject back around to which former players might have talked to the *Free Press*. They quickly came up with a list of a half dozen, closely matching the list generated by the administrators in the Champions Center lobby Friday evening. But when they tried to guess who the one or two current players who spoke anonymously might be, Dusty Rutledge cut it off.

"We can't even think about that," he said, ending the speculation. "We have to go on like no one said anything, or else you start suspecting everybody, and your team falls apart."

They agreed, and—somewhat surprisingly—there the matter ended. But that still left the question of which, if any, staff helped the writers with the story. That would become one of the most damaging guessing games played in Schembechler Hall that fall.

The writers' motives, accuracy, and impact would be debated for over a year, but one thing was beyond debate from the moment the papers dropped on readers' doorsteps that morning: Thanks to the *Detroit Free Press*, the team's water had been poisoned, and the feeling of trust they had worked so hard to establish—what the program was based on, Rodriguez had told the players repeatedly—had been compromised. The Rodriguez program would never again be as strong as it had been the previous Friday afternoon. If the article's goal was to bring the program down from the inside, it had just struck a load-bearing pillar, making the whole structure shake.

"In all my years, I've never seen anything like this," said Bruce Madej, whose thirty-one years at Michigan covered the Fab Five, Moeller's last weekend, Bo's passing, and the Horror. "We always know what to do, even when it's bad. And this isn't even bad! It's nothing! But it's just one thing after another. It has a completely different feel to it. It's personal. I feel horrible for Rich. And there's no framework for how to respond. It's partly the nature of the new media, but it's more than that."

When Rodriguez left the room for a moment, Fred Jackson said, "I've never seen him like this before. I think this is really getting to him. The idea that he wouldn't be doing the best for his players—that hurts him."

As the sole carryover from Carr's coaching staff, Jackson had known Rodriguez for only twenty months, but he had already seen him face a few bad days—and he was right. Rodriguez had been bruised from all the battles he'd been through over the previous two years, but on this morning, something fundamental in him had changed, like a slat under your bed breaking. You can't see it, everything looks about the same, but you can hear it, and you can feel the difference every day thereafter.

The coaches kept up business as usual, meeting with each other and their positions, but there was no ignoring the elephant in the room. During the 12:30 offensive coaches' meeting, they went over every play, four sheets of them, but Rodriguez was clearly distracted, pressing his eyes closed at times, biting his lip at others.

Cal Magee was determined to remain positive. "Team meeting's at four, right?" he asked the other coaches, then added with a chuckle, "I bet they'll be on time today!"

But even Magee was affected. "What bothers me is, if these people just knew our hearts, and how we care about these kids, they'd never believe this stuff. Just amazes me."

Outside the meeting room, Rick Leach stopped in Ablauf's walk-in-closet office, clearly upset. "We all know where this is coming from, do we not?"

Ablauf tilted his head and shrugged. He'd already decided that that game led only to a dark place, with no final answers.

When Leach walked into Rodriguez's office, he gave him a hug and broke down, which finally cracked Rodriguez's defenses, causing him to break down, too.

"I'm sorry," Leach said. "This is not the Michigan I know."

That afternoon, Rutledge, who had helped sell Rodriguez on leaving his alma mater for Michigan, walked down to the coach's office to apologize.

"What for?" Rodriguez asked.

"When I told you Michigan was a first-class place, I was wrong."

"This can be a great place," Rodriguez replied. As much as the article hurt him, he was far from abandoning his faith in his decision to come to Michigan. But it was the first time I had heard him say "can be" instead of "is."

The two freshmen who had been tricked into speaking for the story on Media Day, Brandin Hawthorne and Je'Ron Stokes, made their own walk down to Rodriguez's office that afternoon. Of the six "current and former" players quoted in the piece, they were the only ones quoted by name.

"They came in with tears in their eyes," Rodriguez said afterward. "I told them, 'You didn't do anything wrong. They just misrepresented what you said.' I had to make sure they knew I wasn't mad at them."

Hawthorne and Stokes made it clear that if the *Free Press* writers had been up front about the thrust of their story—exploitation and abuse—they would have refuted it, not supported it. Stokes's dad was particularly upset, telling *The Wolverine*: "My wife and I talk to Je'Ron every day . . . I know [the allegations] are not true, because I know how Mike Barwis cares for these kids. He's taken my son to Bible study and to church. These are the kinds of things that impress us about the program and Rich Rod and his staff. They are good people, and I hate the fact that every negative thing put out there brings the wrong perception to the Michigan program.

"They took and twisted and misconstrued [his quote], when Ronnie was just simply saying he's doing the regulated hours required by the coaches within the rules."

Stokes's dad was not alone. Many players' parents called and e-mailed all day, and their sons walked down to Rodriguez's office by the dozen to let him know how angry they were and wanted to speak out. Mark Ortmann, David Moosman, and even the cool-tempered Nick Sheridan were outraged.

All but one of the players showed up unannounced: Jared Van Slyke, a walk-on, whom Rodriguez had asked to see a few days earlier. When they kept the appointment, Van Slyke felt compelled to take on the article that had broken that morning. "I wanted him to know we completely disagreed with the whole thing, and we got your back," he later told me. "And I told him I wasn't just speaking for myself. That's how we *all* feel."

Rodriguez was touched, but he had summoned Van Slyke for a completely different reason. Rodriguez wanted him to know he had earned a scholarship for the season. Having been a walk-on himself, Rodriguez loved giving this sort of news. Van Slyke didn't disappoint. "I was jacked! I hugged him—and it was cool to see his genuine happiness at my reaction."

It was a rare bright spot in an otherwise bleak twenty-four hours.

They conducted the position meetings right on time, followed by the team meeting at four. Bill Martin, who'd heard about the story Friday night when the *Free Press* asked him for a comment while he was at the family's cottage in the Upper Peninsula, flew back in time for the Sunday meeting.

Rodriguez addressed the story with the team briefly and obliquely and mentioned again how they had achieved the highest grade point average in Michigan's recorded history—clearly a point of pride. The message was simple: The program is working, and you guys are doing a great job.

He got choked up a couple times, talking about how much he cared about them and how much he'd seen them grow together, as tight as any team he'd ever coached. He apologized to them for having to go through all this—"You deserve better"—and told them not to worry about it but to focus on football and school.

"I'm proud of the way you've come together," he said, "and now it's time to show 'em what we're made of.

"Seniors, I'll meet you at my home, as scheduled."

The seniors drove ten miles to the Rodriguez home—a small castle south of Saline, to which they had all been before—where Rich and Rita met them at the door. They ate salads and steaks and shrimp and chicken and Miss Rita's famous nachos, followed by plenty of cheesecake. Then they retired to the basement sunroom facing the pool, where they lounged in chairs and on couches.

Rodriguez sat on a barstool and gave them a different talk from the one he had planned a few days earlier. Rather than discuss the season ahead and the leadership he needed from this senior class, and ask what they needed from him, he decided to face what everyone was thinking about. If you had to pinpoint the exact minute when the *Free Press* article started to affect the way Rodriguez coached his team, this would be it.

Just about any successful college coach knows the team depends on the seniors. They set the example for the players behind them and the tone of the team when the coaches aren't around, whether it's off-season workouts or off-campus fun. Rodriguez knew if they were going to repair the damage the article had already inflicted on the team's morale they had been bolstering every day since the Ohio State game, it would have to start with the seniors, and it would have to start immediately. If he didn't have them, he wouldn't have the rest.

He began by debunking the article's primary charge. "Claiming we're breaking the time limits, using anonymous sources—it's just not true, it's just not fair." Then he embraced the two freshmen the *Free Press* had exploited: "They came into my office to apologize, and they looked like they'd seen a ghost. Man, that's not right." That was his way of letting the seniors know there was to be no witch hunt among the players. The two were victims, not traitors, and would have the support of the entire team— reinforcing the basic principle of any team.

He then reminded the seniors of all they'd accomplished. "You guys *do* work hard, you *do* come in on Saturdays, you *do* do all the things Michigan Men are *supposed* to do! And they *punish* you for it!"

The seniors were nodding. Rodriguez downshifted a bit, lowering his voice and slowing his pace. "What *really* bothers me is that we care about you guys—a lot." He paused to collect himself.

"Mike Barwis—" He could not finish the sentence. He got up and went to the bathroom for a minute or two, then returned, red eyed but more resolute.

"Mike just wants you guys to get better. Has he ever refused you extra help? He's got two young kids. I'm sure he'd like to be home, but he works twelve-hour days, at least. Because he knows that's what it takes.

"We don't coach for a living. We live to coach. I want you to know, if you ever have a problem, you can come and see me. I think you do know that, and I have seen some of you."

The seniors were still and respectful, with a few wiping some tears of their own. Punter Zoltan Mesko was one of them. "All the guys who didn't want to work," he said, "we knew who they were, and they're gone."

"We just need to take care of business," Kevin Grady said.

"I can't wait," Brandon Graham said with his infectious enthusiasm, eyes alight. "I can't wait to get started. I can't wait for Saturday!"

Probably nothing Rodriguez heard all week made him feel better than that.

On ESPN, the announcer mentioned that Michigan had scheduled a press conference for the next day, adding, "Many Lloyd Carr loyalists don't approve of the fact that Rodriguez is not a Michigan Man. No doubt this just turns up the fire on Rich Rodriguez."

No doubt.

The press conference was actually the first of the regularly scheduled meetings they held every Monday throughout the season. But this one had an entirely different feel to it, with national news trucks filling the parking lot. They had not come to discuss the Broncos of Western Michigan.

The national newspapers sent a reporter, as did just about every major sports outlet, including ESPN's Joe Schad. Rosenberg and Snyder made a conspicuous entrance.

"I think both he and Snyder came in that day with a kind of 'Hey, look what we did!' bounce in their step," recalled one reporter, who asked to remain anonymous for fear of retribution. "I remember Snyder walking up to a clump of writers with an expectant look on his face, and everyone just kind of rolled their eyes."

The sense among most journalists there, twenty-four hours after the *Free Press* story ran, was that it was overblown at best and unethical at worst, particularly in regard to the use of the unsuspecting freshmen players.

"I remember walking into the press conference," another said, "and the first thing I saw was Mark Snyder and Rosenberg, looking smug—that's the only word to describe it. We usually all socialized before the press conference, walking around and making small talk, but I remember them sitting by themselves for a while before the presser started. They definitely hadn't made any friends in the media that day. None of the other reporters wanted much to do with [them]."

Things would get weirder before the day was done.

Neither Mary Sue Coleman nor Bill Martin attended, so Bruce Madej went up to the podium to lay out the format. Then Rodriguez rose slowly, wearing a white golf shirt with the block "M" on it, to take the stand.

"Normally, I don't bring notes," he said. "I just kind of speak from the top of my mind. But I have a few notes for obvious reasons. I want to talk the majority of the time about Western Michigan, but obviously we need to address the situation that came out.

"First and foremost, I want to tell everybody I am very proud of the way our players have worked the last seven, eight months."

With this, Rodriguez established that he, at least, would not be backing off. He also provided a strong defense of Mike Barwis. "I have complete trust in him, and I think he is absolutely the best strength and conditioning coach in the country."

He extended the same support to his entire staff: "We know the rules and we comply by the rules. We have a very transparent program. You guys that follow us know that. You've been out to practice several times."

Then things veered toward the emotional.

"I guess the thing that bothered me the most about the things that were recently written or said, or maybe some things in the last eighteen months, is the perception that's out there that we did not care as much for our players' welfare, and that is disheartening."

At this, Rodriguez choked up, looked down, and clutched the podium. He had to pause before continuing, with forceful deliberation.

"That is misleading . . . inaccurate . . . and goes against everything that I have ever believed in coaching."

He spoke of his family attending every practice, his pride in his sixteen years as a head coach helping lots of first-generation college students become great success stories, and his commitment to Michigan.

"When I have two young freshmen come into my office yesterday upset, saying, 'Coach, what did I do? What did we do? We just said we worked hard, and it was harder than it was in high school and we were committed to helping win a championship.' I said, 'You didn't do nothing wrong.

"'You did *nothing* wrong.'"

He paused again to collect himself before stressing the positives of the program and asking, "Why try to tear that up?"

Then, finally, he got to Western Michigan and questions.

Drew Sharp, a columnist with the *Detroit Free Press*, raised his hand. "The fact that you have certain players and their parents willing to basically call out your program, is there a potential disconnect there?"

"The response from our parents, our current players' parents, has been overwhelmingly positive . . . We have an open door, and the parents always know that they can call."

They actually discussed football for a bit, before Rodriguez closed by saying, "Our players are working very hard. Our players have done a whole lot to build this program. And so I'm sure they're not happy to have to deal with this."

As usual, the reactions to Rodriguez's presentation were mixed. He certainly could have done worse—but he could have done better. He did a capable job defending his players and his ethics, but a poor job addressing the *Free Press* piece itself. He said how hard they worked, which did nothing to weaken the *Free Press*'s case, but never once mentioned the article's glaring omission—which all the coaches had immediately pounced on the day before—about the difference between countable and uncountable hours.

He also could have mentioned the one-sided quality of their anonymous sources. When I asked Rosenberg if they had made any attempt to talk to players with different views, he replied, "Did we keep calling until we got guys to say, 'Hey, it's fine?' No, we didn't."

Although many of the players didn't know my name or exactly what I was doing, over a dozen sought me out that week to tell me the anonymous players were not speaking for them. Such players were not hard to find. They were hard to avoid.

Four of them volunteered to speak after Rodriguez left the podium.

Mark Ortmann talked about the coaches changing their summer practice schedule to accommodate their classes and how "personally, I don't think we're working hard *enough*. We can always improve."

"Last year was just a tumultuous time," offensive guard David Moosman said. "We just think we had a lot of guys—a lot of older guys—having their own agendas . . . I don't feel like we have anything like that this year."

None of the comments, taken individually, added up to much. But taken together a picture began to emerge of a team determined to stick together and get Michigan back to where it belonged—one with a very different character from the year before.

Some of the most dramatic moments happened after the cameras turned off.

When the reporters started packing up, Brian Cook, the founder of MGoBlog, approached Michael Rosenberg and Mark Snyder individually to ask if they knew the difference between countable and uncountable hours.

Both seemed as surprised by the questioner as they were by the question. Because I was sitting right there, it was easy to record their conversation.

"I don't know if I'm allowed to talk about that," Snyder replied.

"So you just write the article—and that's it?"

"I was on radio and TV talking about this," Snyder said.

"But you won't talk to me? I've got a direct quote from Brandin Hawthorne saying—"

"This is not something that I'm addressing with you."

During the next few go-rounds, Cook repeated his question about countable and uncountable hours, to which Snyder repeatedly replied, "You're a competitor," then ended the interview.

Cook caught up with Rosenberg on the way out, in the anteroom between the main meeting room and the parking lot. Rosenberg remembered the encounter vividly.

"A guy comes up to me after the press conference," he told me, "and starts *barking* questions at me—practically *yelling* at me. I've never seen him before, to my recollection. He won't let me speak, always cutting off my sentences.

"He's talking about countable hours, and I'm trying to explain to him, 'Of *course* we know the difference between countable and uncountable hours, even if the players don't know the difference. I didn't catch your name,' and he just glares at me. He won't respond. So I reach out my hand and say, 'I'm Michael Rosenberg.' He says he's Brian Cook. But he has no recorder, no pen."

Cook recalled the exchange a bit differently. As he remembered it, he asked Rosenberg if he knew the difference between countable and uncountable hours. "He said yes, and so I tried to get him to explain why the words 'countable hours' never appear in the article. He just kept asking me what my name was, which was totally irrelevant, as I kept asking him why his article claimed that Michigan was forcing players to spend over twice the allotted daily hours when common sense suggests that cannot possibly be true, that any coach who so brazenly flouted NCAA regulations wouldn't have lasted seven years anywhere."

Cook remembered that it had actually been Craig Ross, a local attorney and author of *The Obscene Diaries of a Michigan Fan*, watching the exchange with bemused interest, who told Rosenberg who Cook was, "after about the fourth time I asked him if his story made sense.

"I think we were both right in the end," Cook told me. "My name is Brian Cook, and Rosenberg did know what countable hours were."

If Rosenberg and Snyder expected to be greeted as liberators—fighting for the downtrodden players against their powerful oppressors—they must have left disappointed. But if their goal was to spark a story that would get the entire sports nation buzzing by lunchtime and reverberate for over a year, they had succeeded wildly.

By day's end, the story was burning in every direction, with no one in control of it anymore—not Rosenberg, not Rodriguez, not the *Free Press*, not the University of Michigan.

When ESPN ran a report later that day, they added a graphic, listing Rodriguez's problems since leaving Morgantown:

- Buy out. Michigan paid $2.5 million.
- Accused of shredding documents.
- Notable players have left. Mallett, Boren, more.
- Accused of excessive practice time.

And nationally, that's how the story played: New coach takes hallowed Michigan football program from the penthouse to the outhouse in eighteen months.

Most Michigan fans, however, were more circumspect. The websites blew up with comments, some accusing Rodriguez of ruining Michigan football, but many expressing anger with the *Free Press*—even on the *Free Press*'s own site. The e-mail boxes of just about every Michigan administrator and coach with any connection to the case filled up overnight.

In the weeks that followed, thousands of Michigan alums and fans wrote to Rodriguez, his staff, Bill Martin, and President Coleman professing their support of Rodriguez and his methods—confirming his view of the people he met every day. It didn't take long for many national commentators, including former Ohio State greats Kirk Herbstreit and Chris

Spielman, to conclude that the story was missing some important pieces. Jim Tressel and a few other Big Ten coaches expressed misgivings over the story and support for Rodriguez.

But the most powerful reaction came from a former *Michigan Daily* editor named Jonathan Chait, now at *The New Republic*. Writing for *The Wolverine*, Chait titled his piece "Violations Truly Worthy of Firing."

Chait wasted no time clearing his throat. "*Detroit Free Press* columnist Michael Rosenberg's exposé on Michigan's workout program revealed a shocking breach of rules that should cause somebody to lose his job. That somebody is Michael Rosenberg's editor."

Chait's central charge was that Rosenberg, who hated Rodriguez "from the moment he appeared on Michigan's radar," had written an opinion piece dressed up as investigative journalism. He obviously had a right to his opinion, Chait wrote, but not to publish "a prosecutor's brief, determined to make the case against Rodriguez, rather than present the facts in an evenhanded way . . . Letting him write and report the article himself is journalistic malpractice."

I asked Rosenberg about the controversial decision to assign a columnist to write an investigative piece, particularly on a subject about which he had already published strong opinions. He replied that, due to budget and staff cuts, the *Free Press* no longer had an investigative reporter dedicated to the sports department. So, in the current era, such double duty is harder to avoid.

But with any journalism, objectivity is paramount. When Larry Foote encountered Mark Snyder after the story came out, he asked, "Why didn't you ask me about him? You know I know him."

To which Snyder replied, "I just don't like the guy."

On Thursday, Rosenberg visited the Detroit Lions' facility for Media Day, when Larry Foote—who had left Pittsburgh for his home team that spring—sought him out, asking why he was so harsh to Mike Barwis, among others. Rosenberg confessed that he knew how positively the players felt about Barwis.

"Then why didn't you write *that*?" Foote asked.

Rosenberg answered by telling Foote how bad his own week had turned out and all the duress he was under. If Rodriguez didn't deserve to be unfairly attacked—even demonized—Rosenberg obviously didn't deserve to have his book *War as They Knew It* dishonestly rated down on Amazon.com. "I poured my heart and soul into that [book] for three years," he told me. "The shots at me on Amazon.com bothered me. There's nothing I've ever been prouder of than that book—so for them to trash the book really hurt." Telling all this to Foote, who had considered Rosenberg a friend, Rosenberg became teary-eyed.

By that time, however, neither response could stop his story from spreading, having generated a momentum all its own.

After the *Free Press* story, the Wolverines' already strong need to redeem themselves for the 2008 disaster had been multiplied many times over. They felt both determined and defiant.

When Rodriguez met with the team the night before the Western Michigan game, he told them, "I'm tired of all the drama, I'm tired of all the talk," sounding much less upbeat and enthusiastic than he had exactly eight days earlier. "I just want to play ball. And that's what you came here for: to get a degree and play ball.

"When people ask, 'How's your team handling it?' I think about you guys walking down the tunnel together, with your hands on each other's backs. That's it: We've got each other's backs."

He had no choice but to hope it was true and that it would last all season.

An echo of that was evident in the room shared by true freshman Craig Roh and sophomore Brandon Herron, in and of itself a potentially awkward situation because they were both competing for outside linebacker. The coaches pulled them over after practice that day to tell them Roh had won the position. But the two had worked it out, partly due to a shared interest in the Bible.

"I've been attracted to the psalms lately," Roh said. "Psalm Twenty-seven is the best one. David's being attacked from all angles, but God's his rock.

"'The Lord is the strength of my life; of whom shall I be afraid?'" he recited from memory. "'When the wicked, even mine enemies and my foes, came upon me to eat up my flesh, they stumbled and fell. Though a host should encamp against me, my heart shall not fear: though war should rise against me, in this will I be confident.'"

By the time he got to false witnesses rising up and breathing cruelty, I didn't need to ask him where he stood on the *Free Press* article.

The scene was different a floor below, where senior Nick Sheridan—the previous starter—shared his room with Tate Forcier, the freshman who would be taking his job. Forcier wore his trademark oversized baseball hat down low on his head, working on the playbook all the quarterbacks had to fill out every week, while Sheridan reclined on his bed, munching chips, drinking Gatorade, and watching ESPN. He had finished his playbook much earlier.

Forcier was trying to cram before his final, which he would be taking the next day at the Big House in front of 110,000-some graders. Sheridan was nice enough to help him.

"On Ram Flex Trojan," Forcier asked, "what side of the field do I work when the defense comes out with two high?"

"Is it Trio?"

Forcier checked. "Yes."

"Then you work the weak side," Sheridan said, while Forcier filled in his answer. "Understand that?"

"Yeah, thanks."

"And then you throw to the open guy who's wearing the same color jersey you are."

"Got it." Forcier smiled. "Thanks."

Was Forcier nervous?

He looked up and grinned his Tom Sawyer grin. "Never nervous," he said, and returned to his workbook.

After a 9:00 a.m. wake-up call and a hearty breakfast consisting of bins of scrambled eggs, bacon and ham, potatoes au gratin, biscuits and gravy, and French toast, the players went through their morning "walk-through"—one room for defense, another for offense. Forcier took his first "snaps" without an actual football, under a chandelier, surrounded by his coaches leaning against textured floral wallpaper, going through his steps on Victorian-style carpet, in a comfortable air-conditioned room. Beyond the cadence, all you could hear was the swish of nylon sweatpants.

The actual exam room would look a little different.

———

None of them were surprised that the *Free Press* had picked Western Michigan to beat the Wolverines 31–27.

The coaches got dressed at the stadium in dead silence. A few leaned forward on their metal chairs, heads down, as if in prayer. They knew what this game suddenly meant—and they also knew that, at this hour, their collective fate was largely in the hands of a group of former backups and walk-ons and a kid from California who'd just turned nineteen.

Someone turned on the TV, and inevitably the Michigan game—and everything attached to it—came up on ESPN.

Former Indiana coach Lee Corso opined, "You can lose some games, but you can't lose your football team. Rich Rodriguez is about to lose his football team."

Out in the locker room, an unlikely leader stepped up: walk-on junior Mark Moundros. "The only thing that matters," he shouted, "are the people in this room. So today we fight for each other, we fight for our coaches, and we fight for Michigan!"

When the game finally arrived—where no one mattered but the eleven players on the field—the Wolverines were ready. Michigan's defense forced the Broncos to punt after three plays, giving the ball to Michigan's offense at its own 48.

So here it was: the debut everyone had been waiting nine months to see. Tate Forcier jogged out to the field while the crowd rose to its feet.

Forcier took the shotgun snap, faked the handoff, rolled out, and found Junior Hemingway for a 5-yard gain. In just about every Michigan game since Schembechler took over, the first play went straight up the middle. But on this day, in this situation, that calm progression of options and execution hit the faithful like a bucket of baptismal water.

They were reborn—and cheered like it.

A few plays later, the Broncos flushed Forcier out of the pocket. But, once again, he found Junior Hemingway, this time for 28 yards—and a touchdown.

Just 2:52 into his collegiate career, Forcier had three completions for 47 yards, with no incompletes, no interceptions, no sacks, and one touchdown—and 109,019 instant believers.

Just like that, it seemed Michigan's nightmare was over.

———

With 4:07 left in the quarter and Michigan holding a 7–0 lead, Rodriguez sent Forcier's understudy, the talented but raw Denard Robinson, in at quarterback. It was risky, but not much riskier than starting a freshman in the first place. Rodriguez was not yanking Forcier. He just wanted to see what Robinson could do.

After being penalized for a false start, Robinson dropped the next snap, picked it up, and then took a few steps to the right instead of the left, which is where the play was supposed to go. Recognizing his mistake, he stopped, looked up, and saw that his teammates had already abandoned him, running their routes downfield, leaving him to face a rush of Broncos by himself.

And then, just as suddenly, he seemed to remember he was the fastest man on the field.

What happened next was something Michigan fans might long remember. Robinson saw a seam and, from a dead start, simply took off, flying past would-be tacklers as though they were treading water and he was driving a Jet Ski.

He was as gone as gone could be.

Michigan 14, Western 0.

When Robinson ran back to the bench, Forcier rushed out to the field to meet him for a spontaneous chest bump. "The best thing I saw all day," a relieved Bill Dufek said afterward.

They were young, with a lot to learn. But the unbridled joy they brought to this successful but stodgy school was unmistakable. Michigan fans had never seen anything quite like it since Crisler's Mad Magicians— and it was all encapsulated in that one play.

The halftime score: Michigan 31, Western 0. It was a good old-fashioned butt kicking.

During halftime, Forcier was sitting in his stall when Sheridan walked past him, gave him a fist bump, and said, "Good job, man!"

When I walked past, Forcier said, "I told you, man!"

I turned around. "Told me what?"

"Not nervous. *Never* nervous. I told you!"

On TV, however, the news wasn't all good for the Wolverines. During the first intermission, ESPN condensed the *Free Press*'s allegations in a chart:

- 6 players give allegations
- Sundays, worked 9 hours

The chart did not note that most of the nine hours would not count against the NCAA's limit of twenty. In other words, they were repeating the same mistakes the *Free Press* had made. The story was already recycling itself.

When the game ended at 31–7, the team ran over to the student section to sing "The Victors"—the loudest the crowd was all day, which was saying something. But before they started the song, the students started another chant, "Rich Rodri-guez," and afterward, "Beat the I-rish!"

When the Wolverines headed toward the tunnel, they ran under an eight-foot sign: IN ROD WE TRUST.

"Must be my kids behind that," Rodriguez joked.

The Wolverines packed more into that one wild week than they had in most months. The retreat showed them they were much closer and sharper than they had been the year before. The *Free Press* piece piled more pressure on them and their coaches, and while it surely shrank their margin of error, it hadn't affected their play. If they could still win games, they could still escape their detractors.

Hope was very much alive.

Against Western, the Wolverines had everything to lose.

Against Notre Dame, they had everything to gain.

The game came with two side stories: Charlie Weis's status at Notre Dame, which was more in doubt than ever, and the Wolverines' almost uniform contempt for the Irish's flashy quarterback, Jimmy Clausen.

"I've known him since we started going to camps," Forcier said after practice. "He loved the attention—too much. I don't like his ego. He's a pretty boy. Go look at Martin's locker."

Mike Martin had taped up six color photocopies of Jimmy Clausen in various poses: one of him sitting on a helmet with a football in his hands, like a cheesy yearbook pose; another displaying his gaudy rings; and a third of him decked out in a big fur coat, posing with a limo.

Martin's engine usually idles pretty low, but he got revved up for Clausen. "He better not be showing up at our place in a stretch limo with some spiked hairdo," he said, "and expect to get out of here alive."

"He represents pretty much everything we don't want our team to be," Ryan Van Bergen added. "You can tell someone's behavior on film. You see him get sacked and he tosses the ball in the guy's face.

"Asshole."

"Men, the entire country is watching us tomorrow afternoon," Rodriguez told his team Friday night at the Campus Inn. "That's just one reason why you came here—games like this.

"Bottom line, what this game comes down to is respect.

"And isn't that what we're all fighting for right here?"

A few minutes later, in the room he shared with Martin, Van Bergen observed that the previous season Rodriguez would say, "'We've got guys in here we *can* win with.' Now he says, 'We've got guys who *will* win.'"

Tate Forcier shared their confidence. "They're gonna blitz a lot," he said, studying his playbook in his room. "But as they say, 'You live by the blitz, you die by the blitz.'"

Forcier's world had changed quite a bit since classes had started that week. "I walked into one of my lectures, the professor says my name, and eighty heads turn to look at me. It was awkward.

"If we win *this* one, you'll see a big change, a lot of guys getting on the bandwagon. And we'll get a lot more respect, nationwide, because people will start thinking Rich Rod is doing something special."

For the upperclassmen, like walk-on turned starter Mark Moundros, there was no point pretending. "Every game is big. But this is Notre Dame. We know what we're capable of. No one came here to be in the middle. That's what Michigan is—at the top."

The next afternoon, the crowd lining the Victors' Walk was even louder than it had been the previous week. In the coaches' room, the usual pregame silence was broken by the Central Michigan–Michigan State game on TV, which pitted Rodriguez's good friend and former assistant coach Butch Jones against the considerably less well-liked Mark Dantonio.

At the Big Ten luncheon in Chicago a month earlier, Dantonio announced to the thousand or so people in attendance that the Spartans' rallying cry that year was "Play up!"—play up, that is, to the best competition in the Big Ten, "Penn State and Ohio State," he said, with no mention of Michigan, which he now apparently considered beneath them.

Even privately, Dantonio was prickly. At a Chicago steak house the night before that luncheon, the Wolverine contingent coincidentally got seated next to the Buckeye bunch. Jim Tressel could not have been more pleasant, and ditto actor Jamie Foxx, a true sports fan, who was sitting nearby and who engaged Rodriguez in a twenty-minute postdinner conversation. But earlier, when the Michigan folks first arrived, the Spartans brass was—amazingly—at a nearby table, and Dantonio wouldn't say two words.

On the day of the Notre Dame game, when Central scored a touchdown with thirty-two seconds left to close the gap to 26–27, the Michigan coaches had no trouble deciding which team to pull for.

"Gotta go for two!" Tony Dews said, to which new defensive coordinator Greg Robinson—the only other man in the room who'd been a head coach—quietly added, "Easy to say from here."

Central missed the two-point conversion but executed a perfect onside kick to set up a chance for a game-winning field goal.

In the Michigan locker room, the players had taken a knee by the door and wondered what was holding up their coaches.

"All that work we did, all winter, all summer, that's money in the bank," Brandon Graham said. "Well, this is where we *spend* all that money we saved up. Don't save a cent." Then he added, "Damn, this is the longest five minutes of my life!"

Back in the coaches' room, they had all gathered to watch Central's field goal attempt sail just wide. Game over.

But no. The referee called the Spartans for roughing the kicker. Central's do-over went straight between the uprights to seal the 29–27 upset.

"'Play up'?" Rodriguez asked, recalling Dantonio's rallying cry. Rodriguez stood and adjusted his cap. "Think you forgot Central, Coach!" He marched out of the room, already pumped up.

When the coaches finally emerged from their cave, they told the players, "State lost!"

There was something in the air that day.

When the two head coaches met at midfield before the game, the equally weary Weis shook Rodriguez's hand and said, "So, are we having fun yet?"

They both laughed, proving a maxim: Only head coaches can understand what head coaches go through.

"No kidding," Rodriguez said. "We're the mayors of the two drama capitals of the country."

Michigan mounted a 79-yard drive to open the scoring 7–0. After a Notre Dame field goal, Darryl Stonum caught the kickoff at the 6, then cut straight up the middle for a 94-yard return. A true gift for the Wolverines and a contrast to all the dropped kicks in South Bend a year earlier.

But Clausen engineered two touchdowns and a field goal to go ahead 20–14, outgaining Michigan 302 yards to 119.

"They're kicking the shit out of us!" Dusty Rutledge said on the sidelines. "I mean *physically*. We're working hard, but man, it's seniors versus sophomores out there."

On the final drive of the half, however, Michigan took over at its own 30-yard line, where Forcier hit Stonum for 24 yards and Denard Robinson ran for 14. On fourth-and-11, from Notre Dame's 37, Rodriguez decided to go for it. For all the storms he'd endured over the previous two years, his confidence was clearly intact.

Forcier rolled out, found Greg Mathews, and connected for a 15-yard play down to Notre Dame's 22-yard line. Jason Olesnavage lined up for a 39-yard attempt—and hit it, making the score 20–17 at the half.

"We are in *better* condition," Rodriguez told his team before the second half. "This is *our* half. We're gonna get the ball first, take it downfield, and *stuff* it down their throats! Every man, every play!"

"Time to beat these bastards!" Minor added.

When the third quarter ended, Michigan had a 24–20 lead, and had compiled 320 yards to Notre Dame's 329. They were battling the big boys. The team ran down the field, just like Rodriguez had been exhorting them to do for two years, but for the first time they seemed to do it with pleasure.

The Wolverines finished a 17–0 scoring streak to give them a 31–20 lead in the fourth quarter. It was time for Jimmy Clausen to show if he really was a Heisman candidate after all. He was, masterfully directing two long touchdown drives—picking on cornerback Boubacar Cissoko every chance he had—capped by a perfect Statue of Liberty play, to go ahead 34–31.

With 3:07 left, Notre Dame took over again on its own 16-yard line. Michigan's defense had to get a stop, and soon, or it would end there. Everyone on Michigan's sidelines stood up to cheer them on.

After gaining a quick first down, Weis inexplicably called for two consecutive pass plays, both incomplete, to set up a fourth-and-10. The man who once claimed his players would enjoy a "decisive schematic advantage" in every game they played was making the kinds of mistakes no self-respecting high school coach would commit.

Greg Robinson told his defense, "You guys stepped up *big-time* right there!"

Michigan got the ball back on its own 43-yard line with 2:13 left and two time-outs in its pocket. On first down, Forcier's quick toss to Greg Mathews gained 9 yards. It was especially gratifying for Rodriguez, because Mathews was one of the current players who had spoken to the media. He had been urged by Toney Clemons, who had transferred to Colorado, to join a three-way call with him and ESPN's Joe Schad. After the story broke, Mathews went directly to Rodriguez's office to confess and apologize. Rodriguez thanked him for his honesty and assured him all was forgiven.

On first-and-10 from Notre Dame's 28—within field goal range, on a good day—Forcier hit LaTerryal Savoy for 6 yards, but Savoy couldn't get out of bounds, forcing Michigan to spend its third and final time-out. Without Weis's help, that play probably would have marked the end of the game.

On the next play, Forcier scrambled back and forth with the Irish in hot pursuit. A sack that far back, with no time-outs, would either have put Michigan out of field goal range or out of time, or both. The coaches were unanimous: *"Throw it away! Throw it away!"*

But the confident freshman had other ideas. He eluded the tacklers and fired the ball on the run to Savoy on the left sideline. Savoy clamped it down and got out of bounds at the 5.

"That's one of those Tate plays," Rod Smith said, "where you say, 'No no no no no NO! *YES!*'"

At that point, down 34–31, some coaches might have lost their nerve and taken the field goal and the momentum into overtime. But not Rodriguez. On second down, Forcier rolled to his left, saw the recently repentant Mathews running right to left along the goal line with a defender right behind him, and threw the ball exactly where it needed to be so the defender couldn't touch it but Mathews could catch it in stride. Mathews made the catch and glided into the end zone.

His teammates mobbed him, the players on the sidelines leaped for joy, and, thanks to the skyboxes going up, the crowd's cheer might just have been the loudest noise ever heard in the Big House.

Forcier had covered 57 yards in nine plays in 2:02. The spread offense at its best.

Michigan had earned the 38–34 victory—and the respect of the college football world.

The student section was a sea of arms. The players jammed "number one" fingers into the air, with Rodriguez getting mobbed in the middle of it all. When he took the Michigan job, this is surely what he had in mind.

Back in the locker room, a few dignitaries gathered to greet them, including Rick Leach, Bill Dufek, Jamie Morris, LaMarr Woodley, and George Lilja. A few other alums, however, who had been suspected of feeding the *Free Press*, also lurked in the hallways, perhaps as cover. One insider asked, "Where will *those* guys be if we start losing?"

Rodriguez led the players in singing "The Victors" before telling them, "I'm damn proud of you men. *Damn* proud. But that's just one game on the road back to redemption. So remember, stay humble, and stay hungry."

"YES, SIR!"

"Here's a story worth writing," Rodriguez told the press afterward. "They have four five-star players on their team, and we've got Jordan Kovacs, who joined the team when school started. He tries out with the general student body in the spring, and here he is, playing safety against Notre Dame. To me, that's something special."

"Did you feel sorry for Charlie Weis and Notre Dame?"

Rodriguez smiled. "Do you think they'd feel sorry for us? Their linemen are so much bigger than ours, they could eat peanuts off our linemen's heads."

He added, reflexively, "The tradition of this program cannot be beat."

With the sun setting as they left the stadium, Rodriguez did not seek a bar or even a fancy Main Street restaurant, just the quiet of his home, family, and friends, a few pizzas, a couple cold ones—a Coke Zero, that is, and a bottled water—and the USC–Ohio State game on the kitchen TV. He sat watching on a stool, with a freshly socked foot on the counter.

"These two hours," he said, "are like gold. You don't have to think about the game you just played, and you don't have to worry about the one coming up next.

"You can watch some other poor bastard be miserable."

If the win over Western offered salvation, the upset of eighteenth-ranked Notre Dame sparked a celebration: The Wolverines were back.

The AP pollsters put them in the Top Twenty-five—just barely, at number twenty-five itself.

In his second college game, Tate Forcier created 310 yards of total offense, five touchdowns, and completed 6-for-7 passes on the final 55-yard drive. The Big Ten named him the Offensive Player of the Week.

ESPN's veteran college football writer Ivan Maisel wrote, "This was Michigan's answer to the charge that coach Rich Rodriguez wiped his feet on the 20-hour-per-week rule. This was the Wolverines' reply to former teammate Justin Boren, the offensive lineman who transferred to Ohio State, and all the other players and onlookers who believe that Rodriguez is turning Michigan into something it isn't . . . With a freshman quarterback too goofy to be nervous, and a few well-placed seniors throughout the lineup, Michigan stunned No. 18 Notre Dame 38–34 in one of the most exciting games ever played in one of the sport's great rivalries."

Jamie Foxx, Rodriguez's new friend from the Chicago steak house, sent him a text via the Adidas rep: "Tell coach congrats on the win."

The Wolverines had taken two big steps back to respectability, but they were still a young team—for the second year in a row, they had only fourteen scholarship seniors—and more prone than most to getting too high or too low. It would be too easy, Rodriguez knew, for his impressionable players to believe their clippings, get big heads, and look past their lowly cross-county competition, the Eastern Michigan Eagles, who reside just a few miles down Washtenaw Avenue but a lot farther down the rankings. *Sports Illustrated* put them at 114 out of 120 in its preseason listing.

That would be a big mistake. The Eagles had just lost a close one 27–24 at Northwestern, a team that had won four of the last twelve games against Michigan. Further, EMU was coached by Ron English, Carr's defensive coordinator in 2006 and 2007, who had applied to succeed him.

For those given to conspiracy theories—and, thanks to the *Free Press* report, there were growing numbers of them in the department—this game marked the highlight of the season. Many of these detectives traced a link from English to Jim Stapleton, a Michigan alum and EMU trustee who made his living making business deals. Stapleton is also a public figure who often writes editorials for regional publications. In them, he frequently mentions his status as a former student athlete at Michigan. Although Stapleton was also a private critic of Martin's and a public friend of Rosenberg's, just about everything beyond that was subject to conjecture and rumor.

But, in many ways, it would have been much better for Rodriguez and his program if someone actually had proof of sabotage, which they could then address directly. Instead, Rodriguez had to work under a cloud of suspicion—about which he could do almost nothing. But he knew that if they lost this game, that cloud would produce a severe storm.

In front of his team, Rodriguez never mentioned any of their detractors by name or spelled out what they were doing, instead referring to them collectively as "cockroaches." Because, he explained, they were cowards who came out only when it was dark. But when the lights were on, they scurried for cover. And the best way to keep the lights on, of course, was to win football games.

"Now, can you hear that?" Rodriguez put his hand to his ear, from the podium of the team room before Monday's practice. He had a mischievous grin. "Know what that is? That's all them cockroaches . . . *silenced*. Two weeks ago all those cockroaches were sniping at us, talking behind our backs about how bad you are and how bad your coaches are and all this doom and gloom.

"Now, I've got my piss a little hot for the folks right across the street at EMU. I know you know some of their players and some of their coaches. But some of those coaches were across the street talking trash about our team, our coaches, and what's going on at Schembechler Hall.

"Now, I'll play nice, but on Saturday they better know: If you want to talk trash about this program, you better show up and back it up. Because your ass is coming to the Big House. And that's *our* house."

He paused to gaze about the room, making eye contact with the players, left to right. They were leaning forward, alert and alive.

"I can see you're hungry. Big-time. And if you ain't hungry I'm gonna starve your ass the rest of the week!"

That got a good laugh.

"Like I said, you got your respect back, but just as fast as you got it back, you can lose it. If you run down that tunnel like you did last week— boy, those guys across the street are in for something. And I can't wait.

"The cockroaches are out there, men, but we ain't gonna let 'em get to us. Keep working, stick together, and we're gonna keep the lights on."

The coaches had shielded their players from a lot of the stirrings outside Schembechler Hall, but the players spent far more time online than their coaches did, and unlike their coaches, who simply drove from home to Schembechler Hall and back every day, the players were on campus and around town, talking to classmates, dealing with the public. They knew what the buzz was.

At the team dinner that night, receiver LaTerryal Savoy, a kind and thoughtful young man, said, "It was just crazy to hear the stuff that was going on," referring to the *Free Press*. "Took me by surprise, because we're playing by the rules."

Sophomore center David Molk picked up where Savoy left off. "All the shady characters are gone," he said, plowing into his dinner. "Mass extermination. It's weird how close we are as a team now, almost eerie. No outsiders. No cliques. Everyone's in sync."

"I think in the next couple years they're going to win a national championship," Moosman concluded. "And if Molk doesn't," he said, nodding to his dinner partner, "I'm going to kick his ass."

It was a week to savor. Or it would have been, if the school wasn't Michigan, and the coach wasn't Rich Rodriguez.

In the second quarter of the Irish game, Notre Dame's Eric Olsen had knocked Jonas Mouton down with a clean hit, then leaned over him to rub it in after the play had ended. Mouton responded by shoving the heel of his right hand against Olsen's chin and face mask. The referee saw the entire exchange and told both players to settle down, which seemed about right. It was, in short, nothing.

But Weis had apparently complained to the press and Big Ten commissioner Jim Delany. By Thursday, right before practice, Delany's office let Rodriguez know they would be imposing some form of disciplinary action against Mouton. They didn't say what, but if they ruled for a game suspension, it was too late to prepare to start someone else. Mouton had been practicing on the first team all week.

"You lost to a bunch of freshmen, Charlie," Rodriguez said to his assistants over dinner. "Just admit it! Instead of crying about some nonpunch."

The next day Rodriguez woke up to find still more bad news on his doorstep: the *Detroit News*, this time, printed its own front-page story, whose headline U-M COACHES BORROWED FROM ATHLETIC DIRECTOR'S BANK ran over a large color photo of Rodriguez's home.

"Michigan football coach Rich Rodriguez and seven of his assistants have received $3.3 million in mortgages and lines of credit from the bank founded by U-M athletic director Bill Martin, records show.

"The disclosures raise questions about whether Martin can be objective about the coaches' performance at U-M when their dismissal could affect their ability to repay the bank."

Martin, with his tin ear for public relations, made matters worse when he told the paper, "'Now that I know, I don't like it necessarily,' he said. 'When you don't know, you don't have a conflict.'"

The *Detroit News* reporters did a good job looking at all sides of the story, however. They sought out a "recognized expert on conflicts of interest" at Carnegie Mellon University, who said, "In the scheme of conflicts of interest, this doesn't seem that major."

Nonetheless, it was another front-page story calling Rodriguez's integrity into question, and it reinforced the sense that he and his staff were under siege and that nothing was off-limits.

It was certainly feasible that everybody within the department was "all in," and the local media was simply on an enterprising streak. But on a deeper level, it really didn't matter if anyone was leaking to the press or not. The mere possibility made everyone a suspect and got everyone in the department gossiping about who the leakers might be—and that's enough to break down the bonds of trust that keep any organization healthy and disease-free. The endless stories sorely tested the immune system of the athletic department.

The banking story might not have been the worst news of the day.

A little after lunchtime that Friday, Rodriguez got word that the Big Ten was going to suspend Mouton for one game—the next day's—so Rodriguez called Delany.

"You're caving to the press," Rodriguez told him.

"No, no, this has got nothing to do with that. We just need to do what's right for the league."

"What's right for the league? When Joe Tiller called me a snake-oil salesman, I don't recall you rushing to protect the league's honor then."

Then Rodriguez lit the fuse on a little bomb that would blow up later. "And I'll tell you something else: I'm going to be watching every Big Ten game from now on, and the next time I see a six-inch jab, you're going to hear about it.'"

In another context, from another man, such a statement would be taken for what it was: an idle threat from an aggrieved coach just blowing off steam. But from Rich Rodriguez in 2009, it would have repercussions.

It was the head coach's job to defend his players, his team, and his program. But when Rodriguez did it, he struck some as petulant, defensive, or just plain passing the buck. But if he didn't take a stand, who would?

Countless Michigan veterans told me that if Canham were still the AD, there would never have been a *Free Press* feature, an NCAA investigation, or even a Big Ten suspension for Mouton. Any internal saboteurs would know they would be discovered and fired, and the NCAA and Big Ten would trust Canham to handle his department himself. He would call them, tell them the situation, and assure them he had it under control. And the media loved him—a relationship lubricated by his famous Friday night pregame parties at his company's office down on State Street.

Martin did not know how to intervene on behalf of his coach, instead emitting gaffes about how, if they went 3–9 again, he and Rodriguez would be posting For Sale signs in their lawns—just the kind of statement opposing coaches loved to use against Michigan in recruiting.

The power vacuum was filled by the university's lawyers and public relations people. They almost always advised Rodriguez to keep quiet and let them handle it. Which, all too often, was tantamount to advising him to disregard the fact that someone was pissing on his leg. Among the lessons Rodriguez had taken with him from Grant Town, following such advice wasn't among them. But out of respect for Michigan, he usually went along—and just as often regretted it.

Rodriguez knew he would have to tell Mouton that night that he would not be playing against Eastern, and he also knew Mouton's mom had already bought a plane ticket to watch him play.

Rodriguez put his feet on his desk, waved the air, and concluded, "Shit."

In the locker room before the game, Dan Ewald relaxed outside Big Jon Falk's stadium equipment room. Ewald is a well-respected, mild-mannered former Detroit newspaper writer turned Detroit Tigers public relations man turned author, who cowrote one of Schembechler's books, *Michigan Memories*, and was working with Falk on his memoirs. "In all my years," he said, "I have never seen anything in the Michigan media like what's been going on the last year. There were so many holes in [the *Free Press*'s] piece, I'm surprised it could hold ink.

"You have to wonder if there's an agenda there for all this to happen."

The theme continued up in the press box, where Bruce Madej pulled me into a little-known utility room filled with ladders and pipes. He clearly had something he wanted to get off his chest but couldn't say publicly. "I've never seen anything like this," he told me, marking the third time that day I'd heard someone express that thought. "I've never seen such a good guy take so much shit. And it's *endless*.

"The Mouton shit—Jesus! How does Weis get to override the Big Ten refs? They saw the play and they were right on it. And if you look at the film you'll see a Notre Dame guy slug one of our guys in the groin on the same play!

"And the bank story? Jesus! How does a reporter come up with *that* one? I've got university officials calling me up: 'Why don't you tell us this stuff before it hits the papers?' Because we didn't know! Who would?

"This whole thing makes me sick."

The "Battle for Washtenaw County" didn't matter to anyone who couldn't find Washtenaw Avenue, but insiders knew the stakes.

After Michigan opened the scoring with a field goal, Eastern came right back with a 49-yard drive—occasionally picking on Cissoko, which suggested they had studied the Notre Dame game carefully—that ended in its own field goal to tie the game.

Michigan countered with an impressive 60-yard drive, capped by Carlos Brown's 9-yard touchdown run. 10–3 Michigan. But once again, Eastern fought back with a similar drive and tied the game at 10–10. Forcier's offense countered with another strong touchdown drive: 17–10.

"We want respect, we've gotta go get it," Van Bergen told his teammates.

"The offense is doing their job," Stevie Brown said. "We gotta go do ours!"

"C'mon, D!" Kevin Grady told the defense as they were taking the field. "Look at the scoreboard! Let's knock 'em out."

They did as Grady commanded, stuffing the Eagles and giving the offense the ball back on their own 10-yard line. On the first play, Carlos Brown cut straight up the middle, virtually untouched, and busted 90 yards to the end zone.

With Michigan up 24–10, it looked as though the Wolverines were poised to deliver the knockout punch. But when Denard Robinson took over, he threw an interception that the Eagles converted to a touchdown two minutes later to close the gap to 24–17—burning Cissoko once again—and that's how the half ended.

If it wasn't for Brown's 90-yard run, the game would have been tied.

The fans hanging over the tunnel didn't seem to care.

"You get 'em, Blue!"

"You guys are playin' great!"

The players knew better. Not one of them returned the high-fives.

If ever there was a good opportunity for this team to panic, this was it. Back in the locker room, Brandon Graham summed it up best: "Ain't got no swagger. Nothin'!"

The coaches didn't need to be reminded how costly a loss to Ron English could be. When Rodriguez addressed the team, it was clear his goal was to avoid worrying his players at all costs.

"We're all right. Don't hang your heads. Let's have a little fun out there!"

On second-and-goal from Eastern's 13, Forcier gave the ball to Tay Odoms on a reverse. He made a great cut and trotted into the end zone to give Michigan a 31–17 lead. It also marked Odoms's first touchdown from scrimmage, elevating his nickname from State Street, where he excelled in practice, to Main Street, where they played their games.

On Eastern's next possession, the Eagles faced a third-and-6 from their 23-yard line when Andy Schmitt's pass was tipped by Obi Ezeh and landed, quite by accident, in Craig Roh's outstretched hand.

"I didn't even realize I had it until 'Whoa, what's this?'" he said later. That didn't stop the freshman from starting a rather spastic dance, for which he was roundly razzed in Monday's film session.

Three plays later, Denard Robinson ran up the middle for Michigan's second touchdown in a little over three minutes.

Michigan 38, EMU 17. The game was finally out of reach, the danger passed. The game would end 45–17, with Eastern shut out the second half. There were no moral victories here, and nothing for English or anyone else to hang their hats on.

After the game, Rodriguez found English. "He shook my hand but didn't say anything. Man, that's low."

But three weeks into the season, the overriding fact was the Wolverines had three wins, no losses. Rodriguez soon found out, however, that he had no center, either.

"They say my best lineman is out," he said in the coaches' room, referring to David Molk, who not only didn't miss a single game as a sophomore, he did not miss a single *play*. What knocked out this iron man was not some bruising defensive lineman or a concussion or even a twisted knee. Sometime in the second quarter, Molk simply planted his left foot to block his man—and that was enough to snap the fifth metatarsal.

He told trainer Paul Schmidt, "Something popped," but he was walking fine, so he went back in, played, and played well. Everyone figured he was okay. He wasn't.

"He'll be out only three to four weeks," Rodriguez said, taking off his coaching clothes. "That's the good news. The bad news is, he'll miss our first three Big Ten games—Indiana, Michigan State, Iowa, and maybe Penn State, too. And his backup's out, too," referring to guard David Moosman and his chronically screwed-up shoulder.

"Right now, we've got two seniors on defense and four seniors on offense. We don't have a lot to spare."

When Rodriguez walked into the coaches' meeting the following Sunday, you would not have guessed he was coaching an undefeated team. Head coaches at this level are not in the business of kidding themselves. They hadn't played very well, they weren't healthy, and harder games were ahead.

Paul Schmidt started the injury report with center David Molk: Surgery Monday, out four to six weeks, twice as long as hoped. "Might be back a little sooner, due to his position and toughness." Rodriguez growled, but there was nothing he could do. In some ways, Schmidt was the most powerful person on the staff. He was the only person no one ever questioned.

Schmidt continued. Forcier had a bruised rib, cornerback Donovan Warren had a sore ankle, and tailback Brandon Minor was just plain beat-up. But David Moosman would return and fill in for Molk at center.

"Game evaluations," Rodriguez said. "Quarterbacks."

"Tate," Rod Smith started. "I wasn't too pleased with some of his decisions. Not looking very sharp.

"Denard played thirteen snaps. His reads were not very good at all."

On defense, Cissoko had bombed again. "He used to be aggressive," Rodriguez said. He acknowledged Cissoko had been injured, but he was fine now and had not returned to form. "I need to talk to him and tell him, 'You're just embarrassing yourself.'"

After they finished giving every player who saw the field a grade, Rodriguez said, "We have to understand who we are. We are an undersized team that runs well and usually plays hard, but if we're not good fundamentally, we're in trouble."

What he didn't have to tell those assembled was that if they suffered too many injuries, they'd be in more trouble.

One of the support staffers mentioned that Michigan was ranked twenty-two in the *USA Today* poll and twenty-three in the AP poll, but that barely got a grunt out of the coaches present. The polls mattered to them only when they were recruiting, or when bowl invitations were at stake. Still, it must have been a bit reassuring to this beleaguered bunch to see Penn State ranked fifth, Ohio State thirteenth, and Michigan twenty-third—the usual Big Ten teams all in the Top Twenty-five, just like old times.

Or more like it, anyway. A decade earlier, as many as nine Big Ten teams would pop up into the Top Twenty-five at some point during the season, and seven could be listed at once until conference play started, when the Big Ten began eating its own. With Michigan's 1997 national title and Ohio State's 2002–03 crown, and a handful of BCS bowl wins in between, for a while the Big Ten had been on par with the SEC and ahead of just about every other conference in the country.

But the new millennium had not been kind to the nation's first athletic conference. Since Ohio State upset Miami in the 2003 Fiesta Bowl, Big Ten teams had been invited to fifteen BCS bowls and won only six. If you took out the Buckeyes' seven invitations, the rest of the Big Ten's record falls to an anemic 2–6, with all six losses suffered in the Rose Bowl, just barely ahead of the ACC's 2–7 record and far behind the Big 12's, the Pac-10's, and especially the SEC's mark, which was 10–3 over that same span.

How bad were the last eight years for the Big Ten? If you replaced all eleven conference teams with just Boise State, Utah, and West Virginia, you'd be 6–0 in BCS bowl games, not 6–9.

What do almost all those title teams since Ohio State have in common? The spread offense.

"The hardest thing to do in football is tackle in space," Rodriguez explained. "The spread is designed to make you do exactly that. If you see your opponent tackle in space consistently, you're in for a long day. But if not, you're in for a good day—and not many teams can do that all day long.

"The hardest thing to find in the Big Ten is a fast defensive lineman. You see plenty of those in the SEC. Down there, those guys were tailbacks in Pop Warner, and they just grew up. When they do, you've got a first-class D-lineman: fast *and* big. To pull them out of their backyard, you need to sell them on academics here or a connection you might have. It's not easy for us."

Nor for the rest of the league, apparently.

Rodriguez was worried about the future, but the players were enjoying the present. "We're getting a lot more questions this year," Van Bergen said about his classmates over Sunday pizza. "This year, you're a status improver. They not only want to see you, they want to be seen *with* you."

Mark Huyge laughed at that. "Not on North Campus, man." Huyge was enrolled in naval architecture and marine engineering, whose classes were a ten-minute bus ride from Central Campus, along with the art, architecture, and music students—an odd mix if ever there was one. "I don't think people up there even know what football is. The professors *definitely* have no idea."

"Yeah, well, that's better than having them hating on you," Van Bergen said.

For Patrick Omameh, a 6'4", 299-pound redshirt freshman lineman with a 3.7 GPA, anonymity was the ideal. "I never wear my letter jacket," he said. "I don't want anyone to know I'm a football player. And I can usually pull it off."

"I just want to be there to *learn*, man," Martin said. "I don't like people knowing who I am. I get sick of it."

"I don't like people knowing I'm a football player," Van Bergen said. "I'm less likely to speak up. Because if I get one wrong, it's not just wrong, you're a dumb football player."

"Exactly, man," Martin said. "That's *exactly* it."

When they started clearing their trays, Van Bergen summed it up: "It's all kinda cool, but we haven't really been tested. I don't even know how good Notre Dame is. Michigan State should have beaten them yesterday. Apparently anyone can beat anyone. Look at USC losing to Stanford. You can't look past anyone.

"We're 3–0 in nonconference, but we're still winless in the Big Ten. I think Indiana will be a good test, especially with all the injuries we have."

At the Monday afternoon team meeting, Rodriguez announced that Carlos Brown had won Offensive Player of the Week, not only for Michigan, but also for the Big Ten, following in Forcier's footsteps.

"This other guy had an outstanding game and we didn't realize he had a bad foot, David Molk.

"Defensive Player of the Week goes to a young guy, a freshman, who plays hard every play, and he had a big sack and a *surprising* interception! Craig Roh!

"We had these T-shirts made up a year ago but they've been in mothballs, so it's good to pass them out: Our offense, for the first time, had six scoring drives. Go Offense!"

They passed out blue T-shirts with OFFENSE on the back.

"The goal on defense is six three-and-outs, and we had seven! Go Defense!" Their T-shirts had 3 AND OUT on the back.

They weren't fancy, they weren't expensive, and they probably wouldn't mean anything to people on campus. But before the week was out, just about every player could be seen wearing his new shirt at dinner.

Before the first Big Ten game against Indiana arrived, Rodriguez would have to wade through more muck—some of it silly, some of it serious.

Sure enough, Rodriguez's offhand comment a week earlier to Delany came back to bite him in the backside. Purdue offensive lineman Zach Reckman hit a Northern Illinois player after the whistle. Someone sent the tape to the Big Ten, which gave Reckman a game suspension—same as Mouton—prompting Rodriguez to call Purdue coach Danny Hope directly. "He blamed me for it. I said I had nothing to do with it. That was Jim Delany's decision. I never sent anyone any tape. We've got other things to worry about around here!"

This is probably as good a place as any to say that, in my three years watching Rodriguez at close range, not once did I catch him in a lie. From everything I've gathered, he told me the truth every time—even when it was not flattering, including his description of his conversation with Delany the previous week. And, as it turned out, I learned later from Adam Rittenberg's column on ESPN.com that the person who sent the tape to the Big Ten was someone at Purdue.

Despite the drama surrounding the program, the town was abuzz with the resurgent Wolverines. Outside Moe's Sport Shop, which had been selling Michigan gear next to the Diag since 1915, the sandwich board announced:

WOLVERINES ARE 3–0!
FOOTBALL'S BACK!

On a Michigan football website, someone posted a photo of a proudly overweight tailgater wearing a too-tight blue T-shirt spanning his gut that said, ROSENBERG SAYS I WORK OUT TOO MUCH.

But inside Fort Schembechler, no one was taking the *Free Press* story lightly—even if they found it absurd—because it had sparked an investigation by Michigan, and finally the NCAA. For its part, the *Free Press* was not backing off, filing FOIA requests for everything short of used Kleenex, and printing a front-page defense of the piece a week later from publisher Paul Anger himself.

With the launch of the NCAA investigation, a public relations headache grew into an impediment to Rodriguez's core job of coaching players and winning games. Investigators started pulling Rodriguez, his coaches, staffers, and players out of meetings, practice, and even class the coming week and especially the next, leading up to the Michigan State game.

In public, Rodriguez repeatedly claimed the *Free Press* story and its endless ripples had no impact on him or his team. Of course, he had to say that, and he had to believe it, too, or else his players never would. But watching it all unfold from within, it wasn't true, which in Rodriguez's private moments he conceded. "The bottom line is, all it's doing is hindering us from coaching and helping these kids. They're the ones who suffer. We're not giving them our undivided attention like we should be.

"All I want is for everyone to get the hell out of our way and let us coach, and do it the right way." But once the NCAA investigation started, Rodriguez would not get his wish.

On Friday morning, September, 25, 2009, Bill Martin, Lloyd Carr, and Rich Rodriguez all received a four-page, single-spaced fax from the desk of James F. Stapleton.

> Dear Bill,
>   After a good deal of thought and (above all) out of love for a school and Athletic Department that has meant the world to me for as long as I can remember, I write on this occasion to address an astonishing level of lunacy associated with rumors involving you, Coach Carr, me, Coach Rodriguez and Mike Rosenberg.

Among other things, Stapleton sought to explain why he met Rosenberg at the Chop House the night before Michigan's season opener, five days after the big story came out. "Rosenberg has been a friend of mine for years," Stapleton wrote, though he added that he often disagreed with his stories and had "serious issues with this latest story on our Program, including its timing and true motives (which was the purpose of our meeting, since I was, as you know . . . at my home in Scottsdale when the story broke) . . ."

The rumors of his collaboration with Rosenberg had hit the blogs, he said, and he wanted to clear the air. "In recent days," he continued, addressing Martin, "as this nonsense has continued, it has come to my attention from people whose credibility I trust that they had heard you or a person in the Department were behind the spreading of a story that Coach Carr and I were trying to ruin the Football Program. Me, I am told, because of my relationship with Rosenberg, and Coach Carr because of his alleged disdain for Coach Rodriguez."

Stapleton then defended himself, listing the times he had helped Martin by publicly supporting the plan to build stadium suites, by addressing Jim Harbaugh's attack on Michigan's bachelor of general studies degree (which Stapleton holds), and by speaking out in Martin's defense, too, when he had been attacked.

> I make no apologies for loving Michigan Football and offering to support Coach Rodriguez in any way I can . . .
>
> I also make no apologies for being a friend and confidant of Coach Carr, who I have known personally for over a decade and admire like few people I know . . . I make no apologies for using my influence, expertise, network and stature as a Regent to facilitate an improvement in the Football Program at Eastern Michigan University that led to its hiring of Ron English.

He closed by telling Martin, "You are the titular head of the Michigan Athletic Family. And, it is a family that desperately needs healing within its most important unit. This has gone on long enough. I stand ready to do my part if asked but, all of us need to follow your lead."

The letter was notable as much for what it said as for the author's apparent need to say it. Rodriguez wisely let it pass without comment—but he didn't forget it.

Rodriguez met briefly with the team, as he always does on Friday afternoons, wearing his jacket and tie. They had a homecoming pep rally scheduled at 4:30 at Crisler Arena, but because it was so far from campus, with most students and alums deep in happy hour, they expected fewer than a hundred people. But when they walked down the tunnel at Crisler, they heard the band kick into "The Victors" and an estimated one thousand fans break into a now familiar chant, "Rich Rod-ri-guez!"

"I want to thank you for your support," he told them, "not just in the last three weeks, but in the last twenty months. What your support has meant to me and my family, I cannot put into words.

"I can assure you, our guys are 'all in' for Michigan! We have the best atmosphere in the country. We've got the best HOUSE in the country. And we've got the best university in the world!" Cheers followed each sentence.

"Doesn't matter what the outside world says, so long as the Michigan Nation knows who we are and what we stand for.

"GO BLUE!"

Later that night, while the players watched their movie, Magee and offensive line coach Greg Frey were hunkered down as usual, watching TV.

"Wait till we get this thing going," said Magee, the optimist.

"If they let us," said Frey, the pessimist. "If they let us."

"I know how badly you want those Big Ten title rings," Rodriguez told his team before releasing them down the tunnel. "Well, it starts right here."

The Hoosiers weren't scared. On two of the their first three plays, they went right at Boubacar Cissoko—the Notre Dame tape was apparently getting around—and took the early lead 7–0.

Greg Robinson pulled out his whiteboard, but Cissoko was off on his own, fifteen feet outside the semicircle. "Boubacar! Get your ass over here!" Cissoko slumped over to the huddle, in full resentment. They were losing him.

After Michigan went up 14–7, Indiana came right back with a deep pass, once again burning Cissoko, to set up a tying touchdown: 14–14.

"Two-minute drill!" Brandon Graham yelled. Then, seeing Cissoko sulking, he said, "Don't make that face! Don't let that shit get to you!"

After Michigan's defense stuffed the Hoosiers, they returned to a sideline celebration—but Cissoko, who had been pulled for freshman J. T. Floyd, was having none of it. He had dropped his helmet and sat far away.

At halftime, Rodriguez worked furiously at his desk.

"Let's simplify the playbook," Magee said, "and get Tate on a roll."

"He ain't *seeing* it!" Rodriguez countered. "He's not staying in the pocket. He's leaving too soon."

For a quarterback to play the position properly, he needs to sense when the 280-pound linemen who want to break his back are coming after him like enraged bulls—and then *ignore them*, focus completely on his receivers, and commit to a perfect delivery. The proper follow-through will leave him exposed, of course—which is exactly what defensive linemen dream about all winter when they're pushing the big weights: the chance to knock a quarterback ten yards into Tuesday.

That's why coaches have a special regard for those quarterbacks who can ignore the rush to finish the job. A quarterback can have everything else going for him, but if he doesn't have the guts to stand in the pocket, make the throw, and take the hit, he will never be great. Tate was good, and getting better—but he was not yet great.

In the second half, Mouton made hit after hit, tackle after tackle, extracting a few installments on his pledge to "make Indiana pay" for him having to sit out the Eastern game.

The Hoosiers kicked another field goal to lead 26–21, but Michigan's defense was not breaking.

On third-and-4 from Indiana's seven, Forcier faked the handoff, rolled out, and made a mad dash for the right corner. The Hoosier defenders met him at the goal line. Forcier jumped in the air, broke the plane—and smashed his shoulder.

Ahead 27–26, Rodriguez decided to go for two. A false start put them back on the eight, but Rodriguez didn't flinch. Forcier bravely dashed up the middle, his path cleared by tiny Tay Odoms.

Indiana's Darius Willis countered by turning a simple running play into an 85-yard touchdown, giving Indiana a 33–29 lead, and two records: its longest run since 1977, and the most points against Michigan . . . ever.

Michigan got the ball back with 5:36 left, 52 yards and 4 points to go. The crowd sent Forcier and his teammates out to battle with a standing ovation. Perhaps figuring Forcier had only so many throws left in his shoulder, the coaches went for the whole enchilada. The Hoosiers blitzed, but Forcier was "seeing it." He ignored the rush and found Odoms wide open. But thanks to his shoulder, he had to sling the ball almost sidearm. Odoms had to slow down for the ball, but it slipped just past the defender's fingertips, into Odoms's soft hands.

Touchdown. Michigan, 36–33, with 2:29 left.

On Indiana's first play, Donovan Warren simply wrestled the ball from Ben Chappell's intended receiver—and the Big House boomed.

After three kneel-downs—"the best play in football," Rodriguez liked to say—Michigan had sealed its fourth straight victory of the season.

The student section belted its now familiar chant: "Rich Rod-ri-guez!" The team sang "The Victors" with the students, then they ran, not walked, up the tunnel, where they were met by Jon Falk: "The ring dream is still alive!"

Back in the locker room, a new chant went up from the players: "Keep the lights on! Keep the lights on!"

"Now, we know we've got to play a lot better than that," Rodriguez said, "because you know who we have next!"

They knew.

"Ohhh, yeah!"

"Bring 'em on!"

"C'mon, Sparty! Let's see whatcha got!"

Local sports radio host Steve Clark said, "Rich Rod said you can't play poorly and beat Indiana? Yes, you can!"

"I'd rather win ugly," Rodriguez told the press, "than lose pretty." When every game is practically a playoff game, it's a rational perspective.

When he returned to the coaches' room for his shower, he was clearly in a good mood—they were learning how to win close—until he saw Bruce Madej.

He was there to chat not about the game, or even the investigation, but about the *Free Press*'s latest FOIA to look into Rodriguez's claim that the team had just achieved the highest grade point average.

"What's the problem?" Rodriguez asked, untying his shoes. "We got the numbers from the academic people."

Rodriguez was not reassured to learn the people on the Hill had taken over this task, too. When that happened, Rodriguez's distractions tended to breed more distractions.

The Wolverines were 4–0, and 1–0 in the Big Ten. And, except for David Molk, no starters were expected to be out of the lineup the next week.

But cracks were visible: a defensive backfield that was still unsettled a third of the way into the season; injuries to a dozen players, including both starting tailbacks, Carlos Brown and Brandon Minor; and a freshman quarterback, now among the injured, who freelanced too often, from his sloppy three-to-five-step drop to his panicked checkoffs to his inconsistent throwing form.

On the outside, Michigan looked good to go, but Rodriguez knew his problems were piling up—along with the pressure.

"Tate Forcier," Rod Smith said, starting the grading. "In the first half especially, his eyes and feet were everywhere. We've got to get that fixed. Fourteen loafs, ten MAs. He didn't play very well, not compared to what he can do."

Tony Gibson gave the rundown on the defensive backs. "Boubacar played eighteen snaps and gave up 14 points. Same old shit. Just killing us." In his estimation, walk-on Jordan Kovacs was playing better than the former five-star recruit. Much better.

"They've all tried to support him and rally around him," Greg Robinson said of Cissoko's teammates. "But nobody wants him around anymore."

"If he's pouting," Rodriguez said, "but he's still doing what he's supposed to be doing, don't give up on him. Keep coachin' 'em up."

He then shifted to a frank evaluation. "Our offense is screwing around too much. Fourteen knockdowns is a joke. We're not intense enough. Our concentration's not there.

"On defense, we looked confused at times. They got us with some hidden formations, but we're still too passive. Too often we'll let them catch it and run 10 yards before we close the gap. We're playing hard but not with enough intensity on every play. We're not even breaking on the ball consistently."

It was their job to solve those problems. They got the first step right: an objective assessment of the cold, hard facts.

By 12:47, it was time to put the last game behind them and focus only on the Spartans for six days. Well, almost. Before the staff broke into their groups, Rodriguez asked Brad Labadie, "Do we have the data on the GPA—the 2.61, best in twenty years?"

"We don't have that," he said, "but we have the data for the last few years."

"We asked the academic center for that," Rodriguez said. "That's where we got the information in the first place."

"Those figures were for full years," Labadie said. "We don't have it broken down by semester."

"Well, I've been bragging about it for three or four months, and not just because of that *Free Press* article. I don't want to look stupid on something I was told by the academic center was true."

Labadie promised he would check, which brought Rodriguez to the next problem on his agenda: The NCAA investigators had scheduled meetings with dozens of coaches, staffers, and players the coming week—while Rodriguez would be trying to get his team ready for revenge against the 1–3 Spartans. They would be conducting closed practices for the first time in his tenure at Michigan, in the hopes of minimizing distractions.

Rodriguez wanted to know who decided who gets sideline passes. "Seems like anyone in the country can get on our sidelines," he said. "To me it ain't a big deal, but if someone has not been the best to our program, like Jim Stapleton, then why do we need to give them a sideline pass? What do we owe those guys? Can you look into that?"

"Yes, I can," Draper said, writing it down.

"He gets his pass from Denise Ilitch," Dusty Rutledge said. "She's a regent."

Denise Ilitch's parents founded Little Caesar's Pizza and own the Detroit Red Wings and the Detroit Tigers. They had earned great respect for their business savvy and civic pride. Denise had been elected a regent in

2008, with Stapleton serving as her campaign manager. After the 2009 season, she was one of several regents pressing to fire Rodriguez, but President Coleman insisted on giving him another year. So the normally discreet Ilitch, along with a few other regents, often referred to Rodriguez as "Dead Man Walking." Rodriguez couldn't do much about that, of course, but he hoped to do something about Stapleton's sideline pass.

"I don't care," Rodriguez said, declaring himself in a way he could not have without a 4–0 record. He never discussed Stapleton's fax, but it had apparently not assuaged his concerns the way Stapleton had hoped. "When regents are giving out passes to people who aren't supporting us, I've got a problem. That stadium is my office. That's where we do our work. If you're against me or my coaches or my players, you can buy a ticket just like anyone else, and you can scream at me all day long for all I care, just so long as you're not doing any of that shit on my sidelines or in my building."

If Rodriguez was so intent on reducing distractions, bringing this up in front of his staff might seem counterproductive. Of course, it was convenient, with Labadie and Draper right there, but more likely Rodriguez needed to vent his spleen, put those two on notice, and let his coaches see he was fighting back. It was another distraction, but it was almost certainly a calculated one, designed to reduce distractions in the future.

It's a safe bet, however, that if Canham were still the athletic director, the head football coach would not have to worry about who was getting sideline passes. "When I was standing in the tunnel at Crisler [Arena] and there was a dirty agent standing four feet behind me," he told me, "I could *smell* him—and he was gone." This is the essential piece Michigan lost when it hired five straight athletic directors without any experience coaching or administering college athletics: knowing what to look for and keeping the department safe.

Rodriguez paused to take the measure of the room. "Right now the lights are on, so the cockroaches are hiding a little bit. But they're still there, and I don't want you guys to get caught in the middle of it, so let's close this circle.

"This week, I've got to deal with some more bullshit with this investigation, during State week of all weeks, and I just want them to let us coach. I've been saying that for twenty months: Just let me do my job."

Rodriguez paused again, separating the drama around them from the work in front of them. They would not discuss the former again the rest of the day.

"Okay, let's watch the special teams."

The lights went out, the screen came on, and the coaches, once again, settled in to do what they liked doing best: preparing their team.

An hour later, the door cracked open. Bruce Tall poked his head in and said, "He's here, Coach."

Much to Rodriguez's relief, Tall was referring not to the Compliance people or the NCAA investigators but to Will Hagerup, younger brother of Chris, who had punted for Indiana the day before. Will was ESPN's third-ranked punting prospect. Rodriguez left the room.

Zoltan Mesko, who had had only two punts returned in the first four games, had worked hard to recruit Hagerup. "He liked the B-school, way into that," said Mesko, who got his BBA before pursuing his master's in sports management. "So I said, 'If that's your thing, why wouldn't you go to a top ten B-school? And you don't want to miss out on the Big Ten championships to come.' That pretty much did it."

Fifteen minutes later, the door opened. "Hey, we found our punter!" Rodriguez announced. "Gentlemen, please meet Will Hagerup, future Wolverine!"

Hagerup's commitment gave Michigan nineteen for the recruiting class of 2010. For a team that had gone 3–9, breaking almost every school record in the wrong direction and having an NCAA investigation hanging over its head, it was an impressive effort.

For all the obstacles, Rodriguez knew that if his team kept winning and recruiting, his problems would eventually fade away, along with his critics.

In Schembechler's day, the players would hit on Tuesdays and Wednesdays—"full line," as they called it, twenty plays a day, and more if he felt they needed it. But since scholarships were capped at 125, then reduced to 85, few coaches felt like risking injury that often. They hit only on Tuesdays—and even then quarterbacks were off-limits, no one left his feet, and once you got close enough to tackle the ball carrier downfield, the whistle blew and he was "down." Even so, most coaches considered Tuesday the most important day of practice.

On Tuesday, September 29, 2009, with Michigan State looming, Rodriguez watched dozens of coaches and players go in and out all day to talk with the NCAA investigators. And then, during practice, he noticed a cabal of university administrators collect on the sidelines. He'd coached only sixteen games at Michigan, but he already knew that was never a good sign.

His instincts were correct. Before and after dinner, Rodriguez had to meet with Scott Draper, Bruce Madej, Dave Ablauf, and another PR official from the Hill.

The previous December, Rodriguez had asked the academic counselors a simple, direct question: What was highest GPA the football team had ever achieved? He had to ask several times before someone finally came back with an answer: 2.60.

"So that's the highest ever?"

"Well," Rodriguez said he was told, "it's the highest in the last five or six years."

"What about before that?"

"No team would have been close before that."

Rodriguez left the conversation with the reasonable interpretation that 2.60 was the highest grade point average the team had achieved since the most veteran academic advisers started at Michigan more than two decades earlier. It wouldn't have mattered much if he'd been told it was 2.3 or 3.2; all he needed was the right answer, something to shoot for.

When the players came back in January 2009, he started writing that number on the whiteboard and mentioned it at just about every team meeting when school came up—which was just about every team meeting—telling them it was their job to beat it. Rodriguez knew football players responded to numbers and peer pressure, and he knew this was an effective way to get athletes to take school more seriously. He hammered this home all semester, especially as finals approached, and the players responded, finishing with a 2.61—again, according to the people in Academics.

But the *Free Press* questioned Rodriguez's claim. And to Rodriguez's surprise, Michigan's public relations and academic people decided to back off, partly out of fear of receiving another stream of FOIAs asking for the collective GPAs of every Michigan varsity team, which the academic people wanted no part of. Given the scrutiny Michigan had received from the time Harbaugh's comments made news in 2007, their skittishness was understandable. But their solution—throw Rodriguez under the bus—naturally did not sit well with the head coach.

They sat in the big comfortable chairs circling the new annex to his office, built for recruits and their parents. The meeting was civil, professional, and occasionally lighthearted, but Rodriguez's frustration was often plain, especially after they showed him a draft of a press release in which they had him saying the GPA was only "an estimate," and "I regret any misunderstanding about this matter."

"This is bullshit," Rodriguez said flatly. "I asked for a number, they gave me a number, and we beat it. End of story. What do they mean, they can't calculate a team grade point? They estimate it by eyeballing it? How lazy is that?"

"But they don't calculate [all] GPAs," the PR person from the Hill said. "They know which ones are not worth calculating."

"What does *that* mean?" Rodriguez asked. "And anyway, that's still a calculation. It might be a rough one, but it's still a numerical assessment. And also, I regret nothing! What should I be regretting here?"

They had no answer. Rodriguez continued. "It bothers me that this release makes it look like I'm just saying it, now, as a response to the *Free Press* article, out of thin air! I'm not making this stuff up, and I've been saying it since the spring—when none of us knew anything about all that *Free Press* crap."

In short, Rodriguez was doing exactly what any Michigan alum would want him to do, and what every player's parent hoped he would do, and he was being punished for it. They compromised by hashing out a new press release, and the meeting ended amicably. Rodriguez closed it with "This is just mouse turds" and a smile.

Over dinner, he said, "I spent five hours today on nonfootball stuff, on the one hitting day of State week: three hours talking with Compliance, one hour talking with my attorney after that, and one hour on the whole grade point thing.

"But this is the first time in twenty-one months the university asked *me* how we should respond, so I guess that's progress."

Or it would have been, if the university had not later scrapped the new press release they had created and returned to the original without consulting Rodriguez.

Rodriguez had enough perspective to recognize that the NCAA investigation, which had just kicked into high gear, was of a different magnitude altogether. Initially, Michigan's compliance director, Judy Van Horn, interviewed the coaches, staffers, and players herself—in a clear conflict of interest, since the quality of her performance was one of the central questions to be answered. Yet she did not stop the practice until Rodriguez's lawyer—not the university's or the NCAA's—insisted that the U-M and NCAA lawyers should conduct the interviews. When the investigators asked Van Horn directly if she had told Rodriguez of the missing CARA forms, she replied, "I wish I had." If she had, it's doubtful Labadie would have been able to put them off for more than a year, that a university audit would have been deemed necessary, and that *Free Press* reporters would have learned about the situation, prompting their FOIA request—and sparking the bigger story, and the NCAA investigation that followed.

Van Horn's reply didn't answer the question, but it was apparently enough for the investigators to drop the issue. And then things got a little stranger. The only coaches kept from Carr's staff were tailbacks coach Fred Jackson and strength coach Jim Plocki, and neither the university nor the NCAA asked to interview Plocki, and no one asked Jackson, or anyone else, about anything before 2008, including policies and practices that had been constant throughout.

Around this time, Mike Parrish discovered on his university computer the résumé of one of Carr's quality control people, Tom Burpee, on which he boasted about all the coaching his role required, one of the very NCAA rules Rodriguez's regime was being accused of violating.

After Parrish showed it to Rodriguez, he faced a dilemma. If he turned it in to the NCAA, he risked the entire university being found guilty of the dreaded "lack of institutional control," which would hurt him more than anyone else and for which he would no doubt be blamed. But if he kept it from investigators, he would violate the legal pledge he signed at the outset of the investigation, stating that he would dutifully report any potential violations he came across—which was one of the rules Jim Tressel broke, launching his investigation in 2011.

Rodriguez concluded that he had to submit Burpee's résumé to the Compliance people at Michigan and the NCAA. He did so with some trepidation, fearing the consequences, but to his surprise, no one cared. Burpee's claims of coaching were assumed to be simple résumé padding—and the NCAA agreed. No one ever considered the possibility that Burpee was telling the truth—which he was. In the words of one former player, "Burpee coached his ass off."

For whatever reason, Michigan and the NCAA had no interest in investigating Michigan, just Rodriguez.

But it's also true that after the scope of the investigation had been limited to the 2008–2009 school year, no rock within that time span was left unturned. Van Horn told me that President Coleman insisted their mission was simply to "find the truth," wherever it led.

"That really impressed me," Van Horn told me. "I have such great respect for President Coleman."

"With Compliance," Rodriguez said, while finishing his meal, "it was pretty clear that the NCAA person was there to find any little thing she could to make sure she looked like a tough guy. They spent about two hours asking about the role of quality control. I said, on the record, that U-M Compliance should know exactly what they were doing, since they were there for plenty of the practices."

During the six weeks I worked out in the weight room and Oosterbaan Field House, I saw every member of the compliance team pass through many times. The doors were always open, and the coaches were not hiding anything. While the coaches should have had a better grasp on the many rules regarding quality control and seven-on-seven drills, if they were committing violations, they were doing so in plain sight of the people whose sole job it was to make sure those violations didn't occur.

"And I also said," Rodriguez continued, "on the record, that the only reason the NCAA is here is because of some completely irresponsible story in the *Detroit Free Press*.

"'Oh, no, no,' the NCAA person said. 'We look at all our schools.'

"Bullshit," Rodriguez said at the table, digging into his dessert.

His response was not elegant but accurate. The Big Ten and the NCAA might have started as governing bodies, set up by university presidents solely to ensure that all players on the field were unpaid amateurs, bona fide students, and safe, but their roles had fundamentally changed since then. For decades, the Big Ten's and the NCAA's main source of money had been members' dues, which they used to enforce the rules. Simple enough. But their roles started growing when the Big Ten discovered that enormous profits could be had through expanded bowl bids, conference basketball tournaments, TV contracts, and now its own TV network, while the NCAA's current TV contract for March Madness alone is worth more than $10 billion.

The sheriffs had become the saloonkeepers, and nobody can do both jobs equally well.

The Big Ten and the NCAA now seemed less concerned with actual integrity than the appearance of it. That's what sells. It's image, not substance, that those organizations are now designed to protect. Truth might have been on Rodriguez's side—time would tell—but one question had already been settled: The marketers who run modern college sports had far more power.

"I think this will all be done in a few weeks," Rodriguez said. "They might get us for secondary violations, about Quality Control supervising seven-on-seven drills, but I might fight that, too."

He was wrong about at least one thing: In the NCAA's twisted lexicon, even those violations are called "major." But he had made up his mind about something else: "I've been run over too many times. So I'm going to speak for myself.

"I haven't been able just to coach football for two years. That's all I want to do. *That's* why I came here, to get rid of all the distractions building up at West Virginia. That was our *goal* in coming here—to get rid of the distractions! We figured Michigan was the place."

He didn't say it, but he didn't have to: He would have been hard-pressed to name any school with more distractions than the one he had picked.

Another problem: Rodriguez knew his players were being called in for NCAA interviews all week, but he didn't grasp what this was doing to his team.

"In my opinion," Brad Labadie told me, "none of the players knew the rules, even when they were being interviewed. They were just pissed about having to deal with the whole thing."

Because they didn't know what the rules were, they weren't sure what to say. Had they been violating one of the NCAA's countless and often senseless prohibitions, which allow the school to offer players a breakfast of bagels and butter, but not cream cheese or jelly? (I am not making this up.) Were their off-season workouts voluntary or involuntary? Were the Quality Control guys conducting seven-on-seven drills or not? The average player didn't make distinctions among assistant coaches, graduate assistants, volunteer assistants, or Quality Control personnel in the first place. They didn't know what to say, and they didn't know what their teammates were saying, either.

"We were 4–0, with Michigan State coming up," Labadie continued, "when all these players get interviewed. And they come back and they're talking about it in the locker room. How much did that matter? A lot."

The team unity they had forged heading into the season was strong enough to withstand the *Free Press* and the negative media response that followed. In some ways, it only reinforced the us-against-the-world mentality.

But these interviews were different. They were all conducted separately, and they created divisions. Some kids knew some of the rules. Some thought they did. Most were uncertain. They were understandably confused, since even Compliance didn't know what the rules were. When Mike Barwis called the office to ask about stretching—months before the *Free Press* story appeared—Ann Vollano called back to tell him stretching didn't count. Barwis let the call go to his machine and saved the message, which he later played back for Dave Brandon. A few days after the *Free Press* story broke, Vollano met with the entire team to repeat the same mistake, saying stretching didn't count. Except, of course, it did—or it usually did. In fairness to Vollano, even the NCAA couldn't give a straight answer when Compliance first called to check.

So, when the players entered the interviews, they were almost completely confused. Did stretching count or not? What about taping? Or team meals? When did watching film count, and when did it not?

And more important: What did you say? Is that going to get us in trouble?

"It was not the same as a guy screwing another guy's girlfriend, which will break up any team," one staffer said, "but you need to be pulling in the same direction, and after that week, you're not. You could see it on the field."

Jim Plocki woke up early Saturday morning at the team hotel, which was a stone's throw from the state capitol, and three miles down Michigan Avenue from Michigan State's verdant campus.

He opened the drapes, saw the rain turning the old asphalt a rich black, and said, "Crap. This is just what I didn't want to see."

How would two green quarterbacks, from San Diego and South Florida, handle the ball on a cold, wet day, working with a substitute center who was just learning how to snap the ball? Plocki shook his head.

Yes, the Spartans were 1–3, and probably one good loss from throwing in the towel, but they weren't 3–9 the previous year. They didn't have dozens of players being pulled from practice all week to be questioned by NCAA and university attorneys. And Coach Dantonio wasn't constantly on the hot seat—even at 1–3 in his third season.

"I don't get it," said another staffer, waiting to board the buses. "All these people bad-mouthing Rich and his staff. I want to tell them; 'You think you're taking Rich Rod down. But you're taking the whole program down.'

"When the old players ask me about them, I always say the same thing: 'Have you met these guys? You know who they are? Have you watched them work? Once you meet him, you like him. He's genuine.'"

To those ends, alumni were always welcome, with a few celebrated as honorary captains at each home game—one of several "traditions" Rodriguez initiated, along with the alumni flag football game and locker room tour on the day of the spring game, the Victors' Walk and the post-victory sing-along in the student corner. The honorary captains ate breakfast at Rodriguez's table Saturday mornings at the Campus Inn, and as focused as he tended to be, he always made the effort to connect with them.

"And after they meet him," the staffer said said, "they always tell me, 'You're right. He's the real deal.'"

On the way to Spartan Stadium, the buses passed a Michigan fan wearing a T-shirt that said BIG BROTHER IS BACK—a far cry from the sign seen on the way to the Purdue game last year: OUR 2–6 SIX TEAM IS BETTER THAN YOUR 2–6 TEAM.

When Rodriguez's Wolverines took a knee in the Big Ten's most hated visitors' locker room, Jon Falk said, "Let's get that trophy back, Blue! It's right next door. Paul Bunyan wants to come home."

"Get him outta jail, Jonny!" Brandon Graham yelled.

"Let 'em talk," Brandon Minor said. "We don't play that game. Let's just go out and kick their asses."

"C'mon, Rod, get on out here!" Graham begged. "We wanna go!"

Whatever fault lines Labadie had sensed starting that week weren't visible in that locker room.

"This is a different Michigan team than they played last year," Rodriguez said. "We're going to stick together no matter what. That's who we are. That's the men who wear the winged helmet."

But Dusty Rutledge, sitting in his usual spot on the Michigan bench, was not so sanguine. How did he feel? "Scared to death. I wasn't last year, because we knew we weren't very good, and next year we know we're going to be very good. But right now, who knows? I guess we're about to find out."

Just 98 seconds into the game, Ryan Van Bergen tipped Cousins's pass, which linebacker Stevie Brown ran back to the Spartans' 18-yard line. It was easy to think that if Michigan could get to the end zone, it could be a short afternoon. Michigan State's season could quickly go down the drain, and the Wolverines could take Paul Bunyan home with a 5–0 record and a top-twenty ranking. They would also have the breakthrough victory Rodriguez and his players needed to get ahead of the avalanche chasing them, once and for all, and focus on football. It was Rodriguez's first shot at match point.

But Michigan looked out of sorts, losing yards, getting sacked, and at one point throwing a simple screen to Tay Odoms—who hadn't even turned around. They had to settle for a field goal.

On the Spartans' next drive, facing fourth-and-inches at the goal line, Dantonio took his chances. Larry Caper vindicated his decision with the game's first touchdown, 7–3.

After Forcier's receivers dropped two more passes, Michigan had to settle for another field goal, which the Spartans matched before heading into halftime with a 10–6 lead. Labadie was right, after all: The Wolverines were not the same.

Back in the closet-sized coaches' room, Calvin McGee read the stat sheet: nineteen offensive plays. Anemic. "We're just dropping the damn ball. We just need to pitch and catch and make the reads. And we got to put Shoes [Denard Robinson] in there sometime. I don't care if it's too predictable—everyone knows he's going to run—we just need to get going."

In the main room, Greg Robinson was working the board. "How's their offensive line?"

"Weak as hell," Mike Martin said.

"We're just beating ourselves," Brandon Graham added.

"They had the ball damn near thirty minutes," Robinson said, "and we only gave up 10 points. That's it."

"Listen up, guys!" Rodriguez told the team. "We have not even made them play defense yet, and the tide is already turned. Let's go!"

But Michigan was just as sloppy in the third quarter, relying on Donovan Warren to make a red-zone interception. After another failed drive, Forcier turned to Minor and Brown and said, "We haven't played football all day. Let's get going!"

But right as Forcier said this, Glenn Winston slipped into the end zone to expand the Spartans' lead to 20–6, just 11 seconds into the fourth quarter.

A refocused Forcier started hitting short, sharp passes to find his rhythm, including a nice toss to Darryl Stonum, at the Spartans' 17-yard line—only to see him fumble it 5 yards later. Michigan's student equipment managers started emptying the coolers on the sidelines. But after Michigan's defense stopped the Spartans again, Forcier went right back to Stonum, who gathered the ball, made a couple nice cuts, and dashed all the way to the end zone. With four minutes left, Michigan had cut the Spartans' lead to 20–13.

"The lights are back on, baby!"

As if on cue, the sun came out in full force.

After yet another defensive stop, the Wolverines got the ball on their own 8-yard line, with 2:53 left and no time-outs. They did not deserve to be in this game, having been thoroughly outplayed for fifty-five minutes, but there they were, with the same chance they had exploited against Notre Dame and Indiana.

Forcier passed for 9 yards, ran for 11, and took a roughing-the-passer penalty for 15 more, leaving 2:02 to cover 42 yards. The rain came down again, forcing the managers to scramble for dry towels for the footballs and the ball handlers. "Towels! Towels! Get some dry towels, damn it!"

On third-and-8, with just eight seconds left, Forcier rolled out and saw Roy Roundtree in the back of the end zone. Forcier threw a perfect strike, and Roundtree came down with the ball inbounds. Touchdown!

The celebration on the bench was like no other in this already wild season. Players were jumping up and down, chest bumping, hugging, and high-fiving each other. Total mayhem.

Someone on the bench yelled, "That guy is unbelievable!" To which Greg Banks said, slapping his chest, "No, *we* are unbelievable!" Confidence is contagious.

The scoreboard read Michigan State 20, Michigan 19, with 00:02 left. There must have been some temptation, with the Spartans' defense clearly gasping for air, to attempt a 2-point conversion. But Rodriguez, uncharacteristically, resisted his gambling instincts and took the tie.

Dusty Rutledge, sitting on the bench, just kept shaking his head. "If [Michigan State] had any discipline at all, they would've won this game a long time ago."

Phil Johnson, one of the trainers, agreed. "We just got our asses kicked, and now we're going into OT."

The sun had returned, but it was still raining. It was that kind of day.

In overtime, the Wolverines faced second-and-6 from the 9-yard line, comfortable territory for this team. In the unlikely event their suddenly hot offense couldn't get to the end zone, even a field goal might be enough for Michigan's resurgent defense to stop the struggling Spartans.

There was, of course, a third possibility: After Forcier gave a halfhearted fake, he left the pocket, then fired a pass to Odoms, running through the back of the end zone. But State's defender grabbed the tail of Odoms's jersey and pulled him back for an instant, costing him a step. And that, in a tight offensive scheme, was enough to put the ball just out of reach—

and allow another defender to tip it off Odoms's pads and up in the air, high enough for State's Chris Rucker to grab it before it hit the grass.

Interception.

All Michigan State had to do was score, but they fumbled on the first play. They recovered, and two plays later, Caper ran 23 yards for a 26–20 victory.

Paul Bunyan was staying in East Lansing for another year.

Tate Forcier sat on the bench alone, head in hands, agonizing over his first loss as a college quarterback.

In the visitors' locker room, almost every player had his head down, buried in sweaty, dirty hands. Rodriguez was back in the tiny coaches' room, writing a few thoughts on his index cards, before getting up and slamming the little green swinging door against the tile with a bang.

"First, you got *nothing* to hang your heads about. Nothing. You worked your asses off. And that's the only reason why, as bad as we played, we could've won that game. But we lost, and I take responsibility for that.

"The lights are still on, men! The cockroaches want to come around, they can. Nothing to hide here, but they don't like the light, so they won't stay long. This is gonna hurt, and it should hurt. But only for twenty-four hours. Then we'll get back to work.

"So let's shower and get the hell out of this hellhole. 'Michigan' on three."

"Michigan!"

Rodriguez walked back to the coaches' room, his face tight as a drum. Everything he had told his team was true, and he believed it. But he left something out: In their biggest game to date, with the most to gain against arguably their weakest conference opponent, Michigan had missed reads, missed throws, and just plain dropped the ball.

He banged the swinging doors again, then knocked a wooden chair against the wall. "Fuck me!"

Rodriguez might have preferred winning ugly to losing pretty, but there was no consolation in losing close and ugly.

The forty-five-minute bus ride back to Ann Arbor took days.

If Michigan was looking for a break, they weren't going to get one the following week in Iowa City. But if Michigan wanted to atone for the loss to Michigan State, a nationally televised night game on ABC against the thirteenth-ranked Hawkeyes in one of the league's loudest stadiums—and, on this night, one of the coldest—would do very nicely.

It wouldn't pack the emotional punch rescuing Paul Bunyan would have, but it would serve the same purpose: launching Rodriguez and his players beyond the gravitational pull of their detractors. They would be out of reach and on their way.

In Iowa's infamous pink-walled visitors' locker room, the players took a knee near the door, waiting for their head coach.

"All I'm saying is, who wants to come in on Monday *waiting* to see this film?!" Brandon Graham asked his teammates. "Who wants to fight for each other? We do it in practice every day. Let's do it right here, right now!"

"They didn't lift the way we did," Van Bergen said. "They didn't run the way we did. They ain't us. Make 'em pay!"

Rodriguez kept it short and sweet. "Okay, men, two things: First, you are going to get physical on every snap.

"Second, I want to see some smiles on your faces. You've got the national stage tonight. Let's have some *fun* out there." He held their collective gaze a beat longer, then cut to the conclusion. "Every man, on every play. Because *they better understand*," which cued the players to start slapping their hands and helmets in rhythm, and begin their pregame call-and-response mantra: "When they play Michigan!"

"Oh, yeah!"

"You better tie your shoes a little tighter!"

"HELL yeah!"

"Put a little more tape on!"

"BRING it!"

"YEAHHHH!"

"And put a little more air in your helmets! And—"

"STRAP IT ON!" they yelled.

"Because Michigan's coming! Let's go!"

They ran down the tunnel looking for trouble, their hoots and hollers echoing the entire way to the field. He still had them.

They showed the nation on Iowa's second play, when Ricky Stanzi dropped back and threw a perfect strike—right to Donovan Warren, who caught it cleanly, then dashed 40 yards straight into the end zone. 7–0.

The sidelines erupted.

But a few plays later, Stanzi floated a pass right over the defensive line to his tight end, Tony Moeaki, who all but walked the rest of the way. 7–7.

The Iowa fans, well lubricated from a full day of tailgating in the cold, leaned over the railing close enough to touch the players.

"Review *that*, bitch!"

"I slept with your mom last night!"

"Ann Arbor's a whore!"

The Hawkeyes added a field goal before Forcier led his offense on a 12-play, 72-yard drive to pull ahead 14–10. On the other side of the ball, Michigan's defense reverted to its 2008 form, forcing the Hawkeyes into repeated third-and-longs, only to let them off the hook, most egregiously on a third-and-24. That drive led to another touchdown to give Iowa the lead again, 20–14.

"We got this shit!" Barwis yelled to his guys as they ran up the tunnel for halftime. "We got 'em, Blue!" Tony Dews agreed.

But they were outraced by Rich Rodriguez, who barged through the players. "We should be kickin' their ass!" he yelled. "We're better than they are! *We're better than they are!*"

Back in the coaches' room, he told his assistants, "Tate's not looking downfield. He's looking at the rush—every time! And can we play some defense? Can we get a fucking stop? Third-and-fucking-24—are you *kidding* me?"

Coach Robinson started to respond but was quickly cut off—rare, for Rodriguez.

"Everyone's got a fucking answer, everyone's got a fucking excuse. Can't everyone just fucking coach? If Williams can't cover his man, put someone else in there!" He punctuated his complaint by knocking a chair against the wall.

Rodriguez's final words to his team were simple: "We're in great shape. The only thing beatin' us . . . is us! We're strikin' 'em. If we keep strikin' 'em for thirty more minutes, this son of a bitch is ours! Let's go!"

The idea of another heartbreaker, followed by a late-night flight home, wasn't appealing to anyone in that room.

Forcier continued to miss his marks, but Brandon Minor covered 44 yards on seven carries to close the gap to 23–21. But the mistakes piled up. Mike Williams roughed the punter. Troy Woolfolk let his man run straight at returner Greg Mathews, who dropped the fair catch, which Woolfolk's man gobbled up. And then Michigan's defense made the exact same mistake it had in the first half—leaving Tony Moeaki wide open in the middle for his second scoring jog. The drive took exactly one play, ten seconds, and 42 yards to give Iowa a 30–21 lead with 12:56 left in the game.

The Wolverines still had plenty of time, but Forcier took so long to take the first snap of Michigan's next possession that he was called for delay of game, followed by more bad reads and off-target passes. When Forcier got to the sidelines this time, Rodriguez finally let him have it. "We are a *spread offense*! We're supposed to be *fast*! And on our *first* play from scrimmage, we get called for delay. This is just *embarrassing!*"

Rodriguez's outburst was, naturally, captured on national television. While Forcier sulked on the sideline, ESPN's Lisa Salters asked Paul Schmidt, "Is Tate hurt?"

"Just his pride," he said, and as usual, his diagnosis was dead-on.

Rodriguez looked down the sidelines, found Denard Robinson, pointed at him, and yelled, "Get ready!"

"I've *been* ready—all year!"

He was about to get his chance to prove it.

Robinson got the ball on Michigan's 41-yard line with 7:42 remaining and went right to work, passing twice and running eight times for 58 yards. The last, a 3-yard dive over the goal line, put his team just 2 points down, 28–30, with 3:16 left on the clock.

There were 70,585 freezing people in Kinnick Stadium that night, and at that moment, probably every single one feared Michigan would get the ball back and roll down the field for a last-second score. They had seen what Michigan could do.

Rodriguez, his well-developed brinksmanship bolstered by the comeback, called for the onside kick—but his guy knocked it straight out-of-bounds, giving them no chance to recover it. With 3:16 left, Iowa needed only one first down to ice the game. But surprisingly, Michigan's defense held.

Michigan got the ball back on its 17-yard line with 1:30 left, no time-outs, and 3 points away from a stirring victory on national television,

Rodriguez had to make one big decision: Who should get the ball?

Forcier, who was 8-for-19 with an interception, a fumble, an unforced trip, and an unnecessary time-out, but had already performed the very same last-minute heroics three times that season? Or Robinson, who was two-for-two passing, a far better runner, and had just orchestrated a 59-yard touchdown drive in his only possession that day, but had never run a two-minute drill in college and didn't know the playbook? Rodriguez set his jaw, looked down the sideline, and barked, "Denard!"

Robinson didn't need to be told twice. On first down from the 17, Robinson found Odoms in the right flats for 14 yards and a first down, stopping the clock. A good read, a good throw, a good sign. On the next play, from the 31-yard line, Robinson dashed right for 7 yards.

Offensive lineman Mark Ortmann said the next day, "When I got down into my stance for that last play, I believed—hell, I was *convinced*—that we were going to throw the ball downfield once, maybe twice, kick the field goal, and walk off winners."

But on the next play, with Odoms wide open again in the flats and plenty of room to get a first down, out-of-bounds, or both, Robinson looked past him, rolled out, and saw Junior Hemingway running up the right sideline. Robinson launched the ball off balance and from his right foot, creating a predictable floater, just as Hemingway pulled up, hoping Robinson would find him under coverage. Hemingway watched helplessly as the pass sailed over his head toward three Hawkeyes camped under the ball. The only question remaining was which one would catch it.

Two plays later, the game was over. The student section emptied onto the field like sand pouring out of a dump truck.

A minute later, Rodriguez addressed his team in the pink locker room. "Men, we beat ourselves tonight. We could have won this one—we played hard enough—but we just made too many mistakes. We need to go watch the film and see where we can be better. That starts with the coaches, and that starts with me.

"The first half of the season is over, but everything we want is still in front of us. Follow me?"

"Yes, sir."

"Follow me?"

"YES, SIR!"

The assistants could all head to the steaming-hot showers, warm up, clean up, and change, but Rodriguez's day was not over. The worst part was ahead: the press conference. After a tough loss, such "gangbangs," as they're called in the media, are probably the worst places to generate incisive reporting. It is less poker game than ritual, with the reporters trying to get the coach to say something, *anything*, and the coach trying just as hard not to.

The questions started right where Rodriguez knew they would:

"Why'd you pull Tate?"

"What did you say to Tate when he came off the field?"

"How did he respond?"

"Should you have put Robinson in earlier?"

"Why not use Forcier on the last drive, given his success?"

"Who's going to start next game?"

After each question, Rodriguez gamely tried to respond with a grin, defuse the situation, and say nice things about both quarterbacks. But one local reporter couldn't resist repeating the question: "Why not put Tate in at the end, given his history?"

Rodriguez turned to Bruce Madej, exasperated, but again managed to grin and give a benign nonanswer.

The tension between coaches and sportswriters has long been noted but little understood. Working on this project confirmed what I'd long suspected: The problem isn't that sportswriters are so insightful and ask the tough questions, as we'd like to think. No, most coaches don't hate sportswriters. They simply *dismiss* us as unathletic, pompous fools who have no idea what it's like to play a competitive sport, let alone coach one.

The late David Brinkley wrote that most senators had less respect for *The New York Times's* leading columnist than the local dog catcher—because *that* guy had the guts to put his name on a ballot, and the wits to win an election. Likewise, most coaches would rather talk to the offensive line coach from the local high school than the Pulitzer Prize–winning sportswriter.

Right when things were winding down, a reporter entered the back of the room, breathless, and said, "Coach Rodriguez, I apologize if you already answered this question, but when you made the switch to Denard Robinson—"

The ride to the airport, the flight home, and the ride back to Schembechler Hall were all completed in darkness and silence. The fact was, however, that Michigan had probably played its best game under Rodriguez. It wasn't perfect, and it wasn't enough, but if the Wolverines had played half as well against the struggling Spartans, they probably would have crushed them.

When everyone started looking for his car in the Schembechler Hall parking lot at 3:30 in the morning, all had the sheepish look of dogs who had just gotten into the garbage. They knew they were guilty of something, but they were not quite sure what.

The answer was simple: losing.

After spending weeks poring over films from Notre Dame, Michigan State, and Iowa—replete with future NFLers and professionally produced from three angles in great stadiums with packed houses—looking at film from Delaware State was like watching a two-bit high school squad.

Michigan paid Eastern Michigan $800,000 for the right to beat up on the Eagles but had to up the ante to $1 million for Delaware State, because DSU had been forced to forfeit a league game to make the date—another good argument against the superfluous and cynical twelfth game.

Delaware State earned every penny, losing 63–6. Every Michigan walk-on got in, including senior game captain Ohene Opong-Owusu—"The Big O!" as Rodriguez called him—who made his debut. All the starters stopped to watch when Ohene took the field, and he didn't disappoint, making the tackle on one kick return, and blowing up his man on another.

Rodriguez would honor Ohene's hits by replaying them at Monday's team meeting, where his teammates gave him their ritualistic lead-up—"ZzzzzzzzzzzzzzzzzzzzZZZZZ—POW!" It wasn't fifteen minutes of fame, just a moment, but Opong-Owusu would never forget it.

Beyond notching the fifth win, the game was almost completely inconsequential. But what happened off the field that day would have a much greater impact on Rodriguez, his staff, and his team.

Bill Martin, on his way to the Regents' Guest Area in the press box—where big donors and VIPs get schmoozed by President Coleman and others—

was asked by a student security guard to show his pass. According to *The Michigan Daily*, Martin said, "I am the athletic director. I can go in." Then he walked past the young man into the room. Whether he brushed by him, shoved him, or grabbed his shirt depends on who's telling the story. But no one disputes that, later that day, the student related the incident to a fellow student security guard, who told him of a similar incident earlier in the season.

The two students decided to file reports with U-M chief of police Ken Magee. As one regent told me, Magee might consider you a close friend, "but if one of his officers gives you a parking ticket, you're paying the full amount."

The by-the-book Magee processed the complaint the way he would any other. Although no charges were ultimately filed, four days later, on Wednesday, the university sent out a press release announcing Martin's retirement. Whether the reports had any impact on the announcement is difficult to say, though the timing—midweek and midseason—seemed unusual. Martin has maintained throughout, however, that he planned to retire with the opening of the skyboxes in 2010, and there certainly is a logic to that.

Martin's already limited power to guide and protect Rodriguez would be all but eliminated, and whoever followed Martin would be less committed to a beleaguered coach whom he hadn't hired. For Rodriguez, it was just more snow on the rooftop, threatening to cave it in.

And it was against this backdrop that Martin, whose support for Rodriguez had always been sincere, sat down the very next day to a previously arranged lunch at the Michigan Union with Rodriguez and Carr. All three walked up State Street together, with horns honking the whole way up the hill, and fans shouting their names. When they made their way up the steps to the Union, Martin recalled, Denard Robinson happened to be walking out. Carr had never met him, so they had a brief chat. At lunch, they sat next to former Purdue quarterback Mark Herrmann, whose daughter was considering Michigan.

Otherwise, Martin says, "there was a lot of small talk, and some football talk. There was tension."

Although stilted, it would be the longest conversation between the two since Carr had called Rodriguez in December of 2007 to sell him on the job.

After the chilly pleasantries were dispensed with, Carr sent the first volley. "Tell the people in your camp to quit attacking me in the press," he said, as Rodriguez remembered it a couple hours later. The catalyst for this was undoubtedly Rick Leach's public lambasting of Carr on the radio that week for sitting with Iowa's coaches and dignitaries—people Carr had known for years—in an Iowa stadium luxury box, instead of sticking with the Michigan contingent. Leach, who had no more media training than Rodriguez or Martin, quickly suffered a backlash.

"I don't have a camp," Rodriguez replied, "and whatever they're doing, they're doing on their own. Rick Leach speaks for himself."

Rodriguez ticked off all the reasons Carr shouldn't feel any threat from him, including Carr's five Big Ten titles and Michigan's first national championship in a half century. What Michigan football needed now, Rodriguez said, was Carr's unambiguous support. "When the *Free Press* came out with this story," he told Carr, "saying how hard we are on the players, we could have used you speaking up."

Carr said nothing.

"You're either all in or you're not," Rodriguez continued. "You're either inside the Michigan family or you're not." But the closest he came to accusing Carr of anything more than silence was this: "Somebody inside the department is talking to the press and doing us harm."

The suggestion was that, if there were moles in the department, Carr most likely knew who they were, and Rodriguez would appreciate it if Carr told them to knock it off. As Rodriguez recalled, Carr remained silent at that, too.

Walking back down the hill to their offices, Martin asked Rodriguez, "Why don't you ask him to talk to your team before the Penn State game?"

"Because I've got my team right where I want them," Rodriguez replied. "Gary [Moeller] comes to practice every Thursday—he's a regular—and we're not even asking *him* to talk to our team."

This little exchange might be more telling than the strained conversation over lunch. It displayed the blind spots of both men. Martin was naïve enough to think Rodriguez would have no problem asking Carr to speak to his team after that ice-cold lunch, and that the clearly reticent Carr would accept. Likewise, Rodriguez failed to take advantage of what the Michigan family could do for him by declining to invite respected and supportive Michigan Men to address his team.

The latter echoed Rodriguez's refusal to visit the M-Club for their Monday luncheons during the season, too, which every coach had done going back to Schembechler's early days. The club's members are not, as a rule, the big money donors or power brokers—the VIPs tended to live in the suburbs or on the coasts—but their passion and loyalty were un-equaled, and they served as opinion leaders for the Michigan community. It was, in many ways, an ideal setting for a new coach: a home crowd, with a strict no-press, everything-is-off-the-record policy. Further, it would give Rodriguez, an effective public speaker and a genuinely likable guy, a plat-form to earn some brownie points with the faithful. Here was help he could have used, in a format in which he could excel.

Yet Rodriguez typically sent Dusty Rutledge in his stead. When a patron asked Rutledge why Rodriguez rarely came, he said, "Would you rather have him here or recruiting next year's class?" It was a good point, especially because Rodriguez was the lead coach for both the offense and the special teams. Ultimately you could argue getting even one blue chipper outweighed a season of speeches, but it robbed Rodriguez of the support he would need when the *Free Press* story hit. A few hundred influ-ential character witnesses and amateur PR workers couldn't have hurt during an investigation that would drag out for a year.

Back in his office, reflecting on the day's events, Rodriguez said, "Well, that didn't accomplish a whole lot. We're going to extend an olive branch one more time—ask [Carr] to be the honorary captain for Penn State—and then when the season ends, that's it."

Nothing, of course, could help Rodriguez more than winning another football game. With center David Molk finally returning from his broken foot and many pundits calling the upcoming Penn State game for Michi-gan, there was good reason to hope. Once again, the incentives were many: a 2–2 Big Ten record, bowl eligibility—and proof to the rest of the nation they were back.

In the two weeks since the Iowa game, still more drama swirled around the program. From Leach's outburst to Martin's retirement to suspending Cissoko for missing class to the NCAA investigation, Rodriguez's options for surviving the experience were becoming narrower by the day. He had only one way out: He had to win games, and fast.

Forcier looked good against the Nittany Lions, not forcing anything. But when PA announcer Carl Grapentine told the fans a man was down on the field—and it was center David Molk—they let out a collective "Oooh." They understood immediately.

Everyone assumed Molk had refractured his recently healed right foot. But on the sidelines, a team of four orthopedic doctors began testing not his right foot but his right knee—touching it here and there, seeing where it hurt and what Molk could and couldn't do. The same man who had not missed a single play the previous season had suffered his second serious injury just minutes after coming back from his first—and the two were, amazingly, unrelated.

Moosman moved back to center, and Michigan marched all the way to the end zone. 7–0 Michigan, just 3:49 into the game.

After Michigan's opening drive, Rodriguez walked past the offense's benches. "Tempo, tempo, tempo!" he said, rolling his left hand over and over. "Keep it fast! Make them play *your* speed—they can't keep up!"

Greg Mathews nodded. "They weak, man, they weak!"

But Penn State's offense needed only four plays to tie the score 7–7.

Just when it looked like the two teams were poised for another classic battle, the Wolverines seemed to forget everything they did right on their first drive. Forcier looked rough, from his inconsistent drops to his missed reads; no one seemed capable of blocking anyone; and the receivers ran sloppy routes. When Forcier did manage to get them the ball, they often dropped it.

For the next twenty minutes, Michigan managed only four first downs.

In the waning minutes of the half, down 19–7 but facing second-and-goal, Forcier dropped the snap, fell on it, and lay there while the clock was running. By the time he got up, he had to spike the ball to set up the field goal, which cut Penn State's lead to 19–10 at the half. For anyone keeping count, which included everyone on the Michigan sideline, the Wolverines were two botched snaps from going into halftime down just 17–14.

Of course, such would'ves, could'ves, and should'ves marked Michigan's last three games: a lot of almost. They were slipping backward on the Bowden scale, from winning close to losing close.

At halftime, Rodriguez steamed over Forcier's lack of game awareness. "Where's the sense of urgency!" he asked. "Get up! He's got to get rid of the ball sooner, too. Throw the seam hitch every time. Every time! He's open!"

Rod Smith, who exhibited the patience of Job with his young quarterbacks, told Forcier, "Quit being a robot and start being a football player. Trust yourself!"

Meanwhile, in the next alcove over, the normally cool Calvin Magee blasted the tight ends: "Catch the fucking ball! Catch. The. Fucking. *Ball!*"

———

Just four plays into the new half, however, the Lions invaded Michigan's end zone again to go up 25–10, then 32–10.

The game was over, and everyone seemed to know it except Brandon Graham, who charged in to block a punt, then raced to recover it not once but twice. He was playing for his school, he was playing for his teammates, he was playing for his future. He simply would not stop.

But it didn't matter. Two plays later, Michigan fumbled it back. The Michigan sideline, normally as active as an ant colony, had lost all life. With seven minutes left, the football staffers started packing the trunks. They are the vultures of college football. When you see them circling, you're done for.

After Penn State finalized the deal 35–10, the cold, wet Wolverines trundled back to their locker room.

"I thought I had you prepared, and I was wrong," Rodriguez said. "That's on me. We can't beat teams without playing our best. And we were not at our best today. We just made too many mistakes to win. We've got to get it right—in a hurry.

"I don't want to feel this feeling anymore. I don't like it for the seniors. I need every one of you to get back to your best. I know everyone in this room is *all in* for Michigan. So get in here. 'All in' on three."

"ALL IN!"

In addition to covering the slaughter, *The Detroit News* ran a postgame story with the headline LLOYD CARR PRAISES RICH RODRIGUEZ.

"Former football coach Lloyd Carr appeared on the Michigan radio broadcast during the first quarter of Saturday's Penn State game, praised Rich Rodriguez's spread offense, reiterated he's not a candidate for U-M athletic director and proclaimed his love for Michigan.

"Carr, who has been criticized by some fans and former players for not being publicly supportive of Rodriguez, spoke highly of the new coach and the program, and singled out freshman quarterback Tate Forcier for being 'simply outstanding in every game.'"

On the same day, Drew Sharp of the *Free Press* wrote a column titled, "Lloyd Carr's Support Won't Save Rich Rod Forever."

Sharp asked about Rick Leach's recent comments.

"I'm not going to worry about stuff like that," Carr replied.

The trouncing, coupled with Molk's second injury, a quarterback who was not taking coaching, and a team that had seemingly become timid, had all conspired to foul Rodriguez's mood more than usual by Sunday.

"Game evaluation," Rodriguez said a few minutes before noon, with all the joy of a high school teacher reading off names for detention. "Quarterbacks."

"Tate got sixty-five snaps, worst fucking game he played this year," Rod Smith said, his patience finally failing him.

"Does he ever come in to study film?" Rodriguez asked. The answer: not much. Same as most of the players.

Rodriguez then provided the reason. "Guys are so paranoid about going past their [NCAA allowable] hours, they're afraid to come in here to watch film. We've got plenty of time under twenty hours. They can all afford a couple hours a week to learn their assignments, study their opponents, learn what the hell is going on. And I'll bet you straight up every goddamn guy at Penn State was in the film room this week, learning every damn thing about us that we *weren't* learning about them."

When your team is in a tailspin, you have two options, neither great. You can try to calm the players, to take some pressure off—which risks not bringing the necessary intensity to the next game. Or you can crank it up another notch, in an effort to stop the slide *now*—which risks them getting rattled and not playing their best.

Rodriguez, not surprisingly, opted for the latter. That meant everyone's margin of error—from his coordinators' to his assistants' to his players' themselves—had just been cut in half. He had taken this tack before, of course, and almost always gotten good results, but no one was going to get any breaks that week, and only a freshman or a fool would have expected any.

But there was a method to his madness. He knew his team was young, inexperienced, and struggling to learn new systems. He also knew that, on some deeper level, they were fragile. So while he gave them no quarter, he focused every one of his criticisms not on ability or even performance but on toughness, focus, and effort—all the things even freshmen could control, every play.

Redshirt sophomore Mike Williams, for example, had been struggling at safety, which created tension between Rodriguez and Greg Robinson. Although Rodriguez would have pulled Williams himself if he was the defensive coordinator, he was reluctant to pull rank on Robinson, for whom he felt a great deal of respect. But that didn't mean he would get a free pass. Not that week.

When Robinson graded Williams, he said, "His eyes get him in trouble more than anything. He doesn't know what to watch for and gets sucked in."

Rodriguez grunted but didn't interject until much later, when they broke down a special teams play featuring Williams. "I'm telling you that guy cannot tackle," Rodriguez said. "Or he simply *will* not—take your pick. And that possibility pisses me off more."

After every player had been graded, Rodriguez said, "Here's my impression: We looked poorly coached.

"On defense, we were tentative. We had a lot of technical errors— higher than it's ever been—with everyone either doing their own thing or not listening to coaching. On one play, Stevie [Brown, a senior] lined up at three or four different places. He had no idea where he was supposed to be. And we had twelve guys out there on a field goal block.

"Same thing on offense. We had more MAs than we've ever had, and it wasn't a very complicated defense we were going up against. First play of the game, Moose goes the wrong way. Our center, first play! Later he snaps the ball off Tate's chest and says, 'I couldn't hear anything.' Then don't snap it!

"We didn't play with a sense of urgency. I can't explain that. We played soft, as a team. That's embarrassing to me, more than anything else. We got punched in the mouth and didn't respond.

"And I'm gonna call Tate and Denard both in. Tell them either start becoming quarterbacks or start looking over your shoulder."

When they moved on to the weekly awards, Rodriguez was no happier. "No crunches, no hammers, no nails," he summed up, leaning back in his chair, manila file in his hand, clearly disgusted. "No turnovers, two weeks in a row—and we weren't even close to getting one.

"That's it," he said, slapping the file down. "Let's watch special teams, so I can get in an even shittier mood."

For the coaches, a bad loss means bad moods, bad press, bad pressure. It is part of a coach's wife's compact that her husband is allowed to brood over a loss for twenty-four hours, but then he has to drop it.

For the Big Boys, it means bad fans and bad Facebook.

"There's always a different feel on the streets, around town, even online, after a win or a loss," John Ferrara said over Sunday pizza at the Commons. "After Notre Dame, there's a little more pep and excitement. And after Penn State, it feels dead."

"After a game like that," Perry Dorrestein said, "I get e-mails—lots of them—explaining why I suck. Not just *telling* me I suck, but *explaining* why. That's helpful."

"The worst," Jon Conover said, "are the ones in the Victors' Walk cheering you on and shaking your hand and patting you on the back, and that night they're on their blog ripping you a new one. And what really pisses me off is these are people who don't know much about the game and know almost nothing about what it means to be a college athlete. The greatest adversity they face is running into a traffic jam on the way to work.

"Facebook's worse. I have to deny a dozen people a day who want to friend me, who I know are fans. You feel bad, you don't want to be unappreciative, but they're not your friends, and I'm just too hard-pressed for time. Then the same guy will be on some blog saying what a jerk you are. And then that gets back to your parents—and who needs that? So now I have six hundred 'friends' on there, and probably one hundred are my real friends."

"Cut the Facebook, mon," said Renaldo Sagasse, a lineman from Montreal known by his teammates as "the Big Maple." "Too many people you don't want to talk to."

"My mom was saying some people behind her were swearing all game, F-in' this, and F-in' that, 'You guys F-in' suck,' all that," said Ferrara, from Staten Island. "When Junior [Hemingway] was hurt, they said, 'Drag his ass off the field! We want to see the game!'

"So she finally turns around, right? And she says, 'Do you know you're sitting in the Friends and Family section?' And this guy says, 'I've been coming here thirty years! There is no fucking friends and family section!'"

Linda Ferrara, the wife of a New York fireman, remained poised. "Where'd you get your tickets?"

"The trainers."

"Right," she said. "And that means?"

"They didn't get it," Ferrara said, ending his story.

"A fan who'd stayed for the whole game came up to me and said, 'Keep working. We're proud of you,'" Dorrestein said. "I said, 'Thanks. We appreciate it.' People like that, they make it all worth it."

Just in case the past week wasn't bad enough, the next one started out with another press release.

"ANN ARBOR, Mich.—University of Michigan President Mary Sue Coleman today (Monday, Oct. 26) announced that the University has received a 'Notice of Inquiry' from the NCAA, indicating it will continue its investigation of allegations made about the U-M's intercollegiate athletics football program."

In other words, the NCAA had concluded that the initial round of research warranted digging deeper. Not unexpected, necessarily—the threshold for such decisions was pretty low—but not good news, either. It would provide enough fodder for the media to write whatever it wanted and force the players to wonder who had said what to the investigators, and why. Those questions would remain in the air for twelve more months.

A few hours later, Rodriguez learned center David Molk hadn't sprained his knee. He had torn his ACL and was gone for the season.

At 5–3, and 1–3 in the Big Ten, the Wolverines' early optimism had diminished, but they could still go to a good bowl game. All they needed was one more win to qualify, and they were not likely to get a juicier target the rest of the way than Illinois. For all those reasons, Rodriguez felt his team simply had to make a stand that Saturday and stop its three-game Big Ten losing skid.

From the offensive meeting to the team meeting to the practice, Monday set the tone for the entire week: Get your act together, *now*, and get back to Michigan football—before it's too late.

In the offensive meeting, while going over the game film, Rodriguez interrupted his dissection of another broken play to call Forcier out in front of every offensive player—a last resort. Calling out your quarterback in front of his teammates can always backfire, but Rodriguez figured the way Forcier was playing, he didn't have a lot to lose.

"All we ask is that you run *our* offense and quit making shit up as you go along. Penn State did not do *one* fucking thing we did not see on film—not one fucking thing!—and you'd know that if you ever saw a second of fucking film. But you didn't because you're too worried about going out on the town instead of doing your actual work to be a better quarterback and lead this damn team.

"And it ain't just him," Rodriguez said, pointing his laser to the screen, frozen with football players. "It's all of them. *All* your quarterbacks are letting you down." He didn't actually mean that. Sheridan had been an ideal role model for Forcier, and Rodriguez knew it. But he also knew Denard Robinson hadn't been working much harder than Forcier, and he wanted Robinson to know that he was on notice, too.

"And look at this, Tate," Rodriguez said, showing a play in slow motion, then stopping it. "How many steps are you supposed to take?"

"Three."

"Three steps. That's right. And is your man open after three steps? Yes, he is! Imagine that! You know why? Because the play is *designed* that way. We've actually done it before! We *designed* this fucking offense twenty years ago—before you were born!—and I can assure you it works! But it only fucking works when you do what we tell you to do."

A shaft of light came from the doorway into the dark amphitheater. An assistant poked his head in. "It's 2:45. Defense is ready, Coach."

"Well, I'm not. Tell them to go watch some film. Probably be the first time they see film this week too."

When he showed the play again, the anger built up in him, then came out: "DAMN IT!" He threw the remote at the screen. This time, it was no act.

On the next play, just three seconds after the snap, Rodriguez stopped the tape. "Tate, you are in fucking Division I football. You drop back *three* steps—not four or five or fucking *six*!—THREE! You hitch up and hit the seam in cover-fucking-three. And if they're not open, if their guys run with our guys, you hit the pull-up. Just that simple. That. Fucking. Simple."

The next play was the last before the half, when Forcier squandered their chance to take another shot at the end zone.

"Now, this is what *really* pisses me off. You fumbled it, but you got it back, and we have enough time to try another play left in the half before we have to kick it. That'd be nice, wouldn't it? Cut it to 19–14 going into the locker room?

"But no. Look at this. You're just lying there.

"Get up! Get the fuck up! The clock is running!

"Everyone's milling around and we've got no time-out because we had to waste one because we had twelve guys on the field earlier in the half. So get up!"

At 3:15, Rodriguez had finally finished with the offense and asked Phil Bromley to turn the lights on.

"Crissakes," he said to himself. Then, to the team: "And this was our *good* half!"

Rodriguez wasn't much happier when he addressed the entire squad. He expressed his general discontent with the way things were going— more angry and determined than hurt and defeated—and how that forced him to apologize for the team whenever he had to address a group of alums or a local Rotary Club.

But not with them, he clarified.

"You want to be Leaders and Best? You want to be Big Ten champs? Let me tell you something right now: You cannot hide from that fucking field. It does not lie.

"I saw enough of this shit last year to last me a lifetime. I hated walking off that field—and I never want to again—when I think: They didn't beat us at our best.

"We've got bullshit investigations here, we've got freshmen there—all this shit, none of it matters. It's just eleven guys on the field. I got rid of all the soft asses, I got nothing but men who care about each other and want to go into battle.

"We are *not* reverting back. We are *not* reverting back!"

It was stated as an order—but it was also his greatest fear.

The players and coaches got dressed, then jogged out through the doors of their state-of-the-art practice facility to meet a picture-perfect fall day—Ann Arbor's best season. They had about twenty seconds to enjoy it before Rodriguez got them running and stretching and warmed up. He was all over them, all day long. He installed Sheridan at quarterback ahead of Robinson, and Robinson ahead of Forcier. He was out to make a few points. The players, including Forcier, all responded as Rodriguez had hoped they would. Football players respond better than anyone to "attitude adjustment." They seem to welcome it.

But the fracture lines within Schembechler Hall were now visible.

Dave Ablauf, for one, was not in a better mood. "I'm sick of all this," the normally upbeat football spokesman confided, and he looked like it. "Every time my phone rings I cringe and think, 'What's next?' There are too many factions and they're all working against each other. Why can't they all just pull for Michigan?"

Inside the building, Jon Falk pointed to the floorboards. "Bo always told me, 'Jonny, we're winning, and we've got a strong foundation. But you look close at that foundation, and you'll see a lot of termites in there. You start losing, and those termites come out, and start eating away at your foundation, and try to take over.' And that's exactly what's happening."

The next day, Rodriguez had the unpleasant task of kicking Boubacar Cissoko off the team—something he loathed doing, even when a kid wasn't contributing—while the *Free Press* probably had more fun reporting it.

On Thursday nights, offensive line coach Greg Frey led a group of players over to Mott Children's Hospital. On the way, Frey asked me, "Who's bad-mouthing us? The guys at State? You expect that. But the former *Michigan* coaches? What's up with that?"

They had learned this from their recruits, who told them which former coaches were telling them not to come to Michigan, and why.

"The thing is, all these rumors, all this crap—the underclassmen don't care about any of this. It won't affect them too much. But I think about guys like Moosman and Ortmann and Brandon Graham. Man, those guys work their asses off. They care about their teammates. They *stayed*. They get pushed aside in all this, and that's all right? That's sad.

"If it *is* former coaches going after us, what about the kids *you* recruited? The families you visited and the living rooms you sat in and the promises you made that you would make him a better player and a better person and look out for him. Where are those promises now? You broke them just to take a few swipes at the guys who came after you?

"You know, all these people who say they hate us, do they even know us? All I ask is you get to know me before you start hating me. After that, go right ahead!"

He shifted gears. "I always wanted to meet Lloyd Carr. I'd heard a lot of good things. I looked forward to meeting him when we came here. But I still haven't met him."

The rain let up for the Friday walk-through in Illinois's grand old Memorial Stadium, the same field where Red Grange had run wild on the Wolverines in 1924, costing first-year coach George Little his job.

While Rodriguez addressed each unit about their assignments, a few insiders were treated to an update of Rhett Rodriguez's school spelling bee final, which had taken place that morning. Although only a fifth grader, he competed against the sixth graders in a schoolwide contest. Under pressure, onstage, the kid was ice—and won. For his tutors, Dusty Rutledge and Mike Parrish, it was the first good news they'd had in weeks.

"Hey, Spell Check," I said. "If you're so smart, spell 'cat.'"

"Use it in a sentence," he said, not missing a beat.

"The DOG chased the CAT."

"Cat. C-a-t. Cat."

"Lucky!"

The same kid his dad had described as being "too damn serious" the year before was loosening up.

At the hotel the night before the Illinois game, Rodriguez told his team, "I was given a family name. My kids have my family name. I want them to represent the family name with honor. Nothing wrong having that sense of pride. No matter where you come from, you've all got a name— you should be proud of it. Every time you sign your name, I hope you sign it with pride.

"What I hope you sense now is that when we come together, all of a sudden we have one name—Michigan—that we represent. You need to have as much pride in Michigan as your own name, and if you do, we'll have no problems.

"We'll stick together."

The biggest guys on the team can eat 13,000 to 14,000 calories during two-a-days. Yet it's never enough. These guys can eat anywhere, anytime. Even after their huge team dinner and a postmovie snack—which would be a normal dinner for you—the big guys liked to sneak pizzas up to their rooms whenever they were hungry, which was pretty much every Friday night.

Brandon Graham was enjoying a large pepperoni with the self-described "fat boys" when he started talking about two big events in his life: when Rodriguez's regime showed up in 2008, and when his mom was mugged that past summer.

"I can say I had the opportunity to play under Coach Carr and Rich Rod," he said, and he had respect and affection for both. "When I first met [Rodriguez], I just felt he was going to fight for Michigan. I knew people were going to pressure him, and I didn't want to make it that much worse.

"Before Barwis arrived," Graham continued, "I was just big. Gittleson called me fat every day. He never let me run the golf course. Said I'd kill myself. I never ran it. Coach Rod came in the next year and said, 'No more of that.' Then I went from 300 pounds to 260. That was the hardest thing ever—but I did it.

"I used to bench 300. That was it. Now it's stupid." Graham was on his way to increasing his bench press to about 500, more than doubling his squat from 275 to 625, and tripling his clean. "Mike [Barwis] takes us to a place we hadn't been before. I like my body a lot more now."

Given his improvement, some thought Graham might apply for the 2009 NFL draft. But he was already leaning toward coming back to get a better draft position—and a degree. During Graham's first two years, he was a shaky student at best. But since all the academic reports started going directly to Rodriguez's desk instead of Draper's, Graham's attendance was near perfect, and he was scheduled to graduate in four years that May.

But the decision to return came with a price. That summer, when his mom had just gotten in her car in their Detroit neighborhood, two local thugs busted the glass on the passenger side and reached in to take her purse—a clear indication they had not met Mrs. Graham before.

"I know my momma, I know her!" Graham said. "We're the same way. If someone's trying to take something that's not theirs, we're gonna fight."

In the melee that followed, they got her purse and broke her arm.

Carr, Rodriguez, and Barwis are all great motivators, but there is simply nothing any of them could ever say or do to equal the incentive that scary scene had given Brandon Graham to get his mom out of that neighborhood. "That's why," Graham said, "I play like you're taking my lunch money."

Barwis knew the personal stories of most of the players, including Graham's, and what motivated them—and he used that information to great effect. During the Iowa game, Barwis talked with Graham for six minutes on the sideline—thanks to a good drive and TV time-outs—reminding him what happened to his mom last summer and what he was playing for.

"This is your chance," Barwis recalled, telling him, "you need to fight for it. Don't give up, and don't give in. This is your chance to make it all right."

During the Rodriguez era, however, few good deeds went unpunished. After the game, Judy Van Horn called Barwis to discuss ABC's broadcast. She had already told the entire staff that none of them could discuss football with any of the players anytime outside the allowed twenty hours. That meant, she said, if a player in the hallway or on the team plane asked, "How'd I do today?" the coaches were not permitted to answer.

Apparently, someone watching at home had called Van Horn, concerned that Barwis was "coaching" Graham. Barwis told her he wasn't coaching football—"We have coaches for that, and I never played football"—he was motivating players. "That's what I'm *paid* to do."

"Yes," Barwis recalled her saying, "but it's the perception."

If there was one lesson to be learned from Rodriguez's first twenty-two months in Ann Arbor, it's that perception trumps everything.

In Van Bergen and Martin's room, the concerns were more immediate: Save the season. "If we start dropping the ball and making the same mistakes," Van Bergen said, "we could lose, and it'll be a lot harder to rally and finish strong. There could be some doubts growing on the team.

"I think this is a determining game for how the rest of the season is going to go."

Tate Forcier was doing some thinking of his own. "I have to go back to playing the way I was in the beginning of the year," he said, going over his worksheets. "I haven't been playing well. I haven't been making my reads, and even when I do make the right read a lot of my throws have been late. Especially at this level, you can't be late, you've got to make them right away."

Rodriguez's decision to crank up the intensity seemed to be having the desired effect. But, as he often said, you can't hide from the field.

Friday's rain clouds gave way to sunny skies in Champaign on Saturday, October 30, 2009.

Paul Schmidt spent the warm-ups watching Brandon Minor run plays, seeing if his ankle looked better, while sharing some of the wisdom he had gained over his long career.

"I was telling Molk, 'You played every snap last year because you're tough, and you're lucky. You start twenty-four games, you're *really* tough, and you're *really* lucky. You start fifty-three games like Jon Jansen—you are a *beast*, and you are *damn* lucky. You're telling me Tom Brady isn't tough?'" he asked, referring to the former Michigan quarterback who had suffered a season-ending injury during an exhibition game a few months earlier. "It was just his time."

"I think if we had Molk, we beat State and we beat Iowa. He makes that much of a difference. We'd be 7–1 and in the hunt for a lot of good things. We still wouldn't be a great team, but we'd be that much better.

"He's tough, but he wasn't lucky. Not this year. It was just his time."

And, partly as a result, it wasn't Michigan's.

When they gathered by the door on one knee, Brandon Graham said, "This is gonna be our sixth win—not their second!"

Rodriguez took a more serious tack. "Listen to me clearly. Don't dare take your ass out on that field unless you are fully prepared to lay it all on the line for Michigan. All out, every snap."

The Illini were lead by Juice Williams, the same quarterback who had set records at the Big House the year before. He looked just as good opening the game with a ten-play drive straight to Michigan's end zone.

"Hey, Blue!" one fan wearing an Illinois No. 7 jersey said, hanging over the railing by the bench. "Don't be fooled by the record! We comin' after ya!"

Forcier wasn't rattled. He looked calm, confident, and decisive, connecting on all three of his passes for 31 yards. On first-and-goal from the Illinois 2-yard line, Michigan blocked and read the play so well that Carlos Brown—filling in for Minor—simply walked into the right corner.

The Wolverines added two field goals through a wild wind to take a 13–7 lead into halftime.

"This is when you start having fun," Jon Conover said, "when you're playing well and kicking ass!"

When the teams trotted back to their locker rooms, the home crowd booed the 1–6 Illini, and the game already seemed over.

The stat sheet didn't lie. The Wolverines had bested the Illini in every offensive category, including eleven first downs to five. They had to punt only once.

But Rodriguez was in no mood to let up. He was an experienced general who sensed the moment, a crossroads for their entire mission. "So let's get after 'em *now*. They don't want this like *you* want this! So let's keep hittin' 'em and grind 'em down!"

The Wolverines had shown they could take a punch, time and again. But could they deliver one with their opponent on the ropes?

On third-and-7, from Michigan's own 23, Forcier dropped back with plenty of time to look around. He found Roy Roundtree cutting across midfield and fired it to him right in stride. Roundtree caught it and cut down the middle of the field, going hell-bent for the end zone on as straight a line as any geometry teacher could draw. The defensive players on the bench interrupted their conference to turn and cheer him on, thrusting their helmets into the air.

This was it, the moment when the Wolverines would break the Illinis' backs and put them away. It would mark their fourth scoring drive, putting them up 20–7. The Illini, their season ruined, would take out the dangerous Juice Williams and put in their backup, who was already warming up on the sidelines, and surround him with underclass understudies, hoping to get them ready for the next season.

For the Wolverines, this play would mark the Continental Divide of their season—and Rodriguez's reign. They would end their Big Ten losing streak, getting their sixth win and the monkey off their backs. They'd sing "The Victors" in the locker room once more, with gusto, and enjoy a happy bus ride to the airport in the fading fall sun, take a little hopper home, and still have plenty of time to get out for Halloween parties. The next day's film sessions would be lighthearted, and on Monday, they'd start to think about improving their 6–3 record to 7–3 by beating 3–6 Purdue. Then— who knows?—maybe their momentum could push them past Wisconsin and perhaps even the Buckeyes.

But there would be no overwhelming pressure. The heat would be off. They would start a new streak of bowl games and get the vital fourteen extra practices that come with it. That, in turn, would give a great boost to recruiting, and the train would be rolling.

The particulars didn't matter right now. Just get into the end zone—win match point—and all good things will come your way.

All those visions were riding on the slender shoulders of Roy Roundtree, the freshman receiver running straight to the end zone—but Illinois's Terry Hawthorne had other ideas. Instead of conceding the footrace, the touchdown, and the game—like all his teammates behind him—Hawthorne decided to give full chase to Roundtree, closing the gap bit by bit. When Roundtree crossed the 5-yard line, Hawthorne knew that was his last chance. So he made his move, leaping at the skinny receiver and—incredibly— bringing him down right around the goal line, where Roundtree fumbled the ball into the end zone, and an Illinois player recovered it.

All eyes turned to the referee—who thrust his arms into the air. Touchdown! The Wolverines' cork popped off, and they celebrated, knowing almost everything they wanted was going to be theirs. Their season was saved—and so were their coaches. They had outrun the avalanche.

But just as Jason Olesnavage went out to kick the extra point, the all-too-familiar scenario repeated itself. The referee faced the stands and announced the play was under review.

After several minutes—which in itself might suggest whatever they saw was not conclusive—the same ref went to midfield to announce it was not a fumble, but not a touchdown, either. Michigan would get the ball at the 1-yard line. It all seemed like it wouldn't matter much anyway. Four tries from the 1? Please. Carlos Brown had already walked it in from the 2. No one ever fails in that situation. Right? Even without Molk and Minor, no one seemed worried about this.

On first down, Carlos Brown ran up the middle—and was stuffed by two Illini.

On second down, Brown went over the right end—and got stuffed again. On the bench, the defense became concerned. "We better fucking get this in!" Mouton said.

On third down, Brown ran right again—and was stopped by Illinois's Ian Thomas.

Finally, on fourth down, Rodriguez put Minor back in, by far their toughest runner, even if he was "limited" due to his high ankle sprain.

No matter how much interference and obstruction and undermining Rodriguez had faced in his twenty-two months in Ann Arbor, if they punched this in, none of it would matter. And if you are the game's greatest offensive mastermind of the last two decades, getting it in from first-and-goal with four bites at the apple would seem like child's play.

They had to score.

The play started with Minor back and right of Forcier, which gave him a running start before Forcier handed him the ball. Minor kept slashing to the left—but someone missed his man, who smothered Minor.

But not, it seemed, before Minor crossed the goal line—and fumbled the ball. Michigan's Steve Schilling recovered it in the end zone, and the ref once again thrust his arms into the air: Touchdown!

The Wolverines celebrated again, though not with the same enthusiasm, because they knew, as Olesnavage headed out to kick the point-after-touchdown again, the ref would once again announce that the play was under review.

The debate was not, it turned out, about whether Schilling had scored the touchdown but if Minor's elbow had hit the turf before the ball crossed the plane. The modern game had been reduced to such questions, which would be answered not by players or coaches or even referees but technicians staring at a monitor in a booth hundreds of feet above the field.

After several minutes of deliberation, the head official announced that Minor's elbow had, in fact, touched the ground first.

No touchdown.

The scoreboard remained stuck at 13–7.

Illinois's ball.

They needed five plays to go from the 1-foot line out to the 30. From there, Mikel Leshoure ran over the left guard but was quickly swarmed by a half dozen Michigan helmets. From the end zone camera, you couldn't see Leshoure, just white jerseys. But then Leshoure suddenly and mysteriously popped free from the pack, went wide, and dashed 70 yards down the left sideline, in front of the disbelieving Michigan players.

When Leshoure crossed the line, the Wolverines on the sideline, almost to a man, dropped their heads and turned around to walk back to their bench, as though a furious dust storm had come through and they had to shield their eyes.

The scoreboard said "Illinois 14, Michigan 13," but the faces of the Wolverines on the sideline told another story: The game was over.

The Wolverines trailed by only a point, and because they'd moved the ball well on almost every possession, there was no rational reason to believe they couldn't come back again. Except *they* didn't believe it. As Van Bergen predicted the night before, doubt had crept in.

Those few plays, it turned out, actually did constitute the Continental Divide of Michigan's season and possibly Rodriguez's tenure. But not by separating struggling from sailing, as it seemed just a few plays earlier, but from confidence and hope to fear and doubt.

The coaches tried to reinvigorate their players, and some of the leaders did the same. But it was in vain. They were done.

Van Bergen shouted, "Wake the fuck up! Wake the fuck up!"

Illinois scored 21 unanswered points to end the third quarter 28–13. The swoon was absolutely stunning.

"Hey, Rich Rod!" the loud fan wearing No. 7 yelled, "you've only got 13 points against the worst defense in the fucking country!"

The Illinois fans, satisfied the win was in the bag, started filing out of the aisles to go home. They missed Jason Ford, facing third-and-9 from Illinois's own 21, take off for another long touchdown run. 38–13.

The insult was complete.

The Wolverines had to wait for the Illini to crisscross in front of them to their tunnel. The contrast from the same run at the end of the first half could not have been greater.

Rodriguez was almost speechless. "I don't know what to tell you guys, except *that* ain't us out there. But those were *our* winged helmets, so I guess it must have been.

"Every man needs to evaluate himself and his performance. And that starts with me.

"I don't see enough intensity out there.

"I don't see enough commitment out there.

"I don't see enough hunger out there.

"So we got beat. And we deserved to get beat.

"I thought we were ready, but we weren't, and that's on me.

"You think the haters hated you before? You haven't seen nothing yet.

"We've got to play our best game this Saturday. We've got to get us a bowl game this week. And that's what we're gonna do.

"'Michigan' on three."

"MICHIGAN!"

Back in the coaches' room, Rodriguez slammed his locker. "FUCK!" Then slammed it again. "FUCK!" Then collapsed on his chair, hands behind his head, letting the inevitable waves of pain seep in.

On Facebook that night, one Michigan alum, Stacey Schwartz, probably spoke for the masses when she wrote simply: "Head in hands."

Against team rules, a lot of the players went out that night, "and they never go out after a loss," one of the student managers said. "They were just that demoralized."

The next day, after they had completed the painful tasks of breaking down the tape, grading the players, and reviewing the game, the coaches and a couple dozen players ate their Sunday night pizza in the Commons.

"Why couldn't the plane just go down?" a graduate assistant asked.

"Because," Rutledge replied, "we just can't catch a break."

The Friday night before the Purdue game, Rodriguez dug at his meal like a hungry prisoner who was sick of eating the same gray food every night.

When I told him I was surprised that the guys seemed loose, like they were still having fun and staying positive, he stared at his food, paused, and said, "I don't care.

"I don't care anymore about trying to analyze the psychology of these guys, especially for the press. I just want them to freakin' *play*. I'm sick of it."

Sick of what?

"Everything. I'm sick of the situation I'm in. I'm sick of the crap I've got to deal with every week. I'm sick of people not taking responsibility."

A case could be made that all happiness is feeling like you have possibilities. When someone wins the lottery, he's happy not because he won the lottery but because he suddenly has dozens of options he didn't have the day before.

But the corollary is also true: All unhappiness is feeling like your options are shrinking and the world is closing in on you. That you're trapped.

Rich Rodriguez's options were shrinking. By the time he arrived in Ann Arbor, it was clear he could not go back the way he had come. But after only twenty-one games at Michigan, it had become just as clear there would be only one way he could stay: winning football games. And fast.

Every Friday night, between the dinner and the movie, the offense and defense met separately with their coaches to go over the scouting report one last time. But this week, instead of reviewing the opponent, they reviewed a tape of their practices that week. The message was simple: The Illini didn't beat the Wolverines. The Wolverines beat the Wolverines.

Job 1: Hold on to the damn ball. There was a reason John Heisman famously showed his players a football and said, "Gentlemen, it is better to have died a small boy than to fumble this football."

But John Heisman never met Tate Forcier. On one play Rodriguez showed that night, Forcier held the ball like an oversized sponge and swung it around like he was washing his windows with it. Sure enough, the defense soon forced a fumble.

"High and tight, high and tight, high and tight," Rodriguez said with relative calm. "Anything else is selfish. It shows disrespect for your teammates, and I know you're not selfish, and I know you don't want to disrespect your teammates."

Here he was, going into the tenth game of the season, reviewing something they had covered on the first day of spring ball, the first day of summer practice, and just about every day since. It was pretty clear Rodriguez was tired of that, too.

But he knew it came with coaching young players, and he usually enjoyed the teaching process. But they were repeating the same lessons too often, which became especially aggravating when he had no idea how many lessons they would get.

Job 2: In the spread option offense, the quarterback has to take three steps and *throw* it. Not four steps. Not five steps. And no hitches, either. Three and throw. Three and throw. The timing was simple but exact—and it was everything. Any freelancing and incompletes, sacks, and interceptions soon followed.

And that's exactly what Rodriguez saw next on the practice tape: Forcier taking three steps (an improvement), seeing his receiver open— but then hitching, which allowed the linebacker to cover the receiver. Rodriguez was calm but firm. "I'm sure I will *not* have to see on Monday any tape of any Michigan quarterback taking three steps and a hitch when he should be taking three steps and *throwing*."

Next play, same thing, but this time Forcier threw it behind the receiver. The linebacker just missed making the interception.

"That one's late. Why? Three and hitch instead of three and *throw*. I've been doing this for *twenty years*! I didn't just wake up and come up with this thing. We have refined this over time. We *know* what works. We're not *guessing*! Three steps and *throw*! THROW! You've got to *trust* the timing!"

But it was really more than that. The quarterbacks had to trust the system—and the coaches who had created it. The flipside was just as simple: The coaches had to remember that Forcier was still a freshman. And even though Rodriguez's quarterbacks on every team he'd coached eventually won Conference Player of the Year, not one of them did it his first season.

If the Illinois game could be reduced to Michigan's four tries from the 1-yard line, Michigan's season likewise boiled down to four great chances to win just one game to secure a bowl bid: Michigan State, which ended in overtime; Iowa, which ended one pass short of a winning field goal attempt; Illinois, which broke on the 1-yard line; and Purdue, which looked like an eminently winnable game. But like the fourth-and-1 play against Illinois, the pressure mounted with each failed attempt. This was Rodriguez's last best chance at match point.

Blow it against the Boilermakers, and the odds would only get taller against Wisconsin, and taller still against Ohio State, still in the hunt for a national title. Collars were tight in Ann Arbor.

The quarterbacks didn't think Purdue would be a pushover, either. "They're good, they play hard," Sheridan said later that night in his hotel room. "Much harder than Illinois." And then, unable to let Illinois go: "I still can't believe we lost to those guys."

"Don't let 'em beat you twice," Forcier said, as a half-joking warning they'd all heard a hundred times. "Man, we just got to win again. That's been driving me fucking nuts. We just got to win again."

Adding to the intrigue were the running tensions between the two programs. It was then-Purdue coach Joe Tiller who famously accused Rodriguez of being a snake-oil salesman when Rodriguez recruited Roy Roundtree away from Purdue. It was current head coach Danny Hope who publicly blamed Rodriguez for sending in the infraction on Zach Reckman.

Given the stakes, losing this game would be unbearable for Rodriguez. But that was, of course, exactly what the 3–6 Boilermakers had in mind when they elected to receive the kick—another show of disrespect for the Wolverines' defense that they were starting to get used to.

Clearly, Purdue had studied Michigan's previous game. The gambit quickly proved to be the correct one. Four plays, 80 yards, in 1:45. 7–0 Purdue.

But Forcier put on a spread offense showcase that put Michigan up 17–10, then found Roundtree over the middle. The Purdue defender gave chase, but this time Roundtree gave the defender a stiff-arm and bolted for the right corner. This was not the previous week. Touchdown. Michigan 24, Purdue 10.

With six minutes left in the half, J. B. Fitzgerald tipped a pass to Donovan Warren for an easy interception at midfield, against a team that was ready to quit. But the pattern held: The Wolverines couldn't throw the knockout. They lived their lives on the edge of losing close and winning close, refusing to give up—or take control.

At halftime, there was more fear in the Michigan locker room than during any other intermission that season.

"Don't relax!" Van Bergen yelled. "Don't make the same mistake!"

"It ain't over, Blue!" Stevie Brown said. "We ain't done!"

On the first possession of the second half, Forcier rolled to his right and pitched the ball to Minor. But Purdue's Brandon King knocked it away and recovered the ball at Michigan's 19. One play later, the scoreboard read: Purdue 17, Michigan 24. Illinois all over again?

Perhaps not. On Forcier's next option, he wisely kept it and dashed to the goal line. Purdue 17, Michigan 30.

If the pressure that had built with every headline and every loss got to all the players, as it surely did, it got to them all differently. Quarterbacks dropped more snaps, receivers dropped more passes, but Michigan's walk-on kickers seemed especially vulnerable—which helped explain why they kicked so well on Tuesdays and so inconsistently on Saturdays. Jason Olesnavage, the same walk-on who had knocked a 51-yarder through the uprights earlier that day, missed the extra point.

The Boilermakers countered with a 91-yard, 14-play drive that cut Michigan's lead to 30–24.

Michigan's defense returned to the bench, took off their helmets, and reached for the towels and water bottles, thinking they'd have a few minutes to collect themselves. But Purdue pulled off one of the gutsiest plays of the Big Ten season: a perfectly executed onside kick.

The exhausted defenders dropped their water bottles, grabbed their helmets, and rushed out onto the field. Purdue wisely went deep on the first play for a 54-yard touchdown. After the extra point, the scoreboard read Purdue 31, Michigan 30. Michigan's missed PAT loomed large.

"There are two ways this can go," Van Bergen told his teammates. "We can lie down and take this loss. Or we can fight and take it over. Which way you gonna go? Let's go!"

Early in the fourth quarter, Michigan missed another field goal, while Purdue had added another touchdown to go up 38–30 with ten minutes remaining.

But Michigan's defense, so unlike its second half against Illinois, rose once more. Hemingway caught a punt, then bolted 33 yards down to Purdue's 11, with 3:31 left. In a game chock-full of parallels with the previous week's debacle, Michigan faced third-and-1 from Purdue's 2-yard line. Would they be stopped again? Not this time. On the first try, Minor got the 1 yard needed for a first down. And on the second, he busted through for the touchdown.

Purdue 38, Michigan 36; 2:10 left.

Michigan set up for the two-point conversion. Forcier dropped back and looked and looked, failing to see two receivers wide open, and got sacked. He looked every bit a true freshman.

When the game ended, the normally composed Stevie Brown couldn't hold it in. "God DAMN IT!" In the stands, and on the sidelines, there followed complete silence. The unthinkable had happened. The Wolverines had blown a 14-point lead, with the ball, at home, to a weak opponent. They had blown a 4–0 start to the season, reducing it to a 5–5 knot in just six weeks. They had converted a virtual lock on a bowl game into a long shot.

The handshakes were quick, except for one: When Rodriguez congratulated Purdue head coach Danny Hope, Hope held Rodriguez's hand and yelled for one of his players, Zach Reckman. "Come on over here, Zach, and meet the man who got you kicked out of the Notre Dame game!" Rodriguez stood there seething while Hope pulled off his little stunt.

The locker room mood was a combination of disgust and despair.

In September, this team was the cat that kept landing on its feet. And now it was the cat that kept landing on its head: Michigan State, Iowa, Illinois, Purdue. In each game, they'd had an excellent chance to win—and each time, they'd found a new and creative way to lose.

"We are not gonna give up. That's not gonna happen," Rodriguez told his team. "Nobody'll expect anything from us the next two weeks. Nothing's gonna break us apart. NOTHING. Nothing. Nothing."

He started to get choked up.

"We will stick together. And we will come back. We are DAMN close to getting it. Damn close.

"When you talk to the press, give 'em credit. They played hard. We just gotta get better. We just . . . gotta get better. And we will.

"Don't let the bastards get you. We're gonna have the backs of every man in every way.

"'All in' on three."

"ALL IN!"

Rodriguez left the players in silence to meet Rita in the side room, sitting with Raquel and Rhett. She looked taut. She stood up and gave her husband a big hug. He told her what Danny Hope had said, then blurted out, "Bullshit! I gotta get my ass beat by a junior high school, no-class asshole?!"

He picked up a football lying on an end table and kicked it, causing it to ricochet around the tiny space, then picked it up again and threw it in the corner.

"Call him on it!" Rita said. "Why do we have to be so politically correct when no one else is with us?"

Of course, Hope's gesture was adolescent at best. Likewise, Rita could not be blamed for supporting her husband and getting fed up with the endless stream of criticism while they were constantly being told to turn the other cheek. But it was not hard to foresee what would happen if Rodriguez did, in fact, call Coach Hope out in public.

A few minutes later, at the postgame press conference, Rodriguez explained what Hope had done—and, sure enough, that quote eclipsed everything else. While some readers, bloggers, and fans would take Hope to task, it largely backfired on the man making the complaint. If Hope came across as classless, Rodriguez came across as petulant.

It might not have been fair, but it was predictable. And avoidable.

On his way back to his locker room, Rodriguez stopped in the Crisler Arena hallway, as he always did, to see the hospital kids. A reporter who had just asked some pointed questions about his job security stopped him and said, with a big smile, "No hard feelings, Coach. I think you're doing a great job. I'm your biggest backer!"

Rodriguez forced a smile, shook his hand, and said, "Thanks."

But that was his last good deed for the day. Two overweight autograph seekers, middle-aged men wearing Michigan jerseys, tried to interrupt his time with the young patients to get autographs. He stayed focused on the kids. And when he finished, he walked past the two men into Crisler's wood-paneled hallway, with Rita at his side.

Rodriguez didn't get far, however, before running into Bill Martin. They ducked into the nearest open doorway, which happened to be the boiler room, and talked privately. Rita then walked in, and gave Rich a big hug.

But the door was slightly ajar, allowing the middle-aged autograph seekers to sneak a peek.

One said to the other, "Rich Rod is cryin'!" slapping his friend in his gut—though it wasn't true. "He's fuckin' *bawlin'*!"

"Well, good," his friend said. "He should be."

On Sunday, the grading was finished, but Rodriguez was not. The defense was so bad in this game, Rodriguez concluded, that there was no point giving an award for the Best Defensive Player.

"We better be recruiting our asses off," he said, looking at recruiting coordinator Chris Singletary. "We need some guys who can get after their man and make a tackle. It's no surprise that everyone who wins the toss takes the ball first. They see what we see.

"Damn it!" he said, the frustration boiling over. "We can't run, we can't tackle, we can't block. We are the worst fundamentals team in America. Embarrassing."

Later that day, Jon Falk said, "I feel horrible for that guy. Never have I seen such shit. It's the perfect storm—Bo's gone, the AD's gone, all this NCAA crap—and he's got to deal with all of it.

"I try to leave him alone these days."

Rodriguez spent a few hours that Sunday going over every single play with the defensive coaches. Again, you could feel the tension between him and Greg Robinson, with Rodriguez walking a fine line between respecting Robinson's autonomy over his defense and making his frustration plain.

"We must be insane," he said at one point, "to do the same things and expect a different result. But I'm just trying to understand. I'm looking for answers."

By the time he met the players on Monday, November 9, at 3:00, Rodriguez found his message.

"To accept losing is unacceptable," he said, jaw clenched. His body looked tight, ready to pounce. "I hope you guys understand that. But the nice part is, we're playing a nationally ranked team this weekend, on the road, and no one thinks we've got a chance. This is a game where, if you're not a man, don't show up."

They showed up.

Built in 1917, Camp Randall Stadium is the oldest in the Big Ten. At the outset of the Civil War, the site had been home to an actual camp built to train Union soldiers. It had long since morphed into one of the toughest, and drunkest, places to play college football.

Michigan fell behind the twentieth-ranked Badgers 7–0, but came right back to tie the game. At the end of the first quarter, Michigan had outgained the Badgers, 108 yards to 50, and could have outscored them if they had not roughed Wisconsin's punter.

Rodriguez's speeches had achieved their goal: Despite the heartbreaking setbacks and long odds, they continued fighting. But they still had no knack for capitalizing on their efforts. If the 2009 Wolverines were a baseball team, they would have led the league in runners left in scoring position.

Michigan held leads of 10–7 and 17–14 before the Badgers scored the last points of the half, going into intermission ahead 21–17.

"Keep striking their ass!" Rodriguez told a jacked-up bunch in the locker room. "They're starting to feel it now. Keep after 'em. Get what we want *now*!"

Wisconsin scored on its first possession of the second half to go up 28–17, but once again, the Wolverines came back: Forcier to Roundtree on the bubble screen, to close the gap to 28–24.

But there they stalled. Michigan's offense couldn't muster any more points, while its defense couldn't generate any more stops, and they fell apart. 45–24.

Long before the clock had run out, the party had started in Madison.

In the coaches' room, Rodriguez said, to no one in particular, "They're running the same goddamn play twenty times in a row and we can't fuckin' stop 'em. Fuck *me*!"

But he was not giving up. He walked out into the locker room. "Everyone STOP what you're doing and get in here—every coach and every player.

"Now, here's the deal. We are going to get ready for the biggest game of the year. Nobody is going out tonight. Nobody. We are getting ready for Ohio State immediately. Immediately!

"We can do it. When we execute like we did in the first half, we can beat anyone. I'll be right there with you, every step of the way. *Every* step.

"Now, 'all in' for Michigan."

"Say it like you mean it!" Brandon Graham shouted, and others added, "If you don't, get out!"

"ALL IN!"

Rodriguez retreated to the coaches' room, where he bent over, with his hands on his knees, as though someone had just punched him in the gut—and held the position for well over a minute. He was in physical pain.

But the indignities were not over. Back on the field, with fans filing out, longtime Michigan cameraman Pat McLaughlin looked around and said, "In the old days, if they beat Michigan, they'd be crying, rejoicing. Now they don't care. There's no awe, just disrespect and vulgarity. I don't like it."

On the bus ride to the airport, the caravan got stuck just a couple of blocks from Camp Randall, among the rows of two-story wooden houses typical of almost every old neighborhood surrounding a Big Ten stadium. This being Madison, the residents were drinking, blasting music, and dancing on the porch roofs.

When a few of them realized Michigan's football players were in those buses, they started yelling, flipping them off, and simulating masturbation. But after a while, even they got tired of all that and crawled back through their second-floor windows.

Nothing to see here. Move along.

In the week before the Western Michigan game, the *Detroit Free Press* came out with its sensational story.

In the week before the Michigan State game, the NCAA conducted its interviews and the GPA mess surfaced.

In the week before the Illinois game, Rodriguez learned that David Molk would be out for the rest of the season, and the NCAA sent its Notice of Inquiry.

Those were all pretty bad weeks, but the week before the Ohio State game was right up there.

On Sunday night, Rodriguez's attorney called to let him know the university was going to send out a press release Monday. The *Free Press*'s FOIA request for the CARA forms audit was expiring, and by law, the university had to deliver the goods. The documents they were forking over to the *Free Press* would show that football staffers had failed to submit the internal documents charting the hours athletes spent on football for the entire 2008–2009 school year.

This, in turn, forced Michigan to respond to the stories it assumed would follow, from the *Free Press* in particular. The people on the Hill promised Rodriguez he would get a chance to revise their press release before they sent it out.

At eleven o'clock Monday morning, however, Rodriguez discovered that a press release had already been sent out. It stated, in part, "The audit does not identify where the system broke down," even though the university knew exactly where it had broken down: among Labadie, Draper, and Van Horn.

The release did not point out that: the CARA forms were unique to Michigan; they were not required by the NCAA; and the communication problems had nothing to do with the coaching staff. The forms had also not been lost or shredded. In fact, it said, they had been "misplaced," which sounds shady and was true only if by "misplaced" they meant "Labadie had them in his office the entire time."

Thanks to the lack of clarity, however, the *Free Press* could lead with this: "University of Michigan football coaches failed to file required forms to school compliance officers that document the hours put in by its players for the entire 2008–09 school year, U-M announced today," even though the coaches had had nothing to do with it—by design.

Rodriguez went "ballistic," according to the people in Schembechler Hall: talking so loudly in his office that people outside his door—closed for once—could hear everything, and occasionally stomping down the hallway to see this person or that. The outburst marked the maddest he had ever been at Michigan.

Remarkably, he managed to calm down before he met with his team that afternoon, belying none of the fury he had been feeling just a few hours earlier. In front of his team, I cannot recall him saying anything egregious. He usually blamed himself while extolling Michigan tradition—all things he was accused of not doing at the press conferences.

He knew that whatever he was facing, more distractions were the last thing his team needed before trying to upset Ohio State in a last-gasp attempt to save a bowl bid, and the season.

"This week, we will give Ohio State our undivided attention. This is all you'll be thinking about this week, except for classes—and as you know, we expect you to attend." The last bit was a reference to Carr's policy of letting the players skip class during rivalry weeks. By Rodriguez's second year, they knew not to ask him anymore about that.

"There is no game on our schedule that is bigger than Ohio State," he said from the podium. "Never will be, never can be—until we play for the National Championship. And that will happen, sooner than you think.

"If you want to be remembered for years and years and years, you play well in this game."

With that, Phil Bromley started a special DVD he made of some of the greatest moments in the rivalry—from Michigan's perspective, of course:

Tom Harmon, Desmond Howard, Charles Woodson. The big plays, the big wins.

Rodriguez then spoke about the seniors—how proud he was of them, and how much this game meant to them. Then he turned the room over to the seniors so they could address the team without the coaches present.

"We don't ask for much," Mark Ortmann said. "I'm just asking you all to give all you can. None of us have ever beaten Ohio State. So let's start a new streak."

"We haven't had the kind of season we worked for," Brandon Graham said. "Winning this game would cancel out all that. Everyone's thinking they're gonna blow us out by fifty-something. They're just slapping us in the face and saying we're weak as fuck. We ain't weak as fuck! We've been in every game we've played. So let's get out there and embarrass those boys."

At the team dinner, Rich and Rita couldn't ignore the events of the day.

The people on the Hill told Rodriguez they didn't want to give out more information than necessary, fearing it would lead to more questions about the investigations and more FOIA requests. The concerns were real, but their solution—be as vague as possible—made things worse, especially for Rodriguez. Further, they told him they didn't want him to comment on it, instructing him not to answer any questions.

"That's just gonna lead to more questions and make *me* look guilty!" Rich said that night, ripping into a chicken leg.

"It's like taking the Fifth," Rita added.

"Here's an idea," Rich said. "Maybe here at Michigan, we should get off our high horse and *answer some questions*. They're too worried about politics—and not the truth!"

The chicken leg went momentarily forgotten as he openly wondered whom, exactly, the muzzle order was intended to protect.

"Since when is telling the truth a bad idea? Why are we so scared of the regents? Why are we so scared of the NCAA? Why are we so scared of telling the *truth*? For cryin' out loud—we haven't done anything *wrong*!

"They *have* the fucking forms! They're not even *required*!

"And you want to protect them, at my expense? I'm always taking the hit. 'Oh, he can take it.' Well, I'm reaching my limit. And they seem to forget, I'm Michigan too! On my hat there's a big block 'M,' and that stands for 'Michigan!'"

"If people want to question my play calling, go right ahead. But my integrity? At some point you've got to defend yourself."

After Rich left to watch film, Rita admitted her own sense of guilt. "Rich was going to stay at West Virginia, but we were all excited to come to Michigan. An elite school that will treat him right and give him the resources he needs to be among the top, every year. What kills us is we had such *undying* faith in this place—the *integrity* of Michigan.

"This place is special. I know it's special. Even after all this, I *still* believe we were meant to be here. We'll get through this. We want to win *here!*"

Back in his office, after fielding scheduled interview calls from Mitch Albom, Dan Patrick, and other national stars, Rodriguez took a call from President Coleman.

"I wish *I* could be calling *you* just to say congratulations on being named the number-three U.S. college president in *Time* magazine!" he said.

He listened for a bit, then Coleman turned the topic to the business at hand. You didn't need to hear the questions to know what they were.

"I didn't know about this until August of 2009," he told her, clearly referring to the CARA form situation. "This morning they said, 'Here's the press release.' I said, 'This is going to make it look like I'm to blame.' 'Oh, no it won't.'

"Well, sure enough, today's paper has a picture of me with the headline, COACHES FAIL TO SUBMIT PAPERS. I'm tired of eating it. I've been eating it for two years."

He listened.

"I'm just sitting here trying to get ready for Ohio State, and I'm gonna be asked about it tomorrow and Wednesday. What am I gonna say? I can't discuss it? Then I look guilty, like I'm trying to hide something.

"It makes it look like it's Rich Rodriguez over here and the university over there. It makes me look like the bad guy."

He listened for a while.

"I know it's a big-boy business, and you have to have thick skin. Well, I've got rhino skin now, but I'm human. And so is Rita. And it's not our fault. We haven't done anything wrong!"

The president was wrapping things up. They managed to generate some small chuckles, then Rodriguez brought it to a close. "All right. I know you've got to get on your plane. Have a safe trip."

He hung up.

"Same old bullshit."

Once again, he compartmentalized the distractions to rally for the Senior Walk-Through on Thursday, when he gave lavish announcements of each senior, who then ran out of the field house through a tunnel of teammates.

By Friday evening, he was ready for the pep rally on the Diag before a crowd of about a thousand people. They had not given up. When Rodriguez arrived with the four game captains, the cheer went up: "Rich Rodri-guez!"

"I tell ya, from the bottom of my heart, THANK YOU!

"I love coming to work. I love the people I work with, and I love our fans!"

He introduced the captains, each of whom said a few words before giving the microphone back to Rodriguez. "As coaches, we love to practice— but not too much!" The crowd laughed. "Just enough! So let's practice 'The VICTORS'! And let's sing it so loud they can hear you in Columbus!"

"Thank you! We love you!"

If you had seen what he had gone through that week, you had to wonder how he did it.

On November 21, 2009, Michigan entered The Game without three of its most important players—Molk, Minor, and Carlos Brown—making the already long odds even longer. But after Michigan's defense stopped the Buckeyes' first possession at midfield—punctuated by Stevie Brown picking up Brandon Saine and throwing him to the ground like a rag doll—the crowd went crazy, and hope was in the air.

But when the Wolverines faced third-and-8 from their 9-yard line, Forcier rolled out to the right, across the end zone, carrying the ball like a loaf of bread and swinging his arm as he ran—exactly what they'd told him not to do a thousand times. He was carrying the ball so carelessly that he didn't need a defender to knock it loose. He did it himself, bouncing the ball off his right thigh and fumbling it in the end zone. Cameron Heyward recovered it for the easiest touchdown ever recorded—truly, a gift.

Things could have gone south fast, but the Wolverines kept fighting. The offense got the ball to Ohio State's 5-yard line at one point—where they failed to get the touchdown or the field goal.

They were down 14–3 at halftime, and, as usual, it could have been much closer. But the defense was holding up—something no one expected—giving U-M a slight edge in overall yardage.

Brandon Graham, of course, knocked himself out on every play, making those who knew his situation pray that he didn't blow out a knee in what would probably be his last college game.

But if it wasn't? If Michigan found a way to beat Ohio State? What problem did Rodriguez and his team really have that beating the Buckeyes wouldn't solve?

Forcier engineered an impressive drive to start the second half, ending in a touchdown. The defense did its job, limiting the Buckeyes to a single score that half to leave Michigan down only 21–10. The offense was doing its job, too, matching Ohio State yard for yard. But Forcier committed five turnovers—*five*—including three interceptions in the fourth quarter alone. And that was the difference: freshman mistakes.

In the locker room, there wasn't much to say.

"I'm proud of the way we fought today," Rodriguez told them. "We can beat anyone when we don't beat ourselves.

"Don't embarrass the program tonight. You still have classes this week, and we expect you to be there.

"You seniors, I'm *proud* of you. You played your asses off. You set a foundation for all our future success. This program will be back, ON TOP. And when we win the Big Ten championship next year, we'll give *you* the credit. You deserve it.

"People are trying to divide us, and it ain't gonna work. Nothing and nobody—*nothing and nobody!*—will divide this team, this family.

"Let them cockroaches stay out there. They got nothing to say to us. And we don't have anything to say to them. What we have to say, we'll say in nine months.

"UNDERSTAND THIS! You guys have come a long way and overcome a lot, and if they don't understand that, I don't care. And our ass will be back next year, on the top!"

Graham yelled out, "Let's sing 'The Victors' one more time!"

They sang it loudly, not with joy but with conviction—exactly what the circumstances warranted. When Forcier hugged each senior, he apologized: "I'm sorry. I'm sorry. I'm sorry." He was crying. Rodriguez interrupted the process to give Forcier a big hug. Before it was over, they were both crying.

At the press conference, Rodriguez was asked if he had gained some humility.

"Got humbled last year. Been humbled before and will be humbled again. In this profession, there's enough humility to go around for everybody . . . I'm getting tired of being humbled."

The questions kept coming: "At what point does patience run out?" "Have you been told anything about your job?"

He brushed them aside.

But Rodriguez's fatal flaw flared: saying too much, and saying it artlessly.

While trying to explain how they got to 8–16 after two years, he mentioned his small senior class this year and the next, and having to start a true freshman at quarterback.

A reporter asked, "What have you learned in two years about what you'll need to—"

"It didn't take me two years," Rodriguez interrupted. "It didn't take me two years to figure out what we needed and what we needed to do. I knew it after a couple of games."

That's when someone should have pulled him off the stage with a hook. If he had stopped, he might have avoided another national lambasting. But when reporters asked follow-up questions, he eventually offered the following: "The last three Februaries, or four Februaries, have hurt us," he said, referring to recruiting. In politics, Michael Kinsley has defined a gaffe as being caught telling the truth. This was a gaffe.

More questions drew more answers. "There's a faction—and certainly I wouldn't accuse any of you-all—of creating a negative type of environment that wants to see drama, and wants to see people pointing fingers." As usual, it was all true. And as usual, it would boomerang on Rodriguez himself, who felt compelled to go to Carr's office to apologize.

These answers gave the writers what they needed, perhaps best captured by CBSSports.com columnist Gregg Doyel. In a column titled ROD-RIGUEZ SPOILS IMAGE WITH SPOILED DISPLAY IN DEFEAT, he wrote: "After the loss Saturday to Ohio State, Rodriguez knew exactly where the blame should go.

"At Lloyd Carr.

"And at the media."

He concluded: "Longtime football coach and athletic director Bo Schembechler never specified what he meant in 1989 when he made his famous 'Michigan Man' proclamation.

"But he didn't mean someone like Rich Rodriguez."

As was usually the case when it came to Rich Rodriguez, however, there was a gap between the mainstream media and the bloggers, and an even bigger gap between the fans, who generally supported Rodriguez.

In a poll taken by Annarbor.com (which had replaced *The Ann Arbor News*) hours after Michigan's seventh loss, a surprising 72 percent of respondents said Rodriguez deserved more time, something most pundits would never have guessed.

At the end of Rodriguez's second year, two things were certain: He wasn't giving up, and time was running out.

After Bill Martin announced on October 21, 2009, that he would be step-
ping down effective September 4, 2010—coinciding with the season opener
and the debut of his luxury suites—the search for his successor was on.

Three strong candidates immediately surfaced who were all Division I
athletic directors with close Michigan ties: Buffalo's Warde Manuel, Oregon State's Bob De Carolis, and Miami of Ohio's Brad Bates. It speaks to
the strength of the program Canham and Schembechler built that Michigan had no trouble finding three alums with such pedigrees. Any of them
would have been a good selection.

But there was a fourth, less conventional candidate, who seemed to
have the inside track. Schembechler often stated that he hoped one day
Brad Bates, one of his former players, would be the university's athletic
director and Dave Brandon, another former player, the state's governor.
While Brandon was building a world-class business résumé—which culminated in an eleven-year run as the CEO of Domino's Pizza and enough
wealth to start his own charitable foundation—he had also been deeply
involved in Republican politics. Many considered his election to Michigan's board of regents in 1998 the first step toward bigger things, including a run for either governor or the U.S. Senate. But his failed reelection
bid for regent in 2006, in the wake of a Democratic landslide, showed him
just how vulnerable any campaign could be to forces beyond the candidate's control.

Although Brandon had never ruled out running for public office in the
future, he shifted his attention to Michigan's athletic department. Brandon

had never coached or worked in college athletics, but that was also true of the four ADs who followed Bo Schembechler. Thanks to Brandon's eight years as a regent, he had much closer ties to President Coleman—to whom he often lent the Domino's corporate jet—and the regents than any of the other candidates, all working in different states.

When the search officially started, Michigan interviewed Manuel, De Carolis, and Bates, but often at inconvenient times, just one indication that the job was Brandon's if he wanted it—and he did. And that is how Michigan would end up hiring its fifth straight athletic director with no experience leading college athletics.

Some criticized the selection as simply another manifestation of Michigan presidents giving more weight to their comfort level than the candidates' credentials, a list that includes the Duderstadt-Roberson duo and the Bollinger-Martin pairing, too. (James B. Angell, at least, would understand.)

While there was something to it, Brandon was not Bill Martin. The campus and accounts Martin left will serve Michigan athletics for decades to come. In fact, you could argue that because Bill Martin had done such a good job being Bill Martin, Michigan did not need another one, allowing Michigan to focus on other needs, including public relations, marketing, and unifying the fractured Michigan family. Running a private company with a staff he could count on one hand had not prepared Martin for managing 250 employees, especially coaches, in the fishbowl that is Michigan athletics.

Brandon, in contrast, had spent eleven years running a company that operates over 9,000 stores in 65 countries run by 175,000 people. His job entailed dealing with millions of customers, thousands of stockholders, and dozens of board members, executives, and Wall Street analysts every day.

If there was one thing Brandon could handle, it was public relations. And if there was one thing Michigan and its embattled coach could use, that was it.

The most important day of the year for a college football coach is not the home opener, the game against the big rival, or even January 1.

It's National Signing Day, which falls every year on the first Wednesday in February.

On this day, the end zone is not grass, Astroturf, or FieldTurf but a Xerox FaxCentre 2218. And only when a signed National Letter of Intent hits the receiving tray can you count it.

It can all be traced back to 1945, when Crisler concocted the platoon system. That spawned specialization, and that in turn gave birth to year-round nationwide recruiting. It was no longer enough to round up the best athletes on campus and teach them football. You now had to get the biggest offensive tackle from Dallas, the fastest receiver from Florida, and the quickest quarterback from California. When the competition for those specialists heated up, schools felt compelled to offer scholarships for athletic prowess, something unheard-of before the platoon system. (Even Heisman trophy winner Tom Harmon washed dishes at the Union to make ends meet.)

The race for the biggest and the best was on—and Crisler hated it. He even despised the idea of athletic scholarships, and tried to put the genie back in the bottle. In his long tenure on the NCAA rules committee, he attempted to limit substitution—starving his own baby—but he couldn't control the monster he had created or its many offspring.

In the battle between Crisler and recruiting, recruiting won in a landslide.

Recruiting season now lasts all year, and is far more exhausting than football itself.

It starts with collecting information on over a thousand high school football players, watching hundreds of hours of film, then making the entire coaching staff take dozens of trips each across the country, from Pasadena to Pahokee, to meet with hundreds of high school players, parents, and coaches. They follow that up with thousands of calls, e-mails, and texts, all in the hopes of getting the twenty-five players you think will help you win a national title three or four years down the road.

During Lloyd Carr's last three seasons, ESPN ranked Michigan's recruiting classes eleventh, tenth, and thirteenth, respectively. In Rodriguez's first full season, Michigan finished tenth, a pretty remarkable effort, given the Wolverines' 3–9 season. But despite Michigan's marginally improved record in 2009, recruiting was harder because of the ongoing NCAA investigation. Most coaches knew better, but some of them were not above telling recruits Michigan could lose scholarships, bowl games, TV appearances, and even its head coach.

Rodriguez sought to get the skill position players he needed to run the spread before doing anything else. But given the team's progressively weak defense in Rodriguez's first two seasons—which finished sixty-seventh and eighty-second in total defense, due partly to a bare-bones twenty-five scholarships devoted to defensive players, where most teams use about forty—he knew he now had to load up on the other side of the ball.

The one exception Rodriguez made was quarterback. After the injuries and inconsistency of 2009, he decided to recruit one serious quarterback candidate every year. This year, it was Devin Gardner, one of the top two players in the state. The fact that Michigan had two capable quarterbacks ahead of him didn't scare him—or Michigan.

Michigan was happy to let Gardner, a good student, along with six other recruits enroll early. But Romulus High School, hard by Detroit's Metro Airport, held up approval until mid-January, when Gardner's principal called him into his office.

"You need to get your stuff and go."

Gardner wasn't sure what that meant.

"The school board approved your graduation. You're going to Michigan."

"That," Gardner said on signing day, "might have been the happiest day of my life."

———

It wasn't that long ago that Dan Dierdorf told his parents over breakfast he had decided to go to Michigan—and that was it. No press conference, no hat ceremony, no mention in the Michigan papers. Schembechler would simply give the list of his recruits to Bruce Madej, who sent that out to the beat writers.

Just a few years ago, it was not unusual for a team to have ten recruits still on the fence on signing day. But ESPN and the recruiting websites have made the process so public that fewer recruits flip-flop. Those outlets have transformed recruiting season from a sleepy insiders' game into an intense full-blown season in its own right.

Why the fuss? As the veteran coaches say, it's not Xs and Os, it's Jimmys and Joes.

On Tuesday, February 2, Rodriguez made a final round of calls to his remaining twenty prospects. They had all pledged their fealty to Michigan many times over, and most recruiting experts predicted Michigan would have a top-twenty class. But as Rodriguez knew too well, until that signed fax comes through, all you have is air.

Michigan's recruiting class rank could jump up dramatically if three recruits signed with the Wolverines.

They all played safety, Michigan's weakest position in 2009, which looked even weaker for 2010 after junior Donovan Warren declared for the NFL draft. There would be no getting Boubacar Cissoko back, either. After he was kicked off the team in the middle of the 2009 season for missing class, he then dropped out, held up a cabdriver with a pellet gun, and was sentenced to nineteen months at Jackson State Prison—an already sad story turned much sadder. As bad as it had been, getting these recruits could turn Michigan's weakest position into its strongest, literally overnight. They were:

Rashad Knight, from Jacksonville, whom ESPN ranked the nation's twelfth best high school safety. He would decide between Michigan and Rutgers.

Sean Parker, out of LA, whom ESPN ranked fifth at safety and forty-ninth among all players. He was also considering USC and Notre Dame.

And Demar Dorsey, from Fort Lauderdale, whom ESPN ranked second at safety and twelfth overall—thanks partly to his 4.25 time in the forty-yard dash.

Not surprisingly, Michigan coveted Dorsey the most.

Dorsey looked like a lock for Florida, which dominated the 2010 recruiting wars nationwide, until Gators assistant coach Vance Bedford,

Florida's point man on Dorsey, left to become Louisville's defensive coordinator. Dorsey cooled on the Gators and finally wrote them off when they told him they would rescind their offer if he visited any more schools.

Suddenly, Florida State, USC, and Michigan were scrambling to get this phenom. But there was a catch. Two years earlier, Dorsey had been involved in three burglaries with some high school friends and was arrested for two. Although he had been acquitted of one charge and the other had been dropped, in the era of FOIA requests and Internet recruiting research, any coach pursuing him would have to assume that Dorsey's past would get out, and the coach would have to answer for it.

That didn't stop them from beating a path to his parents' door, however. USC and Florida State could offer Dorsey warm weather and winning records. But Bedford, a former assistant coach under Carr, felt he couldn't ethically recruit Dorsey to Louisville, so he told Dorsey he should go to Michigan. It so happened that one of Dorsey's cousins was Denard Robinson, one of Michigan's best student recruiters.

But Rodriguez knew no school would scrutinize such a recruit like Michigan, and no coach would receive more media attention than he would. So he followed up Cal Magee's visit with his own.

Because Dorsey was behind in his studies, he was attending two schools at once to catch up. Rodriguez went to both to talk to his coaches, principals, teachers, classmates, and even custodians, plus his parents and Vance Bedford.

"They are all vouching for him," Rodriguez said. "We're taking a chance, but not as big a one as it looks from the outside. We know him. We know the people around him. And this is not the first time we've taken a chance on a kid."

When Rodriguez and his staff were still at West Virginia, they recruited Pat Lazear out of Bethesda, Maryland, even though he had served ten days in jail for stealing $463 from a Smoothie King. At the time, Rodriguez said, "We have talked to a number of people, and after a thorough review, I am reassured that Pat Lazear will be a successful student athlete and a positive member of our university community."

Two years later, Lazear made the honor roll at West Virginia.

"There's a reason they call them juveniles and not adults," Rodriguez said, back in his Ann Arbor office. "They do dumb things sometimes. So when we get them, we've got to accelerate their learning and their development."

In 2007, Jim Harbaugh got national attention when he accused Michigan's athletic department of having "ways to get borderline guys in." This is true: It's called admissions—the very same means, we learned in 2011, Stanford used to get Harbaugh's borderline players in.

To its credit, Michigan has never denied giving student athletes preference in admissions, just as it does for children of alumni, kids from Alaska, and, until the courts recently outlawed it, racial minorities.

The question is, how far should Michigan—or any school—lower its standards to get a talented athlete? In Michigan's case, the answer has long been: not as far as its peers.

While it's undeniable that many Michigan football players, from Oosterbaan's era to the present, would not be admitted without special consideration, the majority of them have been solid students who get Bs and Cs—and often better—and a degree from the University of Michigan. Just as important, these Michigan Men do exceedingly well after college, generally outpacing their classmates in grad schools and especially the workplace, thanks to their uncommon drive and support system.

But it was also true that Rodriguez took more at-risk students than Carr had—usually about eight or nine per class, roughly twice as many as his predecessor.

Rodriguez did, however, have a plan, which entailed pushing his players harder once they were on campus. Academic reports went directly to Rodriguez, not Scott Draper. Rodriguez ended the policy of allowing players to skip class during rivalry weeks. And lost in the controversy surrounding the team's grade point average—when the academic and PR people backed off Rodriguez's claim that his team had earned the highest GPA in team history—was the fact that Rodriguez's team had, in fact, earned a 2.61, and no one could remember a higher team GPA. In the classroom, his players were doing as well as or better than any in recent memory.

Brandin Hawthorne is one of three players Michigan recruited out of Pahokee, Florida, on Lake Okeechobee, where they race rabbits through the sugarcane—and catch them. It is a tiny, impoverished town, which produces two principal products: mud by the truckload and world-class football players. There, Hawthorne told me, he had no trouble getting a 3.8 GPA, and he picked Michigan partly due to its strong academic reputation.

"I realized you have to compete here, and that made me a better student," he told me. "And I know the type of student I am. I got a 2.6 here, and I was sad when I got that. Being here, I know I'm not Einstein, but some kids here are! So if I get a B minus, I'm appreciative of that. I worked *hard* to get that, going against students who've been making As their whole life here. So I can accept that."

When the coaches went home late Tuesday night, they thought they had an outside shot at Rashad Knight, who was leaning toward Rutgers, about a fifty-fifty chance at Sean Parker, and better-than-average odds at getting Demar Dorsey.

But none of that meant anything until the faxes started rolling in.

To make sure he woke up on time for National Signing Day, Wednesday, February 3, 2010, offensive line coach Greg Frey set eleven alarms: two clocks on the left nightstand, two on the right, and two battery-powered clocks on his bureau "in case the power went out," plus three cell phone alarms spread around the house and two more alarm clocks downstairs— all set at five-minute intervals. That is how important this day was for college coaches, and how tired they were by the time it arrived.

It was the dead of winter, with everything covered in snow and ice. When the coaches' cars began pulling into the Schembechler Hall parking lot, it was still dark. The coaches opened the silent building and turned on the lights on their way to the meeting room. They put ESPNU on the big screen and dropped three boxes of doughnuts and two huge bags of McDonald's on the table, and enough coffee for everyone. It would not be a healthy morning.

Sitting and waiting, they started looking up the calories and fat grams of all the junk food they were eating. The news was not good.

"This job's gonna kill me," Gibson offered.

"Gimme one of them doughnuts," Magee said, pointing to the box. As he munched on it, he said, "I lost thirty pounds before recruiting started, and recruiting season put it right back on."

Bleary-eyed and exhausted from six weeks of nonstop, no-days-off recruiting, the coaches settled in for a long day, waiting for seventeen-year-old kids to determine their collective fate.

"We had Demar rock solid until last night," Magee said. "But now you've got the kid double-checking everything, and his parents asking the same questions all over again. And then they stop answering the phone, so then you start getting as nervous as they are. 'He didn't sound like that on Monday!'

"You look at what this does to us," Magee continued, waving an arm

over the exhausted troops, wolfing down glazed doughnuts and Egg Mc-
Muffins, "and you figure this has got to wear kids out too. Got to."

You'd think each position coach would recruit the players who play
his position, but in the cross-country, six-week sprint that is the final leg
of recruiting season, assigning each coach a territory is far more effi-
cient. This creates the somewhat odd scenario of quarterback coach Rod
Smith recruiting defensive lineman Richard Ash, receivers coach Tony
Dew recruiting defensive back Sean Parker, and offensive coordinator
Calvin Magee recruiting safety Demar Dorsey. Then the position coaches
hope like hell the guy assigned to recruit their future players comes
through.

Chris Singletary, Michigan's recruiting coordinator, who looked as
though he'd aged ten years in the last month, walked in with a cell phone
in his hand.

"Demar's dad," he whispered to Magee. Singletary handed the phone to
Magee, then collapsed in a chair, equal parts fatigued and anxious. "This is
my Rose Bowl," Singletary said, which was no small thing from a man who
played in one, beating Washington State to win Michigan's first national
title in a half century. "But if we get that one fax from Demar, it's my National Championship, my Super Bowl, and my Pro Bowl all wrapped into
one. That'd be bigger than my *wedding* day!"

"Don't tell your wife that," one coach cracked.

"Oh, she knows," he said. "She's with the program."

Magee spoke to Dorsey's father in a calm, soothing voice. "No, no. No
problem. Always happy to talk with you." He listened for almost a minute.
"I understand. This is a hard decision. But don't let anyone get into your
head at the last minute. I got my cell phone right there. You can call me
anytime. Okay. Sure. All right. We're right here."

All eyes were on Magee, who said, "I told him, 'You fax us your letter
first, *then* you do your press conference at one!'"

"Dorsey's a five-star, and a *real* five-star," Greg Frey said. "ESPN's got
him ranked number twelve player overall nationwide, and I think that's
about right. You know when you're a D-back in Southern Florida, you can
cover some guys, because they have the best receivers in the country."

Tony Gibson dragged a desk chair into the copy room so he could baby-
sit the fax machine three feet away. Nothing, but nothing, would be left to
chance on this day.

"This is like game day, man," Gibson said. "It's miserable."

Secretary Mary Passink, who's worked for every Michigan head coach since Schembechler hired her in 1979, appeared in the doorway of the War Room.

"Big hand for Mary Passink, everybody!" They eagerly cheered for the woman who had fought through a four-hour traffic jam the night before to travel about twenty-five miles to Livonia, a Detroit suburb, just to get toner for the fax machine—which it turned out they didn't need anyway, but they were not taking chances.

"It's something every year," Draper said. "You test everything the night before, then the fax machines jam, or they're not getting the signal, so you have to haul the one up from the training room. Always something."

Just a few minutes past 7:00 a.m., Gibson opened the door to the War Room waving a freshly sent grainy fax. "Courtney Avery's in!" Avery was a three-star cornerback from Lexington, Ohio, whose commitment to Michigan was never much in doubt. But the nods around the table were vigorous. One-for-one. They were on the board.

At 7:54, Fred Jackson opened the door. "Dorsey just came in!"

"I need to see this!" said Gibson, who would be coaching Dorsey, and ran back to the copy room. He picked up the fax and admired it as though it were the Rosetta stone. He pointed to Dorsey's signature. "Right there, you've got the future of Michigan football's defense."

Even Rodriguez left his office to examine the fax. He looked as tired as the rest, having gotten no sleep the night before, but he permitted himself a slight grin, then quickly recovered. "We're waiting on quite a few more," he said. "One or two guys don't make a recruiting class. That's how they rank you, but that's not how you win. Takes a lot of guys to make a good team, and you're only as good as your weakest link."

Another maxim: Fans follow stars; coaches count seniors. The flash and dash of a marquee player sells tickets, but the solid unsung heroes making tackles win games.

"We'll know in a few years what we have," Rodriguez said.

Could Dorsey really be an impact player that fall?

"Did you see us last year?" Gibson replied.

With that gem in their hands, they could sit back and see if the news would leak before Dorsey's press conference at one that afternoon.

By 8:25, Rashad Knight had chosen Rutgers—which broke Rod Smith's heart; Smith had spent two years recruiting him—but almost all the other commitments had sent their faxes in, allowing their recruiters and future coaches to relax. A little.

Only a few questions remained, the biggest being Sean Parker, who would be holding a press conference on ESPN from Los Angeles at 10:00 eastern time. "He hasn't said anything to us," said Tony Dews, who recruited him. "He wants the drama."

They also still hadn't heard from Richard Ash, a four-star defensive tackle from Pahokee, who had told his recruiter, Rod Smith, "five times this week that he's coming, he's coming." But without the fax in hand, it didn't mean anything. By 9:17, Fred Jackson retired to his office to start watching tape of the class of 2011. The interim between recruiting classes lasted exactly nine minutes.

Cory Zirbel, surfing the recruiting sites, laughed, then announced, "Rivals has Dorsey going to Florida State!"

"This is always the best part," Mike Parrish said. "When everyone's saying some hotshot is going somewhere else, and you've got the fax in your hand. Now you just sit back and listen to all the BS until it's time for the press conference. Then you just smile."

They killed the time by telling a few more war stories.

"Last night I was making love to my wife," one coach said, on the condition of anonymity in the hopes of remaining married, "when the cell started buzzing. 'Um, I need to get that.' Five minutes later, it goes off again. My wife says, 'You need to get that?' 'Um, yeah, is that cool?'"

There is no group of men anywhere in America who have more pressure to come through on Valentine's Day than college football coaches.

At 10:00, ESPN's full-blast signing day show started. They teased Michigan's coaches by running down the national scene, starting with the Florida Gators' 15 recruits in the top 150 overall. Michigan had two—Demar Dorsey and Devin Gardner.

Finally, they cut to Sean Parker's press conference. Parker, sitting at a table with his parents and with an unnamed adviser behind him, had three baseball hats in front of him: Michigan, Washington, and USC, in that order.

After a too-long preamble, Parker asked his adviser to pick the cap of the school he would be attending. He reached over Parker's shoulder and picked the purple hat with the "W" on the front, prompting the small group gathered there to cheer.

"Would somebody go make sure Dews hasn't got a rope?" Gibson asked the room. "He worked like hell for that guy. He had his mom, his coach. He had everybody."

"Everybody except Sean, apparently," another said. "And whoever that adviser is."

The entire recruiting process now centered on just one player: defensive tackle Richard Ash.

By 10:30, Magee was restless. "I can't watch all this shit anymore."

Even Gibson had had enough. "Go work out, C-Mag?"

"Sure, let's go."

Twenty minutes later, while the coaches were starting their workouts, Richard Ash's fax slid into the tray.

Well before lunch, Michigan's 2010 recruiting class was complete. They had lost out on Sean Parker and Rashad Knight but had gotten everybody else on their list—six four-stars and twenty-one three-stars, some of whom could probably be counted on to help in the coming season. Dorsey alone elevated the class from good to very good—and when you considered that Michigan had finished dead last in the Big Ten in 2009, it was exceptional.

The four major recruiting services ranked Michigan's class from twentieth to tenth—which worked out to a twelfth overall ranking, behind only Penn State in the Big Ten.

The coaches also took solace in the fact that the two big fish that got away were not "public losses," meaning only they knew Parker and Knight had at different times orally committed to Michigan before Washington and Rutgers pulled them away. Avoiding such public embarrassments matters greatly to college coaches.

And if they had to pick one of the three safeties to sign up with Michigan, Dorsey would win hands down.

"What we gained is greater than what we lost," Dusty Rutledge said. "They say Dorsey could be another Woodson."

After hosting a catered thank-you lunch in the Commons for the hundred or so people who had helped with the recruiting effort—from campus tour guides to hotel owners to pilots—Rodriguez and his entourage drove to the Junge Champions Center to conduct a press conference about their recruits.

They figured the tone of the event would be a rather matter-of-fact recitation of the recruiting class. But this was Rodriguez, this was the new media, this was Michigan football in 2010. No press conference could ever go that smoothly.

He ran through his twenty-seven recruits, starting with the seven who were already on campus, taking classes and working out with Barwis and company.

"Where are we lacking?" he asked rhetorically. "Last year we had only twenty-five scholarship players on defense, where normally you'd have between thirty-eight and forty-four." So that, Rodriguez said, was clearly his team's most urgent need, and he felt this class would go a long way toward filling it.

When Rodriguez got to Demar Dorsey, he handled him no differently than the rest. "Demar Dorsey, defensive back out of Fort Lauderdale. He had been committed to another school for a long time, and he came open only in the last few weeks. We found out because he's Denard's cousin. Cal was his main recruiter, but Denard was a close second. Denard pointed out that he's 100 percent on his recruits."

Mark Snyder of the *Free Press* asked if Rodriguez knew of Dorsey's arrests.

The smile left Rodriguez's face, but he was still composed. "Every guy we've recruited we've researched. We get to know them. We've been in their homes, and they've been up here. We get to know the whole story. We feel every guy we've recruited will be a whole fit, not just on the field but in the community."

If Rodriguez believed that closed the issue, he was badly mistaken.

"Are you confident the charges were not true?"

"Anytime we look at a situation, there's more to the story than people understand. A guy's in the wrong place at the wrong time, then you have to look at why he was at the wrong place at the wrong time."

More questions, more answers.

"There is no one on this team that has a felony conviction or a misdemeanor conviction."

After a repeat question from another outlet about Dorsey's record, Rodriguez lost all humor and patience. He grabbed the podium, paused, and finally said, "It's amazing. We have such a great place here, we have such wonderful people, we have such a great university, and players who are working hard and doing a good job in school."

The questions stopped, but Rodriguez had to know, when he left the podium, that any relief or joy he felt about this recruiting class would soon be wiped out by the stories that were certain to follow.

Sure enough, the next day the *Free Press* rolled out three pieces on Michigan's class: a scathing column by Drew Sharp, another column by legendary prep sportswriter Mick McCabe, and a big feature by Nicholas Cotsonika and Jim Schaefer.

Cotsonika had traveled to Florida to get some answers, and he returned with a thorough, thoughtful piece that was truly "fair and balanced." From their story, you could understand why Dorsey represented a real risk, both academically and socially—one that previous Michigan coaches would likely have passed on—but also why Rodriguez might reasonably consider assuming it. It did not provide any final answers, giving the readers the information necessary to come up with their own.

But Cotsonika and Schaefer's fine work on that piece was soon overwhelmed by the cacophony of criticism for Dorsey and especially Rodriguez, who was depicted as running a renegade program with no feel for what Michigan represented.

A popular blog authored by a Florida fan, "Every Day Should Be Saturday," provided another perspective: "The Michigan press is the polar opposite of SEC press corps, and we mean that in the good and bad way: not fawning, but also convinced there's a potential Watergate beneath that Gatorade bucket over there.'"

By the time the Demar Dorsey saga ran its course that summer, the coaches might have wished they had never landed him.

After the 2009 season ended, businessman Pete Nichols approached Rodriguez about staging a "Victors' Rally" in late February to show his support for the coach and his program. So on Sunday, February 21, 2010, an estimated crowd of six hundred to seven hundred filled most of the lower level of the Michigan Theater. Rick Leach emceed the event, which lasted a couple hours and included a video of Michigan's teams under Schembechler, Moeller, and Carr.

Lloyd Carr himself did not attend, while Dave Brandon, who had been named Michigan's next athletic director on January 5, sat near the front but did not speak. It was an accurate symbol: He would not go out of his way to help Rodriguez, but he was not out to hurt him, either.

The supporters heard speeches from Jim Brandstatter, Frank Beckmann, Brandon Graham, and Larry Foote, who said, "I'm down there working out with Barwis. It's true what they say, he's a lunatic. [But] there's no cheating going on . . . They do it by the books. We do it right here. So stick with them—and Go Blue!"

The crowd also heard from longtime assistant Jerry Hanlon, and Moeller himself, who flew up from Florida for the occasion.

"As I look at it and see what Coach Rodriguez is doing, I have all the confidence he's going to do it. But again, everybody—you're in, or you're out."

With that, Moeller had publicly declared himself in.

Of course, Rodriguez was the one everyone was waiting to hear.

"I knew it would take a special place to leave my comfort zone," Rodriguez said of his alma mater and home state. "When you have an opportunity to play or coach at a place like Michigan, you have to listen. And even though the last couple years haven't gone nearly like everybody wanted, I'm still glad I made the move, because I know what's going to happen in the future.

"What is a Michigan Man?" he asked. "I've heard that a lot. I'm not from Michigan. How do I become a Michigan Man?"

He then said, as he had heard it described, "If you work hard and you're passionate, you give everything you got to the cause, which is having the best football program in America, to developing young men who will represent you right on and off the field, and you're a good guy and you have good guys around you and you believe in the university and its ideals, then you can be a Michigan Man.

"Well, I think I'm a Michigan Man.

"I don't know if I can express in words how much I appreciate the opportunity to coach here."

This marked a shift from his introductory press conference, when he had joked that he hoped being a Michigan Man was not a prerequisite for being the head coach. He was getting it, and reaching out.

The difference between Martin's strengths and his predecessor's was immediately apparent in Brandon's press conference two days later when he, Rodriguez, and Coleman addressed the latest report from the NCAA investigation. The NCAA said it was looking into five findings, regarding the number and involvement of the quality control staffers, whether Rodriguez promoted "an atmosphere of compliance within the football program," and if the department "adequately monitor[ed] its football program." There would be plenty more to say about all of those concerns, but Brandon's performance was the story that day.

The crime novelist Scott Turow has written that a good trial attorney knows how to send a message to the jury without coming out and saying it. Brandon has that skill.

He said all the right things—Michigan takes great pride in the sterling reputation of its program, and therefore any allegations are taken seriously—but he also managed to hint that "major" is a misleading adjective, and back in his day, Schembechler had no problem punishing players any time of year for missing class, which was one of the violations the NCAA was investigating.

The message: We're on top of the situation and handling everything by the book, but it's clear we're not looking at a wanton disregard for the rules here, or a sinister exploitation of our players, contrary to the original story. Given the state of Michigan's athletic department at that time—financially flush but getting publicly trashed—the timing of such help couldn't have been better.

What Brandon's hiring would mean for Rodriguez, however, was less clear. On the one hand, if there was one area in which Rodriguez needed help, it was public relations. Brandon could also help Rodriguez build bridges with the regents and President Coleman. On the other, Martin had hired Rodriguez and his own legacy as AD was wrapped up in seeing Rodriguez succeed. Brandon, however, hadn't hired Rodriguez and would be less reluctant to pull the plug.

Rodriguez would sink or swim on his own.

A little sunshine broke through the clouds camped out over Schembechler Hall that spring, however, when Brandon Graham and Zoltan Mesko entered the NFL draft.

Graham had transformed himself from an overweight underachiever to a lean, mean pass-rushing machine, bursting from the middle of the pack to become the Big Ten's co-MVP and the MVP for the Senior Bowl. High honors for anyone, and especially for a defensive player, which would draw a half dozen NFL executives and coaches to Ann Arbor at a time for the sole purpose of testing the defensive end for themselves. As one NFL executive told me, "If you're prepared to write a check for a few million dollars, you should probably spend a few thousand first to make sure you're getting what you pay for."

The tests were very specific; they knew exactly what they were looking for. Graham excelled at all of them save one: The Big Ten co-MVP cannot throw a football for his life. He doesn't hold it properly, his motion is atrocious—"throws like a girl" came to mind, though I didn't dare say it out loud—and the results make Garo Yepremian's infamous effort look like Tom freakin' Brady. There isn't a twelve-year-old kid playing backyard ball who can't throw the ball better than Brandon Graham.

But then, as one team official told me, "quarterback is the one position we know he will *not* be playing."

They left the field pleased and impressed.

Six days later, however, another team, the Philadelphia Eagles, would select Graham with the thirteenth overall pick—ESPN captured the explosion in Grahams' hotel room crowded with friends and family. The Eagles would offer him a five-year, $22 million contract, obviously more than enough to move his mom and his sisters out of their dangerous neighborhood.

He had made it. His family had made it. He would never have to go back.

Mesko's story might be even more unlikely. He spent Christmas Eve 1989 ducking on the floor of his parents' apartment in Romania to avoid getting hit by cross fire during the revolution. After his parents, both engineers, moved to suburban Cleveland, he got lured into playing football by accident—literally—when he smashed a ceiling light with a kick ball in his junior high school gym. His teacher gave him a choice: pay for the light or join his football team.

Easy call.

Zoltan's parents didn't believe him when he explained you could earn a college scholarship by kicking a pointy ball in the air—who'd heard of such a thing?—but after Lloyd Carr gave him a full ride to Michigan, they believed. Five years later, he had set school records for gross yards per punt at 44.5, and net yards per punt at 41, and earned two degrees with no debt.

While teammate Brandon Graham was wowing the scouts at the Senior Bowl, Mesko was blowing his chance with the same people thanks to a horrible performance in a mini-tryout a couple days before the game. But he refocused and redeemed himself at the combine. His stock bounced back.

On Saturday, April 24, Zoltan Mesko watched the third day of the 2010 draft with his friends and parents. During the fifth round, Mesko's cell phone rang. "Unknown Caller" is all it said. When he picked it up, he found himself talking to the New England Patriots' head coach, Bill Belichick, and the owner, Robert Kraft. While they talked, ESPN announced, "with the 150th pick, the New England Patriots select Zoltan Mesko of Michigan." The room burst into cheers.

On July 16, Mesko signed with the Patriots for the minimum wage. In the NFL, that's not $7.25 an hour but $325,000 a year, and they tacked on a bonus of $187,250.

He might have been the poorest player in the NFL, but probably the richest kid from Timisoara, Romania.

There was another success story developing down at Schembechler Hall. It wasn't big money or big news, but it was very big to the players on the Michigan football team.

Brock Mealer was not a Michigan football player. He wasn't even a Michigan student, attending Ohio State, of all places. But he had become as much a part of the team as any man wearing the winged helmet.

On Christmas Eve, 2007, twenty-three-year-old Brock Mealer was riding home with his family from their cousin's house. Brock's younger brother Elliott had just accepted a scholarship from Lloyd Carr to play on the offensive line at Michigan—which Rodriguez honored when he took over a few weeks later—and Elliott and his girlfriend seemed headed for the altar.

But on the way home, a ninety-year-old driver ran a stop sign and struck the Mealers' SUV. Elliott's girlfriend and the Mealers' father were killed instantly. Brock was paralyzed from the waist down.

Doctors gave Brock less than a 1 percent chance of walking again. Rodriguez told Brock he should come to the U-M hospital's world-class rehab unit. But after a few months, a nurse there told his mom to consider buying a specially equipped van for about $100,000 and to be prepared to change her son's diapers. Hope was officially discouraged. They had their reasons. In most cases like Brock's, there really isn't much chance of walking, and to pretend there is can often set the patients up for a demoralizing return to the reality of their situation.

But Brock's will to live hinged on walking again. With little hope for improvement, he had fallen into a deep depression, made worse when his insurance company cut him off in the fall of 2009.

He still had family, though, and Michigan football. Near the end of the 2009 season, strength coach Mike Barwis invited him to work with them.

The guy had no idea what he was in for.

Barwis turned the job over to Parker Whiteman, who gave Brock his daily lunch hour, but not an inch of slack, especially when the going got tough—which it did, every day. Within a month, as Christmas approached, Brock had relearned how to stand up—just for a second, at first, and then for a moment, and then for a minute. Then he started walking with arm crutches. And then, by the time Graham and Mesko were drafted, just canes.

And that's when Rich Rodriguez called Brock into his office and told him they wanted Brock to help open the renovated stadium for the rededication game.

Leading up to the big day, Brock was as nervous as any player on the team—maybe more so.

The Griese/Hutchinson/Woodson charity golf outing for C. S. Mott Children's Hospital is one of the many events Carr's former players—and Carr himself—attended that raised millions for the hospital. You'd be hard-pressed to find another college football program that made the effort these Michigan Men did for charity.

But, as always during the Rodriguez era, there was an undercurrent to the event. Held at Michigan's golf course on May 15, it played out like yet another Rorschach test. The buzz that day—even with all the parties, including Rodriguez, on the course—was the now familiar subjects of cultural fit and Michigan Men.

Depending on who was talking, Rodriguez either didn't fit the mold or the Michigan Men wouldn't let him—though, if you polled the people on the course, the former probably would have won handily. Either answer put you on one side of the divide or the other, with the middle ground shrinking every day.

For those who felt Rodriguez simply didn't belong, there was a follow-up question: What did he need to do to keep his job, and if he didn't, who might replace him? The most common answers among the bad-fit crowd that day were eight wins, and Brady Hoke, who had coached the defensive line on the 1997 national title team. Carr had earned his players' loyalty by handling a deluge of criticism with complete restraint—he could be abrupt, abrasive, even angry, but never gave off a whiff of self-pity—then proved his critics wrong. Hoke couldn't claim all that, of course, but the players he coached in the mid-1990s were the ones leading the charge. He had earned some loyalty, too.

Hoke was hardly a national name. Whenever fans and pundits discussed replacement candidates, Jim Harbaugh came up most often that spring, and Les Miles second. The lesser-known Hoke seemed like a long shot at the time, but among this influential group, he was the clear favorite.

How much sway the Carr contingent held over the process was entirely debatable, but no one could deny that some of Rodriguez's problems were his own doing. As spring turned to summer, Demar Dorsey was becoming one of them.

For all the hits Rodriguez took on signing day for taking Demar Dorsey, by June it appeared he would not even get the payoff of having the fleet-footed five-star phenom in his depleted defensive backfield. The sticking point, it turned out, was not Dorsey's checkered past. That could be rationalized as something he'd learned from, an argument Michigan had used a few times over the years with the occasional reformed player. No, the sticking point was Dorsey's academic present.

The night before National Signing Day, Rodriguez, Chris Singletary, and Brad Labadie went up to the Hill to meet with director of admissions Ted Spencer, newly hired provost Phil Hanlon, and, by phone, Dave Brandon. They met to discuss five academic risks Rodriguez was recruiting, including Demar Dorsey.

Brandon and the people on the Hill might have been a bit uncomfortable, but they gave Rodriguez permission to offer all of them scholarships, though that did not guarantee admission. Brandon let it be known, however, that at Michigan such candidates should be the exceptions, not the rule, and the unofficial cap going back to Schembechler's regime had always been kept at about four or five. Rodriguez's first two full classes had had about twice that, so Brandon made it clear this would be the last year. Rodriguez accepted that.

For just about everyone involved, there were risks. If Rodriguez didn't get some players who could help on defense—fast—he would have great difficulty getting the seven or eight wins most people thought he needed to keep his job. Of the four players on the table that night besides Dorsey, one played quarterback and the rest played linebacker. But Rodriguez also knew if they embarrassed the program, the problem would be his. He was betting on his ability to get the best out of borderline candidates, which had already resulted in a few of them achieving 3.0 GPAs, but a few of them dropping out, too.

As the spring unfolded, the players tended to determine their own fates, with only Jake Ryan making it to the fall in uniform. Two failed to meet NCAA requirements, so they enrolled in prep schools to improve their grades and scores. (One signed for Marshall in 2011, and another for Miami, Florida.) Another was admitted but flunked out of school by the end of summer term.

That left Dorsey, by far the most vital to Rodriguez.

Knowing he was squarely behind the eight ball academically entering his senior year, Dorsey enrolled in two high schools to make up ground as fast as he could run, one being an alternative high school called Life-Skills. He also took a few online courses, for which he received all As. But Michigan told Rodriguez that Dorsey would not be admitted. Rodriguez gave Dorsey the bad news.

Because Dorsey didn't submit his application, admissions never had to make an official ruling one way or the other. Dorsey subsequently enrolled at Grand Rapids Community College.

Whether Dorsey should have been admitted, whether he could have cut it academically, and how much he might have helped the team will never be known. It is certainly possible, if he had been admitted, that Rodriguez's tough-love approach would have produced respectable results off the field, and Dorsey's speed spectacular results on the field. Considering Rodriguez's detractors' prediction that eight wins would have earned Rodriguez his fourth year, it's a tantalizing what-if.

But in the end, we know only this: Rodriguez and his staff spent time, effort, and lots of political capital with the very people who would determine his fate and got almost nothing in return—except another public bruising.

The buildup to the 2010 season opener against Connecticut might have been the greatest of any game since Rodriguez arrived thirty months earlier—which was saying something, given the endless talk of do-or-die games and sports talk show hosts declaring, "I have it on good authority he'll be gone by December/February/August"—take your pick.

It didn't help that the Wolverines were coming off two consecutive losing seasons for the first time since 1963, the year Rich Rodriguez was born. If they suffered a third, it would mark the first time that had happened since . . . well, since Michigan started playing football in 1879. It would also surely mark the departure of head coach Rich Rodriguez, his assistants, and his strength staff.

Throw in an ongoing NCAA investigation, the incessant derogatory drumbeat of the *Detroit Free Press*, and the rededicating of the Big House after a $226 million renovation, and you had the most pressurized position in all of college football.

But those rumors were nothing new, hounding Rodriguez almost from day one. What *was* new, however, was his response to it all.

Well before the 2010 season started, Rodriguez had made up his mind about a few things that had been floating around Schembechler Hall for longer than he liked. He intended to put an end to as much of it as he could, in the hopes of allowing him and his staff to focus on football.

———

"WELCOME!" Rodriguez said to his coaches on Monday, July 26, 2010. It was the first day of their staff retreat, held in the Schembechler Hall Commons. They would spend five days going over every one of the 162 pages in the binders they had just received. On the covers, Rodriguez had printed 2010 HIDEAWAY above a famed mantra from Schembechler himself, THE TEAM. THE TEAM. THE TEAM, and one from Rodriguez, ALL IN FOR MICHIGAN, against a backdrop of the newly renovated stadium. It marked a nice summation of where they stood, juxtaposing past and present—with plenty of pressure.

"The purpose of the hideaway," Rodriguez explained to the people seated at the square of tables, "is to go over every single aspect of the program to make sure we don't miss a thing about what we want and who's in charge of what. It's about the same as last year. Of course, we have a little more to talk about this year because of all we've been through.

"On the first page is our schedule. It won't be easy."

During the retreat, Rodriguez would cover everything from how they recruited, to how they conditioned, practiced, dressed, and traveled, and a couple dozen more tasks in between. But even if their players aced every class and carried themselves like Eagle Scouts, the coaches knew they would all be judged on the outcome of those twelve sixty-minute contests. But it was even less than that, because the average football game has only eleven minutes of actual action, thus boiling down the annual evaluation of every person in that room—and a hundred others not present—to a grand total of 2:12 of plays produced by kids not old enough to buy a beer.

If you want a definition of pressure, that's not a bad one.

"'THE STATE OF THE UNION,'" Rodriguez said, reading from page four.

"'The worst is behind us,'" he read. "'We must demand excellence.'"

That would start with Rodriguez. If 95 percent of the message hadn't changed from the year before, the 5 percent essentially boiled down to two points: The buck stops with Coach Rodriguez, and no more Mr. Nice Guy.

"Here's what I've learned the last two years," he said. "Like everyone else, I came here with great respect for Michigan. When people here did things differently than I'm used to, or not the way I would do it, I've been very trusting, figuring this is how they do it here. I said, 'Let them do it that way. It's the way they've done it for years.'

"Well, guess what? That got my ass in trouble, and I'm still paying for it. So is Michigan.

"The head football coach is in charge of everything. If I ask you to do something, I'll trust you to do it. From now on, if I say we're going to wear pink wristbands, we're going to wear pink wristbands. I'm not going to ask. My decisions will not please everyone, but I'm the head coach, so that's the way it is. If something is iffy, I'll ask Dave Brandon.

"I don't want anyone here to feel that I'm micromanaging you. But if anything goes wrong, the first guy they're going to blame is me. Is that clear to everyone? Good.

"Another point: Never keep from me anything I'm going to be account-able for. Got it? Good."

The people sitting at those tables knew exactly what Rodriguez was talking about: the *Free Press* front-page story of August 29, 2009, and the NCAA investigation that followed. Rodriguez had been taking slings and arrows since he left Morgantown, but that story penetrated his armor like no other, particularly the suggestion that he had no regard for his players' well-being.

"I have to sleep at night knowing that there's nothing we did or didn't do that day that is going to come back and bite us in the ass. And I'll be the first one they bite."

What he didn't tell them is that he hadn't had a good night's sleep since he had left West Virginia, and it was getting worse. "I'm tossing and turning at four o'clock in the morning," he told me. "And all I'm thinking is, 'I'm *not* a bad guy. I'm not a liar, I'm not a cheater. I *care* about our guys. So why am I going through all this?'"

He had, by his own account, become less trusting of people in general and some local reporters and Michigan insiders in particular. He had also become world-weary, visibly aging. But he was not about to give up. If any-thing, he had become more determined to prove his critics wrong. His glare, his jaw, and his defiance had all grown stronger.

That brought Rodriguez to sideline passes and media access. "The last two years every man in the state of Michigan and his mother had a side-line pass," he said. He didn't mention his name, but most present knew the one pass that bothered him most was Jim Stapleton's.

"No more. We're taking charge of this. Brandon's on top of it."

Carr had been so protective of the program's privacy that the building was jokingly referred to as "Fort Schembechler." Rodriguez was initially the opposite, opening up every practice not only to former players and coaches but also to the media. That had been his policy at West Virginia, but glasnost had worked a lot better in Morgantown than in Ann Arbor.

"I've been nice and accommodating from the day I got here," he said, "and they screwed me.

"Well, we don't have to be nice anymore. We just have to be accommodating. They will not have the access they've had. I've trusted others' judgment about what reporters are fair, which ones we should help, and it got us in trouble. I'm not delegating that anymore."

When they got to the tab addressing the coaching staff, the top item on the first page was "Loyalty."

"We're good here," is all Rodriguez had to say, and he meant it. If Rodriguez had become more suspicious of some people, he had become more appreciative of most, especially his assistants. "When I hired you, I hired you *and* your family. I know you. I know your families. And I think your families are outstanding."

It was not hyperbole. Of the nine assistants, all but two were married, and none of them had ever been divorced. They had almost two dozen children among them, some adults now, and none of them were screwups. In modern America, the staff must have set some sort of record for stability.

Rodriguez, as he did every year, asked all of those present to tell something about themselves, their spouses, and their children.

"I'll start. You all know Rita, of course. She's always around. We've got two kids, Raquel, fourteen going on nineteen, and Rhett, who's twelve. Both my parents are still alive. My dad is a retired coal miner, and my mom's a retired teacher's aide.

"I have two brothers. One's a middle school principal, one's a lawyer, who only has to work twice a week. I think he's the only lawyer in the country I've not hired."

That got a laugh and sent the subject circling around the tables. "I'm so proud of my brothers," defensive line coach Bruce Tall said. "My oldest is an orthopedic surgeon who graduated from Dartmouth, the other two are law grads from Case Western, and the youngest is the smartest. He was in med school, but when my parents got ill, he took care of them, and now he's a schoolteacher."

Cal Magee took it from there: The youngest of six siblings raised in a shotgun shack in the shadows of the New Orleans Superdome, he was the first in his family to earn a college degree and had been thinking about going to law school when the coaching bug bit him.

Rodriguez enjoyed these stories—one of the only chances they had for such things—and frequently asked questions during their introductions.

Next, Rodriguez asked video coordinator Phil Bromley to start a slide show of some 120 head shots, every player on the roster. When a face popped up, the next guy at the table had to give the player's name, position, hometown, high school, and anything else about him he could remember. Rodriguez expected every coach and staffer to know every player, from All-American to walk-on. Through the entire show, no one drew a blank except on the occasional freshman, and they usually had a quick comment or story about each player.

When it was Calvin Magee's turn, he didn't hesitate. "Maaaad Jack Kennedy!" he bellowed. No one was quite sure why they started calling him "Mad Jack"—except perhaps because it was completely counter to his sunny personality—but it had stuck, and spread.

"Walk-on quarterback from Michigan."

"Where in Michigan?" Rod Smith asked, testing his friend. "Big state!"

"Ah, geez. Lake something."

"Lotta lakes, too," Smith said.

"Ah! Walled Lake!"

"Walled Lake *Central*," Smith said, "but we'll allow it."

"Thank you, Rod. Let's see. One run for six yards against Delaware State. Very high average. Hockey player—and a hell of a rapper. Go figure!"

That brought him to "Captains!" which had become another source of friction when Rodriguez ended the 129-year tradition of naming at least one full-time captain for the entire season. Instead, he had brought to Michigan a system of rotating captains for each game to ensure that every senior gets to be captain at least once and leadership comes from the entire class. When the old guard started giving Rodriguez a hard time about this, one big donor told him, "There's a difference between tradition and best practices. Respect tradition, but follow best practices." But drawing that line had proved to be one of Rodriguez's greatest challenges at Michigan.

So, when one of the players suggested to him that they have two permanent captains selected by the team and two game captains, Rodriguez decided that sounded perfect.

If Rodriguez had come up with such a simple solution in the first months of his tenure, he probably would have avoided a few headaches.

"If they don't pick Steve Schilling and Mark Moundros," he said, "they got the wrong guys."

That Steve Schilling was a strong candidate for captain was hardly a surprise. He had been a five-star lineman out of Washington State and was about to enter his third season as a starter. Mark Moundros was a little more surprising.

Moundros had turned down a scholarship from Eastern Michigan to walk on at Michigan. He let his teammates know that playing for Michigan was a privilege, not a right, something he underscored during their summer workouts and seven-on-seven drills, which the seniors directed.

"We were disappointed with the past two years," he said, "and we knew whatever we were doing wasn't working."

Inevitably, that meant dealing with players who took the word "voluntary" at face value. The seniors couldn't do much about it—thanks to strict adherence to all NCAA rules, they couldn't take attendance or tell the coaches—but they didn't have to treat them equally, either.

That included the quarterbacks. Forcier had started all twelve games the previous season, making it his job to lose. But after the 2009 season ended, the former wunderkind had slacked off—in the classroom, in the weight room, in the film room, and in spring practice.

While Forcier was out having fun, Denard Robinson was dedicating himself to learning the spread offense.

That spring, when some of the student managers ran into Roy Roundtree at a party, they'd asked him, "Who's going to be the quarterback?"

He motioned for them to come closer. "Sixteen's ready," he whispered, citing Denard's number. "Trust me."

"Denard bought into the system right away," Rodriguez said. "He just had to *learn* it. I don't know if I've been around a guy who cares more about the people around him and wants them to feel good. Nothing phony about that guy. Denard is not a good kid. Denard is a *great* kid."

So when Tate Forcier missed many of these voluntary spring workouts, the seniors felt they needed to do something—and they picked Moundros to do it.

The next time Forcier showed up for a seven-on-seven game, he naturally walked up to the quarterback position to take the snap. That's when Moundros stepped up and said, "No, it's not your turn," and pointed to the sidelines. Forcier looked befuddled at first but said nothing and walked to the sidelines. Moundros waved in Denard Robinson to take his place.

Forcier then walked back out, but once again Moundros waved him out, sending in true freshman Devin Gardner. Forcier went to the sidelines, then returned again—but for a third time Moundros sent him to the sidelines in favor of Mad Jack Kennedy, who had never missed a workout.

"I think Tate understood what was happening," Moundros said. "He didn't say anything, and that was that."

"It's easier to kick a kid off than try to save them," Rodriguez told his assistants at the retreat, "and I'd rather save them and get them to go our way. But if they show no interest or desire in being part of a team, and accepting what that means, they're not Michigan Men, and they don't belong here.

"No one is indispensable. No one."

And then a bit of a bombshell. "There may be five or six players that will not be on our team at the end of the first week of practice. I hope not, but that's what I'm predicting right now. Whoever's not all in will be gone."

He listed a few candidates, including five-star defensive back J. T. Turner and Tate Forcier.

Rodriguez asked Mike Barwis if he could help him design the first day of summer camp so the guys who had been working out would have little trouble—and those who came to camp in bad shape would be in . . . well, *bad shape*.

"No problem," Barwis said. He seemed to savor the assignment.

"Jonny, are the wings painted on the helmets?" Rodriguez asked Falk.

"Yes, sir."

"Can we get helmets without wings? Because I want them to earn their wings. What would that cost?"

"About $25,000," Falk said. They laughed.

"Hmmm, okay," Rodriguez said. "What about blue beanies, or tape?"

"Let me work on it."

Of course, the real business of coaching was coaching, but that would be coming up soon enough.

One week later, the first day of the 2010 season consisted of two grueling practices in the summer heat and timed runs at the end. As promised, it was a killer, particularly for those who hadn't done the voluntary workouts that spring and summer. For those who had, like supersized nose tackle Mike Martin, "it was nothing. Walk in the park. I felt fine." Even the offensive linemen, the biggest guys on the team, had no trouble finishing the run in time.

But a few players didn't make it—and looked like death trying.

Off-season workouts were supposed to be voluntary at all NCAA schools, but it was a big enough loophole to drive a bus through. Since the NCAA had started investigating the Wolverines' practices, however, Michigan was probably the only school in the country that could claim its workouts truly were voluntary. But being in shape for the start of summer camp was not optional.

The cast of the damned included Austin White; J. T. Turner; Jeremy Gallon, the diminutive kick returner; and Tate Forcier. Actually, Forcier had finished the run under the time limit by a few seconds, literally diving across the line to beat the clock. But his landlord had called the football office, letting the department know that Forcier and his roommates were behind on their rent. That minor violation of team rules was enough to add his name to the list.

"They were just looking for a reason to make me run," Forcier said with a wan smile, and he was probably right.

Turner might have thought he'd get a pass, knowing how desperately his coaches needed help in the defensive secondary. His teammates warned him camp would be brutal if he didn't prepare for it, but he repeatedly told them the coaches "can't break me," that they couldn't make him conform. Word of his boast had gotten back to the strength staff.

The coaches told the five players on the list to meet at the weight room at 6:30 for "Breakfast Club," something Rodriguez used whenever the players needed a little "reeducation." "And don't even think about being late."

At 6:15 on Tuesday, the show was about to begin. Rodriguez dressed for the workout, too, which would start on the StairMasters at level 20, the maximum, for twenty minutes. Hopping on his machine, Rodriguez threw down the gauntlet: "You're not going to let a forty-seven-year-old man beat you, are ya? Start the clock, Mike!"

Although only one strength coach was needed to ensure the safety of the players, who all wore heart monitors, they all attended the Breakfast Club. They were from working-class families and got their chance for a degree—and then a good job—through athletics. With the exception of Dan Mozes, who had been named the nation's best center at West Virginia and played in the NFL before joining Barwis's staff, none of them had won scholarships.

During the three years I watched them work, I had never seen them run out of energy or turn down anyone who asked for help—whether players, former players, or people recovering from serious injuries like Brock Mealer. They never charged anyone, not even the NFL players, a dime. They were not afraid to get in your face, but they always did so with humor, with the expectation you would ultimately be glad you fought through your limitations.

But their goodwill had been stretched to the limit by these five players, who had been given full scholarships and every resource to succeed on the field and in the classroom, yet seemed to appreciate none of it. For the first time since I had met them, their expressions held no warmth, no humor. Their jaws were set, their gazes were cold, their expressions belying their thinly veiled disgust.

Jim Plocki, whose father and grandfather had worked in the steel mills outside Pittsburgh, stared at the five guys flailing on the machines and thought awhile. "Makes me sick," he finally said. "So soft. Such a waste."

All of the players heard it from the coaches at some point—"Getting kind of hard, I guess, but Coach Rod looks fine"—but their main target was J. T. Turner, who had the worst attitude of the bunch, as evidenced by his boast, "They can't break me."

"Can't break ya, huh?"

"Don't look too good to me!"

"Can't break what's already broken!"

After ten minutes, every player was bent over, hanging on to the rails for dear life. A few got shot off the back of the machines. They all had to stop at some point and be coaxed to get back on. Only Rodriguez's legs continued pumping, steady as a metronome.

After the coaches called out the last ten seconds, the players slid off their StairMasters, held on to the rails, and dropped their dripping heads, thinking that—at last—they had survived.

"Ready for Phase Two?" Rodriguez asked. "Plyometrics! Let's go!"

With Rodriguez leading the way, they started with a set of 50 sit-ups on the big exercise balls, then 100 sit-ups, then 150. At 250, Rodriguez was working alone. The rest had slowed down or stopped.

"Are you broken yet, Turner?"

"You don't look too good, J.T. Think I see a crack in there. Maybe two?"

"You know, Concordia College has got a football team this year, right down the road. Think maybe it's more your speed."

Turner didn't look back at the coaches, because his eyes were pressed closed in pain.

They finished their forty-minute workout a little after seven. Rodriguez looked fine. But none of the players had enough energy left to say a word to the coaches or each other.

At 2:00, J. T. Turner entered Rodriguez's office to ask to transfer to another school. Rodriguez agreed, and wished him well.

When Rodriguez had told his coaches a week earlier that "no one is indispensable," he meant it. Just as former Glenville receiver Chris George had said, "With Coach Rod, being a star isn't a hall pass."

Rodriguez had promised his assistants that if any coach, staffer, or player wasn't "all in," he would be out—and he was backing it, no matter what it cost him or his team.

The night after Turner left, I asked the coaches over dinner in the Commons to name the player they could least afford to lose. One joked, "Don't phrase it that way!" But four out of five agreed: not Forcier, not Denard, but senior cornerback Troy Woolfolk, son of Butch Woolfolk, former Michigan All-American and NFL tailback. He wasn't their best player—he was very good, not yet great—but he was virtually the only experienced defensive back they had left.

Later that week, on a routine play, five-foot-seven slot receiver Tay Odoms bumped shoulders with Woolfolk. Troy stumbled and landed awkwardly on his left foot and crumpled to the ground, holding his ankle. It was dislocated, and Woolfolk would be out for the season.

A few weeks later, near the end of summer camp, safety Jared Van Slyke, son of former major-league baseball player Andy, bumped shoulders with tight end Kevin Koger at the end of another routine play. Nothing.

But at dinner, the trainers told Rodriguez that Van Slyke had broken his clavicle and would be out for the season, too. For the first time in months, Rodriguez's resilience, which had shored him up after Woolfolk's injury three weeks earlier, appeared to fail him. He looked somber, barely talking to Rita, or anyone else.

Michigan's defensive backs were dropping like flies. The list was growing so long that a reader of MGoBlog created a page, "Never Forget!" featuring the faces of the fallen, transferred, or rejected defensive backs. It was already approaching double digits.

"It hurts us, and it's horrible for him," defensive coordinator Greg Robinson said. "But we can't think about it too long. No point. This is football—this happens.

"We'll be all right."

It was hard to tell if he truly believed it. But then again, he had to.

A few days later, Rodriguez admitted, "If there ever was a year you'd want an easy opener, this is it."

Easy or not, the season opener against Connecticut was coming their way. Some pundits called it a do-or-die game for Rodriguez. Normally, that would seem a little extreme for a season opener, but in Rodriguez's case, they might have been right.

He had lost big his first year and lost close his second. He was hungry for the third bite of the apple, winning close—and if they were lucky, maybe winning big a few times.

At the Campus Inn on Friday, September 3, 2010, the night before the game, Rodriguez closed his talk with a simple question: "Guess what time it is?"

"GAME WEEK!"

"Stand up and say it!"

The players went crazy—so much so that even the coaches were surprised, sharing wide-eyed looks.

"You've busted your ass the last nine months for this moment. You've seen the countdown clock in the weight room ticking down to this game. Well, this is it!"

If they needed more reasons to get up for the game, Rodriguez listed them. ABC would be covering it as the major regional game. It marked the rededication of the Big House, complete with military flyover. And Brock Mealer would be leading them out to touch the banner.

There wasn't a man on that team who didn't know Brock Mealer. They had seen him working out, sweating as much as they did, every day in the weight room, before he made his way out to the field to watch them practice.

When the players left practice that day for the showers and then the buses to the Campus Inn, Brock stayed behind to sit on the practice field, bask in the sun, and recount his journey. He told me the whole story, laughing about the ways Barwis and Parker Whiteman motivated him, and getting choked up when he talked about what they meant to him.

At one point he digressed to ponder Justin Boren's comments that Rodriguez's regime lacked "family values." "I guess I don't know what kind of family values he was talking about," Brock said in an even voice. "I've thought about that. I wonder—maybe to some people family values are basically just spoon-feeding you your whole life, and carrying you all the time instead of pushing you. But I've always just kind of laughed. This big athlete was partly, I guess, driven away from here by the amount of work he had to do, and that's just what drew me here from Columbus. He's running from adversity, and I'm going towards it."

After our conversation, Brock Mealer showered and drove home.

But, like Rodriguez and his brother, he would barely sleep that night.

"When you look at UConn's schedule—Texas Southern, Temple, Buffalo—you can see who they're focused on," Rodriguez told his team. "They finished 8–5 last year, with a bowl victory over South Carolina. Randy Edsall's been there about ten years, he's a good coach and a good guy. They've got eighteen starters back, the most in the Big East, among the top ten in the country.

"Trust me when I tell you: They're going to be ready for us."

He let that sink in.

"Well, that's fine. We're gonna be ready for them!

"Everyone's always asking me, 'How're you going to do?' The fact is, until we play a game, you can't tell. But I can tell you this: We are closer than ever, and we are better than ever—individually and as a team."

The players nodded and murmured. He had hit a note.

The keys to victory, he said, were simple. On offense: no turnovers. "That is not the ball you have in your hands," he told them, "that is the program. You don't take care of it, we're all going down. But if we have no turnovers, we will win. Mark my words.

"On defense: punish the quarterback."

He then showed them Phil Bromley's motivational video, ending with the words "MICHIGAN TRADITION." The guys jumped to their feet and started shouting.

"DAMN STRAIGHT!"

"HELL YEAH!"

"Get in here!" Rodriguez said, and they were only too ready.

"We are ONE!" he yelled, and they followed suit.

"We are MICHIGAN!"

"Again!"

The night before the 2010 season started, Forcier admitted to me that he had failed to do "what I should have done over the summer—the workouts, the schoolwork." But he seemed to have learned his lesson. "I'm just hoping that I get in, because I truly think if I get in—the game has slowed down for me so much this year—that if I get in, I won't be giving that spot back."

Forcier was not dead yet. His attitude had improved since the Breakfast Club Massacre, and he had regained some of the respect of his teammates—but he was not yet all in. Would he get to play against Connecticut?

"Guess we'll find out tomorrow," he said, sitting at the desk, working on his weekly quarterback quiz. "I'll tell you one thing: If I don't, I might shoot up some fireworks with my dad about transferring."

Which left Denard Robinson, who had never started a college football game. Could he do it? Rodriguez's future depended on the answer.

The next morning, more people than usual crowded the hotel lobby. They cheered for their team boarding the buses, with more yelling and screaming for them along the bus route to the stadium than ever before.

Since David Molk suffered a season-ending knee injury against Penn State in 2009, he was especially eager to play again. "It's been almost eleven months," he said, making a fist repeatedly. "Someone is going to pay."

In the locker room, Barwis yelled in his trademark rasp: "The last two years, you've been through more shit than anyone at any level of football—high school, college, or pro. Nobody's been through what you've been through. You go through the hardest workouts of any team in the country, and you just say, 'That's nothing. Just how I live my life.'

"You got one guy," he said, referring to senior Jon Bills, "he gets in a car wreck, breaks his neck, and he's coaching you today. You got another guy, Brock Mealer, he's walking you out of the tunnel today.

"So this is us right here. You take what those assholes have given you, and you stuff it down their fucking throats. This is our chance to fight back—in the only place that matters!"

A few minutes before kickoff, the players gathered on one knee by the door. Mark Moundros, the walk-on turned captain, stood up.

"The experts said Brock Mealer would never walk! The experts say we're done! And the experts are wrong about us, too!"

He slammed his chest. "They can't take this away from us. They can't take away our pride. They can't mess with this. Today is ours!"

A minute later, Rodriguez stood before them, speaking with a calm intensity. "Mark's right. They don't decide who we are. We have a great opportunity to show the whole world who we are. You've earned the right to have a little fun, on the biggest stage around.

"But remember this: We are one. And we are Michigan. No matter who's trying to tear us apart, it ain't happening.

"You play every play the way you know how, and you show them what your heart is.

"Because when you play Michigan—"

"YEAH!" In Rodriguez's third year, the players knew this set piece by heart.

"—you better tie your shoes a little tighter!"

They were shouting now.

"You better put on a little more tape!"

The players were so loud, yelling and slapping their helmets and shoulder pads, they could barely hear Rodriguez.

"And you better—"

"STRAP IT ON!"

The time had finally come to start the 2010 season and see what they had.

They burst out the door, then walked down the tunnel together, restraining their enthusiasm, because they had one more order of business: Brock Mealer. They remained in the tunnel's darkness during the video that covered Brock's journey from accident victim and paraplegic to man on the cusp of walking across the field to touch the banner.

When the video finished, the players walked down the tunnel, right behind Brock, while the announcer invited the crowd to turn their attention to the man in the wheelchair in front of the tunnel.

Elliott told me he was more nervous that morning about his brother's walk than he was about his own play. "I couldn't sleep," he said. "I can only imagine what Brock's going through."

When the introduction was complete, the overflowing crowd got on its feet to cheer him on. Brock Mealer got out of his wheelchair, gripped his canes, and did something the experts said he never would. He took one step, and then another. And then another. He was so pumped, walking between his two brothers, he was more concerned about going too fast and losing his balance than he was about being able to walk.

Since the famed banner was first raised in 1962, Michigan football players have touched it over thirty thousand times—and every single one of them got there faster than Brock Mealer did. But as Mealer approached the block "M" in the center of the field, stopped, and reached up to touch the banner, no All-American or Heisman trophy winner ever received more affection and respect from the crowd than he did.

Rodriguez stood in front of his team at the tunnel. Only his wraparound sunglasses prevented the camera from seeing his red eyes.

After that scene, it probably wasn't necessary, but the military sent two more planes overhead for good measure, to ensure the crowd was ready to boil over. The fans would soon get their chance.

When the PA announcers told the crowd Michigan had won the toss, it erupted as if Jonas Mouton had made an interception. If ever there was a team that might choose to take the ball first, this was it—but by choosing to defer, they set up the first challenge of the season: Could their decimated defense stop anyone?

Three downs later, the Wolverine defenders were running off the field, showered in cheers. Mission accomplished. "Now *that* is a Michigan defense!" Jim Plocki yelled at them.

Denard Robinson took over, hitting two passes and running six times to set up Vincent Smith's 12-yard run into the end zone. Just that easy. After the defense shut down the Huskies again, Robinson took off through a hole on the right, cut right again, then just kept running 68 yards for Michigan's second touchdown, 14–0.

It was hard to look at Forcier, sitting on the bench, and not think: Michigan has just found a new quarterback.

The Wolverines tacked on another one in the second quarter, to push it to 21–0, and it looked like the rout might be on. "These bastards are *tired*," Tony Dews said. "They *cannot* run with you. Keep pressing them!"

But Michigan's defense gave up a field goal and, with just seventeen seconds left in the half, the Huskies' first touchdown cut Michigan's lead to a mere 21–10—well within reach, given Michigan's recent history. Had the 2010 Wolverines learned their lesson?

The Wolverines jogged up to the tunnel but had to wait for the Huskies to lumber up the path to their locker room. Michigan finally headed up in a full sprint alongside them, the contrast obvious.

In the locker room, the Wolverines were pumped, eager to get back on the field, and not even sweating. Whatever they had done in the off-season seemed to be working.

"We can run all day!" one yelled. "ALL day!"

"Don't even *think* about letting off the gas pedal!" Van Bergen exhorted his teammates.

The Wolverines started the second half with a methodical nineteen-play drive, six of them third downs. It lasted over 8 minutes and got them 3 points. Michigan 24, Connecticut 10.

But the Huskies came right back with a strong drive of their own. Facing fourth-and-1 from Michigan's 7-yard line, Randy Edsall decided to take his chances. When D. J. Shoemate cut through the left side for a 4-yard gain, Edsall's daring appeared to pay off—until sophomore defensive back J. T. Floyd jammed his helmet right on the ball. It popped loose, bouncing off Craig Roh's hands and into Obi Ezeh's.

Ten plays later, Robinson tossed a slip screen to Vincent Smith, who spun around, then zipped past the Huskies into the end zone. Michigan missed the extra point, but the 30–10 margin looked solid.

But something else happened on that possession, far more significant than any missed extra point. Three plays into that drive, Denard landed hard on his backside and came out for a couple plays. With the game on the line—a game that, if Rodriguez lost, would result in the football world coming down on his head—he had to make a decision, which would be no decision at all for most coaches. On the bench he had Forcier, who had started every game the previous season, and true freshman Devin Gardner, who had never taken a snap in college. But Forcier had done almost nothing the coaches and seniors had asked of him in the off-season, while Gardner had done everything and then some.

Rodriguez did not hesitate. He motioned for Gardner to grab his helmet and go in. On Gardner's first play as a college quarterback, he made a poor read and suffered a 4-yard loss, while Forcier stopped warming up, returned to the bench, stuck his helmet underneath it, and a wrapped towel around his neck. He was done for the day.

As the clock ticked down Michigan's first victory of the season, a convincing 30–10 triumph, Forcier told me, "Write this down: I'm outta here." Forcier repeated his comment to Annarbor.com, where it got plenty of attention—eclipsed only by the stunning performance of Denard Robinson, who had run for 197 yards and completed nineteen of his twenty-two passes for another 186 yards, good enough to earn Big Ten and national Offensive Player of the Week honors.

Rodriguez's Wolverines, perhaps for the first time, appeared to have a clear game plan and followed it to perfection.

A little icing: The crowd had broken the NCAA attendance record, with 113,090 fans that day. The players rarely paid attention to such things, but they thrust their helmets into the air with the news. When the final gun sounded, about a dozen Wolverines jumped up on the rail by the student section, Lambeau-leap style, and sang "The Victors" with the crowd.

Running up the tunnel, Mike Martin said, "I'm not tired. I'm just hungry!"

"That was the happiest win since we got here," assistant coach Tony Gibson said later. "Just because of all the bullshit: the NCAA crap, the losing, the bad press. And you throw in the rededication of the Big House, Brock walking—man, our guys were just happy. *Just happy.* For once. Finally.

"The last ten seconds of that game, I looked over, and Rich was just smiling, hugging the guys. It looked like it *should* look."

Hours later, back at Rodriguez's house, twelve-year-old Rhett sprawled in the recliner in the living room watching the big TV. His father sat on a barstool on the other side of the counter, next to the refrigerator, wearing a gray MICHIGAN FAMILY T-shirt and blue Michigan gym shorts. He propped his right foot on the counter, in front of the small TV he preferred, watching the LSU–North Carolina game.

For three hours, he was content—perhaps the most content he had been since moving into that house thirty months earlier.

The coaches had managed to wipe off their smiles long before the players returned on Monday, September 6, and they expected the players to do the same.

The man with the hardest job in this regard was quarterback coach Rod Smith. Denard had just been named the AT&T All-American Player of the Week, and his name was already being used in the same sentence as the Heisman. The task before Coach Smith, therefore, was to find fault wherever he could. And at this, Smith was a pro. "Look here," he said to Denard, pointing to the screen. "The corner hasn't turned his hips yet to chase the wide out, so he's still able to break on Roy [Roundtree]. It's *your* job to see that."

Robinson's failure to do so set up Roundtree for a crushing hit, resulting in a bruised lung. "I hope you call Roy and apologize for this."

After a half hour spent bringing his star down to earth, Smith tossed his remote on the table and said, "Everybody says we kicked their ass. We didn't. Our O-line was average. Our backs and receivers were below average. But when you make the right reads in this offense, you cover a lot of mistakes.

"We won this game because we had no turnovers, twenty-eight first downs, and were 14-for-17 on third down, which is astronomical. You do that, we'll win a lot of football games."

After he dismissed his quarterbacks to join the team meeting, he said, "When you win, food tastes better. But we can't get complacent playing average football. We should have won 50–10. We're not as good as we think we are."

Rodriguez was in no mood to let up, either. "Just remember," he told his team, "all these people who are patting you on the back and telling you how great you are are the same people who were telling you that you weren't worth a damn last week.

"You freshmen better understand what a rivalry week is like around here. When you cross that line, you better flip a switch—especially this week, because you're going to see a lot more intensity out of Notre Dame than you saw out of UConn. Don't wait for us to yell at you.

"Are you all in?"

"YES, SIR!"

"You're starting to get people's attention and respect. You can get a lot more of it by beating Notre Dame."

Forcier's sideline scene during the UConn game had stirred speculation that he meant it when he said, "I'm outta here."

Forcier admitted he thought about it. "My dad went ballistic on me after the game," he said. But Mike Forcier also did his son a considerable favor, refuting the story that Tate was transferring and explaining his comment was intended for the media, as in "I'm outta here because I don't want to talk to you guys."

His father couldn't stop the inevitable backlash, however. "You don't know how many messages I got saying, 'You're not a Michigan Man,' all that. From people I never heard of."

Forcier got the message. At practice on Thursday, Rodriguez pulled Forcier to the side and said, "You've had a hell of a week, and I'm not getting any bad reports, so be ready."

"Dude, I just want them to throw me out there for *one play*," he said the night before the Notre Dame game, "and I swear I'll make it look so easy."

The 2010 Michigan–Notre Dame game marked the third year out of the last four when neither team was ranked. In an ESPN fan poll, this game fell a distant fourth behind the day's other games—Miami–Ohio State, Penn State–Alabama, and Florida State–Oklahoma. But Kirk Herbstreit said, "This is the game I most want to see. Are [the Wolverines] for real?"

Jordan Kovacs thought so.

"We're ready to go," he said lounging in his hotel room, with preternatural calm for a guy who had walked on just a year earlier and was about to start against Notre Dame on national TV. "You wait so long, especially for us after that long off-season [with no bowl]. You get lost in the media, the stories, and the previews, and you forget it's just a game. It's nice to get out there just to play and to win and to celebrate.

"Before games, I try to keep my nerves down, stay relaxed. I'm not one of those guys who bangs his helmet. But once the ref places the ball down, I get amped up."

Kovacs had grown from Rudy to regular, entering camp as the leading returning tackler. None of this was lost on Rodriguez, who motioned Kovacs over to his table during training camp to sign the papers for his full scholarship.

It was more than an honor. Since Kovacs grew up just across the border in Toledo, he and his parents had to pay roughly twice what in-state families paid to attend Michigan—or about $50,000 a year.

But Kovacs's mind was on Notre Dame Stadium, one of the loudest, toughest places to play. "I like the enemy atmosphere," he said. "Everyone's against you, and you can only do your talking with your pads."

If the walk-on from Toledo was calm and relaxed, the national Player of the Week from Florida was anything but.

It was a little after noon, but Denard Robinson and Devin Gardner, who shared an apartment in Ann Arbor and hotel rooms on Friday nights, had pulled the drapes shut and turned off every light but the table lamp in the corner. They both lay on their backs on their beds, holding up shiny game balls and twirling them in their outstretched hands, back and forth, like basketballs. Seeing this, you appreciate just how many hours those hands have held footballs, like world-class pianists mindlessly playing around before a big concert.

The kickoff to come was one of the biggest of the year and surely the biggest of Robinson's life to date. But Robinson was like this before every game.

"It was the same with me in high school. My coach would put the whole team in a room—lights off—and have us visualize the game.

"And that's what I do now. I just come in, chill, close my eyes, and visualize the game."

In ten minutes, Denard Robinson would leave the sensory deprivation chamber that was Room 276 at the Clarion Hotel in Michigan City, Indiana, and begin a journey that would take four hours and end on ESPN.

When the Wolverines' four-bus caravan rolls into Madison, East Lansing, and especially Columbus, they can be confident they'll be welcomed with a flurry of fingers—middle ones—and worse.

But this was South Bend, where the locals almost always replace the middle finger with a simple thumbs-down gesture. Instead of hearing all manner of profane epithets, or getting their bags sniff-searched by trained dogs—à la Ohio State in 2004—the only thing the players heard any Notre Dame official say the entire weekend was "Welcome to Notre Dame."

After hearing enough of that, they admitted, they longed for a nice loud "Fuck you, Michigan!"

They got off the buses and walked into the same room they'd had two years ago: "Visitors Locker, 1101." Two years later, every inch of that locker room was exactly the same. The coaches' room was exactly the same. And the little room off the coaches' room was exactly the same, too.

I looked above the two rusty head coaches' chairs, and sure enough, the isolation play was still there, drawn on the painted brick wall as if preserved by an ice age.

But at some point in the intervening two years, someone had written, with a blue marker, just below that play: 11 AS 1.

At Michigan, the fans see the players only at the very end of the tunnel. But at Notre Dame, the fans can hang over them halfway down their tunnel, about twenty feet overhead. As a result, the visiting players get to enjoy their Notre Dame welcome a little longer.

"No chance today, Blue!"

"Long bus ride back to Ann Arbor!"

"You're getting your *asses* handed to you!"

Kovacs was in heaven. Just as he had promised, as soon as Michigan kicked off, he flipped his switch, making four solo tackles. The more the Notre Dame fans booed and hooted and hollered, the meaner he played.

But Kovacs couldn't do it alone. When Notre Dame marched down to the 1-yard line, new head coach Brian Kelly called for the quarterback sneak, and it worked. But on Dayne Crist's trip across the goal line, he struck his head against a Wolverine's knee and suffered a concussion.

Unlike in Denard's debut, when he scored on the first possession, he couldn't get anything going against the Irish. Maybe UConn wasn't that good. Maybe Michigan wasn't, either. What was striking, however, was

Rodriguez's eerie calm and how it spread to his assistants and players. No one was yelling, pointing fingers, or slamming hands or helmets. The staffers instead gave the players reassuring hand slaps when they returned to the bench. "We'll get this!"

When the Irish offense returned to the field, Crist had been replaced by backup Tommy Rees. When he stepped back to throw his first pass, Jonas Mouton stepped up to intercept it at the Notre Dame 40-yard line and returned it to their 31.

Michigan's offense hurried out to the field and ran a play Robinson had failed to recognize twice before: fake a run to draw the defense up, then find Roy Roundtree slicing right up the middle of Notre Dame's defense. After Robinson had missed it the second time, Rodriguez came back to tell him, "Cover One, Man Two, Laser Three, remember?" This time Robinson remembered, lofting a perfect pass, and Roundtree cradled the ball and trotted straight into the end zone. 7–7.

Suddenly, it was the Irish offense that couldn't get any traction, even after they put in Nate Montana—yes, son of Joe—who failed to score on six straight possessions. While the scion struggled, Robinson found his rhythm, driving his team to a 14–7 lead.

On Michigan's next possession, Robinson got hit—hard. Forcier, who'd been on his best behavior, started warming up. But so did Gardner, who went in to take the next snap before Robinson returned. A small play, but it confirmed that Forcier still ranked behind the freshman.

After the Irish stuck a punt on Michigan's 2-yard line, with 3:47 left in the half, it looked like Michigan would be lucky to take its 14–7 lead into the locker room. What followed instead was one of the most memorable plays of the Rodriguez era.

On first down from the Irish 13, Robinson took the snap, then saw the gap he wanted on the right side of the line and zipped through it. He ran straight at the next Irish defender before cutting right again, leaving him in the dust. Patrick Omameh threw one defender into a second player to complete a two-for-one bargain. Robinson's race was on.

At about midfield, Robinson was flanked by one Irish player on his right and another on his left, both ahead of him. He also had Darryl Stonum, a speedster himself, right behind him, looking to make a block—but none of those players would have any impact whatsoever on the play.

"It looked like he was slowing down a bit at midfield," kicker Brendan Gibbons said, "when someone yelled, 'RUN!'—and I swear, he flipped a switch and found another gear."

After he crossed the goal line, Robinson took his customary knee to pray. I once asked him what he asked for when he prayed. "I don't *ask* for anything. I give *thanks*."

While Robinson was giving thanks, a member of Notre Dame's celebrated Irish Guard band, kilt and all, leaned over to say, "Fuck you."

Welcome to Notre Dame.

If the Wolverines could score on the second half's first possession and go up 28–7, they could break Notre Dame's spirit like the Irish had broken theirs two years ago. But, characteristically, the Wolverines squandered their chance for the knockout punch and had to punt.

When Notre Dame's offense returned to the field, a big cheer went up: Dayne Crist had returned at quarterback. Two plays later, Crist's touchdown pass cut Michigan's lead to 21–14. When the third quarter ended, Michigan was holding on 21–17, but Van Bergen was breathing hard while Mike Martin splashed water on his face. The Wolverines were getting a workout.

The two teams worked the fourth quarter like boxers, throwing punches but neither able to put their opponent on the ropes. After Michigan's Brendan Gibbons missed his second midlength field goal of the day, Notre Dame took over on its 5-yard line. Crist faked a handoff, then dropped back to find Kyle Rudolph running straight up the middle. Michigan cornerback James Rogers, a converted wide out pressed into action due to the rash of injuries, bit on Crist's fake and ran forward. Behind him, true freshman Cam Gordon started backpedaling when he should have turned around and hightailed it. That's how Rudolph found himself completely alone, running to the end zone for a record touchdown.

Seven quarters into the 2010 season, Michigan's Achilles' heel had finally been exposed: the defensive backfield.

"That's 95 yards!" the announcer said. "With a rainbow in the sky! Michigan 21, Notre Dame 24!"

So this was it. 3:41 left to play, with the ball on Michigan's 28-yard line. On the sidelines, only the backup field goal kicker, Seth Broekhuizen—better known as "Budweiser"—was warming up.

Robinson ran for 12.

Robinson hit Stonum on the right side for 16 yards, then again for 7 more.

Robinson, on third-and-1, tried a sneak but got stuffed.

The officials measured the mark and determined that Robinson had finished short of a first down by "four inches."

On fourth-and–4 inches, from Notre Dame's 35, Rodriguez did not give the slightest thought to kicking a field goal—he'd seen enough of that—or even a sneak. He'd seen enough of that, too. Instead, he had Robinson take the snap from the shotgun formation, 5 yards and 4 inches short of a first down, and run as fast as he could into a small indentation on the right side of the line. Robinson made it—just barely.

On first-and-10 from Notre Dame's 34, with less than two minutes to play, Robinson threw to Shaw on the right sideline; Shaw ran up the sideline for a 12-yard gain to Notre Dame's 22.

Robinson threw again to Shaw for 5 more, though it cost Shaw a bloody nose from a hard hit to his chin.

Then, on third-and-5 from Notre Dame's 17-yard line, Rodriguez's gambling instincts kicked in once more. He remembered how poorly Notre Dame had covered Roundtree all day—and how tough his skinny receiver with the bruised ribs could be. They called Roundtree's number.

Robinson caught the snap, took his standard drop, and saw Roundtree cutting along the goal line, with his man right behind him and no margin for error. Robinson didn't flinch. He fired the ball right on target, to the only spot where Roundtree could touch it, and no one else.

Roundtree dived, caught the ball two feet off the grass, and held on tight.

First down, on the Notre Dame 2-yard line.

On the next play, Robinson ran off-tackle left, took two hits, and bounced into the end zone. Michigan 27, Notre Dame 24.

Broekhuizen kicked the extra point, to give the Wolverines a 4-point lead, with 27 seconds left.

The crowd went silent, while the Wolverines went crazy.

The Irish, with the help of some bad Michigan penalties, managed to get the ball to Michigan's 27-yard line, with just 6 seconds left. Crist dropped back and fired to the end zone—but too high and well out of reach of his receivers. The game was over. Michigan had won again, 28–24.

The press conference was a pleasure for once. "In honor of Denard," Rodriguez said, taking the podium in the nicest pressroom around, a veritable museum of Notre Dame lore, "I'm wearing my shoes untied."

But this being Michigan and Rodriguez, gray linings had to be discussed: How many times did Robinson run this time? "Well, I promised Dave Brandon we would not run him twenty-nine times again. So we ran him twenty-eight. But I guarantee you, if he hadn't made that last run, he'd have made twenty-nine!"

How long could he keep that up? Robinson replied, "Until the season ends."

In the coaches' room, Rodriguez's joy could not be contained. "I wouldn't trade number 16 for anyone!" He tore his hat and shirt off next to that old play on the wall. The "11 AS 1" now seemed prophetic.

When Rodriguez walked to the bus, a man with a Notre Dame hat approached him. "I'm not sure if you're shaking hands with Notre Dame fans, but great job. I'm impressed."

As the buses rolled down the road, cell phones started buzzing with text messages coming in from parents, girlfriends, fans, and even the famous.

The national story would be Denard Robinson, who broke just about every single-game record for a Michigan quarterback on the books. With 455 yards rushing in two games, Robinson led not only all quarterbacks nationwide but all tailbacks, too, and he had yet to suffer a single run for a loss.

PR man Dave Ablauf's phone vibrated like a tuning fork the entire way home, with everyone wanting a piece of Denard, the leading Heisman candidate. Even Dhani Jones and Braylon Edwards, frequent critics of the Rodriguez regime, appeared to want back on the bandwagon. But the best response might have been the tweet from LeBron James—a Buckeye fan, no less—who wrote, "I give credit where credit is due. That Denard Robinson is a monster out there right now."

The Wolverines were undefeated, and headed home for what looked like two easy games before starting Big Ten play.

But Rodriguez didn't give a second thought to any of it. He sat in the front seat with his laptop, breaking down the tape.

"Offensive player?" Rodriguez said, doing his best to sound mildly grumpy throughout the Sunday staff meeting. "Guess we can figure out who that is." It was the first tipoff in forty-five minutes that he had actually seen Denard play the day before.

On defense, Kovacs and Mouton took top honors, but when special teams came up, Rodriguez jumped at the chance to try to take the sheen off the Era of Good Feeling. "Special teams?" he asked rhetorically. "I don't think we have anyone. It was atrocious."

But the good news kept coming anyway. Seven players had crunches, three had picks, and the defense achieved its weekly goal of six three-and-outs. Nonetheless, after they broke down the special teams film, the offensive coaches ran through every play—all eighty-seven, back and forth and back and forth—without cracking a smile.

But when Denard finished his 3-yard run for the winning touchdown—the last offensive play of the game—Tony Dews couldn't restrain himself, jamming both fists into the air. "Man, that *still* feels good," he said, standing up and pointing at the screen. "*Suck it,* Notre Dame!"

Rodriguez himself displayed a a grin worthy of the *Mona Lisa.* No one else said a word—no one dared—until Rodriguez retired to his office. Outside of Dews's brief outburst, if you watched the two-hour meeting, you would have assumed their team had been humiliated.

But when they all walked down the hall to the bathroom, their faces broke into big smiles and they started high-fiving each other and patting each other on the back.

"Oh, man, that was great!"

"We needed that one!"

"That felt good!"

"We've only just begun!"

That five-minute celebration was the last they talked about the Notre Dame game all day, all week, all season. They returned to the den, put their game faces back on, and started breaking down tape of the University of Massachusetts, their third opponent.

Their focus was interrupted only once, when Denard Robinson timidly cracked the door open to see if it was okay to come in.

"Come on in, Denard!"

"Hey, man, you guys see it?" he asked.

"See what?" they asked, assuming he was talking about his now famous 87-yard run, which had been playing on ESPN every thirty minutes.

"You guys all see my knockdown? I got a knockdown! I want my Payday!"

They laughed. "We'll check the tape again. Promise."

"You a little sore today?" Rod Smith asked.

"Yeah," he said, chuckling. "I'm sore as hell right now. Ribs. Neck." He picked up some tapes of UMass.

"Getting hounded by the press yet?" Rodriguez asked.

"I'm getting texts from people I never met. I just ignore 'em."

"Good. Don't talk to anyone who doesn't go through Dave [Ablauf]."

A couple hours later, Ablauf sat down with Rodriguez for Sunday pizza.

"I'm getting pounded," Ablauf said, referring to the flood of media requests for Denard. "We need to come up with a strategy—*now*—to deal with all of it."

"That's easy," Rodriguez said, munching on a slice. "No change in his routine. No hype for the Heisman."

"I agree," Ablauf said. "Of course, they're going to howl."

"You can blame it on me," Rodriguez said. "What're they gonna do, write a bad story about me? Been there, done that. They can kiss my ass. And they can kiss Denard's too—if they can catch it."

While the media showered praise on Robinson, it seemed to regard Michigan's success as a lucky fluke. Few seemed to remember that Michigan was the only big-name program smart enough to recruit Denard as a quarterback and honest enough to keep their word. People had also forgotten how unprepared Robinson—and his supporting cast—had been just one year earlier. Michigan's success wasn't based on just Robinson, or luck. The quarterback and his teammates had been recruited, they had been coached, and they had responded.

Obviously, since Rodriguez had arrived in Ann Arbor, a lot of things had not gone as he had hoped or expected, especially on defense. But if his bosses had reviewed Rodriguez's progression at Glenville State and West Virginia, and analyzed his first twenty-six games in Ann Arbor, they would recognize a familiar pattern: After struggling to learn his system, the offense takes off, then the defense follows.

As *Sports Illustrated*'s Austin Murphy had written, "If past is prologue, the Wolverines will grind their offensive gears in Rich Rod's first season. After that, stand back."

That appeared in the 2008 college football preview. Everything seemed a year behind schedule, for a variety of reasons, but by mid-September 2010, it looked more like the cycle had merely been delayed, not broken.

"Any time you get a win, it's good," Rodriguez told his team on Monday, September 13. "And any time you get a win over Notre Dame, it's even better. But when you see the tape, you'll see that we can play a lot better.

"Now, all of a sudden the cockroaches are hiding because the lights are on. And now the media wants to have *all* these interviews—with Denard, with me, with all of you.

"Well, where the hell were they two weeks ago?

"Remember, all this attention, all this praise—it's just like poison: It's not gonna kill ya unless you swallow it.

"We're not going to coach any different, we're not going to play any different, no matter who we're playing, no matter who's watching."

The next six games represented a perfect progression upward: UMass, Bowling Green, Indiana on the road, Michigan State at home, Iowa at home, and Penn State on the road. Each week they would probably have to play better to win, but that seemed a lot easier than the two-game gauntlet they had just survived.

Everyone expected UMass to be easier, but no one expected Rodriguez to let up. When they were winning, he was at his toughest. At the end of a good practice, Rodriguez told his team: "Do not get behind on your schoolwork. How you start your semester has everything to do with how you finish. We have eleven more weeks of unshakable focus ahead of us. Keep the lights on!"

Quarterback coach Rod Smith was more direct when he addressed his four charges: "Don't you *dare* take these guys for granted. They're good!"

The players were done for the day, but not the coaches. On this warm, sunny day, twenty-nine walk-on wannabes showed up to run, pass, catch, and kick in front of the coaches for forty-five minutes.

The group looked like an intramural flag football team—and not a great one, at that. But Rodriguez noticed a tight end with a Division I build who made a great diving catch. On his next route, he strained for another high pass, tipped it, and then gathered it on the way down, with the defender hanging all over him.

"There you go!" Rodriguez said. "Good job catching my eye! Come over here!" Rodriguez wanted some basic information: Mike Kwiatkowski. Macomb, Michigan. A 3.4 GPA, majoring in neuroscience. Bingo.

After Kwiatkowski made another strong catch, I asked Rodriguez, "Did he just make the team with that one?"

"No," he said, then turned to me. "He made it on the last one."

Throughout the tryout, Rodriguez roamed among the half dozen stations, with his two children close by. They often attended practice—"If I don't see 'em then, I might not see 'em all day," Rodriguez explained—but this was their only chance to walk on the field. They took full advantage, following their father wherever he went, taking turns being sheltered by his big left arm.

Rodriguez's Wolverines were 2–0, ranked twentieth in the nation, with winnable games on the horizon. The Irish had been vanquished, his patented spread offense was humming along nicely with a Heisman candidate at quarterback, the weather was perfect, he was about to give a walk-on the same chance he'd been given, and his kids were under his wing.

When they're happy, cats purr. Dogs wag their tails. Coach Rodriguez spins his whistle string on the first two fingers of his right hand, winds it all the way up, then spins it all the way back, unaware he's even doing it.

Rich Rodriguez was happy.

Back at his desk, he was writing notes on each player he'd just watched. He decided to keep two kickers and the tight end.

Was this the best part of coaching?

"If it's not my favorite day, it's one of 'em," he said, writing away, then looked up. "I love it. I love it."

If you want to get the pulse of the average Michigan football fan, you need to close your laptop, leave the campus cafés, and walk down State Street toward Ferry Field. If you stop halfway down the slope, between Hill and Packard, you'll see such Ann Arbor institutions as Pizza Bob's, Mr. Spots, Big Ten Burrito (though the conference made it change its name to BTB Burrito, everyone still calls it by its original name), and two barbershops: Coach & Four and the State Street Barbershop.

They have a history. Jerry Erickson came down from a little town in the Upper Peninsula called Stambaugh, near the Wisconsin border, and opened Coach & Four in 1972. He hired fellow Stambaugh native Bill Stolberg, whom everyone still calls "Red" even though his hair turned white long ago. Four years later, Stolberg took over the State Street Barbershop, and it's been that way ever since.

Both barbershops cut hair—sixteen bucks, no appointment needed—and serve as mini-museums to Michigan Men, with signed game jerseys and photos covering every flat surface, from legends like Anthony Carter, Jamie Morris, and Jim Harbaugh. Erickson's place features a stuffed bear on the wall wearing a Michigan hockey jersey from 1973, and a photo of Bo Schembechler, who wrote, "To Jerry, the worst barber in Ann Arbor." That didn't stop him from walking up the street for decades. He got his last haircut just two days before he passed away. "I think," Erickson said, "he was saying good-bye."

Both barbershops serve as gossip centers for all things Michigan athletics. The proprietors are cousins, to boot, but that doesn't mean they agree very often.

On Friday afternoon, Erickson was busy shooting the bull with his customers, selling tickets, and watching his barbers cut hair. "Oh, everyone's real happy, everyone's real excited," he said about the team. "They're fun to watch. Keep it up for a few more, and I think the ol' boy is safe."

Red Stolberg was holding court down the street. "The consensus is," he said, while cutting a local businessman's hair, "someone should have sat Rich Rod down when he came to Michigan, and told him what Michigan is all about, the tradition, and the Big Ten. And he should be more visible on campus. You never see him, except for some big pep rally once a year. He needs to come up here! Lloyd was always walking up and down State Street saying hello to people.

"Hard to like someone you don't know.

"Sixty percent of my customers say, if he doesn't come through this year, he's got to go. Other folks are saying it's his third year, and you need to give him more time."

Of course, to Rodriguez, the idea that the danger had passed was, well, dangerous.

On Friday night, September 17, in the team meeting at the Campus Inn, Rodriguez reviewed the keys to success. The previous two seasons, he offered five points each for offense, defense, and the team, but this year he'd reduced that to just one key for each, which he then beat into their heads so often that they could yell them back. It mirrored the coaches' decision to simplify both the offensive and defensive schemes in the hopes of sacrificing complexity for execution and aggressiveness. It was the start of his third season in Ann Arbor, and he was still evolving as a coach.

"On offense?"

"Attack, whack, don't hold back!"

"That's right. And BSA?"

"Ball security always."

"Good. Defense?"

"Strain, contain, and CAUSE SOME PAIN."

"Yeah, you got it! And our team keys?"

"Stay hungry. Don't swallow the poison!"

"I don't think you have swallowed the poison, from what I've seen. You've been humble. Practice has been good." Then he showed a tape that had popped up that day on the UMass website. During their walk-through that day, someone asked one of their players about the Big House. "Well, it's not that big," he said. "It should be called the Little House on the Prairie."

It was just like Dierdorf had warned: They weren't scared anymore.

Rodriguez looked at his players, held up the printout, then said with perfect comic timing, "I can't make this shit up!

"I don't care where you grew up. I don't care how big your house is. You take *pride* in your family, in your home. You guys play in the biggest house in the country—and I've never heard *any* of you guys disrespect any other team or stadium. Ever.

"There was a time, when Michigan ran down that tunnel with that winged helmet, that was worth 14 points. Now we've got UMass calling it the 'Little House on the Prairie.' So somewhere along the line we lost that. But we can get that back.

"And it starts with us.

"They are gonna feel the full brunt of our program. Then I want to see if they still got this shit on their website at four o'clock tomorrow afternoon."

The next afternoon, the players seemed ready, but apparently the Minutemen were, too, jumping out to a 17–7 lead.

Michigan basketball coach John Beilein, sitting in his usual perch in the front row, felt their frustration. "People don't realize it, but UMass isn't bad. You beat Notre Dame on NBC, then come back and play these guys?" He shook his head. "These are nightmare games."

When Michigan got the ball back with just 1:17 left in the half, Robinson hit Stonum on the first play for a 64-yard touchdown. On the Minutemen's kickoff return, Kovacs ripped the ball loose and recovered it. Four plays and 29 seconds later, Robinson took the snap from the 9-yard line, rolled right, and found Stonum again in the right flat; he walked into the end zone, untouched.

Michigan 21, Massachussetts 17.

Denard Robinson returned to the bench. For the first time all day, he smiled.

But the Minutemen weren't giving up. When they walked back down the tunnel to start the second half, one player yelled, "Let's go shock the world!" while another added, "We're gonna win this one!"—and they both sounded like they meant it.

The Michigan mystique was no longer worth 14 points.

The question to be answered was simple: Was Michigan a weak team, or just a young team? The former needed to be fixed, the latter needed nurturing. The seesaw second half provided evidence for both theories. Michigan's *program* didn't need to be rebuilt. No school had a deeper, stronger foundation than Michigan. But even if Rodriguez's critics didn't want to admit it, the team did.

The Minutemen came back from a 35–17 deficit to cut Michigan's lead to 42–37. But their two-point conversion failed, setting up an onside kick with 2:05 left.

A fan behind the bench gasped in horror, "Ohhhh, my god!" She had probably been in that same seat for the games against Appalachian State and Toledo.

And another: "We want Ron English!" The ghosts were far from gone.

But Michigan got the ball back, and Robinson took a knee. Disaster averted.

The next day, when Greg Robinson nominated Mike Martin and Jordan Kovacs for Codefensive Players of the Week, Rodriguez said, "We gave up thirty-seven points to a I-AA team. No one's getting an award for that.

"Did we have *any* three-and-outs?" Rodriguez asked, as if he hadn't already watched the film three times.

"No," Tony Gibson said.

"None?" Rodriguez said. "Not one? Hmm."

From this meeting, you'd be surprised to discover that Michigan was ranked twentieth in the country, one of six Big Ten teams in the top twenty-three—seven if you count Nebraska, which would join the Big Ten in 2011—making up almost a third of the nation's top teams. None of that mattered on Sunday.

Rodriguez had wisely stayed calm during the UMass game, to avoid disaster. But that didn't mean he was going to let that performance slide.

Instead of the usual Monday routine, in which each coach meets with his position group in their breakout rooms, Rodriguez met with the entire defense in the team room. Once Rodriguez made the announcement, the defensive players knew that they were in for something they called "Movie Night with Coach Rod." For this premiere, however, there would be no popcorn, jumbo Cokes, or Milk Duds.

"Everyone gets their ass ripped," Van Bergen explained afterward. "The worst thing you can do is tell him something that sounds like an excuse."

"That's what they're waiting for," Mike Martin said. "One 'But!'"

"Or, 'I thought,'" Van Bergen added. "'You *thought*?!'"

Martin laughed. "Oh, yeah. They're *waiting* for that one."

"What you do," defensive end Steve Watson said, "is just shut up and take it."

"That was our first Movie Night after a win," Van Bergen said. "I guess that tells you something. He expects more. This summer, Coach Rod's big message was: I'm not going to be soft and sensitive about criticizing you anymore. I'm going to get in your face, and if you can't take it, we'll get someone else.

"On Monday, we needed that. None of us objected to what he said. And this week we had more mental focus. We went hard on Tuesday. You're not supposed to tackle them—but there were a lot of tackles!"

"No way we have another game like that this week," Martin said. "No way."

At Coach & Four, Jerry Erickson provides tickets, free beer out of the mini-fridge in the corner, and stacks of *Playboys* on the trunk that serves as a coffee table. It is the man cave of man caves. A woman might have walked in at one point, but I can't remember it.

"There are lot more people out there who like him than don't," Erickson said of Rodriguez, working next to the big window. "The fans like him. Some of the old players don't. There is only a handful of guys who are stirring all the crap up. The thing is, you gotta give the guy a chance. And I think Brandon is going to stick with this guy."

Pressed for a prediction, Erickson had no trouble saying, "They'll go 8–4 easy. And we're gonna win a bowl game. But don't ask me to put a million bucks on it."

He stopped his scissors to make his next point. "Beating Michigan State will save his job. But losing to Michigan State? Hooo boy. Not gonna be good!"

Just a few doors down, Red Stolberg was, as usual, taking the other side. "At the start of the season, I said he'd go 5–7, but I might have to bend a little. Now I'm saying they might pick up six. But I think he's got to get at least seven to save his job. And win a decent bowl game, not the Motor City Bowl."

Would Rodriguez survive the season?

"Hard to say. But," he said, pointing his razor, "if they can beat [Michigan] State, that's going to be the big one this year. I think right now State is more important than Ohio State, even though that's The Game.

"But if they lose three straight to State—hooo boy," he said, unwittingly quoting his cousin. "Not gonna be good. Not gonna be good!"

Michigan football players get very little free time, but what they get, they savor.

Friday afternoon is one of those times. After a walk-through, they have about forty-five minutes to hang out in the locker room or the players' lounge watching TV, playing Ping-Pong or pool, or sitting upstairs on the square of couches, where one kind soul leaves three big aluminum trays of his wife's famous supersize cookies. They evaporate quickly.

But before the players do any of those things, they stand in line at the equipment manager's window to get the gear they deem most important. It's not the $257 helmets or $330 shoulder pads or even the $150 jerseys.

Nope. It's the $4 socks. But not just any socks. Twin City socks—the thickest you can find.

David Molk, at the front of the line, handed me a pair. They are so dense, you could wear them as slippers around the home—or fill them with water.

"Best part of being a Michigan football player," Molk said, holding up a pair, "is these socks." Every one of his teammates—and I mean *every* one—agreed with that assessment.

At dinner Molk approached Mouton, who was enjoying a huge helping of pretty much everything.

Molk asked Mouton if he knew where his Twin City socks had gone.

"I don't know, man," Mouton replied, taking a bite out of his drumstick and chewing very slowly. "Go see Big Jon." Falk, that is, the equipment manager.

"It's dinner," Molk said. "He's not here."

"Go see him tomorrow," Mouton said, picking up a roll.

"I want them now."

"Guess you'll just have to wait, then."

After Molk turned and walked to the back of the buffet, ticked off, Mouton leaned forward and said, "I'm wearin' 'em."

After Phil Bromley showed the weekly highlight film, Rodriguez asked, "What's our record?"

"Three-and-oh," the players replied.

"Right. Life's not so bad, is it? Then why did I have to spend this week answering questions about our team? 'You're not that good.' 'It's all offense.' 'It's all Denard.' 'You won't last in the Big Ten.'

"Well, I'm used to it by now. And I've thought about it, and now I realize why: They *like* it when Michigan struggles. They like it when we're not in the top twenty-five. So when we win, when we're ranked—well, now they're asking about how many freshmen we have starting. About quarterbacks running so much. All the doubting, all the criticism—and that's when we're *winning*.

"A lot of people don't want us to do well. They like it the way it was the last couple years. Well, I've got bad news for the haters: Last year was last year. Those days are long gone."

The players were nodding. There was no dissension in the ranks, and no taking Bowling Green for granted. They looked properly pissed off, which was bad news for the Falcons.

In their hotel room, Denard Robinson and Devin Gardner were in their usual contemplative states: headphones on, heads bobbing, twirling footballs in their hands.

"Most teams wanted me to play tailback," Robinson recalled of his recruiting process. "Florida wanted me to play quarterback, but Coach Smith put it in writing, in a letter to me. And he kept his word."

Robinson had kept his end of the deal, too—and then some. But even his success came at a price. "Ideally, I could just play the game and be with my teammates—that's it. I don't like the attention. But I can handle it, I guess."

He still spoke with his parents almost every day. "They always say, every time, 'Stay humble. We'd like you to act like you're still third string. Because remember last year—you were!' My dad cares about the football thing, but he's mostly about grades."

Denard's dad needn't have worried about distractions. Outside of fans, Robinson didn't have many. He doesn't drink, smoke, or swear very often. Even the night before a game against a mediocre MAC team, Robinson could not relax. He had the butterflies, he said, right on time. And he would have them until the first hit.

But only one thing upset him that week. "The coaches never gave me credit for my pancake, man. I'm mad."

Tate Forcier was focused on an entirely different set of concerns. "I was in the compliance office yesterday, signing my papers to give other schools the permission to contact me. I should have been gone by today. To Washington, probably.

"I went to Coach Rod, and he said, 'You'll be playing this year.'

"'How do I know?'

"'Have I ever lied to you?'

"'No.'

"'Then you need to take my word for it. After this year, if you're still not playing like you should be playing, I'll help you leave. But I think you're going to be a good player and I think we're going to have a special team. You want to be part of this.'

"I thought, 'He's right.' So I decided to stay.

"Then he gave me a big hug," Forcier said with a laugh.

The idea that Rodriguez was a snake-oil salesman didn't have much traction among his young quarterbacks.

A little-known custom: Every morning before a game, each position group goes for a walk around the hotel block. They walk past an important house on the Underground Railroad, and down Ann Street, which is actually the street Ann Arbor native Bob Seger is singing about in "Down on Main Street," but the players were oblivious to all of it—and the people they passed, too.

The three quarterbacks started out an hour before the buses left for the stadium. They wore their baggy blue Adidas sweat suits, their Adidas sandals, and, of course, their brand-new Twin City socks.

Denard put his headphones in his ears and his hands in his pants pockets and started gliding down the sidewalk, very slowly, with his weight back on his heels, deep in thought. When people on their porches said hello, and people in their cars honked their horns and waved, Robinson did not respond. He wasn't being unfriendly. He simply didn't see or hear them.

Two attractive blond students driving past recognized the trio, then turned back to ask if they could take a picture with them. "Sorry," Denard said, speaking for all three, barely looking and not breaking stride. "We gotta keep going." And they kept going.

Gardner literally followed in Robinson's footsteps. He wore his Adidas skullcap and jammed his hands in his pockets, but he didn't bring any music and didn't speak the entire walk. Forcier wore earphones but paid more attention to the people and places they passed.

Even fans wearing number five and number sixteen jerseys, grilling on their porches, didn't notice they were walking by.

It made for an odd scene. These three men, who would be the focus of intense national interest when they performed in the center of a 110,000-seat coliseum in just a few hours, could walk largely unbothered through the streets of their fans.

Five minutes and two seconds. That's how long it took Denard Robinson to lead two straight touchdown drives against Bowling Green to go ahead 14–0.

"Be ready!" Van Bergen told the offense. "We're getting it back!"

They did, and they started their third possession on their own 9. No matter. Robinson took off, cutting up the left sideline by Michigan's bench. It looked like he might go all the way again, but at midfield the Falcons cut off his lane, exactly the situation the coaches had been urging Robinson to avoid: geting out-of-bounds.

But he cut back, trying to squeeze out a few more yards. At the 44-yard line they knocked him out-of-bounds, sending him to the ground. It didn't look like much, but he struggled to get up.

On the sidelines, Dave Brandon said, "He's so used to outrunning everybody, he's not good at getting out-of-bounds. Even *Bo* let the quarterbacks do that!"

The doctors and trainers set him up on the table against the wall and surrounded him with every medical professional they had, about eight in all, plus a couple coaches, the athletic director, and even a regent or two. All the king's horses and all the king's men.

In Robinson's stead, Rodriguez once again sent out not Forcier but Gardner, who needed only three plays to put Michigan up 21–0, just 10:39 into the contest. But the Falcons, playing a backup quarterback, scored twice themselves to tighten things up, 21–14, with 5 minutes left in the half.

That's when Rodriguez sent Forcier in, and a big cheer went up. For all his trials and tribulations, Forcier remained a fan favorite. "I might have gotten the biggest woodie I've had in ten months," he cracked. He was sharp, directing the offense from their own 31 in ten plays to go ahead 28–14.

At halftime, Paul Schmidt made a rare appearance in the coaches' room. "Denard," he said, and all heads turned to the door. "It looks like an MCL sprain, inside of his left knee. He'll be okay." Relieved, the Wolverines came out swinging. The defense scored a safety, Mouton got an interception, and the offense burned Bowling Green for five consecutive touchdown drives, the first four by Forcier, the last by Gardner, for a very convincing 65–21 victory.

Their 721 total yards finished just 6 yards shy of the all-time Michigan record set the previous year against Delaware State. Critics could no longer say the offense was all Denard Robinson. It was the *offense*—when run right. Forcier had gone 12-for-12, setting a Michigan record.

When the Wolverines ran to the student section to lead "The Victors," Forcier and Denard sang it side by side, "Kumbaya"-style.

At the press conference, Forcier—who had filled out the paperwork to start the transfer process just two days earlier—said all the right things. "I love everything about Michigan. I love Coach Rod."

When he left the podium through the back hallway, he ran into Rodriguez heading toward him and returned his big hug from Thursday. Forcier showered and changed, then basked in the attention of the fans outside the tunnel, signing everything they had.

Denard, in contrast, hid in the tunnel with his high school sweetheart, Sarah Chattman, to avoid the very same crowds Forcier was delighting. Chattman wore yellow tennis shoes, blue pants, and a yellow zip-up sweatshirt, topped by a warm smile and bright eyes. If you were Denard Robinson's mother, this is the young woman you'd want showing up at the door for your son.

They met through a cousin, but she was no pushover. Before they started dating, she said, "I want to know who this 'Shoelace' is. What's your real name?'

"I liked his personality, and his smile. And he seemed to have a plan. He wasn't just riding on his talent."

Chattman had goals, too. She was attending Valencia Community College in Orlando, earning a 3.5 in political science, and applying to Michigan. "I've planned this out for a while."

After Rodriguez finished signing autographs, he returned to the tunnel, where he helped smuggle Robinson and Chattman to Junior Hemingway's truck. Some fans gave chase—but as usual, they couldn't catch him.

Rodriguez moved Sunday's offensive film session from its usual spot at 1:00 in the afternoon to 10:00 a.m. The reason had nothing to do with their upcoming game at Indiana. Rhett's second football game was scheduled for 2:00, and his dad figured this might be his only chance all season to see his son play.

After getting their work done, Rodriguez huddled in the cold with his extended family in the stands. Rhett failed to duplicate the magic of his debut, when he'd scored a touchdown on offense, defense, and special teams. He did, however, connect on all three of his passes—to the other team.

"The bad news is, I threw three interceptions," he told his dad. "The good news is, I can clearly throw a catchable ball." Rodriguez liked the line so much he repeated it with a few friends that week.

After the game, Rodriguez walked out to the parking lot with his arm draped around his daughter's shoulders. He had a relaxed smile few fans would recognize.

On a drizzly Friday morning at Coach & Four, Jerry Erickson said the blue backers were optimistic. Even ESPN's Colin Cowherd, who had broadcast from campus that week, was giving Rodriguez credit.

"It's still scary," the barber said. "The jury's still out." But the jury seemed to be tilting in Rodriguez's favor. "I had dinner with [former Michigan hockey coach] Al Renfrew the other night, and he said it's only a few football alums who are down on him, and you know their names. But they're still crushing him, even now. In their eyes, he can't do anything right. That's not fair.

"But I can give him one knock," Erickson added, echoing his more critical cousin's comments. "I cut Bo's hair way back in '69. People don't remember this, but he wasn't popular at first, either! But he got out all the time, and people liked him. We know Rich is busy—we respect that—but he needs to get his ass up here! Whoever meets him likes him."

A few doors down, Red Stolberg had to concede, "People are a little bit more positive in this chair, but everyone reminds me that we went 4–0 last year—and look what happened!

"This is probably a turning point. Win this one, and the ol' boy's almost home. But if they lose, you better start looking over the horizon."

On Friday night, October 1, 2010, in Bloomington, as they twirled footballs in their hands, watching the game on ESPN, Robinson and Gardner had arguably become the epicenter of the Michigan football universe.

What would they be if they weren't football players?

"An A student," Gardner quipped.

That was not an idle boast. Gardner is an excellent student and so motivated that one of his professors felt compelled to tell me his comments in lecture, the best he'd heard in some time.

"I'd probably be running track or playing baseball," Robinson said. "I love all sports. But football was always my favorite. At first I was a running back. I always wanted the ball in my hands. But quarterback is best. It's what I always wanted to play. There's no other feeling like this. The best part? That's easy: winning!"

"Best part?" Gardner said. "Playing on TV."

"Yeah, that's cool," Robinson said. "But I don't like being noticed."

Right on cue, ESPN's Mark May said, "Denard Robinson is the most outstanding player in the nation."

"Oh, jeez," Robinson muttered.

"There you go!" Gardner gushed, bolting upright, knowing how much his roommate hated it. "Heisman hopeful Denard Robinson!"

"A month ago," Lou Holtz said, "he was just second string!"

Robinson clapped and laughed. He had been first string since the spring game in April.

"So here we are with Heisman hopeful Denard Robinson," Gardner said, mimicking a sportscaster. "Mr. Robinson, how is that whole not-being-noticed thing working out for you?"

They both laughed, but Robinson shook his head, chagrined.

"When I was coming out of the Academic Center last night," Robinson said, "the autograph guys were waiting for me. They're there almost every night now, no matter how late we come out. And they all say the same thing: 'It's for my ten-year-old son.' Their kid is *always* ten years old! Is ten the automatic age for charity?"

"Ha! No doubt!" Gardner said. "But that's the price of being the Heisman trophy favorite."

"Aw, man! Why you always gotta bring *that* up! Now *everyone's* doing it!"

When Gardner quit laughing, he admitted, "People say I'm arrogant or aloof. No I'm not. I just don't like talking to random people. I just don't."

"I *love* people, that ain't a problem," Robinson said. "But it's just, like, don't be trying to act like you know me when you really don't know me. What's scary is when they know my birth date and all that."

"Well, that's what happens when you're a Heisman hopeful!"

"Will you *stop* with that?" he said, threatening to throw the football at Gardner's head. "The other day [at Chili's] I thought the waitress was bringing my check, but she wanted my autograph."

"Have you no shame?" Gardner asked.

"Then a lady was following us around the mall," Robinson said, "and she said to her little daughter, 'You better get that autograph, or I'm going to take away everything I just bought you!' This lady just really said that!"

"Have. You. No. Shame?" Gardner repeated.

"So the mall's almost off-limits. But I can still go to the library."

"Class is fun," Gardner said. "We're good there."

"We don't even go out, anyway," Robinson said. "Except to go bowling."

Robinson had his reasons for steering clear of trouble. He'd gotten a reminder the day before, during a quarterback meeting, when his cell phone started ringing. He never picked up in meetings, but this one he had to take. It was from his twenty-two-year-old cousin, who had been a star defensive tackle at Deerfield a few years before Denard and was something of a hero to the younger man.

"They were the first Deerfield team to get ranked in the nation," he recalled. "I was very close to him. He had a scholarship to go to Louisville."

But after their senior season, he and a teammate decided to pull an armed robbery.

"Bad idea," Robinson said softly. "I was very disappointed in him. And his mom took it hard. Real hard. It was hard to see that."

On Thursday, his cousin was released. The very first call he made was to Denard.

"It was good to hear from him," Denard said. "But it's sad, you know, to think about everything he lost. My parents call me every day just to tell me school, school, school, school. 'They can take football away from you, but they can't take your education!'"

Gardner chuckled at the imitation. "Ohhh, yes. One *does* hear that! The hardest part about this is time management."

"The hardest part, for me, is rest!" Robinson said. "We don't go home until nine or ten o'clock, every night, earliest. And you want to have fun sometimes, and you can't have fun. Sometimes you just give up having fun. They get mad at us at the Academic Center when we're laughing with other people, but they don't realize, it's because we're happy to see other people! *We're happy to see other people!*"

Gardner laughed at that. "Too true, too true. Other students can all do whatever they want. We actually can't. We have curfew six days a week.

People think we just got it made—'You guys get all this stuff'—but if you had to do all this, you'd give all the stuff back and pay for school yourself."

Except they couldn't, and they wouldn't. The chance to get an education they probably couldn't pay for themselves—both were from modest homes—and to play football on the world's biggest stage was enough to keep them going.

Fourteen hours. Every day. Six days a week.

But winning helped.

"This week," Rodriguez had announced to his coaches six days earlier, "we're going to use all twenty hours," something they hadn't done since the season started, probably the only team in the country that hadn't. "This is Big Ten time. They've got to feel it's different, a different level of intensity. They've got to know we'll do whatever we've got to do to beat Indiana's ass."

Indiana's two Big Ten titles—outright in 1945 and shared in 1967—placed them dead last in the league. The Hoosiers have finished in the Top Twenty-five just five times, most recently in 1988. But they felt they had a good chance to get it right this time—as evidenced by the 52,929 fans who filled the place, the fourth-biggest crowd in school history.

Before the game, Rodriguez seemed more anxious than usual, pacing back and forth in Indiana's tiny blood-red coaches' room. Playing had been far less stressful for him than coaching.

"Waiting's the worst, isn't it?" he said to Dave Brandon, sitting nearby.

With Michigan ahead 14–7, and the ball about midfield, Robinson hit Roundtree, who twirled around, made a couple cuts, followed his blocking, and dived just short of the end zone. Two plays later, on the 1-yard line, Robinson fumbled the snap, and Indiana recovered.

Indiana quarterback Ben Chappell took immediate advantage, hitting five different receivers en route to a 99-yard game-tying, spirit-sucking touchdown. The ghosts of the Illinois debacle haunted every man on Michigan's sideline. But this time neither team backed off, firing at each other all day.

The Hoosiers trailed Michigan 35–28 about halfway through the fourth quarter, when they charged 80 yards for a game-tying touchdown, leaving just 1:15.

Just 1:15.

That's what every team in the country would say in that situation. But in the Michigan coaches' box, Calvin Magee turned to Rod Smith, smiled, and said, "They left us too much time. We got this."

On the sideline, Denard Robinson told his troops, "Plenty of time."

Roundtree agreed. "Let's go get this," he said, flashing his smile while snapping his chin strap.

At Indiana's 46-yard line, with 29 seconds left, Robinson dropped back to pass with a Hoosier rushing right at him, determined as a bull. Robinson ignored him, standing steadfast in the pocket long enough for Junior Hemingway to get free along the right sideline. Robinson launched a bomb, an instant before getting launched backward.

Robinson didn't see the outcome, lying on the turf 5 yards from where he'd passed, but he could hear it. The sure-handed Hemingway came down with the jump ball, getting to the 4-yard line. From there, Robinson took the shotgun snap and cut through a hole on the right for the score.

Michigan 42, Indiana 35, with 17 seconds left.

Robinson didn't celebrate. On the sidelines he looked his fiercest—"Let's go, D!"

But Roundtree did, always happier when a teammate scored than when he did. "What did I *tell* you?" he asked Hemingway, exchanging a series of complicated hand slaps. "Don't fuck with us!"

The defense held, and the Wolverines got their fifth straight victory.

"We *know* we've got a lot of work to do when we get back," Rodriguez told his team in the crowded red locker room. "But I admire your poise under pressure.

"Do I have to remind you who's next?"

"OH, YEAH!"

"I know it's not good to hate, but it's okay to hate State!"

"YEAH!"

Winning solves a lot of problems, but it doesn't solve all of them. The offense and its star quarterback were getting better every week, but the defense was stagnant at best, and the kicking game had become so unreliable that on fourth downs in normal field goal range the coaches usually opted to go for it or punt. (Where was top-ranked kicking recruit Kyle Brindza when you needed him? Lost to Notre Dame.)

Some of those problems were simply the result of the rash of injuries and departures on defense. In the Indiana game alone, Michigan played a stunning twelve true freshman, seven of them on defense. Another year or two would go a long way toward maturing those players and getting the injured veterans back, but not all Rodriguez's problems could be explained by dumb luck.

One of Rodriguez's good friends, who was well aware of Rodriguez's coaching ability and the treatment he had endured both in Morgantown and at Michigan, said, "I love Rich, but he's made some mistakes." In his mind, these included failing to get Jeff Casteel to come with him, then hiring Scott Shafer and Greg Robinson, and, of course, failing to find another blue-chip kicker after eleventh-ranked Brendan Gibbons lost the job.

There was a logic behind most of those decisions, of course. If Rodriguez couldn't get everything done at once, he should start with what he does best, the offense—and the contracts Michigan offered at the time did not permit him to hire his first choice for many coaching positions, including defensive coordinator. In hindsight, he would probably agree that insisting on guaranteed contracts for his coordinators and cutting $100,000 out of the new weight room's budget to secure Casteel—plus a multiyear contract—would have been wise, as would making recruiting an acclaimed kicker a higher priority.

But there isn't a coach in the country who couldn't look back over his past three years and have reached similar judgments based on facts known only at the end of a season. Of course, the majority of those coaches could safely assume they'd get a few more years to iron out the kinks. By the middle of his third season, Rodriguez labored under no such illusions.

Still, if Michigan was looking for improvement, there was ample evidence. If it was looking for fatal flaws that would undoubtedly show up in bigger games that year, there were plenty of those, too. This was a team in transition. It seemed to be going in the right direction—following a familiar pattern—but it still had a way to go.

But if Rodriguez's bosses wanted to see the second coming of the Leaders and Best, they were bound to be disappointed. It wasn't going to be this year.

Schmidt's injury report didn't have to be very long to inspire fear.

Top on his list: Denard's left knee, which had taken another beating, causing the bursa sac to swell. Otherwise, the team was relatively healthy, but that one knee would generate an inordinate amount of worry in the week ahead.

"Evaluations." Rodriguez sounded somewhere between mildly peeved and disgusted—just where, his staffers knew, he operated when he was at his best.

The Big Ten had named Denard Robinson the Offensive Player of the Week for the third time in five weeks. But that didn't stop Rod Smith from grading him out at 77 percent, including two loafs on center exchanges, one of which led to the fumble on the goal line.

The grades for defenders, however, struck Rodriguez as a bit inflated. "Here are my thoughts," Rodriguez said. "First thing I see is, we took 45 snaps. They took 102. That's ridiculous, and it will kill us against better teams. I thought Denard competed his ass off, but he hasn't reached his peak yet.

"On defense, we were all over the place. Again." Rodriguez was especially critical of linebacker Obi Ezeh, a common source of friction between him and Greg Robinson, mimicking their debates over Mike Williams in 2009.

"And our special teams sucked," Rodriguez concluded. "Other than that, we won the game. Yippee.

"We've got a lot of work to do."

After they finished breaking down game film, they had to face their least savory task: watching the tape from the 2009 Michigan–Michigan State game over and over. But in that horrible performance—the team's worst showing since Rodriguez had arrived—there was a silver lining: If they could play *that* badly against the Spartans, at their place, with all the distraction of the NCAA interviews going on that week, imagine what they could do "with our heads out of our asses," as Rod Smith said.

"Might be a little different this year, with 16 in there," Magee added, referring to Denard.

It could also be a little different if they could figure out how the Spartans had apparently stolen their play signals in 2009, something they had started to suspect after last year's game, and now were convinced of.

"You can see them look at our sidelines," Rod Smith said. "But what are they looking at?"

"Our signals," Magee said, savoring a little sarcasm.

"But they couldn't have all of them, because this is a pass play and they've got eight guys in the box right here."

After watching another hour or two of film, Magee said, "They definitely didn't know the routes, or that guy would be the hell out of there, chasing the slot."

The solution? Watch more film.

Rodriguez had plenty on his mind that night as well. He and the defensive staff had just watched every one of their 102 plays against Indiana. "Didn't make me feel any better."

I suggested that perhaps Indiana's speedy offense might have matched up better against Michigan's defense than Michigan State's more conventional attack would, but he was in no mood to sugarcoat his situation.

"Right now, Saline high school's offense would probably match up pretty well against us."

There weren't too many ways to improve the defense dramatically halfway through the season, but there were ways to make it worse: give in to the tendency to start adding plays, schemes, and packages. No, Rodriguez said, the best thing to do was addition by subtraction. Make it simpler. Let your players *react* to the play in front of them, instead of thinking too much and hesitating.

One distraction they probably would not have to deal with that week was the NCAA ruling, which both Van Horn and Rodriguez expected to be largely good news for the program. "The only remaining question is, will they say I fostered 'an environment of noncompliance'?" he asked. "That's what I really want them to take back."

Rodriguez had a lot of rational reasons to fight the charge, of course, but paying over $300,000 for his own lawyers indicated just how badly he wanted his name cleared for its own sake—and how little Michigan cared about that point. This was one of the lessons he learned—slowly, perhaps—after getting smeared by West Virginia, Michigan's buyout mess, and the *Free Press*: If you want to protect your name, don't expect anyone to do it for you.

But the NCAA's delay also held up any talk of a contract extension with Michigan, or even a vote of confidence. The previous week, one of Rodriguez's advisers called Dave Brandon to ask for just that, to prevent other coaches from using the endless Rodriguez rumors against them in recruiting.

Brandon told the adviser, "'We just need to see a little more,'" Rodriguez reported. Rodriguez's adviser said Brandon hadn't stopped there, reportedly adding, "'Word on the street is he wants to win and leave.'"

"Well, if I did, I'd have my reasons!" Rodriguez told me. "But I've not talked to *anybody*. I don't *want* to talk to anybody. I want to win *here*! And everything that happens to me happens to my assistants. And those guys don't have contracts!"

Michigan hadn't even given them year-to-year deals, which is the bare minimum at most programs. That was why, before the Indiana game, Rod Smith was asking Magee, "All right, Cal, if you were me, do you buy a house, or do you rent?"

"Well, I'm an optimist, and I'm a loyalist. So I'd jump in, if the price is right."

"It's foreclosed. The price is great. Worst case, I lose my deposit."

"Then put it down."

"I told the banker, 'If we beat Indiana, we'll talk next week. We could win four in a row. If we lose to Indiana, I'm out. We could *lose* four in a row!'"

A week later, after beating Indiana, Smith still hadn't jumped.

No one needed to be reminded that the stakes of the game against the seventeenth-ranked Spartans were piling up: bragging rights, the state championship, the Paul Bunyan trophy, the Big Ten title, the national rankings, the growing rivalry between Rodriguez and Dantonio, and a flood of national attention—for the winner *and* the loser.

Everyone was writing it. Everyone was saying it. And everyone at Schembechler Hall was sick of it.

"If *one* more person says to me, 'Big week!'" Rutledge said, "I'm gonna tear their head off. We *know*!"

But, silly as it sounds, it was actually bigger than all that. If the Wolverines beat the Spartans, Rodriguez's team would have slain two of Michigan's three rivals, they would be 6–0, and they would probably be ranked in the top fifteen. For all those reasons, a victory would almost certainly result in a contract extension or at least a public vote of confidence, provided the NCAA report didn't destroy him. And at that point, everyone could relax—a little, anyway—and not face another season of do-or-die games, which was taking a visible toll on everyone from the coaches to the receptionists.

It was, in other words, another match point, the first of 2010. Win it, and Rodriguez would be free to coach football.

But *lose* this game? He would not simply be 5–1, which didn't sound so bad. The critics would become deafening, the ghosts of 2009 would come rushing back, morale would plummet, and from that point on, the team would be working to catch up, not to stay ahead.

At Monday's team meeting, Rodriguez laid out the good, the bad, and the ugly. "Anytime you win on the road, especially in the Big Ten, it's good. We're 5–0. *That's* good. But I'm frankly getting tired of answering questions about the D and special teams, all week, every week.

"Now, some of you aren't from Michigan, and some of you guys are new," Rodriguez told them. "So you need to learn right now: This game is different. It's a hell of a lot bigger than Indiana. The only one even comparable to this one is Ohio State.

"They paint us as the preppy-ass, five-star entitled guys and they're these hardworking, up-from-the-bottom blue-collar guys."

Not surprisingly, the son and grandson of coal miners didn't take too kindly to those stereotypes. He didn't care where his players came from—he believed Moundros and Kovacs, suburban walk-ons, were as tough as anyone on the team—so long as they didn't *act* entitled, one of the qualities Rodriguez couldn't stand.

"It's just wrong," he said. "Do you understand this game is different? Are you prepared to give your all?"

"YES, SIR."

"Saturday, at 3:30, they will see a team coming out of that tunnel they have never seen before. Get it right. Do your job. No excuses this week. No mistakes."

All of which, of course, inadvertently reinforced the incredible pressure they were already under, yet again.

|ı|ı|ı| 43 **DENARD'S DAY**

Michigan's entire athletic department was originally run by an undergraduate named Charles Baird, more than a century ago. He had to do some fancy financial work just to raise a few thousand dollars to pay for a couple dozen sweaters and pants. Helmets and pads hadn't yet been required.

Today, Michigan's athletic department is a multimillion-dollar machine that employs 250 people, supports some 700 athletes, and entertains over a million spectators a year and millions more on television.

In 2010, all that depended on a skinny kid from Deerfield, Florida, and his swollen left knee.

The health of that bursa sac would determine if Rod Smith's family bought a house or continued to rent; whether Tony Gibson's kids had to move again and say good-bye to their friends; and whether the entire "Rich Rod experiment" at Michigan would be deemed a success or a failure.

It was a multimillion-dollar pyramid turned upside down, pointed directly on that knee.

It might not be fair, and it certainly isn't sane, but after building up this athletic empire for 131 years, football had become the public face of the university.

Denard Robinson's day started at 6:30, in his off-campus condo. He hit the snooze once, then twice, before turning on a light and getting out of his warm bed to put on a pair of jeans, a red polo shirt, black Adidas shoes, and his letter jacket. Then he hopped into his roommate Devin

Gardner's family pickup truck, an old Dakota 4×4, with a tool box behind the cab.

Robinson rolled into Schembechler Hall by 7:00, two and a half hours after the strength coaches arrived for their own workouts. When he stumbled into the locker room to put on his team shorts and T-shirt for treatment, he was met by a picture on the locker room door of the Paul Bunyan trophy:

> Home at Michigan State University since 2008.
> Since 1953: 34–21–2.

Robinson looked half-awake when he walked into the training room, but athletic trainer Phil Johnson was fully alert—he'd been there for an hour already—and Denard's left knee was all Johnson needed, anyway, not his brain.

Robinson's knee was still swollen so badly you couldn't delineate his kneecap. When he lifted his thigh, he winced, and that simple motion was the basic building block of every move he had to make to play quarterback— like running and throwing.

So Johnson went to work. He started by putting Kenisio tape, which spreads out like spiderwebbing, on Denard's knee. Next, Johnson attached a few electrodes to Denard's knee and thigh, which sent small shocks into his muscles, forcing them to contract. Phil then elevated the knee to get the fluid draining out of it, followed by low-level laser therapy, pulsed ultrasounds, and Inter-X—whatever that is.

After an hour of treatments that looked like voodoo to a layman, Robinson went to a side room for some rehab work.

"All this stuff helps the swelling some," Johnson said, "but it really keeps it from stiffening up. Once that happens, you're screwed."

Robinson was game for everything they threw at him, except swallowing NSAIDs like ibuprofen, which help reduce swelling. "I don't like medicine," he said.

"On a scale of one to ten, ten being an injury requiring surgery, he's about a four," Johnson said, putting Denard through his paces. "He's got a swollen bursa sac, but at least it hasn't burst. Jake Long burst one of his right before the spring game, and his whole leg turned black. Not pretty." Long played anyway, adding to his legendary status among trainers and teammates.

Next up: the cold tub, which is kept at 50 degrees, the same temperature as Lake Superior in October. It's cold enough to inhibit pain, decrease swelling, increase function—and make Denard's lips turn purple. The trainers provided the players with foam socks to cover their toes, but that's the only mercy they were shown.

"The worst part," said the Florida native, who had never been in such cold water. "I'd rather work out with Barwis than hop in here."

Robinson started to get out after seven minutes, but Schmidt said, "You really should go fifteen." He left it up to Robinson.

"Awwww, no!" But he slowly forced himself down in the water, grimacing the whole way. "'Y'all got it made,'" he said, mimicking the typical comment of his classmates, who would not wake up for a few hours, if they decided to go to class at all. "That's what everyone thinks. They don't see this!"

By nine o'clock, the sun was finally showing through the frosted window by the swim tank, which was Robinson's next stop. After he spent twenty minutes walking back and forth in the tank—which, at 90 degrees, was much nicer than the cold tub—Johnson measured the circumference of Denard's thigh, knee, and calf, all of which were a quarter inch less than when Denard started that morning.

The voodoo of the Michigan medicine men was working.

After Robinson showered, he entered the last phase of the morning routine: taping. Every day, half of the 120 Michigan football players get their ankles taped, which requires one roll of Johnson & Johnson athletic tape for each ankle. The trainers tape 120 ankles a day, from early August to late November, plus fifteen practices in December when Michigan's in a bowl game, plus fifteen more practices during spring ball. That's about 18,000 rolls of tape, or 600 boxes—about $45,000 worth. Before they started wearing custom-fit knee braces in practice, it used to be much more.

But that's a pittance compared to the team's budget for meals. During fall football practice, the training table meals served from Monday through Thursday cost more than $400,000. Tack on the weekend hotel meals, the bowl game meals, and the spring ball meals, and the total passes $1 million (to say nothing of twelve nights in hotels for seventy people and support staff)—or about $10,000 a player per year.

If you divide the cost of salaries for football coaches and staffers by 120 players, it comes to $57,000 per player per year.

But the biggest cost is still tuition. Few fans or reporters realize it—even many of the players don't—but the university does not set aside eighty-five free passes each year for football players. The athletic department writes a check for every single scholarship athlete—some 500 at Michigan—paying the actual tuition for both in-state and out-of-state students each semester, down to the penny. In 2010, that exceeded $15 million, of which roughly $4.2 million went to football players—or about $59,000 per scholarship player who attends school year round.

By the time a fifth-year scholarship senior from out of state graduates from the University of Michigan, his school has spent over $580,000 on him, whether he's an All-American or a fourth-string, long-snap center—and that does not include the Academic Center, strength and conditioning, facilities, administration, athletic trainers, or tape.

When people argue it's time to start paying players, they usually miss two vital points. First, Michigan's is one of only a handful of athletic departments that make a profit, and it had lost money in the years between Bo Schembechler and Bill Martin. If you pay one quarterback, you had better pay the women rowers the exact same, or you've violated Title IX. Once you start doing that, watch colleges start folding teams they can't afford.

For those who say the NCAA has yet to stamp out illegal payments, and therefore colleges should stop the charade and pay the players, would they make the same argument that because the IRS has failed to stamp out all tax cheating, the IRS should be abolished? Should state troopers stop giving out speeding tickets because they have failed to stamp out speeding?

Second, such critics don't realize the athletes are already being paid quite a bit, whether they're any good or not. And if you don't think $295,000 for five years of out-of-state tuition is compensation, tell that to the parent of an engineering student from Chicago. Likewise, ask professional boxers or Olympic triathletes what they pay for coaching and training.

The average player gets a very good deal financially. Only a very few, like Denard Robinson, make more money for their school than their school spends on them. The only sensible solution, I've always believed, is for the NFL and NBA to set up viable minor leagues to give those rare stars a real choice—the same option high school hockey and baseball players have.

What no college athlete has, however, is free time.

While Denard got dressed, the TV overhead scrolled the runner: "Denard Robinson Big Ten Player of the Week for third time in five weeks."

Viewers reading that probably thought Robinson was having a hell of a time.

At 9:40 a.m., Denard hopped back in Gardner's dad's pickup truck and dashed up State Street to grab his roommate.

The modest first-floor apartment was bright, clean, and neat. "That's because we're never here!" Gardner said.

The duo dashed to the truck—with boxes of Hi-C and bags of Hostess Mini Muffins in hand—and headed back down State Street to their 10:00 class: Crime, Race and the Law. They passed Mike Kwiatkowski, the walk-on who made the team during the fall tryouts. He had just won Scout Team Offensive Player of the Week.

"Hey, that's Mike, the walk-on," Denard said.

"Yeah, tight end," Gardner added.

"He can play!" Robinson said. "Got the body, too."

"Now, you got to wonder," Gardner said, "how does a guy like that get missed by *everyone*?!"

The two dashed to the Dennison Building and snuck into the classroom three minutes late. They would be marked up for that, it would get back to Rodriguez, and there would be consequences. Robinson found an empty seat against the right wall of the packed classroom. Gardner sat in the middle among the "normies."

Professor Scott Ellsworth, a middle-aged white man, started discussing a documentary called *Murder on a Sunday Morning*, which explored a case of mistaken identity in Jacksonville, Florida. It resulted in fifteen-year-old Brenton Butler, who was walking by to apply for a job at Blockbuster that morning, being accused of murder, but ultimately being acquitted.

"Was Brenton Butler guilty of anything?" Ellsworth asked.

Most of the white kids said no, but most of the African Americans disagreed: wrong place, wrong time, they said.

"Was he even in the wrong place?" one woman asked.

"He wasn't at home!" Gardner said, getting a laugh. But Gardner was anything but a class clown, raising his hand more than anyone else during the eighty-minute class. Robinson wasn't afraid to speak up when the spirit moved him but was usually content to take notes in his spiral notebook. He used a mechanical pencil with a thin lead and wrote in careful penmanship, which leaned left—a sign of an introvert. By the end of the class, he had written a page and a half, a little more than the suburban student sitting next to him.

"This shows, in part, the weakness of eyewitnesses as proof," Ellsworth said. "Let me show you. Everyone look at me. Right now. Good. Now, without looking back, tell me what Denard is wearing."

Gardner didn't miss a beat. "He's wearing red-and-black shoes, blue jeans, a red polo shirt, and a letter jacket!" His classmates, most of whom knew they were roommates, got the joke.

They broke into groups to answer one question each. When Robinson's had hashed out theirs, he slipped off to the bathroom before the class came back together to go over their questions. It was one of the few concessions he had made to his newfound fame; if he tried to go during the break, he'd be stopped too often to get to his classes on time.

"Okay, Group D," Ellsworth said to Robinson's circle. "Your question: If you were accused of a crime, would you prefer a black or white attorney?"

In the group, Robinson decided he would want an attorney who was the same race as the jury, but he had since modified his answer. "If I was in a racist town, I'd hire a white attorney," he said. "But if I was in a normal town like Ann Arbor, I'd just get the best lawyer I could get."

Ellsworth offered a "closing thought, paraphrasing Winston Churchill on democracy: The American justice system is the worst in the world, except for all the others. What do you think? We'll pick that up on Thursday. In the meantime, read Franz Kafka's classic, *The Trial*."

The class wasn't quantum physics—which was being taught down the hall—but it wasn't rocks for jocks, either.

While Robinson packed his things to go, a coed slipped him a small handwritten note, which he tucked away.

He walked out with Kelvin Grady and Devin Gardner across the Diag for lunch. He peeked at the note: "For your eyes only," written in purple ink. "You seem like a really nice guy and I think it'd be cool to hang out with you. And no, I'm not a creepy stalker! Text me some time."

Robinson grinned and shook his head. Grady demanded to see it, then started laughing immediately. "Ahhhhh! Same note I got!" he said, then pointed to Gardner. "Same note *he* got! Did she go like this?" he asked, tilting his head back as he slipped Robinson the note with a bent wrist. *"This is for you."*

Robinson's grin answered his question.

Robinson wanted to go to Wendy's in the Michigan Union basement, as usual, but Grady argued for Noodles & Company, at the far end of the Diag. "Come on, man, I'm trying to *expand* your horizons!"

"I like Wendy's, man."

"But it's *rivalry week!*"

"Exactly why I don't want to change my routine."

People walking past often looked twice but said nothing, until a frat boy finally asked, "Excuse me, are you Denard Robinson?"

"Yes, I am."

"I just want to thank you for all you do for this university," the young man said, shaking his hand. As soon as the student was out of earshot, Grady and Gardner started laughing.

"Pardon me, are you Denard Robinson?" Gardner asked, wide-eyed. They weren't making fun of the fan but of Robinson's new status.

"See?" Grady asked. "You're a *celebrity* now."

"Oh, yeah, oh, yeah," Gardner chimed in. "Big maaan on campus!"

"Can't be seen eating with the little people at Noodles & Company!"

Robinson grinned but was clearly uncomfortable. "Man, you know that ain't right," he said quietly.

"So long, Heisman hopeful Denard Robinson!"

Robinson got his favorite, Wendy's Spicy Chicken #6 Combo, then sat with his friends and teammates. The woman at the next table looked up from her anthropology textbook to ask, "How's your knee?"

"What? My knee's fine. Where'd you get that?"

"They said on TV—"

"Damn, already?"

After lunch, Robinson walked over the spot where John F. Kennedy had stood almost fifty years earlier to introduce the idea of the Peace Corps, and past a retail tent selling yellow T-shirts with SHOE at the top, LACE at the bottom, and an untied cleat in the middle.

"Think they'd give me one?" he said, walking by unnoticed.

"Only if you want an NCAA violation," I replied, recalling a similar conversation Chris Webber had had with Mitch Albom.

"That's crazy," he said, smiling. I didn't have the heart to tell him a replica of the No. 16 jersey he wore on Saturdays was going for $70 down the street. Paying players might be impractical, but it's even harder to justify why some guy selling Denard's nickname on a T-shirt should make a profit—or EA Sports, for that matter.

Walking back across the street to Gardner's truck, a stranger in a pullover sweatshirt walking toward us struck the Heisman pose with no words spoken.

Robinson smiled and shook his head. "That's crazy, too!"

He asked about Desmond Howard and Charles Woodson. Who struck the pose? When?

Howard did it, I said, in the 1991 Ohio State game. Robinson thought about it, then said, "I wouldn't do it."

Driving back down the hill in Devin's truck, Denard asked, "You been to New York?"

"Yeah," I said. "You'd love it."

"I'd like to go. Is it expensive?"

"Flights are cheap, but hotels aren't," I said. "But you know . . ."

He started wagging his finger back and forth. "Naw, naw, nawwwwww. Don't even go there," but he knew the Heisman ceremony took place in New York.

But if Robinson wasn't going to discuss his newfound status, everyone else was. The previous night, on *Monday Night Football*, Michigan alums Tom Brady and Chad Henne battled it out, but Robinson was still the story. "Both Brady and Henne have lots of Michigan records," Ron Jaworski said, "but neither would be starting for Michigan right now."

While we drove down State Street, ESPN radio's Scott Van Pelt was interviewing Michigan State quarterback Kirk Cousins—about Denard Robinson. The actual Robinson turned the radio off.

"Do you have to pay to go?" he asked, referring to the Heisman trophy ceremony.

"No, they pay for your flight."

"Do you have to pay for your hotel?"

"No, they pick that up, too. Couple nights, probably."

He considered that in silence, then got out to meet his professor for an office hour appointment.

By two o'clock, Robinson was back in the cold tub, up to his chest in frigid water, with his elbows on the deck. He borrowed a cell phone to handle a national press conference with ESPN and others on the line.

"It was a great win for Michigan," he said. "We're all in.

"Scott Shafer offered me as a defensive back, but Rod Smith offered me as a quarterback. That was my goal, to play quarterback.

"I was just in the right place at the right time. The right coaches, the right teammates.

"I wouldn't say I'm famous yet. A lot of people seem to know me around town, but that's about the only difference."

When he hung up, Phil Johnson told him, "You better go—you're going to be late."

It was 2:27, and the quarterback meeting started at 2:30 sharp, as always. Robinson put on his sweats and ran up the stairs to the meeting room, stopping to pick up my dropped pen on the way. The treatments seemed to be working.

When he got to the door, Magee was waiting outside.

"I was in the training room," Robinson said with a half smile, knowing it wouldn't matter much.

"I don't care why you're late," the normally cheerful Magee said. "Late is late."

After going over dozens of plays and pointers, Rod Smith explained to his quarterbacks that the coaches had had a breakthrough during another late-night film session.

"Last year we thought they had our signals. We got word from people that they did. But they don't. They ain't got our signals. They got our *tendencies*.

"Watch this. What they're watching is not our signals but our running back. Look, when Carlos [Brown] sets up inside the tackle, they raise their left hand. That means get ready for [a play called] belly—and the end squeezes hard.

"But watch this: When he's outside the tackle, they point left.

"They covered both plays perfectly. They had us.

"So they didn't have our calls. What they got, they got from our alignment. So this year, we're going to be in the same alignment every time."

Smith went back to the board.

"The back is going to line up right behind the tackle—not inside or outside. Your toes will be at six yards, and so will the back's.

"Then once you yell 'Ready!' you step up *one yard*. Then the back will not shuffle, shuffle and go, like normal, he'll just take off. But you'll have more time to read it because you're a yard up.

"We're gonna fuck these guys!"

Rodriguez laid out the challenge in front of his team: another nationally televised game and probably a new stadium attendance record. The Spartans were for real, with fourteen starters returning, he said, then brought up a slide of the Paul Bunyan trophy.

"The ugliness of the trophy is well documented. It's undeniable. But Paul's ugliness is only acceptable when *we* have it.

"They've had Paul for two years now. Who knows what they're making Paul do? Probably taking him around to every damn frat house on campus and doing God knows what to him." They laughed. "Poor Paul! He needs to be rescued!"

That meant complete focus. Unless you've got a test or paper, he said, that's all you're doing: class, practice, preparation. "Whatever you got to do to get ready, you do it this week. Tell your best friends, your girlfriend, your parents, 'I'll call you Sunday!'

"They say all games count as one. Trust me, this one counts more. This game is different."

He didn't tell them how much rode on the game, but he didn't have to. They read the blogs, they talked to the "normies."

"If you watch that game last year, it'll make you puke. It was the worst-executed game we played in seventeen games. It was *awful*. AWFUL. On both sides of the ball. We *gave* the damn thing away. Well, that's not going to happen this time, because we're going to take care of the ball.

"On offense: ball security always. BSA!

"On defense: Shed, hit, and wrap—and quiet all the crap.

"I am *tired* of hearing about them, tired of talking about it. Tired of answering questions about it. I just want to kick their ass."

His emotional fatigue threaded through his comments and undoubtedly pushed some buttons in his players, too. They were more tired than they let on, every week preparing for a must-win game.

"You turn down a chance to make a play in this game, you'll be embarrassed about it the rest of your life. You leave nothing on the table. We play them *one* time a year, and we hear about it 365 days a year."

Rodriguez had to know that if they lost this one, he could be hearing about it for a lot longer than that. Instead, he said, "I know it's not life-or-death. It's not. But as far as football goes, trust me, this is war."

At practice, members of Michigan's football royalty lined the field to watch, including Dave Brandon, Bill Martin and his wife, Sally, and a dozen or more former players. Like most teams today, Michigan hits only on Tuesdays, and even then it's mostly pushing and shoving. But on this day, you could hear the pads smack, each hit packing more punch.

After practice, Rodriguez told his team, "Turn around and look at that stadium. The Big House. We're going to have the biggest crowd ever, and they're going to be the *loudest* ever.

"Next time we hit someone, they'll be wearing green.

"'Michigan' on three."

Robinson led the quarterbacks in their postpractice chest bump—Forcier joining them—then showered, reached behind the equipment manager's counter to grab a fresh pair of Twin City socks, and headed to the training room for yet more treatment.

It was 6:49, and Denard Robinson had been on the go for twelve hours. He would not be heading home for another four.

Phil Johnson, who was putting in a fourteen-hour day himself, gave Robinson different knee pads to try on, two sizes bigger than normal. Wasn't he afraid the big black rubber pad would let the Spartans know which knee to hit?

Robinson laughed. "They already know. The girl at *lunch* knew!"

Junior Hemingway walked by, then stopped. "Damn," he said, "your knee looks like a balloon."

Next, more ultrasound. "Congratulations!" Phil said, gliding the applicator around Denard's knee. "It's twins!"

The pulsed ultrasound was not to see what was inside Robinson's knee but to generate cavitation, Johnson explained. "Sound waves go in, open the cellular membrane, and, with some joint movement, fluid gets jostled out. Then when you elevate the knee, they hope the fluid leaves the area."

All told, over the course of three sessions lasting three and a half hours, Denard Robinson received the following treatments:

- Kenisio tape, twice
- Cold tub, twice
- Big pool workout
- Stationary bike
- Dead lift, single leg, with thirty-five pounds
- Body weight squats
- Quad sets, four times
- Short arc quad
- Pivot board, clockwise and counterclockwise
- Electric stimulation, three times
- Inter-X, twice

- Low-level laser therapy, three times
- Pulsed ultrasound, twice
- Elevation, three times, twenty minutes each
- Recovery pants, tight spandex
- Electric stimulation at home

"That's all?" Johnson said, when I read back the list. "I'm disappointed. That's not enough."

At 7:30, Robinson sat down with a few teammates in the Commons for some dinner and conversation. In less than an hour, Robinson ate:

- Two biscuits
- One big scoop of rice
- Sixteen chicken wings
- Two Gatorades
- Two caramel cheesecakes

All told, Robinson consumed well over four thousand calories that day—without a Barwis workout—which ranked him among the lightest eaters on the team.

After dinner the coaches, naturally, analyzed more film. First they watched that day's practice, then they watched Michigan State. Rodriguez was largely pleased with the practice, with one snag: On one play Roy Roundtree got wide open on an X-route, but Robinson overthrew him. That was normally an easy toss, which Robinson's overthrow converted into an easy interception.

"That was the first time I saw a bad throw out of him in weeks," Rodriguez said, but he thought he knew the reason: Robinson was not putting full pressure on his swollen left knee, which forced him to put more weight on his back right foot, which in turn caused him to throw floaters, higher than he wanted. And that explained why Robinson had just spent three and a half hours in treatment that day, and would do it again the next.

Thanks to Michigan's paranoia over violating its self-imposed limitations on hours, probably no major team's players saw less film in 2009 and 2010 than did the Wolverines. But on this night, there were players watching film in just about every room on the second floor of Schembechler

Hall. If this game didn't go their way, it wouldn't be for lack of preparation—which is not something they could claim the year before.

In the team meeting room, Denard Robinson, Vincent Smith, Junior Hemingway, and Darryl Stonum hunkered down to watch the big screen.

"They're not bad," Stonum said, referring to State's defense.

Robinson agreed. "They're gonna play ball, man."

When they put on the tape of last year's game, however, they were struck mainly by how badly they had played.

On one play, in Michigan State territory, Forcier had virtually every receiver open—Stonum up top and Odoms and Roundtree straight down the hashmarks, all available for touchdown passes—yet threw to Carlos Brown in the left flat, who had not yet turned around. The pass skipped harmlessly past him.

"Oh, my goodness," Robinson said. "No one was *not* open!"

After the play, the nearest Spartan ran up to Brown and started trash talking, prompting the viewers to start laughing.

"Man, *he* didn't make no play!" Stonum said.

"That guy's woofing on every play," Smith added. "Even when we just drop it."

The last offensive play of the game, when Michigan needed to get 5 yards for a first down or 9 for a touchdown to take the lead in overtime, might have been worse. On the screen, Forcier ignores his checkoffs and telegraphs his pass to Odoms running across the end zone. The State defender actually grabs Odoms's jersey, pulling him back, then jumps ahead to tip the ball to a teammate for the game-ending interception. But that's not what these guys noticed.

"On that play he's supposed to look to Darryl, then to Koger, *then* to Tay," Robinson said. "But he just locked in on Tay right away. And they could see it. Then he throws off his back foot."

They watched it again. "Look at that gap," Smith said, pointing to a hole on Forcier's right side. "Could've run for a first down, too."

"Only needed 5," Robinson agreed. "Not 9."

They watched the ball fall into the hands of the Spartans for the fifth time.

"And therrre she gooooes," Stonum said.

"Wah-wawwww," Smith sounded.

Whether it was the NCAA interviews that had started that week in 2009, or the pressure of a big rivalry game, or just youth and inexperience, or simply a bad performance at a bad time is impossible to say. But looking back at that 2009 game, it was obvious to the players just how badly they had played. They agreed with their coach: That was their worst performance.

"Man, that's my only fumble since I've been here," Stonum said.

"Greg [Mathews] was *wide* open," Hemingway said, "and Tate doesn't throw it."

"Man, we played so bad in this game," Stonum said, "and we still almost won it."

"Whenever we go three-and-out, it's because we stopped ourselves," Robinson said. "We get this going, no one can stop us."

"I can't wait for game time," Hemingway said. "I wish it was tomorrow."

"Any requests?" Stonum asked.

"Third-and-longs," Robinson said.

While Stonum fished around for the file on Bromley's computer, they talked about how long their days had already been.

"Classmates say, 'You look tired,'" Hemingway said. "Yes, I just finished lifting for ninety minutes, before *you* woke up."

"Or they say, 'You walk slow,'" Robinson said. "Yes, I do. It's because I'm dead." And it was true: They run like hell and work like crazy during conditioning and practice, then they walk out of the building slower than their grandparents, barely lifting their feet. They don't waste an ounce of energy getting to their cars.

"Girl calls me up and asks me what I'm doing," Stonum said. "I say, 'I'm watching film.'

"'Oh, what film are you watching?'

"'No, not *a* film. Just *film*.'"

At 10:34, they finally walked out of Schembechler Hall for the last time that day. Normally they would be coming out of the Academic Center, but somehow two middle-aged men carrying a stack of glossy photos figured out where they were and approached Robinson the moment he walked outside to sign their photos of him. It was all for charity, of course, or their ten-year-old kids—they claimed both at various times—so Robinson autographed one each, then said, "That's it, man," and got into Gardner's pickup.

He would be in bed by eleven, then do it all again the next day—plus a workout and study table.

I had only followed him that day—and I was exhausted.

"I've never seen it like this since Bo coached," Jerry Erickson said by his barbershop's picture window, flipping through a stack of tickets the day before the Michigan State game. "I'm getting $100 to $150 a ticket."

The next day, a picture-perfect Saturday, more than two hours before kickoff, it was obvious this day was different. The team buses drove past crowds that were thicker, louder, and more juiced than at any other time during Rodriguez's reign, exceeding the energy levels before UConn and Western the year before. The cheering and honking never stopped as the caravan made its way through tailgate after tailgate, fans drawn to the buses. The Victors' Walk was pulsing with fans yelling and cheering from new perches they had to seek out, thanks to the overflow crowd.

When Mark Dantonio got off his team bus, however, he was not feeling quite as cheerful. He had suffered a mild heart attack shortly after State's overtime victory against Notre Dame and had not been allowed to coach from the sidelines since, but he still went to every game.

A crowd control volunteer greeted all the opposing coaches when they stepped down from the bus, and, he told me, they always appreciated it. Well, almost always.

"Coach Dantonio," he said, extending his hand, "I just want to wish you a speedy recovery and welcome you to Michigan Stadium."

Dantonio brushed his hand away. "Get the hell outta here."

Back in Michigan's coaches' room, the TVs were off, even though a few Big Ten games were already well under way. The coaches radiated more quiet intensity than they had for any game yet. Before they headed out for warm-ups, Greg Robinson stood up and began shaking the other coaches' hands, starting a chain reaction of back claps and man hugs.

"Let's go."

"All in this together."

They knew what this game meant.

While Mike Barwis shouted at the troops—"Today, we start the *demise* of MSU, and the *rise* of MICHIGAN!"—Rodriguez leaned forward in his chair. He was as still as he could be but couldn't stop his feet from tapping a furious beat, like a boxer moments before a title bout.

Someone poked his head in. "Coach, it's time."

He nodded. He took one last look at his notecards, stood up, exhaled, and walked slowly through the door.

The atmosphere was everything they had hoped for—and more.

It seemed like almost every game in the Rodriguez era qualified as do-or-die, must-win, and a career saver or a career killer—so often that it sounded like crying wolf before long. Certainly the players were tired of hearing it.

But it was so often true. If beating Notre Dame could reestablish Michigan as a national power, losing to UMass or Indiana would put them right back in the also-ran bin, just like that. But for all the hyped-up games of Rodriguez's reign in Ann Arbor, this one topped them all.

On the third play from scrimmage, Robinson ran toward the middle, then cut right for an 8-yard gain.

To the fans, this looked like a decent but unremarkable play. The coaches saw it differently. On the right side, the offensive line had opened up a hole big enough to drive a bus through, or about five Denard Robinsons. Of course, they needed only one Denard Robinson to take advantage of it.

If he had, he would have discovered his men had also picked up the corner blitz perfectly, which took a couple more Spartans out of the play. Downfield, Darryl Stonum had blocked out the free safety. The pathway had been cleared for Robinson. Everyone had done his job perfectly, leaving no one to stop him—setting up the kind of before-you-know-it touchdown runs he'd been executing from his first game against Western Michigan to his last game against Indiana the previous week.

But as Robinson headed for the hole, he got caught by the foot of a lineman who had stepped too far back, forcing Denard to pull back, then run wide around the right end. Eight yards.

When a receiver drops a bomb, everyone sees it. Everyone knows what was lost. But the spread offense is set up more for the run than the pass—not 3 yards and a cloud of dust, but long, game-breaking runs that work better than bombs. So when the table is set to rattle off one of those runs, they have to take advantage of it. If they don't, the crowd doesn't see it—but the coaches do.

In this case, Michigan lost a likely touchdown run, the kind that breaks the game open and makes the crowd explode. It was the first of Michigan's many missed chances that day, but only the coaches and players knew it.

On third-and-4 from State's 10-yard line, Robinson rolled right and saw his receiver cutting across the end zone a step ahead of State's Trenton Robinson. Denard hesitated a split second, then fired—late, and behind, but right at Trenton Robinson, who caught the ball in the end zone. It was the kind of mistake a banged-up quarterback starting his sixth game makes in the biggest game of his career.

The Michigan fans deflated, while Michigan State fans let everyone know exactly how many had made it into the stadium that day.

After Michigan's much-maligned defense did its job, Denard picked up where he had left off: four runs for 15 yards, and six simple, quick passes for 35 yards.

From State's 24-yard line, Robinson rolled to his right. He saw State's cornerback come up to stop the run, and Darryl Stonum slip behind him, unnoticed, wide open in the end zone. All Robinson had to do was loft one over the cornerback's head—the kind of pass he'd been making all season—for the first touchdown, which would set off this tinderbox of a crowd.

But his mechanics were off. He instinctively avoided following through to avoid putting pressure on his injured knee, leaving his weight on his back foot and his left shoulder open. The pass flew too high, exactly like the pass he had missed in Wednesday's practice and for the exact same reason. That's why the ball didn't fall softly into Stonum's waiting hands but kept flying over his head. The Wolverines had to settle for a field goal and a 3–0 lead. But it could have been 10–0, or even 14. And with Michigan's porous defense, the offense couldn't afford to leave plays on the table.

On the sidelines, Stonum blurted out, "Shit!" a half dozen times. "I thought it was going to come down, but it kept soaring! Shit!"

When the first quarter ended, Michigan's defense had held State's offense to zero points and minus 8 yards rushing. Reporting from the sidelines, ESPN's Quint Kessenich asked me, "Was this the same defense I saw two weeks ago?"

But in the second quarter, Michigan's defense finally broke, allowing State's Edwin Baker to convert a simple line plunge into a 61-yard touchdown.

Denard countered with a pass to Martell Webb, who had no trouble beating his man to finish the 12-yard touchdown play. 10–7 Michigan.

But Michigan's defense promptly let the Spartan's Le'Veon Bell beat them for another long touchdown, this one 41 yards. Kessenich was starting to get his answer.

"Once our D steps up, it'll be a different game," said LaMarr Woodley, who had taken advantage of the Pittsburgh Steelers' bye week to be on the sidelines, with his face painted maize and blue. He, for one, was all in. "They're close, but you can't give up the big play. That's all it is: two big plays."

After the Spartans kicked a 38-yard field goal and then blocked the Wolverines' 42-yard attempt, the half ended, 17–10 State.

But the Wolverines had reason for hope, plenty of it. They led the Spartans in first downs, rushing, and passing. In fact, just about everything but turnovers—including one crucial one—and points.

The normally reserved fifth-year senior Greg Banks made a desperate plea: "We ain't going out a loser. We ain't going out a loser! This is my last fucking go-round. Let's go!"

To the team, Rodriguez said, "On defense, just a couple big plays got us. Stop those, and we're good. On offense, we're just killing ourselves. Once we get out of our own way, we'll take off. This is it, men. This is our time. Leave everything out there. LET'S GO!"

But after Michigan cornerback James Rogers—one of two seniors on defense—came out with a full-body tension cramp, the Spartans went immediately to his replacement, true-freshman Cullen Christian, burning him for a 41-yard touchdown bomb on the left side.

Only 2:28 into the half, it was 24–10 Michigan State. For the first time all day, the same stadium that had been waiting for a reason to boil over turned cold. There was no energy in the stands and none on the Michigan sideline, either.

Ten plays later, the Spartans scored again, giving them a 31–10 lead—

and all the momentum they would need. "FUCK!" Mike Martin yelled. "Fuck, man!" Then he sat down and yelled "FUCK!" again.

Down 31–17 with just under a quarter to play, the game was not out of range—until Robinson threw his third interception on the next possession.

Later, when Rodriguez elected to punt on fourth-and-9 from Michigan's 30, with six minutes left, he got booed, a rarity in the Big House. For perhaps the first time at Michigan, he didn't trust his gambler's instincts, a decision he would say he regretted at the press conference.

But it hardly mattered. What did matter, however, was a far less significant play, with a far more serious outcome, when a Spartan delivered a chop block to Mike Martin's left knee. The ref saw it and threw his flag, but if the lineman had finished the job, Martin would be out of the game, out of the season, and out a career. It was that easy to do.

After a couple of minutes, Martin stood up and left the field with some help. His face was flushed with pain.

At 34–17, with seven minutes left, the Spartan fans started cheering: "Go Green! Go White!" And the far more humiliating "Lit-tle Sis-ter!"

As usual, Rodriguez was rational and as positive as the facts allowed when addressing the team. "Listen up! We didn't play as well as we can play. We know that. We gotta play better. I gotta coach you better!

"It's gonna hurt. It better hurt! But after we see the tape, it's done. No need to hang our heads. They're a good team. They deserve it. But we made more mistakes today than in the first five games combined. But let me tell you this: I'd rather be in this locker room with you men than over there. No question.

"The cockroaches will be out. All the shit will be coming our way. But don't believe it—any more than you believed all the praise last week. We'll get redemption next week when another ranked team comes into our house.

"So let's get in. 'Michigan' on three, and I want to hear you."

"MICHIGAN!"

Van Bergen started crying in his stall, burying his face in a white towel. Devin Gardner sat down next to him and put a hand on his shoulder.

Rich Rodriguez in front of his team is one thing. Rich Rodriguez in the privacy of his office, where his ambition and frustration and self-criticism can run free, is quite another. The second door was still closing behind him when he yelled, to no one in particular, "We're just getting run over! Run the fuck over!" Then he knocked his chair over.

Trainer Paul Schmidt opened the door slowly and said as quietly as he could, "Tay's [Odom] foot is broken. He's probably out for the season."

It was as good a straw as any.

"God DAMN IT! That's just fucking GREAT!" He grabbed his chair with one hand and tossed it a few feet. With the anger still rising inside him, he kicked the big cooler—filled with a case of Coke and juice and plenty of ice—toward the bathroom tile with enough force to topple it over and send the ice and cans sprawling across the floor.

"What else can fucking happen? What *hasn't* happened the past three fucking years? DAMN IT!"

His anger largely spent, the room went silent, which made an appeal from the locker room audible. Usually, when the coaches could hear someone speaking out in the locker room, it was Mike Barwis, Mark Mondrous, or, the previous year, Brandon Graham. But this time it was Denard Robinson, who had never addressed the team before. "This one's on me. My fault! But we ain't losing again! Got that? Eleven and one! We are not. Losing. Again! All year! Ever!"

Back in the coaches' room, Dave Brandon entered quietly. "Do you want to take a minute?" he asked, referring to the press conferences ahead.

"No, I'm okay," Rodriguez said, collecting himself before going out to greet the recruits and parents. He gave them all hugs and smiles. This was not phony. Rodriguez had an amazing ability to compartmentalize his emotions and get back to the bad ones later.

Sergeant Gary Hicks, who had protected Rodriguez at every home and away game since Rodriguez came to town, escorted him to the press conference. After Rodriguez walked to the podium, Hicks said, "That man is so cordial, at all times. I never see any of the stuff the press is always talking about. I don't know where they get it, but it's not the man I know."

When Rodriguez took his postgame shower a few minutes later, it sounded like he might suffer from a rare strain of Tourette's. "Fuckin' defense! Fuckin' long snapper! Fuckin' LIFE!"

When he emerged, Dave Brandon was sitting in a chair in the middle of the room. He made his sympathy clear. Then he pointed at a three-inch by half-inch gash on the coach's left shin, now bleeding impressively. "How'd you get that?"

Not by kicking the corner of the cooler, as I had assumed, but by a

Spartan's cleat in the second quarter. Only now had his adrenaline abated enough for him to appreciate what he had done.

"Do you mind if I watch film with you tomorrow?"

"Sure," Rodriguez said. "You can share my agony."

After he dressed, Rodriguez stopped by the trainers' room, where one of the interns sprayed his cut, then covered it with a five-by-five-inch bandage.

He knew he would not be sleeping much that night.

On paper, Rodriguez's Wolverines were 5–1, not bad at all.

Though they faced fourteenth-ranked Iowa next, their near miss in Iowa City the year before gave them reason for hope. After that, they would face Penn State, Illinois, and Purdue—all struggling. It looked as though they could still win three of the next four, and maybe sweep, leaving them 8–2 or 9–1, in great position for a good January bowl game, a contract extension, and protection from those who wanted to see him fail.

But the season wasn't played on paper. Even the student managers—who, like butlers, are often ignored but see everything—knew where the team stood.

"At 5-and-1," one told me, when I met them after the season, "right after State, we all felt like it's coming again. All the pressure. All the fear."

The ghosts of 2009, coming back to haunt them.

"Oh, yeah," another said. "Right away."

"We knew, at that instant," a third said. "You had Michigan State coming to your stadium. If you beat this team, you're all set. It's done! All the bullshit—it's over!"

"But all the pressure was on Michigan."

"And Michigan never loses three in a row to State."

"So when we lost, you just knew, that was it. It's over."

Whatever disease they had caught in 2009 that ruined their 4–0 season had not been eradicated; it was only in remission. Now it was back after a single loss in week six of the 2010 season, and more virulent than ever.

No sport fosters myopia like college football, where every weekend is a playoff game. That's part of its charm, of course—but the younger the team, the higher the peaks and the lower the valleys.

Just one loss put the young Wolverines in great danger of crashing.

Ultimately, Rodriguez's critics didn't matter. Not directly, at least.

The *only* thing that mattered was his ability to keep his team.

If they kept working hard, improving, and believing in themselves, each other, and their coaches, they would get better, and the future would be bright. They could endure the press, the critics, and the small but powerful segment of football alums and big-time donors who wanted Brandon to clean house. They could even lose some heartbreakers, so long as they learned from them and came back the next week determined to make it right.

But all that was asking a lot. This group of players had been getting beaten up since they arrived in Ann Arbor, whether their first game was the Horror against Appalachian State, Rodriguez's debut heartbreaker to Utah, or the 2009 opener against Western Michigan—which had been eclipsed by the *Free Press* front-page sensation six days earlier.

Many of the former players—including some of their former teammates—told the current players and the press they just weren't "Michigan" anymore, as if they were orphans. They had been carrying a heavier burden than probably any other group of Michigan players in its long and glorious history—so heavy, in fact, that after just one loss at midseason, the student managers could already feel the foundation cracking.

If Rodriguez lost his players—if they buckled under the weight, splintered, started blaming one another or the coaches, or just plain quit—nothing could save the team. Or him.

And no matter how mentally tough they were—and if they had shown nothing else over the past thirty games, they had surely shown that—keeping the team together depended on winning some games. Not just to get the outsiders off their backs but also to reward the players for their commitment and faith, to keep them working, and to keep them believing.

It would not be easy. Not this week.

Inevitably, there had to be some distractions to make the already difficult task harder. This time, they were largely self-inflicted. At his Monday press conference, held in the Commons, Rodriguez's responses ran some one thousand three hundred words in the transcript, and none of them seemed very newsworthy.

Almost none.

In the middle, Rodriguez repeated his usual comment that he was receiving great support from the university and the fans. "Everybody wants the same thing here," he said, "and nobody's happy with a loss."

If he'd stopped there, his words would have been justly forgotten. But he didn't. "We lost to Michigan State. What? You wanna hang me off the building now? I mean, there might be a few people who want to do that, but that's the same people that probably wanted to do that after the first five games, too, they just weren't saying it publicly."

At that moment, you could hear his supporters around the nation slapping their foreheads. It was, at best, artlessly worded. At worst, it suggested he hadn't taken the loss as hard as the fans did when nothing could be further from the truth—witness the kicked-over cooler in the coaches' room.

It was, however, an accurate reflection of his frustration—he was far harder on himself than the fans could ever be—and his lack of discipline in front of a microphone.

And, as usual, the man who would pay the most would be Rich Rodriguez—followed by his players, who would have to defend their coach.

Just a few hours removed from his gaffe in the Commons, Rodriguez addressed his team in the cantilevered team room behind the blond-wood podium. In front of the press, he was apt to blurt out statements that had nothing to do with what he was really thinking, but in front of his team, he was invariably strong, confident, and on message. The contrast was at times so great as to defy credulity.

"I only ask two things of you," Rodriguez said in his powerful voice. He often gripped the podium—not for strength but as an outlet for his excess of energy, built up through daily workouts on the StairMaster and the speedbag. "One," he said, raising his finger with the back of his hand toward his players, "that you be coachable, which I think you are. And two, that you play ball, *hard*, every time you take the field.

"We're not there yet. You cannot be tentative and be a football player. At some point, it's not about schemes or plays or anything you can draw up on a board. You just gotta go *hit him*. Or he's gonna hit you.

"GO KNOCK THE SHIT OUT OF HIM!

"We don't have soft players. But it's got to be *every* play. *Every fucking play!*

"It's a violent game! You don't need to do anything stupid and cheap. You just need to get after your man like you mean it.

"I hear everyone talking about how tough the Hawkeyes are. I don't hear anyone talking about how tough *we* are. Everyone's talking about how great they are. The best front four in the history of football. Their offense is gonna wear our little defense out.

"And I'll play right into it: 'Yeah, they're incredible, I don't know what we're going to do, maybe we'll show up.' All that bullshit. But I'm expecting us to win the game. Just so you know."

A day later, on the ESPN talk show *Around the Horn*, Rodriguez got roundly ripped by all the panelists for his "You wanna hang me from a building?" comment. They had a point, of course, but if they could see him in front of his team, they wouldn't recognize him as the same man.

If Rodriguez was worried about losing his team—and he was too smart not to be—he had reason to sit up and take notice when he got word that a few of his players had missed class on Wednesday and a couple more were late for their workout that day. Minor missteps, perhaps, but he took them as major signs.

That was what he was fighting when he collected his players after practice that day in the team's new indoor practice facility. They hunkered down on one knee, looking half-bored and worn-out—tired not simply of the physical toll every team feels at midseason but of the entire experience: the doubts, the defending, the demands of facing a do-or-die game just about every damn weekend.

"Listen to me," he said simply and sincerely. Every coach has to be a good actor, but there was no acting in this message. He had the tone of a father who finally had to level with his sons about something serious.

"For too long, I've let you guys off the hook. I've been soft on you guys. And that's not fair to you.

"I'm personally offended when we get outtoughed, and that's what I saw on the film this weekend. I take it personally. Last week we got out-worked, and we got outtoughed. And that wasn't the first week."

That got their eyes up, but some still slumped their shoulders.

"They can be bigger than us, they can be faster than us, but they will not outtough us. EVER.

"If I go into a fight with someone, he may be bigger, I might lose, but damn it, he'll be bloody. I guarantee you that."

Bowed heads rose. They knew what he was talking about and why he was saying it. He had cut through the usual cloud of coachspeak and con-nected with them with some simple truths, the same ones he had to face himself that week.

"Freshmen, I've defended you in the press. But I don't have to defend you here. Between the white lines I can't make excuses for you."

As he continued, his voice grew louder, his pace faster.

"Last year, we went into Iowa for a night game on national TV. Every-one was saying how great they were, how tough they were—and we went toe-to-toe with them. We didn't back off an inch. We did not play scared. We got up for that challenge and gave them our most physical game. They won by a couple points, but they *did not outtough us.*"

Their shoulders rose. Their backs straightened.

"It's good to have Ortmann and Moose here at practice today. They went into Iowa and played the best games of their careers.

"Nothing is going to be easy. You have to put your work in. And that is what you have to do in life. If you lose your job, you have to get back up. Someone may get sick, and you need to help them and keep fighting.

"You can't just lie down. Get up. GET THE FUCK UP!" He tore his jacket off and threw it on the turf. Rodriguez was a naturally good speaker and motivator, and he did a remarkable job after each loss getting them to slough it off before the next kickoff, when they invariably seemed ready to go again—but they seemed particularly mesmerized by this speech. Even the strength coaches, circling the group, were nodding vigorously.

"We're going to go hard on Saturday, so we need to go hard all week! In class, at workouts, at practice. GROW UP. GROW UP NOW.

"WE WILL NOT BE OUTTOUGHED!"

He snatched his jacket off the ground and stomped back to the building.

The players were dead silent, staring straight ahead, most of them bob-bing their heads, pursing their lips.

Walking away, Barwis said, "Best fucking speech I've ever heard."

Denard turned to one of the student managers and said, "Go get me some balls." A minute later, all four quarterbacks were taking snaps under center, soon joined by other players staying after practice to work on their own, the most they had done all season.

Whether the NCAA would consider their extra work voluntary or not, no one, for the first time in over a year, stopped to consider.

"Everyone's sad we lost to State," Erickson said, "but avoid a couple picks and we win the game. Fans are still pretty happy. Hey, we're 5–1. Once in a while you still get some guys who want to run Rich Rod out of town, but not many."

Not surprisingly, the man cutting hair a few doors down saw things differently—a fair representation of the other side of the debate.

"I said turnovers will cost the game, and it sure did," Red Stolberg said, pointing his scissors for emphasis. "They say it's just not Greg Robinson's defense. It's Rich Rod's, the three-man front and all that. And Obi can't tackle. Guy runs right up the middle, right at him, and goes right through him. Well, whose fault is that? Then you've got all those dumb penalties.

"I think some of the guys are getting kind of iffy. A bit demoralized. And I know some of the fans are! If they lose Saturday, it's just gonna blow up the balloon, same as last year. Iowa's gonna be tough. If we're lucky, we'll beat Purdue. Couple weeks ago, those were gimmes. If he gets six games and a lousy bowl, he's out of here.

"People are fed up with our boy Rich Rod. He's had his chances, and if he doesn't pull a rabbit out of his butt, he's gone."

"How many games will Michigan lose?"

That was the question posed on Saturday, October 16, 2010, ESPN's College Game Day.

"Coach Rod was right," said Forcier's new roommate, Teric Jones. "We've got a better record than Iowa, but they get all the respect."

"I think it's bullshit how they're talking about our program," said Forcier, whose improved attitude had been praised by Moundros, Banks, and other seniors. Forcier had largely recovered the respect he'd lost in the off-season. He was engaged.

"We lost *one* game against a team that's beaten two ranked teams, and we're playing against an Iowa team that lost to Arizona, and beat Ball State and Eastern Illinois and Iowa State. What the fuck, Iowa State? Who *isn't* going to look good against those guys?"

Would Forcier get a chance to look good himself? He grinned. "My dad isn't stupid. He didn't fly out here to watch me ride the bench. He knows we're playing a team where you can't just run the ball. Denard got his shoulder popped last week. It doesn't take much. Just one good hit. So my dad sees opportunity. I've been killing our defense all week. I'm ready."

At the stadium, before warm-ups, strength coach Jim Plocki could often be found sitting on a training table with his back against the wall, elbows on knees, staring off, thinking. "This is a critical game," he said. "This team is too fragile. I can't tell if we're focused. If we lose . . ." He didn't finish the sentence.

"They're gonna smack us, too. I know we can't afford to lose Molk or Martin." Plocki didn't bother to add Denard to that list, because it went without saying. "But you never know. If we win this one, we'll be good to go. You just never know."

About ten minutes before kickoff, the players got up, walked to the front of the room, and took a knee.

"Do you want respect?" Rodriguez asked them.

"Yeah!"

"There ain't a better day to get it than today. Ranked opponent. National TV.

"I know you can do it.

"I believe in you.

"I trust you.

"So let's go out there and give them sixty minutes of Michigan football."

He *did* believe in them. He just couldn't tell if they still believed in themselves.

Iowa won the coin toss and made the unconventional decision to receive the ball first, another slap in the face for Michigan's defense. But that wasn't how it played out.

On the first play, Kenny Demens, who—after a season-long debate between Rodriguez and Greg Robinson—had finally replaced Obi Ezeh at middle linebacker, stopped Iowa's runner cold after he'd gained just 1 yard. Two plays later, the Hawkeyes were punting.

But after Michigan's third offensive play of the day, the PA announcer said, "The Michigan player receiving attention is David Molk." The crowd didn't need to be told by Jim Plocki that Molk was one of the players Michigan couldn't afford to lose. They groaned in unison as he was helped off the field.

Denard kept the offense rolling down to Iowa's 8-yard line, where they faced third-and-goal. Would it be Michigan State all over again? Not this time: Robinson, with a better knee and better form, hit Vincent Smith on a slant route for a quick-strike touchdown. 7–0.

It was all Michigan needed to ignite the crowd. Forcier himself had become the team's biggest cheerleader, urging the crowd to crank up the noise every chance he had.

Michigan's defense—which had twice sent the Hawkeyes punting after three downs—trotted back onto the field. But Rodriguez saw something that made him run full speed down the sideline straight to Greg Robinson. The problem? Robinson was sending Obi Ezeh out to replace Kenny Demens. After a brief heated exchange between the two coaches, Ezeh returned to the sideline and Kenny Demens took his place.

When people asked about Michigan's defense, they wondered if the shockingly poor performance was the result of inheriting weak talent, transfers, injuries, youth, or coaching. The answer was yes. It is impossible to field a defense that finished 68th out of 120 teams in 2008, 82nd in 2009, and 110th in 2010 without all those factors playing a part. If the team had to deal with only two of those issues, say, they'd probably rank somewhere in the middle—and Michigan would be a Big Ten title contender.

Of all those variables, coaching was the hardest to tease out. After Rodriguez and Scott Shafer decided they weren't a good match, Shafer went to Syracuse, where his defense finished seventh nationally in yards per game in 2010. Rodriguez hired Robinson, whom, like Shafer, he barely knew personally or professionally and had just been fired from his only head coaching position after finishing 10–37 at Syracuse.

But Rodriguez was not hiring Robinson to be the head coach. Robinson's run as a defensive coordinator included two Super Bowl rings with the Denver Broncos in 1997 and 1998, plus a national title with the Texas Longhorns in 2004. Some pundits debate how much influence Robinson had on those teams and suggest Rodriguez should have asked more questions, but New England Patriots' owner Robert Kraft, for one, was impressed. He told me he had dinner with Robinson in 2002 with the intent of hiring him, but Robinson chose to work for his old friend Dick Vermeil in Kansas City instead. In fact, if Robinson coached one more season in the NFL, he would have the fifteen necessary to earn an NFL pension—no small bonus.

Rodriguez and Robinson clearly respected each other. Robinson was popular with the assistants, and he fostered a fierce loyalty among the student managers who worked with him. But, as with Shafer, Rodriguez and Robinson were not a match made in heaven. If it was the defensive coordinator's responsibility to teach proper tackling, that was on Robinson, even with the decimated roster. Teaching the talented, experienced Broncos and Longhorns the finer points perhaps required different skills than instilling the fundamentals into Michigan's callow underclassmen. More important, Rodriguez favored the 3-3-5 defense that Jeff Casteel had used to great effect at West Virginia, while Robinson preferred the more common 4-3-4. As the vision for Michigan's defense passed from Rodriguez to Robinson to the position coaches to the players, something was getting lost in translation.

It is difficult even now to determine exactly where the responsibility for Michigan's anemic defense should fall, but the easiest problem to identify was the differences in their judgment of personnel. Robinson was more patient with certain players, including Michael Williams in 2009 and Obi Ezeh in 2010. Rodriguez restrained himself about such decisions—resisting but not overruling—until he reached his breaking point.

Because, ultimately, there was one simple answer as to where responsibility fell: the head coach, something he said outright in the first minutes of the staff retreat in July. It was his job to bring the coordinator he wanted, line up another one he knew well, or not come to Michigan at all. He would never take such chances with his strength and conditioning program, but he did with his defense. It might not be fair, but it's the reality all head coaches live with—and he was paying for it now.

The difference between Ezeh and Demens didn't help much this time, however, when Iowa quarterback Ricky Stanzi led his team on a 70-yard drive down to Michigan's 14-yard line.

On second-and-10, Stanzi dropped back, rolled right, and threw to the right corner of the end zone. His pass was off: too shallow and too far to the right. Michigan safety Jordan Kovacs read it perfectly and sprang forward to the ball, which was chest-high. It looked as though all Kovacs had to do was make a simple catch and start running down the right sideline. Although Kovacs was no sprinter, he was still a safety, not a lineman, and it was hard to imagine anyone catching him with a 10-yard head start.

The crowd had already jumped to its feet in anticipation, ready to cheer him wildly as he pumped his way right past Michigan's bench to the end zone, giving Michigan a 14–0 lead before the first quarter ended—and delivering a dagger to the Hawkeyes' heart, just like Toledo had done to Michigan two years earlier in almost the exact same situation.

A 14–0 lead wouldn't guarantee victory, but with the offense looking good, the defense serviceable, and the crowd on fire, few would have bet against that outcome. And with it, of course, would come almost all the prizes they would have received for beating State—including job security for their coach and relief from the relentless pressure everyone worked under.

It was, in other words, Michigan's second straight match point.

It was all right there, soaring directly toward Kovacs's chest. Perhaps Kovacs was thinking all those things, too—they all felt the pressure building week after week—as the ball spiraled right to him with nothing but a hundred yards of green in front of him.

And perhaps that's why the utterly reliable Jordan Kovacs dropped the ball.

The crowd, the players, the coaches, and Kovacs himself all slumped in anguish.

Stanzi took the next snap, then fired over the middle for a 14-yard touchdown pass to tie the game 7–7.

"He should have been gone," former Michigan player Andy Mignery said on the sideline. "You need a play like that in a game like this. This is the whole season. These guys are used to losing like this, and then the slide starts."

If two plays can change a game, a season, and maybe a career—well, there were two more candidates.

Of course, it's not fair to pin all that on Kovacs, who had already done far more for Michigan than anyone ever could have asked or expected. And that was the point: These hardworking, honest, team-spirited players kept finding themselves facing extraordinary demands, week after week. And they were beginning to crack.

On Michigan's next possession, Robinson threw an interception, followed by a rare outburst: "Fuck!" he said, walking back to the bench. "FUCK!"

Four plays later, Stanzi threw a strike to go ahead 14–7.

When the half ended, the scoreboard indicated that Michigan had gained 223 yards to Iowa's 192—but trailed 21–7.

In the locker room, Greg Robinson focused on getting senior Adam Patterson ready to replace Mike Martin, who left the game because his knee had not completely recovered since the Spartan chop-block a week earlier. Thus, by halftime, both players Jim Plocki had said Michigan could not afford to lose were lost. The field of hope had narrowed yet again, with Denard Robinson once more at its center.

On Michigan's second possession of the half, Robinson gained 12 quick yards only to be hit hard by Iowa's Tyler Nielsen, leaving him lying on the field. The team could have collapsed right then and there and called it a season, but this was the moment Forcier had been waiting for, and he took full advantage, giving the fans what they wanted, with Denard standing on the bench, urging the crowd to get into the game. Forcier delivered with an 85-yard drive to cut Iowa's lead to 28–14, with 13:10 left.

Crazy? Sure. But the crowd knew it was not impossible. Not with this team and this offense. After another Iowa touchdown, Forcier countered with a bomb to Junior Hemingway. 35–21, with over 10 minutes left.

He had captured the fans' imagination, and they were with him completely. Feeling total confidence, he led another touchdown drive to cut Iowa's lead to 35–28, with a luxurious 6:55 left in the game.

It was a solid minute before any coaches could be heard over the roar, while the players jumped up and down, waving their hands upward to keep the crowd going. Stonum called Hemingway over and punched him in the chest. "Let's motherfuckin' GO!"

"Write this shit down," Mike Martin hollered over the noise. "We are winning this game! WE ARE WINNING THIS GAME!"

It took three days after Rodriguez's Wednesday speech, and three quarters of football, to conclude without a doubt: Yes, they still believed.

For the second time in a row, however, Michigan hooked the kickoff straight over Michigan's bench—which is what rookie walk-ons can do. As it flew over the heads of the players, each helmet seemed to drop down as if the ball itself had set off a row of dominoes.

It was a surprisingly severe blow to Michigan's shaky momentum. On third-and-8 at midfield, Michigan had a chance to get the ball back with plenty of time to tie the game. Freshman Courtney Avery had the ball carrier lined up in open space—but he missed, allowing the Hawkeyes to kick a game-clinching field goal.

Another Wolverine comeback attempt had fallen short. They were running out of air, running out of gas, running out of hope, running out of time—the very thing this team needed most.

The tunnel was not kind to the Wolverines. When one fan saw Greg Robinson, he yelled, "Your defense sucks!"

Robinson kept his chin up, looked straight ahead, and kept jogging.

Rodriguez kept his own postgame address to the players short. "Today we showed 'em we'll fight," Rodriguez said. "We showed 'em we're tough! But we didn't show them we're smart. Too many stupid penalties and mental mistakes. And that's on us," he said, thumbing his chest. "That's our job! So the coaches are committed to fixing it."

Back in the coaches' room, Rodriguez muttered, "Just ONE fucking stop when it counts would be nice."

An hour later, Rodriguez signed autographs by the barricade, alongside Forcier, who savored the attention, while Rita waited in the cold by their car, clutching the lapels of her winter coat.

"I just want a break," she said. "I just want a break."

Before the Sunday staff meeting, Barwis was hanging out in Rutledge and Parrish's shared office, presenting some surprising numbers. He pointed out they were outscoring teams badly in quarters one, three, and four, but getting "our asses kicked in the second." Through seven games, Michigan was minus 34 in the second quarter, and minus 24 against MSU and Iowa alone. Why was that?

"It's like in Ultimate Fighting. You hear about some new guy who's undefeated, and think, great, I'll kick his ass. Because he's never been hit. Never gotten smacked around and had to shake that shit off and come back harder.

"And that's what happens to us. We come in breathing fire, all jacked up, and we take it to them. But when they start fighting back, we're surprised. We're stunned! And it takes us a full quarter to get our heads back on straight."

It made some sense, and spoke to their intensity and conditioning—and inexperience.

Despite the loss to Iowa, the mood among the coaches on Sunday started out surprisingly light. No one was panicking. No one seemed overly stressed. They had lost two in a row, but both loses had been to very good teams, and both times they'd held their own in the yardage battle, even notching a remarkable 522 yards on Iowa.

Of course, it also helped that everyone was in for a bye week—much needed, physically and emotionally—even if the coaches would spend it traveling the country recruiting. Chomping their Sunday night pizza, Magee stopped chewing for a moment and said, "Man, when I close my eyes, I am seeing *little men* running around in my head. And they're not even running any plays I recognize. Man, I have seen *too much film.*

"This break could not have come at a better time. Well, maybe last week. But that's it."

That night, with no pressure to prepare for practice or a game in six days, the assistants had a rare chance to openly consider the possibilities: No one gets fired, some of them get fired, or everyone gets fired.

Frey groaned at the prospects. "What I find amazing is, we're talking about all this stuff, and we're 5-and-2, and this is only our third year. We had only seven scholarship O-linemen ready to play our first year, and none of them were drafted."

The quality of the cupboard's contents when Rodriguez took over ranks as one of the most frequently debated subjects among Michigan fans. You can very plausibly make a case that if Carr had stayed for the 2008 season, many if not all of the players who transferred, jumped to the NFL, or simply did not return for a fifth year would have played for the Wolverines. And since the team would not be changing coordinators or systems on either side of the ball, they would have the considerable advantage of continuity. Throw in a few breaks, perhaps, and it's not hard to imagine Michigan going 8–4 or even 9–3 in 2008, instead of 3–9.

But even making those concessions, it is much harder to argue that the recruiting classes of Carr's last years would allow Michigan to sustain even 9–3 records.

From 2009 to 2011, the NFL drafted only four Wolverines, and just one—Brandon Graham—in the first three rounds. Even if you count Ryan Mallett and the injured Troy Woolfolk as likely draft picks, the six total is still a third less than the previous low of nine, which is how many Michigan players were drafted from 1984 to 1986.

It's not just the top end that shrank, either, but the middle band of solid starters, too. As a result, in 2010, Michigan played twenty-six freshmen, the third most in the nation. They had only five senior starters, less than half as many as Ohio State, Penn State, Michigan State, and Iowa. On the other end, Michigan started four freshmen, while the top teams listed above all started one freshmen, or none—simply because they didn't have to.

"I don't care what anybody says," Frey concluded. "The cupboard was bare."

The good news for the Wolverines was that in 2011 they would return nineteen starters—or twenty-four if you count the injured players who would be returning to the lineup. Of the record 6,011 yards Michigan notched in 2010, all but 67 of them were gained by players who would return in 2011.

"Iowa had never given up a third-and-seven or more *all year*," Frey added. "On our first third-and-long, we scored a touchdown. They had never given up a rushing touchdown. We scored two. They had only let two runners go over 100 yards in 34 games. Denard did it in the first half. They averaged only 242 yards against their D all year, one of the best marks in the country, and we got 522. More than twice that. They were giving up ten points per game. We scored twenty-eight—and should have scored more, if we could make a red-zone pass or kick a field goal.

"So why is everyone saying, 'It's all do-or-die,' and 'We could be gone?' That's crazy!"

In fact, many of the same arguments were being made by ESPN's Ivan Maisel. "Why Rodriguez is considered on the edge of endangered remains mystifying. Michigan has improved and 18 starters return next season. Michigan will be favored in three of its final five games. Regardless of the outcome down the stretch, would it really be better to start over again?"

All true. Which raised another question: At what point did all the predictions of doom and gloom—and with them, the increased pressure— become a self-fulfilling prophecy?

That was virtually impossible to answer, but no one questioned the importance of the Penn State game on the horizon. The Lions were 4–3, and starting a walk-on quarterback.

It was Michigan's third straight match-point opportunity. Win it, and you're free.

One MGoBlog reader listed the stakes of this nationally televised night game thusly: "Our season, Denard's Heisman hopes, R-Rod's tenure, Bill Martin's reputation, a recruiting bounty, my sanity, Dave Brandon's decision, Mike Barwis' weight lifting program, Joe Pa's retirement, my marriage, our future . . . Let's see how much more shit we can pile on top of the outcome of this game."

Rodriguez did not need to be reminded, especially with his boss's presence in the locker room. The rumor had spread to the coaches that Brandon had circled this game as do-or-die. Win it, and votes of confidence and contract extensions would flow. Lose it, and—well, they were back to the scenarios discussed over pizza.

Whether the rumor was true, they were too afraid to ask, but it seemed plausible enough for them to worry, and they did.

The most intimidating walk in the Big Ten is not at Iowa's Kinnick Stadium or Spartan Stadium or even the great Horseshoe in Columbus but in Happy Valley, Pennsylvania.

When you approach Beaver Stadium, it looks nothing like the classic coliseums you see in Ann Arbor, Columbus, or Champaign, with their majestic arches in brick and stone. No. Beaver Stadium looks more like the scaffolding set up to *build* a stadium than a stadium itself, with sections of exposed girders and crossbeams everywhere. It takes a moment to realize that *is* the finished product. Thanks to seven expansions in the last forty years, every one of which seem to have been designed by a different architect, it is the Erector set of Big Ten stadiums.

If the outside of Beaver Stadium isn't especially welcoming, the inside is even less so for opposing teams, who get dressed in a concrete box under the stands, then walk through a maze of chain-link fencing, between hundreds of loud, drunk Penn State patrons, shaking the fence and yelling the most popular profanities.

"It used to be fun, but it started changing about ten years ago," Ferguson County police officer Ryan Hendrick told me. "The language, the spirit of it. It used to be if Michigan made a good play, no one booed, and some people even clapped. Now they just boo. You're considered a sap if you cheer."

Thanks to the spectators' new habits of spitting and spilling drinks on the players, the security detail added a wind fence a few years ago, which cut down on the worst of it. But it still picks up when Michigan's in town.

"Other teams, you might hear a few shouts. But when Michigan comes through—wow! Caged animals!" Perhaps hearing himself, the officer added, "But that's a show of respect. The students get up for Michigan."

The coaches and players made it a point to stare straight ahead walking through the labyrinth. Once they ran through the tunnel, the Wolverines faced the loudest crowd that season—maybe ever. The Lions prided themselves on hosting the "Greatest Show in College Sports," and they made a fine case. The rock music, the scoreboard, the ribbon bands, the marching bands and—most of all—the raucous student section fully pumped up for a night game on Halloween combined to create the happiest—or most hostile—environment in the country.

It wasn't for nothing Kirk Herbstreit declared Penn State had the best student section in the country two years in a row.

There was only one way to counter it: score early, and score often.

The Wolverines started on their 30-yard line, with a chance to quiet the crowd down. Instead they went three-and-out and gave the ball back to Penn State on its 29. On his first play, Matt McGloin stepped back and launched a bomb down the left sideline. It fell incomplete, but it still scared the hell out of Michigan's underconfident secondary, prompting them to fall too far back the rest of the game. It might have been the most important pass of the day.

After that, it was easy. Whenever the Lions faced third down on that drive—three times—or just about any time thereafter, all the walk-on quarterback had to do was drop back, hit a receiver 5 yards away in the right flat, and watch him turn upfield for 5 more before a Michigan defender caught him.

That's how Penn State cut through Michigan's defense to the end zone on four of their first five possessions, giving them a daunting 28–10 halftime lead.

"Hey, Michigan, you guys suck! You really suck!" Brainless and vulgar, yes—but the man had a point.

The news wasn't all bad. Michigan had notched 201 yards to Penn State's 246. But the defense was utterly unable to stop the Lions, and that would get worse after Mike Martin left the game with a sprained ankle, suffered when his roommate Ryan Van Bergen rolled on it in the second quarter.

"We've got a lot of football left," Rodriguez told his team. "I want to see what you're made of. You know damn well we can play better than that. We're just beating ourselves. Let's go get after their asses!"

But he sounded less confident than anxious, almost pleading with them to perform.

The Wolverines fought back bravely to close the gap to 38–31, but they couldn't get any closer. The walk to the locker room after the game was louder and drunker than the walk out, and seemed to take forever.

"Listen close," Rodriguez told his team. "Y'all didn't quit and I'm proud of you. We're not that far away. Believe me.

"Now listen: Don't you quit on each other. I will not quit on you! And next Saturday, it's in the Big House, our home. Our fans, cheering for us. So let's go. 'Michigan' on three."

On the plane ride back, Rodriguez sat in his customary seat right behind the bulkhead, with Greg Robinson across the aisle, both staring intently at their glowing computer screens. There was no danger of Rodriguez tossing his laptop in anger that night. The ride was quiet, as expected, but without the tension that followed tough road losses against Illinois, Michigan State, and others.

They had just blown their last best chance to save their season, and their jobs. The air was leaking out of their tires faster than they could get around the track.

Rodriguez was not visibly angry. He was not upset. He was something far worse: unhappy—and defeated. Simply beaten. Whether he was beat for the day, or just plain beaten, remained to be seen.

For the first time in the two-and-a-half-year odyssey of setback after setback after setback, Rodriguez looked like he was finally out of answers. He didn't have anything else left to offer.

47 **A PYRRHIC VICTORY**

With Illinois coming to town, the stakes had shifted.

Where the Wolverines had three straight chances to win match point, any one of which would have been enough to secure their future, beating Illinois would not be good enough. The Illini were heading to a respectable 4–4 record in the Big Ten, but they didn't represent the prize that beating MSU, Iowa, or Penn State on the road would have. No, winning would only keep Rodriguez alive. It wasn't his match point anymore. It was his detractors, this time, who would likely be able to wave him good-bye if the Wolverines lost their fourth in a row.

On Tuesday, November 2, after Rodriguez gave his team the weekly rundown on their opponent, he turned the floor over to Mark Moundros, who had asked the coaches to leave so he could address the team. He started out talking normally, but it didn't take long for him to get into a full shout, as he had before many games.

"I just want to take you back to camp," he said. "We're at the Big House, standing in a circle, holding hands, everyone's got that bond, no one's letting go, holding on to each other forever. We've got four more weeks to strengthen that bond.

"These coaches' jobs are on the line—because of us," he said, marking one of the few times players ever mentioned this.

"What are you willing to sacrifice for them? For each other? Maybe a little more time in the film room, or on the field?

"They sacrifice for us. They gave up family, their friends, their homes, to coach us. They're hated back in their state—and they did all that for us. What are you willing to sacrifice for them?"

His teammates weren't sure where he was going with this, but they were listening. Moundros started shouting, his neck straining, his voice almost immediately hoarse, and before long he was marching and stomping around the front of the room. Moundros had only one speed: overdrive. Everything else felt unnatural to him.

"For all the haters: Go ahead and talk shit about this program. You don't know us! You don't know Michigan!"

This hit home. They were all sick of answering questions and defending themselves and their team and their coaches from people who had little idea what was actually going on.

"We've got a chance to make a statement to the world: You don't mess with us. Our coaches aren't going anywhere. They're staying right here!"

"Yeah!" A dozen or so players were getting vocal, others were nodding.

"What are you willing to sacrifice for a program that gives you an education every day, that gives you a future? For them. For that winged helmet.

"Three and a half weeks. What are you willing to sacrifice for three and a half weeks—to beat this team right here?" He slapped the schedule on the wall, which showed only Illinois.

"They don't own us. Only we decide how hard we play. Every play, every day, a hundred miles an hour!"

Moundros was in phenomenal shape, but all the shouting and stomping was testing his lungs.

"Remember the winter, the spring, the summer? All that blood, sweat, and vomit? What was that for? Everyone can be first in line when things are going great. But when shit's not going great, where do you stand? The FRONT of the line, that's where! Bring that shit on! All day! Every damn day! Bring that shit on!

"From the very first play, you knock that bastard over—let him know that's how it's going to be: every play, all day long.

"Where are we going to stand?

"At the front.

"It starts today.

"Michigan football.

"Let's go."

Whatever problems this team had, no one could accuse the players of giving up or bailing on their coaches. Rodriguez may have come trailing enemies from Morgantown, he may have failed to win over certain factions of the fractured Michigan family, and he may have lost Brandon after Penn State, but as of Illinois week, he still had his team.

The practice that followed was, not surprisingly, fast and crisp. Moundros's teammates were responding.

But the very next day, a player left his feet to make a tackle—a definite no-no in practice—diving for cornerback J. T. Floyd, who had become the most valued of a decimated bunch. He fell to the ground, spinning like a lathe, with a freshly broken ankle. Floyd went off on a golf cart, then to the hospital. He was done.

A few minutes later, Rodriguez finally got some good news—sort of. Dave Brandon appeared and summoned Rodriguez to the sideline for a minute or two.

When practice ended, Rodriguez gathered his team around him like he always did, but this time to tell them the NCAA report would finally be released the next day. They had agreed to all of Michigan's self-imposed sanctions except probation, which they increased from two to three years.

Rodriguez left a lot out, however. When Rita walked into his office between practice and dinner, he revealed the rest: The NCAA had been persuaded he had not, in fact, been guilty of failing to promote "an atmosphere of compliance," changing the charge to the far milder "failure to monitor" those who were in charge of the monitoring. Given the possibilities, the ruling represented just about the best possible outcome.

Rita gave Rich a big hug. When they walked into the Commons, Rita was smiling more than she had been after the victory over Notre Dame.

On Thursday, November 4, 2010, the regional press gathered in the Junge Champions Center—the same room where Lloyd Carr had announced his retirement, where Rich Rodriguez had been introduced as his successor, where the coaches' cell phones had rung in unison with the news that a major report from the *Free Press* would be coming out that weekend, and where Rodriguez had broken down addressing the paper's charges the day after they hit the newsstands.

This time, the media—a couple dozen strong—was coming to hear the verdict.

Everyone received a copy of the NCAA's twenty-nine-page report, which actually referenced the *Free Press*'s initial story, noting that "the violations of daily and weekly countable hour rules, though serious, were far less extensive than originally reported and that no student-athletes were substantially harmed." The committee characterized the violations as "relatively technical."

The NCAA officials gave a synopsis of their findings via speakers on a conference call, then opened the floor to questions. Michael Rosenberg, who was in Minnesota, asked the first question over the speakerphone. "If the committee noted that the rules were stated clearly, but the staff willfully ignored the rules, how is that not failure to comply?"

A committee member calmly explained the difference in terms that were dry as dust but unequivocal. They knew this terrain.

Next up, Jim Schaefer, the *Free Press* editor from the news side who had worked on the paper's initial bombshell. "The report seems to be fairly critical of Rodriguez in several important areas," which he listed, then asked the committee to explain, in layman's terms, their findings.

"There were many different facets to it," one committee member said, "but in layman's terms, it's the 'captain of the ship' theory. The captain is ultimately responsible, but that doesn't mean the coach is involved in *any* of the things involved. Some of the things we found didn't get to the coach, but ultimately he bears responsibility."

On and on it went, with *Free Press* editors and columnists dominating the session, focusing almost entirely on getting a central concession: You say he's not guilty, but he really is, isn't he? The committee was polite and patient but never gave them the answer they wanted, which only inspired them to ask the same question in new and different ways.

The conference call complete, Dave Brandon took the podium. "Effective today," he said, "I'm pleased to report that the NCAA investigation is over and done. There will be no appeals, because there's nothing to appeal." He went on to mention that "a local newspaper did a very high-profile story" that suggested players were being harmed due to a wanton disregard for the rules and their well-being. "There was nothing found that even remotely suggested that our players' well-being was at all at risk."

When he finished his statement, he welcomed questions, and the cycle started anew, with the same people asking the same questions, hoping for different results. They had little chance getting Brandon to stumble. He was in his element, the best practitioner of the craft in the room.

Free Press columnist Drew Sharp asked an original question: "Are these grounds for firing the football coach?"

At this moment, Rodriguez shot Sharp a look that would later be described on websites as a "death glare."

Brandon replied that he had made it clear at the first press conference he had seen nothing in the evidence to give any reason to terminate the coach's contract, and "what I see now is even more positive than it was then."

A few minutes later, Brandon closed the event by saying, "Let's just go play the games." That was more than an exit line. It underscored the obvious: Regardless of the report's findings, it would not protect Rodriguez if he fell short at his principal job, winning football games.

As Jim Brandstatter put his bag in the backseat of his car, in the same parking lot where Rosenberg had made his feelings for Rodriguez plain after the coach's first press conference, the former Michigan football player and longtime broadcaster said, "So, it took the NCAA fifteen months to determine that Michigan stretched fifteen minutes too many? Am I missing anything?"

Not much. The NCAA investigated Michigan from January 2008 through the fall of 2009. During that span, the players were allowed to engage in 976 countable hours of athletic activity. The NCAA penalized Michigan for working 65 hours more than it was allowed, 58 of that stretching, or roughly 6 percent. But the NCAA had actually discovered that Michigan had exceed the *daily* limit of 4 hours in-season by 20 minutes of stretching on Mondays only, even though Michigan's *weekly* total was often still below the NCAA limit of 20 hours. Thus, the actual *total* excess was much lower—perhaps a half or a third of the 65 hours. It also found that graduate assistant Alex Herron had helped run the voluntary seven-on-seven workouts in the spring of 2009. In his classic, *Season on the Brink*, John Feinstein reported in 1986 that even the squeaky-clean Bob Knight, whose integrity Feinstein extolled, and his assistants sat high in the stands to watch "captains' practices," "though even doing that is a violation of a universally ignored NCAA rule." Universally ignored or not, it is still an NCAA rule, and Michigan had violated it. Further, the NCAA accused Herron of lying to the panel about it. "When you've got four attorneys firing questions at you," he told me, "they can get your head spinning pretty fast." Michigan had to fire him.

But, on the grand scale, after dozens of people from the NCAA, Michigan, and the football office spent over a year on the investigation—and probably more than a million dollars in legal fees among them—the outcome was undeniably small. Far more common in these cases, once they open Pandora's box, they find money, cars, and other illegalities. It is hard to remember the last time this much time and money were spent on an NCAA investigation that found so little—tantamount to hiring a few full-time plumbers to live in your home, and finding only a leaky faucet on the second floor.

But the consequences would be real enough. In addition to resources devoted to the case, seven people received official reprimands in their personnel files: Rodriguez and Barwis; Van Horn, Ann Vollano, and Joe Parker working in Compliance; and Draper and Labadie. Within eight months, six of them would no longer be working at Michigan.

In the less tangible column, you could list the hundreds of hours everyone had to spend away from their families and the players. The effect on the squad was incalculable. If the reporters were trying to make the players' lives better, as they occasionally claimed, few players would say they had succeeded. The players would have to answer for it the rest of their lives.

Back at Schembechler Hall, Dusty Rutledge had watched the whole press conference on the TV in his office. "Well, we won't get fired today, at least," he said at his office computer. "And now we can go somewhere else if we have to."

He returned to his computer but more bile bubbled up inside him, forcing him to turn back. "But that whole thing pissed me off. They asked eight times, eight different ways: 'Wouldn't you say he's guilty?' 'Why didn't you declare him guilty?'

"You know why? *Because he wasn't guilty!*

"I hope Rosenberg feels like an ass. But no matter what Rosenberg's going through right now, he can't be half as miserable as he's made Rich and Rita the last year and a half. Rich can't sleep, his hands shake, and he can only listen to XM radio, the only place where they're not bashing him night and day.

"The kids like it here! Raquel says there's too much homework, but that's it! And if they're gonna have to move because of that asshole, when I'm walking out of here, I want to punch Rosenberg in the face."

You might think Rodriguez would have returned to his office thrilled—or at least relieved—but he was steaming.

"What did I do to them?" he asked of the *Free Press* reporters. "That's not standard questioning. That's humiliating. That's what it is. To sit there and listen to that is humiliating. 'Oh, it's part of the business, blah blah.' No, *that* is not. They weren't trying to get the truth. They were trying to make it as humiliating as possible. And especially on a day I was proven right? Man, it pisses me off!

"You know, I blew through my life savings to defend myself against that bullshit, three or four hundred thousand dollars. I don't care how much you make. That's pretty substantial.

"Is it good news?" he asked, trying to feel better about it while yanking his tie off to get ready for practice. "Yeah, but the guys who created this bullshit don't care. And you watch—they won't report it that way."

The next twenty-four hours would prove just how much Rodriguez had learned about the media.

That night, Jonathan Chait wrote for *The Wolverine*, "It's interesting to read how different news outlets report the conclusion of the NCAA investigation into allegations of practice abuse at Michigan. Here's the headline of one report:

"'RichRod gets win, but still needs more on field'

"Here's the headline of a second:

"'UM's violations deemed major, but not serious'

"And here's a third:

"'NCAA's verdict: Rodriguez ignored rules; U-M gets more probation'

"Those headlines came from ESPN, the *Detroit News*, and the *Detroit Free Press*. You can probably guess which was which."

When I visited the barbershops that Friday, Red Stolberg was none too optimistic about Michigan's prospects—or the head coach's. "Oh, I don't know," he said, cutting away. "We might keep Rodriguez . . . for another week! The students have been loyal all along, and now they're selling their tickets."

What he and his customers were talking about was less surprising than what they weren't: yesterday's NCAA report, which was making national news. After I prompted him, Stolberg said, "That? Well, it's kind of weak. But most of the customers just talk about the defense."

And with that, he was done with the subject.

At Jerry Erickson's shop, everyone was eager to talk about Rodriguez, the defense, the season, and the future, but once again, no one gave a thought to the NCAA report until I brought it up.

"The NCAA report?" Erickson asked. "I don't think anybody cares about that. It was bullshit from the beginning."

Once I quit asking about it, the subject dropped instantly.

Rodriguez was right: Everyone cared about the *Free Press* headlines a year ago, but no one cared about the conclusion. The NCAA ruling was far too little, far too late.

The *Free Press*'s claims were found to be far off the mark. And yet it didn't matter. The damage had been done, and it was apparently irreversible.

After former secretary of labor Raymond Donovan was acquitted of fraud, he asked, "Which office do I go to to get my reputation back?"

I continued down State Street to Schembechler Hall, arriving early for the 2:00 quarterback meeting but just in time to hear the quarterbacks share stories of their recruitment. One told of visiting a powerful SEC school. When he got to his hotel room to unpack, the quarterback discovered two attractive coeds in his room, already in his bed.

"It was weird, man!" he said, laughing.

Another described an SEC school giving him a rental car for the weekend and telling him, "You don't have to return that."

A third SEC school promised one of them they would pay for his sister's tuition.

"Man, am I the only one to do it clean?" Devin Gardner asked, laughing.

"*We* did it clean!" Denard said. "I didn't take any of that stuff! But the *schools* didn't do it clean! How many visits did you take?"

"Just one," Gardner said.

"That's why, man! You go visit [other big-name schools], they're gonna offer you money and cars and women."

"Man, Michigan didn't give me *anything*!" Gardner said, keeping up his mock outrage. "This place sucks!"

"Jesus," Rod Smith said, shaking his head but grinning slightly. He wasn't surprised—he knew what other schools did—but the contrast struck him, especially a day after the NCAA press conference hashed out every minute his players had spent stretching, and the *Free Press* wanted more. "When it comes to recruiting, we're going to a gunfight with a plastic spoon. And the crazy part is, these guys were offered all that, and they still came here!"

"I know!" Gardner said. "What are we—stupid?"

On Friday night at the Campus Inn, Rodriguez let it all hang out.

"All right, men," he said. "We're in the foxhole, and we're coming out swinging! We're firing every bullet we've got. We're going after their asses!"

He got them all chanting and jumping again, as he had the previous night at practice. They starting shouting and smiling and even laughing. It never ceased to amaze me how the coaches could pull themselves up from the depths of a postloss Sunday, back to the peak on Saturday—and get their players to follow. They had done it again.

Saturday, November 6, 2010, started out cold and gray, but by kickoff, it was another perfect football Saturday.

On the first snap, from Michigan's 25, Robinson took the shotgun on a play designed for him to run. But as he started forward, he saw Roy Roundtree cutting straight up the middle, with the safety coming up to stop the run. Robinson did exactly what he was supposed to do and threw a simple toss up the middle. Roundtree didn't miss a stride, bolting for the end zone, 10 yards in front of the nearest Illini player.

Roundtree was taking no chances this time, running as if his life depended on it, even watching himself in the huge scoreboard above to check on the defenders chasing him. Just fourteen seconds into the game, Michigan had taken a 7–0 lead. After the season, Robinson would describe that as his favorite play of the year.

Michigan's defense let the Illini come back with two touchdowns of their own, and the Wild West duel was on. The game had everything—great runs, passes, and acrobatics—except defense. But the fireworks were well worth the price of admission, including an ESPN top ten play from Junior Hemingway, whose fancy footwork caused three Illini defenders to fall all over themselves, which gave him a free path to the end zone.

"What the fuck happened?" a laughing Stonum asked an expressionless Hemingway on the bench. "That was *stupid*!"

"I didn't know you could dance!" Singletary said.

Roy Roundtree seemed happier about Hemingway's touchdown than his own two. "That was *silly*!" he said, laughing. "Just *silly*!"

Almost as silly as a 31–31 halftime score, with Michigan's offense putting up 394 yards on the twelfth-ranked scoring defense in the country, while giving up 312—numbers big enough for a whole game, not a half.

When Rodriguez addressed his players, they were already standing, all but growling, that eager to get back on the field. "That's right!" he said. "We're in that foxhole, and we're battling. You keep your ass fightin', ya hear me?"

"YEAH!"

Nothing more needed to be said.

They ran out of the tunnel and into the sun. Greg Robinson looked down his bench and saw Mike Martin snapping on his helmet. "Are you going back out?"

"Hell yeah, I'm going!" he said, and that was that. Martin, sprained ankle and all, was back.

With the score tied 38–38, Denard Robinson told the trainers he was feeling dizzy and had a headache. They ran some rudimentary tests, huddled, and decided he should not return for the rest of the game. They did not consult the coaches, and the coaches did not give their opinions. This is the way it should be, of course, even if the coaches' jobs could very well rest on their best player getting back in.

On Forcier's first play, from Michigan's own 35, he dropped back, hitched to throw, then lost his grip on the ball. It floated away, then onto the turf, where Illinois's Clay Nurse gobbled it up. Six plays later, Illinois went ahead, 45–38.

"I don't normally keep my headset on because I'm talking to the linemen," Greg Frey said the next day, after the offensive coaches had reviewed all their plays. "But when Tate fumbled, Rod got on the headset and, let's just say, he owes the swear jar a few bucks."

It begged the question: What did the normally calm, supportive, and infinitely patient coach say?

"Let's see," Frey said, trying to get it right. "'Fuck you, you dumb motherfucker, you haven't learned a fucking thing in two fucking years and you're doing the same fucking shit you were doing fucking last year. When are you going to fucking grow up?'"

"No, Frey, that was actually the *second* thing he said," Magee corrected. "The first thing he said was 'FUCK YOU!' and he threw his headset down and stormed around the box for a while before he calmed down enough to sit down, get back on the headset, and say all that other stuff."

"But you know, that's exactly what Tate needed," Dews said.

Apparently. Forcier settled down and started playing the position the way he'd been coached—quick drops, focusing on his receivers and not the rush, and firing the ball first and scrambling on second. Three steps and throw.

With time running out, he fired a gutsy pass to Darryl Stonum, who dived and caught it in the end zone. 45–44. The snap for the extra point flew behind Doug Rogan's back, but he caught it, put it down, and Seth Broekhuizen made the kick.

The score was 45–45, the yardage 605–486 in Michigan's favor—a total of almost 1,100 yards in regulation, an absurd statistic. The spread at its silliest. But it was far from over.

In the second overtime, trailing 59–52, Forcier threw to Hemingway on the goal line into double coverage. It looked like it could be intercepted—ending everything—but it hit the defender's helmet, and stayed there. Hemingway plucked it off and juggled it twice before gathering it in for a very unlikely—and very lucky—touchdown. 59–59. They were still alive.

By the third overtime, Dave Brandon was standing on the sidelines. Rita Rodriguez sat at the far end of the benches, trying to smile.

After Michigan scored yet another touchdown, the rules required they go for 2 points. Some players looked away. "I can't watch this shit!" one said when Forcier found Hemingway cutting back out across the goal line. Hemingway bobbled the ball, bounced it off his thigh, and almost lost it before securing it for the 2 points on his way to the turf. 67–59.

"I cannot believe I'm seeing this," Will Hagerup said, holding his head in his hands. A few thousand fans were thinking the same thing. No one was leaving.

A couple minutes later, Illinois scored a touchdown and faced its own

2-point attempt to tie the game. "What do you guys have?" Rodriguez asked his defensive coaches over the headset.

There was a pause. "If it's all right with you," Tony Gibson finally answered, "we're gonna bring the house."

"Yeah!" Rodriguez said. "Bring the house!" His gambling instincts were alive and well.

The instant Nate Scheelhaase took the snap, he saw Michigan's Craig Roh running right at him—and to his left, Jonas Mouton running in just as hard. All week in practice, they had worked on the blitz, but too often Mouton would come straight at the quarterback, allowing him to escape to his left. The key was to come hard while sealing off his lateral options.

"Once I saw Mouton cover the left side," Magee said, up in his box, "I threw my arms up. I knew he had 'im!"

Scheelhaase tried to escape, but it was futile. They devoured him.

The second Mouton threw Scheelhaase down, the Michigan sideline dam burst open, releasing a flood of players, coaches, managers, and trainers all exploding onto the field. The team's new pastor, a former lineman, was knocked to the ground. Ryan Van Bergen ended up on his back. And Rita Rodriguez, in a precise, fancy outfit, gave the very sweaty Taylor Lewan a big hug.

The rest came in a blur—the players celebrating, the student corner going crazy, the chanting: "It's great! To be! A Mich-i-gan Wol-ver-ine!"— and the band breaking into "The Victors," almost drowned out by a rowdy crowd. Before they were aware of it happening, two players told me, they had already run back up the tunnel and into the locker room.

After much cheering, the players dragged their coach to his makeshift stage, the leg machine in the middle of the room. He was a little sunburned, a little sweaty, and a lot relieved.

"Men, you work that hard, for sixty minutes and *three* overtimes—you *have* to have heart," he said, pointing and straining his neck for each word. "And YOU have HEART! . . .

"We didn't play great, but we played with great intensity—every play!" He made sure to look at all the players as he spoke, scanning the semicircle of happy faces. "And hey—we are going to a bowl!"

"YEAH!"

"From here on out, every win elevates our status. Let's go somewhere nice! I'm PROUD of you! You have a right to enjoy this—you earned it— but no one screw this up tonight, got it?"

"YES, SIR!"

"Okay, seniors, you know what to do!"

Rodriguez produced a fist, his whole body flexing with every "Hail!"

At the press conference, Rodriguez said, "We had three true freshmen start in the secondary. That's why I'm so excited for the future."

The future—something not discussed in weeks, except in the bleakest terms.

Back at their home, filled with a dozen friends and family members, Rita watched the Michigan game again on the small TV in the kitchen with her cousins. After the players had stormed the field, Barwis walked across the screen and seemed to be pulling a tear. Rita played it back to be sure.

"Awww, would you look at that!"

Rich retired to the smallest room in the basement with an octagonal poker table, a flat-screen TV, a cold beer, and a fresh cigar.

His phone buzzed with friends calling and texting their congratulations. "Yeah, this one felt good. Real good. Thanks, buddy."

We discussed a wide range of subjects, including how much schools spent on football. "You probably don't know this, but Michigan ranks fifth or sixth in the Big Ten! It's less than we spent at West Virginia!"

Certainly, he was surprised to discover that statistic, but only after he had already moved his family to Michigan. He assumed, like probably everyone else, that Michigan must be at the very top of the Big Ten in spending, along with Ohio State, and on a level with Alabama, Texas, and the other elite programs. Not even close.

"I came here to quit swimming against the current," he said. "I wanted to swim downstream. That's what Michigan represented to me. But I've been swimming upstream for three years now, and it gets tiring.

"When you lose a recruit, they won't even call you back. They never tell you why they're not interested or why they picked some other school. But because of the *Free Press* story and the investigation, and all the negative recruiting every other coach is doing against us because of it—'They're getting the death penalty!'—we've probably lost out on four or five players this year who could help us this year or next year. And that's probably conservative."

But even the *Free Press* couldn't spoil his mood on this night. With a bowl game secured, he felt a little relief for himself and a lot of joy for his players.

"It's a business for the coaches, but it's a game for the players. They're not paid. You have to remember that.

"The number one goal I have for my players is simple: I want them to say, 'I'd do it all again.' If they can't say that, you've failed."

It was probably fair to say—on this day, at least—that few of his players would not say they'd do it all again.

I left Rodriguez's home about 10:00 to join Mike Martin's party at his condo down the street from the stadium. It was a modest, modern apartment, the kind of place you'd get with your first job out of college.

As soon as I walked in, I could hear the party thumping downstairs. The small room was packed with football players, friends, and women, all drinking beer and sloppy mixed drinks and head-bobbing to the music. Many of the women were athletes themselves. There were also a number of players' brothers there; if you wanted to know what the players would look like without Barwis, you had their doughy siblings for comparison.

It was a party, for sure, with plenty of drinking by underage students. But when I thought back to my own college days, these people were a lot better dressed—ready for a club, not a campus pub—and a lot better behaved. When it was time to head to the campus bars, they called cabs. They knew they were one cell phone picture away from a national scandal, and their coaches would know everything.

My friends and I were not Division I athletes, but we had more fun. Perhaps that's why.

Monday, November 8, 2010, was another gorgeous day, 65 degrees, not a cloud in the sky. A late fall sun, with long shadows. You could go golfing in a polo shirt, and many were doing just that, right across Stadium Boulevard.

The music blasting out of Dusty's Disco Wagon, a converted golf cart, was all feel-good stuff: Otis Redding, "Sitting on the Dock of the Bay," Jimmy Buffett singing "Brown Eyed Girl" with steel drums, and the team's unofficial anthem, "We're Not Gonna Take It!"

When they started their warm-ups, wearing helmets, jerseys, and shorts, the one-legged hops looked more like dancing than working.

"I've seen these bastards suffer for three fucking years," Barwis said. "They got what they deserved on Saturday. I don't get emotional too much. But when a paralyzed guy walks, or 125 guys get shit on for three straight years, and their faith gets rewarded—well, that'll do it."

So was that him pulling a tear on the game tape?

"Pulling a tear? Me? Naw, man." He toed the turf, stirring up a small cloud of black rubber pebbles. "See this stuff? The black pebbles kick up, get in your eyes. It's just not safe. Someone needs to look into this."

He looked up, and seeing his BS wasn't flying, grinned the biggest grin I'd seen from him since I'd met him.

"All good things come to you now," he said.

Time would tell.

The schedule did the Wolverines a favor the following week, giving them a trip to Purdue. The Boilermakers were mired in the middle of another mediocre season with a 4–5 overall mark and 2–3 in the Big Ten. The day was gray and ugly, cold and muddy—perfect Big Ten weather for mid-November.

"This is what we've been working for," Magee said. "Just us and an opponent, playing football."

Of course, that wasn't entirely true. On ESPN, Kirk Herbstreit and Robert Smith were reporting that the decision had already been made: Jim Harbaugh would replace Rodriguez. Fortunately for the Wolverines, they were in West Lafayette, about as far from the national media as you can get. With even a little less pressure, they seemed a lot more relaxed, though the sloppy field matched the sloppy play.

With 5:59 left in the game, Michigan had the ball and a shaky 20–13 lead. On the sidelines, Rodriguez grabbed Denard Robinson, who had banged his left hand earlier that game. "If you're really hurt, I'll put Tate in."

"Fuck that!" Denard said.

"All right," Rodriguez said. "You're the quarterback. So go in there and *win us the fucking game.*"

And that's just what Robinson did, chipping away at Purdue and the clock with a confidently executed nine-play drive that finished with freshman Stephen Hopkins barreling into the end zone with 1:58 left, for a 27–16 lead. Game over.

"I've been part of a lot of pretty losses lately," Greg Frey said, jogging off the soggy field. "I'll take an ugly win."

In the double-wide, separate-standing locker room, the chant went up: "SOMEWHERE WARM! SOMEWHERE WARM!"

At 7–3, they were all but guaranteed to avoid the dreaded Motor City Bowl and head to Arizona, Texas, or Florida. In stark contrast to the funereal return trip from Penn State, the plane ride home from Purdue was fun, complete with Jeremy Gallon and Devin Gardner singing a duet of a country song Rutledge blasted at practice, "Where Did You Come From? Where Did You Go?" Life was good—and could still get better.

The coaches took advantage of a bit of breathing room to look around the league, and the country. They couldn't help but be amused that USC, Texas, and Florida, which had all won national titles that decade and had consistently landed the top recruiting classes in the country, were, to quote one of them, "in the shitter."

In the Big Ten, an all-but-dead Minnesota team upset Illinois, and Iowa had just gotten surprised by Northwestern, 21–17. It was always interesting when it wasn't you.

Three Big Ten teams were now in the top eleven: Ohio State, Wisconsin, and Michigan State.

"We're about to screw the whole Big Ten race up," said the ever-optimistic Magee, "when we beat Wisconsin next week."

On ESPN radio that morning, however, strength coach Dan Mozes heard Dan Patrick give a less sanguine assessment, reporting a "100 percent chance Rich will be fired."

One of the two predictions was about to get a big boost.

Down at Coach & Four, Jerry Erickson was back on the positive: "The word around here is we're gonna do it. That's what everyone's saying. But we still got guys—*Michigan* guys—who don't *want* us to win, whether they're supposed to or not. What is that?"

His cousin Red Stolberg *wanted* them to beat the Badgers. He just didn't think they would.

"Yeah, it's gonna be a tough one," he said, snipping away. "A lot more rolling on this one than meets the eye. I'd like to see a Wolverine win, but Wisconsin's just too big, too experienced."

On Saturday, November 20, the naysayers were proved right—early and often.

After being forced to punt on its first possession, Wisconsin ripped through Michigan's hapless defense on four straight scoring drives to forge a 24–0 lead while racking up 379 yards to Michigan's 124.

Michigan's vaunted offense showed some glimmers, but they usually ended in the now-familiar missed field goal. With Wisconsin driving yet again near the end of the half, Michigan's James Rogers picked off a pass at the 6-yard line and ran it back to the 15. With thirty seconds left, everyone assumed Rodriguez would do what he does best, throw the dice and take his chances to get back in the game—but he sent Denard on two straight runs to end the half. The fans were disappointed to see his gambler's instincts suppressed, cascading boos down on Rodriguez and his players as they ran to the tunnel.

If the players wanted to give up on the game, the season, their coaches, and themselves, this was the perfect chance. Return to the field with anything less than a full effort, and the Badgers could put 83 on them the way they just had against Indiana, a team Michigan barely beat.

Or they could pull themselves up and fight, knowing there was virtually no chance for success.

David Molk decided to pull himself up, and he wanted his teammates to come up with him. They were slumped in their stalls, ready to concede, when he stood up and marched around the room. "Hey, Michigan! Are we fucking scared? Because we're playing like it! We are all on our fucking heels! ALL OF US!

"We gotta drop our fucking nuts and MAN UP! We are NOT lying down! We are NOT scared! We will fight! We will FIGHT! And we will GET AFTER THEM!

"Everyone STAND UP! Stretch out! I mean it!"

"Get up!" Van Bergen said, and they did.

"We're gonna hit 'em in the fucking face," Molk said, "and they'll cry! They'll bleed! NOW LET'S GO!"

The energy spread. The players went out and drove the ball 71 yards for their first touchdown of the day: 24–7.

Freshman Courtney Avery forced a fumble on the Badgers' third play of the half, and Mouton recovered it at Wisconsin's 38. Denard passed to Stonum for 34 yards, then ran the remaining 4 for another touchdown.

The score was 24–14, just 5 minutes into the second half. Suddenly, anything seemed possible.

The Badgers came back with a touchdown, but Michigan matched it to close the gap to 31–21 when the third quarter ended.

The Wolverines' defense still couldn't stop the old-school Badgers, though, who scored 17 more points Big Ten–style in the fourth quarter by sending the big boys running downhill. But when the game ended, Michigan had recaptured a measure of self-respect by outscoring Wisconsin 28–24 in the second half.

At Michigan, there are no moral victories. The press would bury them for the 48–28 loss. But they could at least walk off with their heads up and look their teammates in the eye. If the ugly first half showed just how mentally worn-out they were, the second showed just how much fight the players had in them.

It was no surprise that Red Stolberg wasn't enthusiastic about Michigan's prospects the next week in Columbus—or Rodriguez's chances of keeping his job. "You're hearing all kinds of rumors," he said between haircuts, sitting in the customers' chair with a newspaper in his hand. "Some say he's gonna stay, some say he's gonna go. And some say they'll keep him but clean house on defense. Who knows? I think they're all gonna go. It's gonna be real interesting to see."

A client came in, which got him out of the chair. "I don't have much hope for tomorrow at all. Not at all. I think we're gonna get pounded. I'm gonna say 45–28. Go Blue anyway!"

No shock there. What was surprising was how completely Rodriguez had lost one of his staunch defenders, Jerry Erickson, up the street. "I thought for sure we were going to win that game," Erickson said, sitting in his chair, enjoying a cold beverage and conversation with his regulars while his assistants worked away. "We were all pulling for an upset, but when you play defense like EMU, that's what you get. It *is* the defense— but *why* is it the defense? That game took the wind out of a lot of people's sails."

He'd been hearing rumors of a press conference scheduled for Monday, which was gaining momentum in the mainstream media. "Supposedly Harbaugh's got his bag packed," Erickson said. "Some say they want another coach before the bowl game. Everyone's pretty down, I can tell you that. Nobody feels good about it. All I can tell you here is we're about to get our butts kicked. I'd say 42–7. I hope they prove me wrong, but I got this bad feeling. If that happens, you might as well head back to West Virginia!"

He stood up to take a customer. "I tell you this: If I was Rich Rod, with all this pressure? I'd leave on my own!"

In the visitors' locker room the following Saturday, Mark Moundros stood up to speak. "Your body will grow old and break down, but your memories will never fade. When you get older and look back on this, how do you want to remember this game, this season, your career?

"Forget those who don't believe—because we do!"

Three years ago it was surprising when the sophomore walk-on talked to his teammates, but now they expected it.

What they didn't expect, however, was senior Greg Banks—who had been saved from living with his family in their car in Denver by a full-ride scholarship to the University of Michigan. When he left for Ann Arbor, his mom begged him to do two things: not come back, because she knew the neighborhood could bring him down, and to take care of his teeth. He took both pleas seriously, always traveling with a bag filled with floss, mouthwash, and an expensive electric toothbrush his first Michigan girl-friend's uncle, a dentist, had given him. On Fridays, at the hotel, he would cut his teammates' hair for free. In a few weeks, he would graduate from Michigan and join his new girlfriend in San Francisco, where she was go-ing to graduate school.

He had his teammates' respect, and their attention.

"It's been an *honor*," he said, "to play with you guys. I've been on a lot of teams, and this is the best of them all: the tightest and the toughest. We've been yelled at by our coaches, but it made us better. We've been cussed at by people we don't even know, but here we are, still fighting. Let's keep fighting today!"

From the back of the room, sophomore Roy Roundtree yelled, "I got you, Greg! Every play! You can count on me! You can count on me!"

Once again, incredibly—after another disheartening week, after more flack from some fans and coaching rumors on the Internet—the players found a way to play their best, at least for a while.

To start the game, the defense sent Ohio State's vaunted offense to the sidelines after three plays. Robinson led a strong twelve-play drive from Michigan's 27 to Ohio State's 28, where they faced fourth-and-8. Most teams would take their chances on a 45-yard field goal. Not Michigan. Rodriguez went for it, but Robinson threw incomplete.

After another Buckeye three-and-out, Robinson rolled the offense from their own 18 to Ohio State's 26. On third-and-17, he cut up the middle all the way to the 9—enough for a first down, with a chance for a touchdown—where he fumbled the ball. He would later call this his most disappointing play of the year.

Michigan outplayed Ohio State in the first quarter—six first downs to two, 133 yards to 97—but, having failed to capitalize early, it was only a matter of time. Dropped passes; penalties; turnovers; injuries to Je'Ron Stokes, Taylor Lewan, and Denard Robinson; and atrocious punting—Will Hagerup was back in Ann Arbor for breaking team rules—all added up to a 24–7 halftime score, despite a 14–9 advantage in first downs and a slight 258–229 edge in yardage. As usual, they could get the yards but not the points, another sign of an inexperienced squad.

And once again, they were done—and they knew it.

In the second half, the Buckeyes scored on their first three possessions to post a 37–7 score, and it would have been worse if Coach Tressel had not shown some mercy in the fourth quarter. The Buckeyes' infamous fans, of course, showed a little less mercy, yelling and screaming profanities throughout the game. In the words of a U-M police officer assigned to guard the players, "If I was given a free pass to shoot Ohio State fans today, I'd have run out of bullets."

But they were far less hostile than usual, which might have been even more insulting. They knew a beaten team when they saw one.

"Let's don't act like they beat us!" Lewan told his teammates back in the locker room. "They didn't. We beat ourselves. We had 'em! We outplayed 'em!" As crazy as it might have sounded, given the final score, he wasn't far off. They made nineteen first downs, same as Ohio State, and lost the yardage contest 478 to 351. Significant, but not reflective of the score. Michigan just made more mistakes—turnovers, bad penalties—which were as foreign to Michigan fans as Rodriguez's high-flying offense.

"We played *hard*!" Rodriguez told them. "And we know we should have been up three scores in the first half. But that's woulda, coulda, shoulda. We know we can *fix it*! You seniors have nothing to be embarrassed about. I'm proud of you.

"There's a new level of commitment here, and we're gonna build on it. That's tomorrow, that's this winter, this spring, this summer. It's the work you do when no one's watching that makes you great. We got rid of the selfishness, we got rid of the laziness. That's what this year's seniors established, and we're gonna build on that.

"Michigan football's not dead. We're coming back."

Probably everyone in that roomed believed him. But no one—not even Rodriguez—knew if he'd be around to see it happen.

Two days later, Rodriguez was taking calls in his office, wearing a jacket and tie, before heading off to Weber's Inn, a venerable Ann Arbor institution. He was going to give a lunchtime speech to the M-Club, something he had done only a handful of times before.

This is the group Michigan coaches had been addressing every Monday during the season for decades until Rodriguez unwisely broke the chain. Not the big donors or the power players, but a good bunch to have on your side. He was doing so in the swirl of yet another media frenzy, kicked off by still more reports that Stanford coach and ex–Michigan quarterback Jim Harbaugh had all but been anointed his successor.

The speculative circus was made all the racier by rumors that Harbaugh would be attending Michigan's annual Football Bust three days later, as part of the twenty-fifth anniversary of the stellar 1985 squad, which finished second in the nation. Ticket sales and media requests soared. Surprisingly, though, the news barely registered on the Rodriguez scale.

"Just another day," he said. His threshold for drama had increased considerably since the Saturday night mess at President Garrison's house almost exactly three years earlier.

He drove with Dusty Rutledge to Weber's, where they sat with a dozen assistants and staffers. After Bruce Madej introduced him, the full house of five hundred or so patrons gave him a standing ovation. He talked about his three seasons at Michigan, 2010 in particular, and the Ohio State game. He was warm and funny, confident but humble, exuding none of the edginess or defensiveness he sometimes flashed in press conferences.

"We are closing the gap," he said. "It may not seem like it, but we are. Right now we're putting out a bunch of freshmen against a bunch of fifth-year seniors. But we're getting better. Trust me. When we've got third- and fourth-year players against their third- and fourth-year players, we'll be right there.

"We're supposed to have five or six guys playing back there who are injured or gone. But we have guys on the scout team starting. The one place we couldn't afford that was the secondary, and that's where we got hit the hardest."

When he said something like this in press conferences, it sounded like he was making excuses. But with the receptive audience, it came across as an explanation—one arguing for more sympathy for the players, not more criticism—and, no doubt, a pitch for giving him more time.

A patron asked him about recruiting. "We'll be getting more defense, especially in the secondary. And did I mention kickers?" They laughed, but again, he would have been hammered for a similar statement in a press conference. "In practice, they almost never miss, but it's not easy kicking with the wind and all that pressure."

Another asked Rodriguez about dropped balls in the Ohio State game, particularly a few by Roy Roundtree. "Roy is one of our most reliable receivers. He makes almost all of the hard ones but dropped two or three of the easier ones. He's young, and he'll get better."

Boubacar Cissoko? "He didn't do what he was supposed to do," he said, and left it at that.

The next question sounded like the sort of nonquestion they plant in political rallies: too good to be true: "I felt when you were announced, and before you ever stepped on campus, 'We got the best coach in America,' and nothing since then changes that." A big cheer went up. "But right now you've got fours, fives, and sixes going against kings and aces."

"I appreciate that," Rodriguez said. "We feel lucky to be here. We've had some obstacles. The NCAA investigation threw us for a loop. I don't want to say it's a victory—whenever you get investigated, it isn't fun—but the truth came out in the end. It made us better. We got better at our procedures and our communication. And I hope you understand that no one in or out of the department was trying to cheat.

"I know you all have a great love and pride about what the school's about, what the team's about, and what the attitude is about. It's still there. I'd even say, more than ever. If you saw my seniors, before and after the Ohio State game, you'd understand how they feel, how deep their passion is.

"I'm not used to this, either, folks! I've been to BCS bowls, been ranked in the Top Ten. I didn't win a lottery ticket to work here!

"I can tell you this: There's not been a day we *ever* cheated the University of Michigan out of an hour of work. You'll get our very best. We have as much pride, intensity, and passion as any staff in America. Because it's Michigan!"

The attendees jumped to their feet and gave Rodriguez a rousing ovation. The emcee returned to the podium and told the club secretaries: "If you write something [for the newsletter], make it nice, because we just *love* him!"

You had to wonder why Rodriguez didn't run down to Weber's Inn every Monday just for a shot in the arm. No one could say the fans were not supportive. They were, as a group, the first to jump on his bandwagon and the last to leave.

If you could break down his backers and detractors into voting blocs—a popular exercise at the time—you'd probably find his biggest critics among the local media and Carr's former players and assistants, and his greatest support among the average fans and the current players, who had bought in and defended him often. There were plenty of exceptions and shades of gray, naturally, but those were the basic building blocks of both sides.

The problem for Rodriguez was simple: Even if those in favor of keeping him outnumbered the naysayers, as polls typically showed, those against him had more power.

Ultimately, however, only one vote mattered: Dave Brandon's. And where that vote was leaning would be the source of much speculation in the days and weeks ahead.

When the Monday myopia wore off—the same phenomenon that had fans thinking Michigan was going undefeated after beating Notre Dame and never winning another game after losing to Penn State—perspective returned, and by Thursday, the arguments for retaining Rodriguez were resurfacing. The arguments for firing him, of course, weren't going away, either, and that set up an even more popular parlor game: What was the tipping point?

The range of opinions about the final straw spanned virtually from the day Rodriguez was hired to the day he was fired. But the candidates most commonly cited include: his initial PR problems with the buyout, West Virginia, the wave of departed players, and the bad press that followed before he had even coached his first game; his streak-breaking 3–9 debut; the *Free Press* feature and subsequent NCAA investigation; the string of four losses in the middle of the 2009 season when they needed just one more win to secure a bowl bid; the transition from Bill Martin to Dave Brandon; the rash of defensive backs lost in the 2010 off-season to the NFL, other schools, and injuries; and the losses in 2010 to Michigan State, Iowa, and Penn State. Take your pick.

Every one of the moments above added to the avalanche that ultimately caused the roof to cave in, but even after seeing all of these events at close range, I'm still not sure it's possible to determine exactly which pile of snow broke the beam. To me, Rodriguez's reign was fatally damaged by two main causes: the harm done by detractors inside and outside the football family, and his own missed opportunities—from PR problems to those four match points in 2009 and the three in 2010, any one of which would probably have been enough to overcome those seeking to sabotage his efforts and deliver him to a new era when he could focus on coaching football.

For Brandon's part, he has been utterly inscrutable in revealing when, exactly, he had made up his mind. He claimed at the press conference announcing Rodriguez's departure that he was still tossing the question over that very morning. For someone who appears to be such a calculating man, that seems very unlikely. I suspect he had made his decision long before that day, but wanted to maintain the appearance of open-mindedness while gaining the opinion-bending benefits of three straight blowouts. But I'm merely guessing. Only he and his closest confidants know for sure.

But if I had to give an answer, and pick one moment as the last straw, I would say this: The moment I thought Rodriguez's tenure was finally coming to an end, fairly or not, occurred on Thursday, December 2, 2010— not on the field of battle, but at a banquet to honor his team. That's when he faced a critical mass of powerful fans, followers, and alums who would judge him primarily on his ability to transform himself from outsider to Michigan Man—and he lost them for good.

After Harbaugh decided not to attend the ninetieth annual Michigan Football Bust, the national media backed out of the event, but most of those fans who had bought tickets to see Harbaugh decided to come honor the seniors and the 1985 Wolverines anyway. The thousand-plus people who packed Laurel Manor in Livonia, about thirty minutes from Ann Arbor, were hoping to see something memorable.

After receiving a generous introduction from longtime play-by-play man and emcee Frank Beckmann, Rodriguez went to the podium. The crowd gave him a standing ovation.

"Thank you!" he said. "I had to stretch my legs, too, so I appreciate that!" The crowd seemed almost as receptive as the M-Club had been just three days earlier.

The senior speeches are usually the highlight of the evening, and the 2010 class didn't disappoint—perhaps the best I'd heard in the half dozen or so Busts I'd attended.

On the lighter side, at least four gave a shout-out to Twin City socks, the "best socks in the world."

All seniors made it a point to thank Coach Carr, who did not attend, even though most had played for him only one or two years. But most of the seniors also seemed to go out of their way to praise their current coach.

Four of them were graduating from the engineering school, and Zac Ciullo, Rodriguez announced, had just been admitted to Michigan's law school.

"I told him, 'You're too late! I already used all the attorneys I need. I hope I never need ya!'" The line got a good laugh and seemed to show that Rodriguez could comfortably joke about the off-field troubles he'd just been through, and that the problems were "in the past."

"Coach Carr," Ciullo said, "you were a hero to me growing up. I'm proud to say I played for you. Coach Rod, thanks for being an unbelievable coach for the last three years. You made me a better man and inspired me to do more than I thought I could."

He turned his attention to the audience, which included a few tables of reporters, and made a strong and stirring case that the defendant, his coach, was, in fact, a Michigan Man.

Ciullo closed by saying, "We received the harshest criticism of any Michigan team. All the fire and turmoil has only made us stronger. My friends say, 'One day, Michigan will be great again.' But in my opinion, Michigan never stopped being great. Michigan was, is, and always will be great!"

The crowd cheered.

"He's good!" Rodriguez said. "Wish I could've used you. Where have you been?"

Many of the remaining seniors sounded like character witnesses following up on Ciullo's testimony. Doug Rogan said, "Coach Rod treated us like his own as soon as he got here," and later added, "I finished one run facedown. But, as a disclaimer, it was all done voluntarily."

"We didn't give up," Renaldo Sagasse said. "The class before, a lot gave up, but we didn't. Thank you, Coach Rod. Thank you for helping us become better men.

"And thank you for making our summers . . . terrible! We couldn't sleep Sunday nights because we knew we were running the next day."

Jon Bills, whose doctors said he would have likely been paralyzed in a car accident that spring if not for his unusually strong neck, also thanked Rodriguez. "When the head coach of the winningest program in college history visits you nearly every day, that speaks volumes." He also thanked Barwis. "Without you and your staff, I would not be standing here."

Fifth-year senior Adam Patterson thanked "Rich Rodriguez and his staff for showing me what it means to be a Michigan Man."

The most passionate speech, not surprisingly, came from cocaptain Mark Moundros. "Thanks, Coach Rich Rodriguez," he said. "Your energy, passion, and enthusiasm never wavered no matter what came out. I want to thank the coaching staff. You are uncommon men—who take the criticism from less-than-average men who could not handle the pressure."

Rodriguez, clearly moved by his captain's speech, said, "Sometimes I get a bit defensive about this class. But it will go down as one of our most important. They hung in there, and they are Michigan Men."

When Denard Robinson received the team MVP Award, he said, "If it wasn't for Coach Rod, I wouldn't be playing quarterback at the best university in the world."

It was an almost perfect evening, more than Rodriguez could have hoped for—one that could go a long way toward quieting his critics on several fronts.

Then Rodriguez got up to give his speech.

He started by saluting the 1985 team sitting in the back. "You're all my age," he said. "So I don't know why you look so much younger than I do!"

He gave a very open and direct account of where he and the program stood, what it had taken out of him, and what they would need to finish the job. "This 'hot seat' stuff is not any fun," he said with some humor. He spoke of the program's work ethic and embraced both the foundation he was given and what he and his players, led by his seniors, had accomplished in building on top of it. "The seniors went through a lot of discomfort and turmoil outside the program. And they *stayed*."

He noted the more than six thousand yards they gained in 2010, a record, and how almost all of those yards would return in 2011. "The worst," he predicted, "is behind us." And the future was bright. They were on the cusp of winning big. "We never quit believing in what we were doing," he assured the crowd, "or who we were doing it with, or where we were doing it, and to this day I am as sure as the day I got hired three years ago that it's going to happen, and happen in a big way."

He turned to Michigan tradition, its decades of extraordinary success, laying out the request that eras not be compared. That no matter how hallowed an era, it should not be used to tear down another, which by clear inference meant his own. Surely, he suggested, if being a Michigan Man meant anything, it meant being all in for Michigan, and supporting the coaches and the players picked to build and maintain that tradition.

"We all need to be ONE Michigan. One Michigan. Proud of every era. Proud of every young man, every student athlete who went through this program . . .

"What truly makes a champion?" he asked. "What truly makes a Michigan Man? The first thing you got to do is build a man and a mindset, and then the next thing that comes is winning a championship."

After giving a nod to Michigan tradition, he was now speaking of what his coaches were doing to turn their players into a team of Michigan Men. Now that he understood Michigan traditions, Michigan needed to extend him the respect he needed to lead the program.

At this point, his speech became increasingly halting. "Seeing these guys grow from high school kids to Michigan Men—that's what I'm most proud of." And while it is common for coaches to say their greatest reward is making a difference in young men's lives, watching them rise up to become more than they thought they could be, he added that they had done just as much for him. "Thanks," he said, "for helping raise me up."

The raw emotion of the speech went up a notch.

"Is this worth it?" Behind that question stood all the personal and professional costs of the past three years. "Is this worth it for your family?" he asked, getting choked up.

The answer wasn't clear-cut. It wasn't a matter of feeling sorry for yourself, he said, though the temptation was always there. It was instead seeing "the pain in the coaches' faces and the worry and anxiety in your kids' faces." He wasn't speaking just of the losses but also of the personal attacks and the seemingly endless public trial he and his staff and players had been put through.

But, unequivocally, Rodriguez said, the answer was yes. Yes, it was worth it. It was worth it because of the differences made in the lives of everyone attached to the program, he said, and because of his unquestioning faith in the future greatness of his players and team.

The speech had some slightly uncomfortable moments—perhaps unavoidable, if he was going to be honest—but it rang true, and it felt like the crowd was with him. If he had stopped right there, it could have gone down as one of the greats. In fact, it seemed that the entire night was building to this moment, and he was on the verge of pulling off a coach's version of Richard Nixon's "Checkers" speech, which could help save his job. Most people appeared to be leaning forward, apparently poised to give him another standing ovation. Whether Brandon retained him or not, it would be a night to remember.

But then he read lyrics from a song with the same theme, "You Raise Me Up," popularized by Josh Groban: "I am strong, when I am on your shoulders; You raise me up . . . To more than I can be." Many present exchanged uneasy glances—*Please don't do this!*—but he continued. Still, it probably would have been forgotten had he not pointed to the soundman in the back of the room and asked, "Do we have that?"

It looked to some as if he had planned to play the song at the end of the night but got carried away and wanted to play it sooner; either way, the song came over the loudspeakers. Rodriguez grabbed Rita's hand, and before long, everyone at the podium was holding hands, then raising them up—with the notable exception of Dave Brandon, who held hands but kept them conspicuously down, along with his gaze.

The crowd felt compelled to follow—some enthusiastically, some reluctantly. This is Michigan, after all—God's Frozen People—where folks don't normally end banquets this way. It might have been the longest four minutes in the ninety-year history of the Bust.

When the song finished, he gave a great closing line: "My name's Rich Rodriguez. I'm proud to be the head coach of the University of Michigan. And I hope you realize I truly want to be a Michigan Man."

The Victors came crashing through, the lights went up, and the night was over—as was, in all likelihood, Rodriguez's tenure in Ann Arbor.

Brandon's secretary told Rodriguez, just minutes later, that she cried during the song and admired his honesty. But the men were less impressed. One of his staunchest supporters, walking out, said with a pained grin, "It's over."

The Internet ignited within minutes, the papers buried him, and even the national sports shows took their shots. Perhaps most embarrassing of all, Josh Groban himself—who makes a towel boy look tough—tweeted the next day, "Coach Rodriguez, I'm very flattered but crying to You Raise Me Up is SO five years ago."

The day after the Bust, at the normally scheduled press conference in the Commons, instead of discussing the team awards from the night before and the bowl game ahead, the players had to defend their coach. Again.

"I get upset when people poke fun at Coach Rod, because I know him on a personal level," Mike Martin said. "I've been at his house with his family, and that man should never be made fun of, because he's nothing but a good person.

"Why would you want to poke fun at a good person? He deserves nothing but the best."

The players had come to Michigan expecting to work harder in the classroom and the weight room than they would at any other major colleges. They had come expecting to play against big opponents in big games with big stakes. They had come not to be second-rate, but the "Leaders and Best."

But they had not come to defend their coach every week—to the media, to their classmates, even to some of the alumni players and their former teammates. Even if a lot of it wasn't Rodriguez's doing, the effect was the same. Instead of talking about their team, they were talking about their coach.

As Forcier told me earlier in the season, "Rich Rod never talks about this story or that problem, just about the cockroaches and all that. But when a bad story comes out, you can feel the difference in practice. How can all that shit not get to you?"

After a while, their coach's burden became their burden. His pressure became their pressure.

And as any general can tell you, if you keep your troops on red alert too long, they get tired and start making mistakes.

The rumor mill had Fox Sports offering $50,000 for the film and another outlet $100,000. Dave Brandon—a world-class whiz at damage control, who had handled the NCAA investigation so masterfully—quickly quashed that problem by telling the film crew that if they did so, they'd never work for Michigan again, though he surely didn't savor having to spend his day fielding calls from the media, alums, and former players.

Brandon—a self-conscious man who cares deeply about appearances—did not like seeing his office the subject of public amusement and hated having to answer for it.

The contrast with the stoic, tight-lipped Carr could not have been more stark—and benefited Rodriguez not in the least.

It is, of course, absurd to say Rodriguez lost his job to the strains of a Josh Groban cover. It is less absurd to say that, for those select and influential few who would judge his transformation into what they deemed to be a Michigan Man, he lost more of them that night, at a time when he desperately needed to add powerful supporters.

When the dust settled, though, a few things stood out. First, Rodriguez had evolved from an outsider who, when asked at his first Ann Arbor press conference in late 2007 if you had to be a Michigan Man to coach the football team, joked, "I hope not!" Of course, he was criticized for that. At the Victors' Rally, held in February 2010, he closed his speech by saying, "I'm Rich Rodriguez, and I am a Michigan Man." He'd been criticized for that, too, for being presumptuous.

Finally, with great humility, he told the crowd in December of 2010, "I hope you realize I truly want to be a Michigan Man." He was even criticized for that, with some saying, "a true Michigan Man would not have to ask," bringing the silliness of the exercise full circle.

But the changes his three different statements represented were real. He had become more respectful of Michigan tradition and more humble about himself. But, for some, it would never be enough.

The speech and song themselves—looked at independent of the responses—were sincere, heartfelt, and ultimately heartbreaking. It was painful to watch a man so plainly and bravely bare his soul and miss the mark at the same time.

It was gutsy and awkward. He was asking Michigan to meet him in the middle. He knew and deeply respected Michigan tradition. He'd never been far from its influence throughout his coaching career. But he not unreasonably assumed he had been hired for who he was, not what they wished him to be.

But it also revealed that, in other ways, Rodriguez had still not learned everything he needed to know to lead the Michigan family. If he had simply recognized that he needed help addressing the faithful in a crucial speech, and sought it out, plenty of Michigan Men who supported him to the hilt would have come running to help him hit the target. Instead, he decided he knew exactly what he needed to do, he worked alone, and he missed the mark.

Like most of his PR problems, this one started with good intentions, and his relatively minor misjudgments were magnified beyond all reason. But his inability to anticipate the consequences of his public statements and actions remained a constant, resulting in a punishment that did not fit the crime. Whatever people's feelings about Rodriguez's message that night, it was the furthest thing from mean-spirited, which could surely not be said about many of the responses that followed.

In fact, the evening served as a decent summary of Rodriguez's three years coaching the Wolverines. So often his defense pushed an opponent to third-and-long, only to allow a big play. His offense was notorious for producing 75-yard drives ending with a turnover or missed field goal. And his last two teams both started out so strong, only to fall one victory shy of having the breakout season they needed.

On this night, an important banquet that had begun with such great promise—from the standing ovation, to the senior speeches, to Rodriguez introducing himself anew—now lay burning in a heap on Internet message-boards.

The coaches knew the case against them was building, but they had a job to do, and they were going to do it. Even with the axes dangling over their heads, they hit the recruiting trail as hard as ever—pulling in their best class of commits—knowing they might well be filling the cupboard for someone else.

They also knew that other schools might be interested in them— particularly Maryland—if Rodriguez would just entertain the offers, but he steadfastly refused. That, too, came with a price.

"Keep in mind," Rodriguez told me at the time, "I have a contract, I have a buyout, but my assistant coaches don't. And instead of calling other schools for jobs, they're going all-out for Michigan. Not one of them has come to me with an offer from somewhere else, and I know they could get them."

Would beating the twenty-first-ranked Mississippi State Bulldogs in the Gator Bowl save them? Brandon, a shrewd poker player, wasn't tipping his hand either way. But around town one day, one Michigan football stalwart told me, "If Michigan starts winning, that's Brandon's worst nightmare. Then what do you do?"

I had heard others make similar statements. No question, Rich Rodriguez had made some mistakes, and Bill Martin had made more. But no one could ever doubt how badly they wanted the Wolverines to win every game—something not every Michigan Man could say.

If this celebrated alum was right, there was good news for Brandon: Michigan had almost no chance.

Some parents and returning players who wanted to defend Rodriguez could not get through to Brandon, much to their dismay. That group included Denard Robinson, who publicly and privately declared his desire that Rodriguez stay. He repeatedly tried to make an appointment with Brandon in Ann Arbor, and later in Jacksonville—site of the Gator Bowl—but could never get Brandon's time.

When the bowl practices started, the seniors began conducting their exit interviews with associate athletic director Greg Harden. Not surprisingly, these interviews focused on the central question: Should Rodriguez stay, or should he go? Their views were mixed, but their conclusions leaving the interviews were not: Our coach is a goner.

"It's all anyone was talking about—Rich getting fired," one student manager said. "No one wanted to be there."

"They knew before the Gator Bowl, Rich Rod was going to be gone," another added. "Even the assistants knew, or seemed like it. One day, during practice, Coach Frey pulls me aside and says, 'I don't know what's going to happen, but I just want you to know you're the best student manager I've had. We should stay in contact.'"

"We knew the guys weren't into it," a third said. "You could just see, they'd had enough of the whole thing."

Given the incessant pressure of the previous three years, the discouraging end to the season, plus the Bust and the exit interviews, they finally realized winning would bring not freedom from their burdens—as it would have earlier in the season—but an extension of them. The way things were set up, they had more incentive to lose than to win.

Right before kickoff at the Gator Bowl, on January 1, 2011, Mark Moundros and Rich Rodriguez spoke to the team at full power. When the Wolverines took the field, it looked, once again, as if it could be Michigan's day.

Denard Robinson wasted no time moving his team downfield, passing for 10 and 6, running for 24 and 22, and finally hitting Roundtree for a 10-yard touchdown pass. 7–0.

The defense gave 10 points right back, however, before Denard found Odoms—making his return after breaking his foot—in the end zone for a 27-yard touchdown pass. Michigan ended the first quarter ahead in just about every category, including the score: 14–10.

But in the second quarter, Mississippi State scored three straight touchdowns to Michigan's zero, taking a commanding 31–14 lead into halftime.

One fan sitting in the stands behind the bench held up a sign that read: EVEN BO SAID IT TAKES FOUR YEARS.

But three other fans held up one sign each: WE. WANT. HARBAUGH. The players had not been able to escape such talk for over a month, even during their last game.

In the locker room, David Molk asked his teammates, "So this is it? After a month of practice, this is what we bring? This is all we got? This is US? Disgusting! Lying down after a half? We laid down after a *quarter*!

"No hanging our heads! Get up! Get up and get after their asses!"

Rodriguez followed Molk: "There ain't nothing wrong with ya! You're better than that! Get your heads up—and let's go!"

But after three years of nonstop drama, after facing just about every obstacle you could throw at a group of college football players, they didn't have anything left.

When they ran out of the tunnel, you could tell they were done.

"I've been 'all in' for Rich Rod from the start," cameraman Patrick McLaughlin said. "But they're down 31–14, and some of these guys just came out of the tunnel *smiling*. You can't allow that—not that he does.

"Unless they pull off a miracle, or lose respectably, I do believe his story ends here today. I finally believe it."

The Bulldogs added three more touchdowns in the second half to stretch their lead to 52–14. That was it.

McLaughlin may have been late to reach his conclusion, but he was right. And back in the coaches' room, Rodriguez knew it, too.

"Today's not our day," he told them. "I thought we were ready to play, and we weren't, and that's on me. We just didn't execute, in any phase of the game.

"But that doesn't diminish my feelings for you, and especially you seniors. You guys busted your asses off all year. You're going out winners in my book.

"Seniors, you laid the foundation for all the teams that follow. We have a great work ethic and a great attitude.

"Your curfew is one a.m. Don't screw this week up by doing something stupid. Breakfast is at eight to nine thirty. Then the buses take us to the airport.

"You seniors, you've given the juniors something to live up to. You have the right attitude.

"Get in. 'Michigan' on three."

"MICHIGAN!"

Van Bergen, Moundros, and a few other players were in tears.

Like most of the assistants, Greg Frey gathered his position players. "Once you're part of my family for one play, you're a part of my family for life. You need me, you call me."

Rodriguez went through the locker room to hug every senior, then handled the press conference and returned to an empty locker room.

He faced his locker for a moment, half slammed it, and said, "Well, I just made Dave Brandon's job a lot easier."

On Tuesday, January 4, 2011, word leaked that Rodriguez was meeting in Dave Brandon's office that afternoon. One news source, which had already erroneously reported after the UConn game that Tate Forcier was transferring, reported that Brandon would fire Rodriguez that day.

Rita Rodriguez had asked Brandon's office to let her know before he made an announcement, so she could be sure her children didn't find out in school and break down in front of their friends.

"Oh, we're not West Virginia," they told her. "We wouldn't do that."

No such announcement came, but Raquel said, "I knew Dad was meeting today. I was ready for it."

Some people in Schembechler Hall were not doing as well. Secretaries Mary Passink and Jennifer Maszatics were crying, and another broke out in hives.

When the meeting ended about 5:00 p.m., Brandon had not given Rodriguez a final decision.

Back at the Rodriguez home, they hovered around the kitchen, snacking, doing homework, and watching TV, but mainly talking about what had happened and what might happen the next day.

Rita discussed the cultural fit question, which might have been more real than anyone had imagined initially. "I should have known we were in trouble when Ivan Maisel [of *Sports Illustrated*] asked, 'How do you think you'll fit in up there?'

"I said, 'What do you mean? Why do I have to fit in? Why *wouldn't* I fit in? I always thought we were pretty likable people. Why wouldn't that be enough?'"

In Christine Brennan's *USA Today* column that day, she wrote, "Rich-Rod knew he wasn't in Morgantown anymore when a Michigan staffer poked his head into his office one day to tell Rodriguez that a university regent had complained about his language at a recent speech in front of Michigan football fans. As Rodriguez frantically racked his brain to recall what he might have said, the staffer sheepishly offered up the offending word: Rodriguez had said 'ain't.'"

"Every time I wanted to love Michigan," Rita said in the kitchen that night, "something would happen to scare me off and put my guard back up."

The next day, Rich and Rita Rodriguez returned to Brandon's office, where he told them he was letting Rich and his staff go. Soon thereafter, Rodriguez addressed his coaches, then his team, while Brandon met with the press.

During his announcement, Larry Lage of the Associated Press asked Brandon if he had talked to the players. "Believe me, I've talked to plenty of players. I've always taken the meeting and it's always been very helpful. If someone wants to have a meeting with me, they can have one—because that's the kind of guy I am."

This would have come as news to Denard Robinson, among others.

As soon as the meeting was over, Rodriguez walked through his office to the coaches' meeting room, where his staff had been waiting for him.

"Well, as expected, they fired me," he told them. "They said they did an evaluation, and they didn't like all the 'negativity surrounding the program.'

"They'll have a press conference at noon. I won't be there. No need to be humiliated one more time. I'm just going to release a statement, and that will be it.

"I've seen how hard you have worked. You have not cheated Michigan out of an hour. I don't know if Michigan appreciates it"—his voice cracked at that—"but I do."

He waited a minute to speak again. The staffers observed a respectful silence, and remained completely still. Their expressions were sadly stoic.

"I had a chance at other jobs last week, but we were not going to sell Michigan or the kids short. I'm a little mad about that now, that they dragged it out so long—but it is what it is. I'm not burnt-out, I don't want to sit out—even though everyone tells me I should. I want to be a coach. I want to be a head coach.

"I feel badly for you guys. You all came here to do your best. I'm sorry it didn't work out. If I can do anything to help, let me know.

"It was a bad fit here from the start. They've tarred and feathered us from the day we got here. But we're still standing.

"You've got pay and benefits through April."

They remained quiet for a while. No one got up to leave, or even move. Finally, Tony Gibson spoke. "I just want to say, I'm sorry, Coach. It's not just you. It's all of us." The others seconded Gibson's sentiment.

"Coach, I'm sorry," Rutledge added. "I said this was the greatest place in the world, all first-class—"

Rodriguez interrupted Rutledge with a wave of his hand. Water over the dam. Not going to go there.

"Coach," Magee said, with his phone in his hand. "It's Denard. He wants to come down to see you."

"Tell him I'll be in my office."

After Brandon's press conference announcing the firing, he arranged to meet with the team first, followed by Rodriguez.

"Obviously," he said, "you're all well aware of the fact I made an announcement today, that we're going to make a transition with our coaching staff. I want you to know it was a tough decision. Coach Rodriguez was a professional—open, honest, good to work with.

"Change is hard. This is not fun. Anyone who likes that has got something wrong with him. I hope you're here because of Michigan—from the classroom to the Big House—where you can get a world-class education and compete at the highest level." He then stated more explicitly: If people start transferring, we have to start all over again.

"Whether we like it or not, we've got all these clowns outside this building waiting for us with their cameras and recorders, looking to perpetuate the drama. I'm asking that you don't give them the sound bite they want. Just tell them you're a Michigan Man and you're ready to play for whoever is the next Michigan coach.

"The world is waiting to hear what you tweet and what you text. They've got us under a microscope again. I ask you to use a lot of discretion. Think about what you say and write."

When he opened the floor to questions, Denard Robinson's hand shot up. "You got a coach?"

"I'm looking to find the best coach I can find."

"Do you have a timeline?" Robinson asked.

"Great question. It's exceedingly important that I move as fast as I possibly can. Having said that, it's not a race about speed but getting the right person."

"Are you keeping Barwis?" another player asked.

"The current strength staff is in place and we'd like them to stay in place for as long as possible. When a new coaching staff comes in, Mike's gonna be here." With that, Brandon nodded to Barwis, standing in the back as always, who said, "Yes, sir."

"What coaches are you talking to?" Denard asked.

"The problem with that is I can't say any names without it being tweeted in ten minutes and on ESPN's fourteen stations, but you have to trust me no one wants the next coach to be more successful than I do."

Following up on one of Brandon's comments, Cam Gordon asked, "What are the negatives we face as a team?"

"We've been playing football here for one hundred and thirty-one years, and we've always had a tradition of winning. We haven't kept pace with the expectations that are Michigan—not from a lack of effort—but we need to get the trajectory right so we're competing for Big Ten titles."

"How fast do you expect us to get back to where you want us to be," Denard asked, "if you bring in a whole new staff?"

Brandon gave a generalized answer about making "significant, positive steps."

"Will you keep the assistants?"

"Absolutely," he said, "if the assistants are interested, and the new staff wants to keep them. But I'm a big believer that leaders must pick their teams."

"Is there anything we can do to help you in the process?" one asked.

"Don't give the media what it wants. Don't say anything about the old coach, about the new coach, about the school. Just be Michigan Men.

"One other thing," Brandon said in closing. "Coach Rodriguez is a good man who tried hard and worked hard. He's operated in a very difficult environment for years. I want to change that environment—big-time."

Before the meeting was over, he already had. Brandon had surely learned some lessons from watching the last transition, and he was eager to prevent the transfers and headlines that occurred during the last one.

After Brandon left, Rodriguez entered the room for the last time.

"I appreciate you guys hanging around. Unfortunately, I'm not going to be able to stay here, and they feel the same way," he said, gesturing to Rita and Rhett standing near the door.

"It's not an easy time for anyone," he said, and paused. "The last couple years I sat in your homes and said I'm going to be your coach. That was the plan. But even though we didn't win every game, I believe the foundation of greatness has been set in this program. What you did in the weight room, the classroom—I've seen your grades from fall semester, you've done well—well, the attitude and work ethic is better than it's ever been. Brighter days are ahead. And I'll be your biggest fan.

"When I start a job, I like to finish it. That's not going to happen. But I'd like to see you all do it.

"Make sure you have my new cell number and my home number, wherever I go. You're going to have to find me to get some of Miss Rita's nacho dip. I'm not gonna mail that shit!

"Some of your families have already called. Tell them I appreciate it and it will take me a couple days to get back to them."

Rita said a few words—"You have been such great role models for my kids. We will miss you tremendously"—before Rich finished the meeting.

"Everyone wants to judge you on wins and losses, and that's the business we're in," he said. "But it's a business for us coaches. It's a game for you all.

"I want to tell you how well you represented your university—always with class. I can't tell you how many times the bowl reps said we've been doing this for years, and they never saw a group like you.

"Remember, life's a lot easier if you're a good guy. Doesn't mean it's always fair, doesn't mean things always go the way you want. But being a good guy still matters.

"I'll be around for a little bit. If you ever need anything, holler."

When he finished, they clapped strongly. Not an ovation, but a sincere thank-you.

After the Rodriguezes left, the juniors went to the front.

"All right, we've been through this before," David Molk said. "A lot of things had to happen to go 3–9—not because of the coach, but because of the transition. Every guy who had a chance to leave, left. That tore our team apart. We lost starters, backups, you name it. There were only half of us left.

"We're a family. I love all you guys. No matter how much shit I give you—I love you. If we don't stay together, we'll never make it. This program stays together. I don't want to see anyone leaving. If you do, we'll be crappy for three more years.

"I love Coach Rod. He did everything he could. But now it rests on us."

Van Bergen followed. "Everyone in this room knows we're pretty close to becoming what we want to be."

"We've got nineteen starters coming back," J. B. Fitzgerald chimed in.

"This could be special for us," Van Bergen said. "But only if we all pull in the same direction."

Like Brandon, the players had also learned a few lessons from 2007.

Outside Rodriguez's office, a thick line of players stretched down the hallway, waiting to say good-bye—plus Brock Mealer, who walked in with the help of two canes.

Rodriguez and his assistants started cleaning out their offices. He discovered how many things you can collect in just three years: souvenir helmets, footballs, framed photos.

Rodriguez and his family came back the next day to finish the job. They began packing a few large boxes, filling them with books of Michigan lore, the painted game ball from his first victory, over Miami of Ohio on September 6, 2008, and the photos of his family. He paused to look at the picture of Rhett running under the banner for the first time, straining to touch it with all his might.

It gave him a wistful smile and made him laugh the smallest of laughs. Then he placed it carefully inside the box, with both hands.

"Rhett, what's our philosophy?"

"What you just told me?"

"Yep."

"When it's too hard for everyone else, it's just right for us."

"That's right."

A week later, with Rodriguez gone, even his supporters didn't have to restrain themselves from speculating about his successor, and the rumor mill went into overdrive.

The most popular candidates, of course, were Jim Harbaugh and Les Miles. According to a well-placed source, becoming Michigan's head coach "was all Jim talked about for the last two years." But Brandon was late to get to him, so even his offer of $5 million a year—double Rodriguez's salary— was not enough to keep him from taking over the San Francisco 49ers, which didn't even require Harbaugh to move his family. Harbaugh wasn't coming to Ann Arbor.

Brandon then approached Jim's older brother John Harbaugh, head coach of the Baltimore Ravens, about the position. Although John was then making less than Rodriguez, he declined, then signed a three-year contract with Baltimore for $12 million. Brandon went down his list, and offered the job to Northwestern's Pat Fitzgerald, who ultimately decided to stay in Evanston after a wealthy NU alum promised to improve Northwestern's outdated facilities.

The one coach who did not receive an offer from Michigan, again, was Les Miles. He had been handled shabbily during the 2007 search, and it appears he wasn't treated much better in 2010, either. All overtures to him were strictly a show designed to appease his supporters. When Rodriguez asked Brandon in December if he already had someone lined up, Brandon denied it but said he would hire Les Miles "over my dead body." The rest was theater.

If Brady Hoke was a dark horse candidate to most Michigan fans and followers, he wasn't to his former players at the Griese/Hutchinson/Woodson golf outing the previous May. They were unified in supporting him as their favorite. When Dave Brandon took to the podium at the Junge Champions Center on Wednesday, January 12, to present Brady Hoke as Michigan's nineteenth head football coach, they got their wish.

In a crucial introduction, the largely unknown Hoke, clearly well versed in Michigan lore and well coached by the PR-savvy Brandon, hit all the right notes to win over just about everyone. He came across, in the phrase of the day, as the consummate Michigan Man.

"Hoke will be successful," Bill Dufek said, "because we're not going to do to him what some of those guys did to Rich."

Brandon, who had learned a few lessons watching the calamitous 2007 transition unfold, would also help his new coach by not releasing Rodriguez until January. Whether it was a factor or not, the late firing had the effect of knocking Rodriguez out of the running for open positions elsewhere, all of which were filled by the Gator Bowl. If Rodriguez had gone to Maryland in December, for example, he would likely have hired some of his assistants, and in turn, players like Denard Robinson would have had an appealing option if they weren't excited about the new coach and his systems—à la Ryan Mallett in 2008.

Brandon made sure Hoke got everyone whom he wanted on his staff. Michigan lured defensive coordinator Greg Mattison from John Harbaugh's Ravens staff with a contract worth $750,000 a year, and incentives that could push it to $900,000—more than three times what Michigan paid Scott Shafer and Greg Robinson.

If Hoke was surprisingly impressive in his introductory press conference, the normally silver-tongued Brandon fell short. He did not name names, but he clearly felt the need to explain why he had not hired the higher-profile coaches who had played under Schembechler: Harbaugh and Miles. He said, "All that glitters is not gold when it comes to some coaches . . . Sometimes the hype or PR does not match the real person."

Even in praising Hoke, Brandon could not resist saying, "Unlike some other coaches, it's not about him, it's about his players and his team.

"He doesn't have to learn the words to 'The Victors.'"

After reaching beyond its famed family for only the fourth time in more than a century, Michigan had officially declared itself: Only a Michigan Man would coach Michigan.

At the spring game in April, Michigan put on its third alumni game. The day attracted record numbers of former players returning to meet the new coach or reunite with an old friend, depending on when they played.

When Angelique Chengalis of the Detroit News asked Ryan Van Bergen how it felt to see hundreds of alums returning to support the new coach, he said, "You know, it's just kind of unsettling . . . It's great that they're back, but it's kind of, where have they been the last two or three years? We've still been wearing the same helmets since they were here."

Van Bergen would be reprimanded for his comment.

When a team goes to a bowl game, each school is allowed to spend $500 on various gifts for their participants, including rings. In May of 2011, Michigan started sending out the 2011 Gator Bowl rings it had ordered for the players, the coaches, and the staffers who made the trip, even those who had since left, like Scott Draper. It was a custom most schools followed, including West Virginia, which sent the 2008 Fiesta Bowl rings to

430 | THREE AND OUT

the coaches and staffers who won the game but had already left for Michigan.

But not all schools. Michigan, for one, decided not to order rings for Rodriguez and the coaches and staffers he had hired, all of whom Michigan had since fired. Only those they considered Michigan Men received rings.

A few months after Rodriguez had been released, I joined Rich and Rita to watch one of Rhett's sixth-grade basketball games at Saline High School, where Raquel was a freshman. They sat in the shallow bleachers, watching Rhett's game, when a parent came up to Rich and said, "I just want to thank you for everything you did for Michigan."

"Thank *you!*" Rodriguez said, shaking the man's hand.

After the game, they approached the gym doors, when a slightly chubby African-American kid saw Rodriguez, stared at him for a second, and blurted out, "Didn't you used to coach Michigan?"

Rodriguez looked down, patted the kid on the shoulder, smiled a small smile, and said, "Yes, sir."

Then he opened the door and walked outside. After months of cold, gray days, the sun had finally come out. He was free.

Tate Forcier traveled with the team to Jacksonville to prepare for the Gator Bowl. One day he was telling *The Detroit News* that if you just go to class, it's almost impossible to flunk out of Michigan. But the next day, he learned that he had flunked out. Rich and Rita Rodriguez met him in the hotel lobby and walked him to the curb to pick up a taxi to the airport. Forcier, in tears, gave them both a hug, and then he got in the cab. He took the next semester off, and by the summer of 2011, he was contemplating where he might transfer.

J. T. Turner, of "Breakfast Club" fame, transferred to West Virginia, of all places, but at the end of his first semester he transferred again, this time to Notre Dame. No, not the "Win one for the Gipper" Notre Dame, but Notre Dame College in Cleveland, Ohio, a Division II school.

While Boubacar Cissoko was waiting for his sentence in the Washtenaw County Jail for three counts of larceny and assault with intent to rob—for which he would receive nineteen months to fifteen years—he pled guilty to assaulting a guard, and received an additional twenty-two to thirty-eight months.

After Michigan hired Brady Hoke, Denard Robinson considered transferring, but quickly realized there was no obvious place to go. With his parents advising him to stay at Michigan to complete his degree and his teammates urging him to stay to lead the team, he decided to remain in Ann Arbor. The new coaches told him he would take most of his snaps under center, but said they still believed he would be the starter in 2011.

Both Brandon Graham and Zoltan Mesko played well during their rookie seasons in the NFL, and appeared to be heading to very solid—and lucrative—NFL careers.

Donovan Warren entered the 2010 NFL draft but injured his ankle before the NFL combine, performed poorly, and was not selected. He eventually signed as a free agent with the New York Jets, where his godfather, Mark Carrier, is an assistant coach. After the Jets waived him in September 2010, the Pittsburgh Steelers picked him up in 2011.

Justin Boren became a two-time All–Big Ten lineman at Ohio State, but was not picked in the 2011 NFL draft. The San Diego Chargers selected Jonas Mouton late in the second round—higher than many expected—and Steve Schilling, Boren's former offensive line mate, in the sixth round.

Calvin Magee, Tony Gibson, and Tony Dews were all hired by the University of Pittsburgh, while Rod Smith and Greg Frey now coach at Indiana University. They got their jobs within weeks, and had to move their families almost immediately. Rod Smith—wisely, it turned out—had not bought his house in Michigan.

Many of the remaining coaches and staffers are still out of work, including Greg Robinson, Dusty Rutledge, and Mike Parrish. In early 2010, the Florida State Seminoles called Mike Barwis with an offer they thought he could not refuse: a multiyear contract to become the highest paid at his position, plus raises for his entire staff. But he turned it down to stay at Michigan. Shortly after the university hired Hoke, who brought in his own strength staff, Barwis was fired. He now consults for the New York Mets, and started his own fitness center with many of his former staffers in nearby Plymouth, Michigan, called BarwisMethods. There he trains a couple of dozen former Michigan athletes who now play in the NFL and NHL, plus Brock Mealer, who has since been joined by several others overcoming serious injuries.

Of the seven Michigan employees who received reprimands in the wake of the NCAA investigation, only one—Ann Vollano—still works for the university.

In the 2010 off-season, Brad Labadie accepted a job at Blue Cross Blue Shield, but when the hiring generated some negative publicity, the company rescinded its offer. Labadie asked Michigan if he could return to his previous position, but Dave Brandon declined. Labadie now works in the area for Kapnick Insurance Group as a client executive.

In late 2010, Judy Van Horn left Michigan to become the senior associate athletic director/senior women's administrator at the University of South Carolina. About the same time, the NAAC named her the 2010 recipient of the Frank Kara Leadership Award, the highest honor in the athletics compliance profession.

In early 2011, Scott Draper became the director of development for Albion College, about a half hour from Ann Arbor. Joe Parker left Michigan to become the athletic department development director at Texas Tech in Lubbock.

As of this writing, three of Michigan's nine positions in the Compliance division remain vacant, including director—unusual for a school in the middle of three years' probation.

In the spring of 2011, Lloyd Carr was inducted into the College Football Hall of Fame and had a wing of Michigan's C. S. Mott Children's Hospital named after him, for which his former players raised a million dollars.

Rich Rodriguez signed with CBS Sports Network to provide color commentary and some studio work for the 2011 season. He hopes to be coaching again in 2012. The Rodriguezes moved to Naples, Florida, where Raquel will be a tenth grader this fall, and Rhett will enter the seventh grade.

Between his release and his move, however, the family put a collection of nine cherished football photos from West Virginia and Michigan on display in a special cabinet in the basement rec room. It includes a picture of Rodriguez standing with Joe Paterno on the sidelines, another of West Virginia quarterback Pat White running through the Georgia Bulldogs in the 2006 Sugar Bowl, and another of Michigan's Brandon Graham crushing Wisconsin's quarterback en route to the Wolverines' record-breaking comeback in 2008.

The photo featuring ten-year-old Rhett jumping and stretching to touch the GO BLUE banner now rests in a cardboard box in their garage.

It's hard to remember now, but at that sun-soaked moment, captured just minutes before Rich Rodriguez's first game as Michigan's head coach, anything seemed possible.

| | | | | | ACKNOWLEDGMENTS

This project started out as a simple three-month stint intended to generate a few magazine articles, and ended as a three-year marathon to produce a book. It's impossible to expand the scope of any journalistic enterprise that dramatically without some serious help.

My first thanks is to my former student, Greg Farrall, who got this ball rolling, and to Mike Wilcox, Mike Brown, and especially Bennett Speyer, who provided expert help at a few crucial junctures.

The relationship between any journalist and his subject is fraught with competing interests. That's all the more true when the journalist is following more than a hundred subjects, wherever they go, for three years.

Rich Rodriguez invited me into the Michigan football program, but the assistants, staffers, and players didn't have to accept me. They could have shut down access to their daily lives and thoughts, especially when things were not going their way. But they remained accommodating throughout. For all this, I remain deeply grateful.

So, to assistant coaches Adam Braithwaite, Tony Gibson, Jay Hopson, Fred Jackson, Greg Robinson, Scott Shafer, and Bruce Tall, and to graduate assistants and interns Alex Herron, Dan Hott, Josh Ison, Eric Smith, Bryan Wright, and Cory Zirbel—thank you. Rod Smith was particularly helpful in the countless quarterback meetings I attended, while Calvin Magee, Greg Frey, and Tony Dews let me eavesdrop on their Friday-night conversations in Magee's hotel room.

The office staffers already worked a minimum of twelve hours a day during the season, and I added to their workload without adding to their paychecks. Thanks to Scott Draper, Brad Labadie, Mike Parrish, Chris Singletary, and Dusty Rutledge; and to Jennifer Maszatics, Mary Passink, Kelly Vaughn, and Michelle Guidry-Pan for cheerfully putting up with my endless presence.

During football weekends, videographers Phil Bromley and Kevin Undeen work from dawn to dusk—and that's before the real work starts, often requiring all-nighters. Yet they found the time to burn me a DVD of each week's game and give me their sage observations.

Equipment managers Jon Falk, Bob Bland, Rick Brandt, and Brett McGinness not only keep the Michigan machine humming, they provided some great quotes—plus one pair of Twin City Socks. I owe you four bucks.

Just down the hall, strength and conditioning leader Mike Barwis and his staff—Chris Allen, Cassandra Baier, Jesse Miller, Dan Mozes, Dennis Murray, Jim Plocki, Kentaro Tamura, and Parker Whiteman—put me through something I'll never forget, and I know a few hundred guys who could say the same thing. Trainers Paul Schmidt, Phil Johnson, and Lenny Navitskis take in the Wolverines' tired, their poor, their banged-up masses yearning to walk free. They also demonstrated infinite patience with my utter lack of medical knowledge.

Across the parking lot in Weidenbach Hall, athletic directors Bill Martin and Dave Brandon were consistently helpful, even when it didn't help them to be so, which says a lot.

I've said it before, and I'll say it again: sports information pros Bruce Madej, Dave Ablauf, and Barb Cossman are the best in the business.

Compliance director Judy Van Horn and her assistant Ann Vollano answered my many questions courteously and clearly—and given the NCAA's byzantine rule book, that was no small feat. The people who run the Academic Center—Phil Hughes, Sue Shand, Shari Acho, and Steve Connolly, among others—were just as helpful.

I'd be remiss if I didn't acknowledge the student managers for their indefatigable good cheer—and I'd be putting them in jeopardy if I did so by name. So here's to Team Atkins. The security men were kind enough to let me roam the sidelines every home Saturday, and university police officers Gary Veld and Gary Hicks kept us all safe in some strange environments.

Many Michigan Men, years after their playing days were over, helped me in more ways than I can count. You know who you are.

A few years ago I had the opportunity to spend a couple of days on the USS *Theodore Roosevelt*, a veritable city at sea. The night before we flew out to the aircraft carrier, the admiral told us, "All the visitors go out expecting to be awed by the technology, but come back talking about the twenty-year-olds who run the ship."

I can say the exact same thing of the players in this book. It was certainly eye-opening to witness the meetings, the workouts, the practices, and the games close up, but the players themselves quickly eclipsed all of it. With few exceptions, they cared deeply about their school, their work, and especially their teammates. They were not only interesting but completely open, honest, and even good-natured about my frequent invasions. A few had to tolerate me more than most, especially on Friday nights at the hotels, so special thanks to Nick Sheridan, Tate Forcier, Denard Robinson, Devin Gardner, Mike Martin, and Ryan Van Bergen.

Stephanie Nicholas, Elise Brown, and my father gathered hundreds of clips, programs, and stat sheets and organized them into boxes of accessible materials, while Nate Sandals proved to be every bit the budding star I already knew him to be, from his remarkable research skills to his savvy suggestions on numerous drafts. Some smart people gave great advice and support when I needed it most, including Neal Boudette, Jonathan Chait, Vince Duffy, John Kryk, Scott Lasser, John Lofy, James Tobin, and Pete Uher. I cannot thank them enough.

My agents, David Black and Dave Larabell, were early believers in this often quixotic mission, from proposal after proposal to draft after draft of a story that seemed to resist ending. Larabell put in coaching-style hours—including weekends, holidays, birthdays, and anniversaries—to see this through. I hope I never need so much of his help again—and I'll bet he feels the same.

Thomas LeBien—like just about everyone else involved in this book—had no earthly idea what he was getting into, but unlike everyone else, it was his job to turn piles and piles of pages into a coherent volume, which required him to get his hands dirty at almost every turn. Without his energy, enthusiasm, and vision, this book would not be in your hands. Zachary Brown, Dan Crissman, Brian Gittis, and Amanda Schoonmaker demonstrated many times why FSG has the sterling reputation it enjoys.

But in a long list of debts, the biggest I owe, by far, is to Rich Rodriguez and his family. I don't know of any sportswriter who ever got the kind of access to a major college football program that he gave to me, and I doubt any writer will ever be so lucky again.

He clearly had the most to lose, yet he never flinched from my many intrusions into his work and his life. His wife, Rita, and their children,

Raquel and Rhett, followed suit. I sincerely hope that when the dust settles, he will see this book as a fair depiction of a good man who made some mistakes but is an inspired, innovative coach, and a truly decent husband and father.

In his final team meeting, he told his players, "Remember, life's a lot easier if you're a good guy. Doesn't mean it's always fair, doesn't mean things always go the way you want. But being a good guy still matters."

It does. And he is.